Students
Data Com

Books in the series

Students' Guide to Information Technology
Students' Guide to Business Computing
Students' Guide to Office Automation
Students' Guide to Expert Systems
Students' Guide to Spreadsheets
Students' Guide to Databases

Students' Guide to Data Communications

Martin Gandoff
Senior Lecturer in Data Communications and Systems, Thames Valley College

Heinemann Newnes

Heinemann Newnes
An imprint of Heinemann Professional Publishing Ltd
Halley Court, Jordan Hill, Oxford OX2 8EJ

OXFORD LONDON MELBOURNE AUCKLAND
SINGAPORE IBADAN NAIROBI GABORONE KINGSTON

First published 1990

British Library Cataloguing in Publication Data

A CIP catalogue record for this book is available from the British Library

ISBN 0 434 90700 6

Printed and bound in Great Britain by
Biddles Ltd, Guildford and King's Lynn

Contents

Preface

Modern methods and techniques for human and computer communications make up what is probably one of the most exciting subjects you can choose for study and careers. Computing has exploded into life during the last 25 years, particularly since the late 1970s with the introduction of the microprocessor into computers.

As a result of the massive increase in the use of computers and the increasing awareness of their potential, communications have exploded as well. Now, almost every organisation knowingly or unknowingly, makes some use of computers in communications even when the only terminal is a telephone.

Looking at my bookshelf, I can see well over 30 books whose subject matter is computing and/or data comms and/or telecommunications. I could quite easily double this number and not have the lot (a selection is given in appendix 5).

Most of the books on the subject are fairly advanced - they introduce many complex and complicated techniques and often a certain amount of electronics. This is unfortunate because as a beginner to the subject, you can be easily put off with the wrong book - a tragedy from the point of view of a career in the industry and your possible future position in computing.

A strange thing about books is that until you spend quite a lot of time with one, you can never be sure whether it will suit you and whether you can cope with the 'heavy' theory. Just to give you an idea, one book in the list is published by Radio Shack in the USA (you may know them as Tandy in the UK). My first reaction was that it would be a trivial book that just scratches the surface. In fact it goes quite deeply into the electricals and electronics of communications but in spite of this, it is really quite readable. Its main drawback, as with most other books on the subject, is that it does not spend much time on applications.

In this book, I have covered as broad a range of subjects as possible and brought in practical applications as often as I can - the first chapter tries to lay a foundation for the rest of the book by introducing as many applications as possible.

The major theme in this book is the importance of data comms as a support for data processing and to make the best use of it, you need to have some knowledge of DP and DP applications. Chapter 1 will touch on much of the DP needed, but you will not gain all the knowledge required - I have assumed that you know nothing about comms, but have spent at least the first term of an HND/C in Computer Studies or Business Information Technology, or as a student on a professional course that has some DP foundation in an earlier part.

Although the book has been designed with students in mind, I am confident that it will be of value to those in business and industry, particularly DP staff who need to consider the possibilities of on-line systems and their relation to telecomms. It will also be helpful to telecomms people who need to know more about the DP side of things.

As to the general style of the book, there are several things I would like to point out:

- I have written the book mainly for students involved with computing or information technology and although telephone applications must be mentioned (as they are closely linked with data communications), most of the book deals with data communications applied to computing, leaving out telecomms as a single subject
- abbreviations - impossible to avoid them, so in particular, DP stands for *data processing*, comms stands for *data communications*, LAN is *local area network* and WAN is *wide area network*
- genderism - I object to *he/she* in print so please, whenever you see *he*, take it to mean *the reader or user, whatever her/his gender*
- diagrams and standards - I have taken a few liberties with standards in diagrams - in several places, I may have used a symbol or picture that is more informative than one in more general use
- using the book for study - I have tried to follow a similar format to the other books in this series and insert student activities after each major section although it is difficult to insert lots of activities for you to carry

out - in most cases, you would not have access to the necessary equipment.

I apologise for the length of some of the chapters - chapters 2, 5 6 and 8 are especially long, because they introduce so many important points, but, throughout the book, you will find the occasional *pause for thought,* designed to break things up. In addition:

- recap - a chapter ends with a recapitulation of what has been covered and a set of short typical questions to see if you have picked things up
- appendix 2 is designed to help you and your lecturers think up further ideas for the practical work that is essential for the proper knowledge and skills acquisition - many of you will be studying on BTEC courses **and I would remind you that practical assignments can count as much as written examinations**
- appendix 3 contains a set of typical examination questions and marking schemes/assessment strategies, while appendix 4 has suggested answers to the typical questions at the end of each chapter
- my favourite hobby-horse - there has been an increasing use of the word *orientated* in everyday speech and in technical English. As far as I am concerned, the verb is to **orient** and the past participle is **oriented.** (In fact, current dictionaries allow both options.)

If any lecturer wants to discuss assignments or projects and their implementation, feel free to contact me at TVC.

If any lecturer or student wants copies of the diagrams for OHPs or for inclusion in notes, contact me at TVC and we can discuss the possibility of supplying them.

If anyone spots any mistakes or wants to put forward suggestions for changes or improvements, I will be very happy to hear.

I would like to thank HND3 students from 1988 to 1989 at the Thames Valley College for the help they have given me, both in collecting specialist information from companies with whom they were placed and in the efforts they put into some of the assignments set as part of their course work. Several have been included in the book to give you an idea of what can be done.

I must also thank the many organisations that allowed me to pick their collective brains on products and services - far too many to list by name.

Stop press!
Two things came up just before final desk-top publishing of the book which were too late to include as detailed case studies. I cannot mention the name of the company in the first application, but a very broad summary will be of interest and will bear out my views on the importance of knowing about the scope for the integration of DP and comms.

The organisation, which supplies its products to a large number of retail outlets, has well over 30 distribution centres. It intends in the very near future, to implement a system whereby all distribution centres will have on-line access to a centralised database of customers, products and delivery resources. In addition, a heavy computer-integrated-telephony front-end is planned. It is hoped that the software will scan the database and automate the making of telephone calls thereby facilitating contact with, for example:

- all customers that must place an order today for their regular delivery in three days time
- any customer that has not placed an order this week
- any customer who has written in with a query.

The other item came from a contact with the company Datapoint based in Neasden, London, NW10. Quite recently, they completed the implementation of a country-wide telephone banking system for Midland Bank plc. The service is called *First Direct* and provides a full retail banking service without the need for branches. Datapoint have also installed DP/CIT systems for wholesale chemical companies and others in the retail trade.

Watch out for many more developments employing a computer terminal with an integrated telephone.

M Gandoff
Maidenhead
February 1990

List of figures

1: What are you studying

Objectives

On completion of this chapter, you should:-

- understand the concept *system* and appreciate the components of a computerised system
- have an overview of data processing and data processing systems
- understand why there is a trend towards on-line and distributed processing and data
- appreciate why data comms is essential for modern DP
- be able to classify the various applications of data comms in computing/DP, text, data and image transmission.

This book is about data communications (data comms from now onwards) - the reasons for, and the means whereby data, in whatever form it is needed, can be made available by sending it to wherever it is needed.

The subject is very wide indeed and I believe that the way to introduce it is to remind you that you need to revise your knowledge of what is involved in the business application of data processing (DP from now onwards). Then you will be in a good position to appreciate how and why data comms is becoming increasingly more widespread in its support for DP applications.

We start with an introduction to systems and computerised systems, showing what they are and what is their purpose. Then we consider how and why computing is linked with the telephone system and the voice applications it was originally designed for.

What is a system

A system is a set of processes put together to achieve some objective and a particular system may be considered as consisting of a number of smaller units, each of which is a *sub-system*: indeed the system itself may be a sub-system of a larger system.

For example, we might be looking at the possibility of computerising a car sales department, so this would be our system. Sales might be thought of as advertising and marketing, order entry, payments etc, each being a sub-system of car sales.

The sales department is a sub-system of the overall company, which might be a sub-system of the 'car industry' which is a sub-system of ...., and so on.

Every system consists of 5 main elements:

Input - items, material or data in some suitable form that is passed into the system for it to operate on

Process - an activity or operation that will be carried out within the system which will refer to and change the contents of stores

Store - a collection of items, materials or data that is used by the system

Output - the results of the system carrying out processes on input, making use of (or referring to) stores

Control - the mechanism that ensures the system 'works'.

Let us consider an example to put these elements into perspective and help us look at how and why some systems are computerised, ie, carried out with the aid of computers.

A Sales and production system

Such a system will receive the following as some of it **inputs**:

- orders from customers
- enquiries about product prices and availability
- payments from satisfied customers
- complaints and goods returned from unhappy customers.

Among some of its **outputs** will be:

- invoices for payment by customers and receipts when they pay up
- delivery notes (showing which goods are to be delivered to which customers)

- lists of raw materials, components, packing materials etc, that are running short (so that suppliers can be contacted for further supplies).

Some of the **processes** carried out may include:

- talking to customers about their requirements
- making the goods, checking their quality and packaging them for delivery
- working out delivery schedules for the drivers
- servicing and maintaining the machines used in production.

As the system operates, the processes will need access to its various **stores**. Some of these will be stores of real items, such as:

- production raw materials and components (eg nuts and bolts)
- production and packaging consumables (boxes, labels, glue, string, lubricating oils, paint)
- office consumables (paper, envelopes, typewriter ribbons).

Others will be stores of data and information - the basic unit being a *record*, a number of which make up a *file*, such as:

- customer payments (so that we can find out those who have not paid up yet this month)
- product sales (so that we can determine which have sold the best this month)
- production machine service records (so that we can service or replace those that are giving us a problem)
- delivery vehicle records (so that we can make sure that renewals of insurance, road tax etc, are carried out promptly)

As you can see, the processes that make up the system need to make use of stores so that materials etc, can be taken out for use, or because information is needed to support other processes - I can't service the vehicles unless I know when they were last serviced, or I have access to the reports handed in by the drivers.

Resulting from these processes, the contents of the stores will change and so must the contents of the files (usually to reflect the changes in the stores) - we say that processes *update* them.

System objectives

As you can see, any business organisation can be thought of as a system and as such, will have certain objectives (otherwise there would be no reason for its existence). To discuss any kind of system and how it is 'managed', we need to know something about its objectives.

Typical business objectives include any of the following:

- continued existence (ie, commercial survival)
- making as much profit as possible
- sales revenue maximisation (selling as many goods as possible)
- growth
- service to its customers.

As part of a system, the objectives of a business sub-system may be to service the system in some way. For example,

- the transport division is there to ensure that goods are delivered to customers (thereby supporting sales and production)
- marketing ensures that the company and its products are presented in the best way in order to maximise sales
- credit control will make sure that customers pay up so that there is enough money to pay staff, buy new raw materials and so on.

Later in this chapter, when we refer to computerised systems, we could be looking at the whole organisation but more often, we will be looking at part of the company, as a sub-system. We will often make assumptions, usually ignoring parts of the overall system in order to concentrate on a particular sub-system.

System inputs

For the computerised business systems we are interested in, the majority of the inputs are documents, each of which represents a business *transaction* ie, any item of business that affect the company accounts:

- for immediate processing and production of results
- to be stored for later use
- to change (amend) data stored earlier.

Strictly speaking the word **transaction** should be separated from **document** which is the form in which the transaction is recognised and recorded. For example, I carry out a transaction when I buy goods from you. The order form or the receipt for payment is the transaction document. **Document** is however, a very loose term. In a manual (non-computerised) system, it could include any piece of paper that records a transaction or starts one off.

In a computerised system, although most transactions have the same documents as a manual system, others are **not** human-readable but carry out the same function as a paper document.

They arise because computerised systems make use of automatic devices, such as:

- magnetic card reader (to read cheque cards and credit cards)
- bar-code reader (bar-code labels are used on clothes, books and groceries)
- optical character reader (for items such as gas bills and postal orders).

So our definition of document can be extended to mean:

> **Any record made, whether human-readable, machine-readable (or both) that forms the basis of a business transaction and which in a computerised system will become a computer transaction and affect data stored in the computer.**

Computer people often call these *source documents.*

Some examples:

- a transport system will get customer delivery schedules, goods packing notes, requests for vehicle servicing and so on
- marketing staff will receive sales figures, completed customer questionnaires, results of advertising campaigns and so on
- payroll staff will receive time sheets, sick notes, notifications of tax code changes.

System outputs

These are the eventual products of processing and are intended:

- to be human-usable - in the form of computer print-out or VDU screens

- for transfer to another computerised system (eg, the output from a sales sub-system could be a magnetic tape containing salesman commissions which is passed to a payroll sub-system.

Figure 1.1 shows a student fee analysis report while Fig. 1.2 show the output from a simple spreadsheet program as examples of typical system outputs.

Pause for thought

Two points to be covered here:

1. Don't get confused over the **objectives** of a system and its **outputs**.

It often looks as if these are the same thing. Think about a college student records system. The outputs consist of things like progress reports, examination results, fee receipts etc but the objectives might be better course management, speedier reporting of student problems, more efficient fee collection. Can you see the difference?

It may look as if we are hair-splitting but throughout the book, we will be looking at methods of reducing errors, improving effectiveness and so on, unlikely to alter the outputs but which go a long way to help a system achieve its objectives.

2. We have looked at examples of completely unrelated inputs and outputs. Now, think about examples of outputs from a business system being used as inputs to the system that produced them. This is not the same as an output going into some other system. There is every reason to assume that our input documents were output from someone else's computer and that our computer-produced outputs will become someone else's input.

Look at a gas or electricity bill such as that shown in Figure 1.3. You probably know that it is produced by computer (can you imagine how many typists would be needed to produce the millions of bills needed each month?) but why is some of the information on the bill repeated at the bottom?

When you pay the bill, either by post or directly at the accounts office, the electricity company will need a source document to accompany your *remittance* (that's why it is called a *remittance*

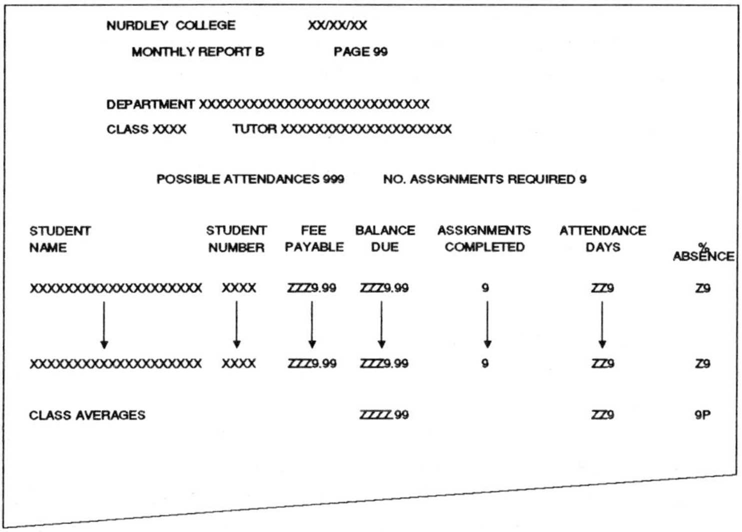

NURDLEY COLLEGE XX/XX/XX
MONTHLY REPORT B PAGE 99

DEPARTMENT XXXXXXXXXXXXXXXXXXXXXXXXXXXX
CLASS XXXX TUTOR XXXXXXXXXXXXXXXXXXXXX

POSSIBLE ATTENDANCES 999 NO. ASSIGNMENTS REQUIRED 9

STUDENT NAME	STUDENT NUMBER	FEE PAYABLE	BALANCE DUE	ASSIGNMENTS COMPLETED	ATTENDANCE DAYS	% ABSENCE
XXXXXXXXXXXXXXXXXXXXX	XXXX	ZZZ9.99	ZZZ9.99	9	ZZ9	Z9
↓	↓	↓	↓	↓	↓	
XXXXXXXXXXXXXXXXXXXXX	XXXX	ZZZ9.99	ZZZ9.99	9	ZZ9	Z9
CLASS AVERAGES			ZZZZ.99		ZZ9	9P

Figure 1.1 Nurdley College monthly student report

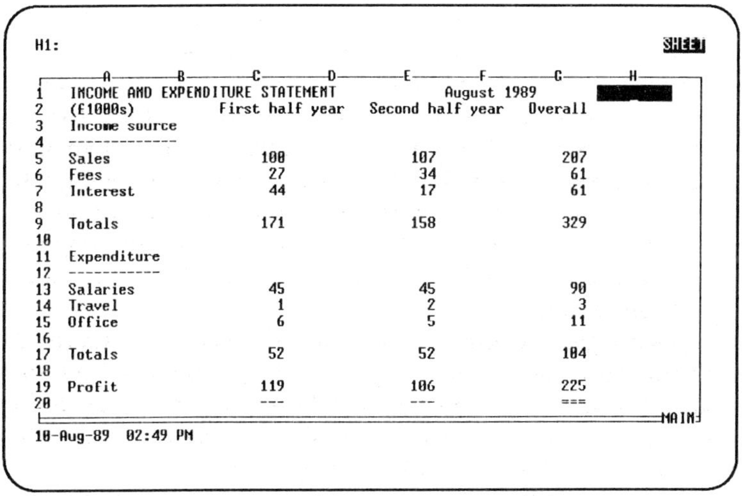

H1: SHEET

	A	B	C	D	E	F	G	H
1	INCOME AND EXPENDITURE STATEMENT				August 1989			
2	(£1000s)		First half year		Second half year		Overall	
3	Income source							
4	-------------							
5	Sales		100		107		207	
6	Fees		27		34		61	
7	Interest		44		17		61	
8								
9	Totals		171		158		329	
10								
11	Expenditure							
12	-----------							
13	Salaries		45		45		90	
14	Travel		1		2		3	
15	Office		6		5		11	
16								
17	Totals		52		52		104	
18								
19	Profit		119		106		225	
20			---		---		===	

MAIN

10-Aug-89 02:49 PM

Figure 1.2 An income and expenditure statement

SPARKS ELECTRIC CO PLC

Account No. 123 234 3456/7 Date 12/08/89

To: XXXXXXXXXXXXXXXXXXXXXXXXXXX
XXXXXXXXXXXXXXXXXXXXXXXXXXX
XXXXXXXXXXXXXXXXXXXXXXXXXXX
XXXX XXX

Balance at period start	12.45
Usage this month	56.39
Appliance rental	8.00
Total due	£ 76.84

please tear off

Account number 123 234 3456/7

Payment date

Due £76.84

Amount paid

Figure 1.3 A Sparks electricity bill

note). You could provide it yourself but there is always the chance that you will make a mistake (in the account number for example). Then, how will the details on the source document be entered into the company computer system?

The bill is a typical example of a *turnaround document*:

- it was produced as printed output from the electricity company computer
- you enter the date of payment and the amount you intend to pay (perhaps you can only afford part of it this week)
- the figures on it are then read into the electricity company computer by means of a document reader.

Try and come up with another example of this kind of document - perhaps that is not a remittance note (hint - think of examinations).

In contrast to the idea of a turnaround document, the next section looks at the very common situation where input and output **are the same thing**.

Computer dialogue

As we will see, many computerised systems involve a user entering data through a keyboard while what is being entered is displayed on a VDU.
This technique of arranging that the user and computer can talk to each other is called *computer dialogue* and you will see examples throughout the book. Figure 1.4 shows what is called a *menu*, whereby making an entry against the relevant shape (or *icon*) informs the computer what action you want it to take.

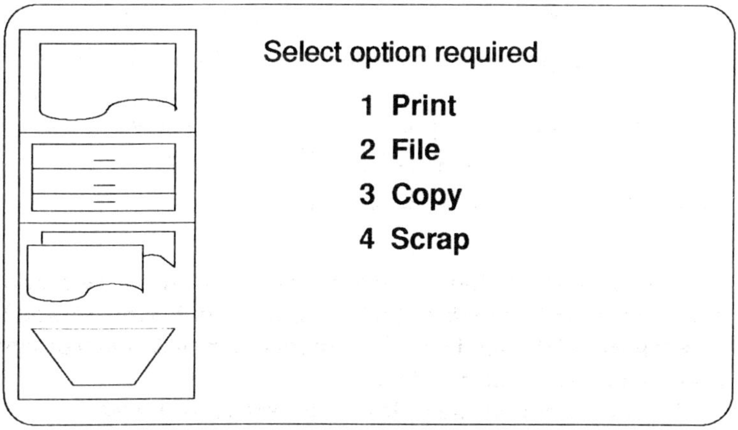

Figure 1.4 A typical menu

In this example, the user can request any of the following:

- running of a print program which will read a file and print the details on a printer
- saving of some data as a new file
- making of a copy of some file, with a name to be supplied by the user
- removing a file from the available list.

```
STUDENT FILE CHANGES

          ENTER STUDENT NUMBER   [217456]

 STUDENT NAME     [A.B. DE MONTEFIORI-JONES     ]
 CLASS            [AC23 ACCA LEVEL 2.2, GROUP 3 ]
 ADDRESS          [21 HIGH STREET               ]
                  [NORTH ACTON                  ]
                  [W6 5JR  ]

 ATTENDANCE:  POSSIBLE [125]  ACTUAL  [113]
```

Figure 1.5 Student file display/amend

Figure 1.5 shows the dialogue associated with a student progress system. It allows the user to make changes to data stored about each student - this screen show the possibilities displayed on the screen, the user enters figures within the brackets to make a change, otherwise the *return* key skips to the next entry.

System stores

Data is stored in computerised systems:

- for later use by system processes, such as:

  keeping a detailed record of all products sold and those returned by customers so that each month we can compare the performance against another and find out if any products are doing badly and why;

  keeping records each week of staff taken and leaving, sickness and holiday and bonuses earned, so that at regular intervals, the personnel department can look to see if there are any problems of motivation or perhaps bad supervision

- for reference, particularly to *decode* data so that, say:

  given a product code, to convert it into description and price

  given an employee number, to find out his tax code and years of service

  given a library book number, the title, author and when it is due back can be made available.

The following are examples of the use of files with various systems:

- if we are running a payroll system, some of the data that we will want in order to pay salaries could include factory production (so that we can work out bonuses) product sales (so that we can determine commissions for salesmen), weekly hours and overtime hours worked by all staff, sick days off and holidays taken.

With this data, not only can we determine gross salaries, but we could produce for example, reports showing which staff had holiday outstanding, which departments were suffering from excessive sickness

- we may be responsible for the day-to-day operation of some complex telephone system. In order to be sure that it is giving the right level of service to users, we must collect data such as, the number of line breakdowns each day/hour, the response times (how long users have to wait for a connection), the number of times that a user cannot get an outside line and the number of times that all lines are busy.

Only if we can access files with this data can we run the analysis programs that will give us some idea of what is going on and when. From this, if we decide that the system operation is unsatisfactory, we can make changes to the way it operates.

Databases

In a conventional DP system, one or more files are likely to be involved with each sub-system and the system as a whole may contain many different files.

Of increasing more importance in DP, is the *integrated system* where we have a series of individual computerised sub-systems linked together employing comms facilities and techniques. To gather information from a set of different files in different locations becomes complicated and inefficient. It is scattered about in different forms in different files, perhaps not updated to the same extent or not to the same degree of accuracy.

This is even more complicated when we look at what are called *distributed systems* where there is no central computer site. Each division of the company, even each branch, may have its own computer, needing access to a mix of local and overall company data.

For this kind of situation, instead of grouping data into files, the whole mass is more or less lumped together (in a highly organised way), designed so that there are many different ways to access it from all the sub-systems that want to get at it. This complex is called a *database.*

(The detailed difference between files and databases is not really within the scope of this book, but to understand how data comms is needed in distributed systems, you must be aware of the difference between them.)

To give you an overview of a typical application for a database, consider an engineering company with manufacturing/sales depots all over the country:

- each depot must access its customer data and own stocks of components and finished goods. DP operations carried out at a depot will involve this data, and that relating to employees, machinery and equipment and expenditure
- head office may need access to all stock data for all depots, so that it can give general instructions. Perhaps it will order one depot to deliver surplus components to another that is short
- personnel and manpower planning may need to know what staff are available at each depot in case there is a need for a temporary transfer of staff to meet a holiday or sickness crisis
- head office needs to keep an eye on company expenditure and it may need to look at depot income and expenditure figures to see if depots are keeping within budgets and not spending too much.

All the data for all the depots and head office could constitute a database. (We will see this environment again when we look at different types of system.)

System processes

Processes are the various operations carried out in a system:

- handling of input - so that it is complete, checked and ready for the computer
- keeping files/databases up to date
- carrying out calculations on data already stored
- producing output - so that users can see and act on the results of processing

- error detection/correction/prevention (we will come to this soon).

Although this book is concerned with computerised systems assisted by comms technology, you must realise that there are very few purely computerised systems. Most system processes are either manual procedures (those that must be carried out by a human) or computer procedures (those that could be or are carried out by computer).

Detailed computer processes include:

- organisation/reorganisation of stored data so that it is in a conveniently arranged form in the right place. This process is called *sorting*
- *aggregation* - collecting together documents or groups of data from several sources, perhaps credit card transaction records from all the branches of a retail company
- *selection* - picking out particular records, such as selecting all customers who need a sales phone call because that have not placed an order recently
- *summarising* - producing overall data, representative of a group of documents/records
- *matching* - taking incomplete input (or stored data) and referring to other stored data in order to complete it
- *updating* - changing the contents of stored data by addition, removal (deletion) or amendment.

However much we make use of computers in business, there will almost always be a human element. But there are many situations where human activities can be partially automated. Since we will be meeting many of these again, a short list of some of the more common might be useful:

- recording entry of stock into a warehouse, where packages have bar-code labels which are read as they pass along a delivery chute
- recording issue of bar-coded goods at a supermarket check-out so that the total bill can be produced and further supplies reordered
- Using a credit card at a petrol station, where the customer account number is automatically read by a magnetic card *wiper*
- using a similar card to record employee 'time on' and 'time off'

- using a magnetic cheque card to get money or order a statement from a cash-point.

Control

However clever we are in the design of a system and however clear we are in the specification of its objectives, we must always assume that things will go wrong. But, how will we know unless we have some way of determining whether the system's objectives are being met?

From its inception, we must decide on the results we want in terms of the required system performance - we can call these the *target, budget* or just the *'expected results'*. We then allow the system to operate as designed. Inputs are entered, processes are carried out, files are updated and output is collected. During its operation, we try to gather information on the performance of the system such as, how easy was it to handle the input without too many errors, how effective was the output; was communication adequate and so on.

At predetermined times, the actual performance of the system must be compared with the expected results. We collect the *feedback* from the system and examine it against what we expected (hoped for). If there is a difference (*divergence*), we must do something about it.

The difference could be for many reasons, such as:

- our objectives were too high, ie, not attainable
- our input is inadequate handled carelessly
- processing is careless or inadequately supervised
- output is inadequate or confusing.

Whatever the reason for poor performance, we must do something about it, or the situation will probably get worse.

We use the term *control* to describe the process of detecting problems and correcting them. The control mechanism must make a comparison between expected and actual results and then make adjustments so as to bring the system back into line or to stop it going out of control. Figure 1.6 shows the application of control.

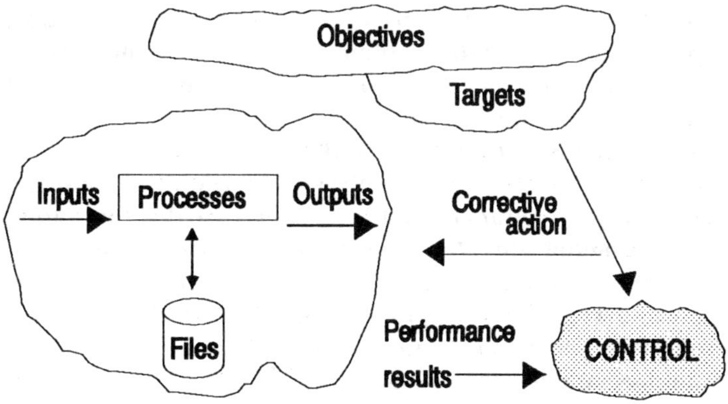

Figure 1.6 The application of control

In a well-designed computerised system, we arrange for the system itself to produce performance results in the form of *management information* - records that will tell us whether the system is performing properly and hopefully what to do about it.

So what do we actually need to do when we apply the corrective measures indicated by the control process? The feedback should tell us **what** is going wrong. It is then up to a manager (or the system itself if possible) to work out **why**. Chapters 2,4 and 5 will have a lot to say about error handling. This is often one of the major aspects of control. Others include:

- trying to make the best use of resources
- trying to reduce inefficiencies and waste
- maintaining security - ensuring that only those who need to, can read or change data.

Once we make use of data comms in a system, there are two additional considerations:

- the communications aspect means that time is important and if there is a problem, we often cannot wait for a human to look through a stack of printed results and decide what action to take
- we may be looking at a completely automatic system controlled entirely by electronics equipment (including computers) - humans design it but are not themselves involved in decision-making at all.

Control means finding out what is wrong and then doing something about it: in these automatic, comms-oriented systems, although we may have built in control measures, it may be necessary to give the system a set of parameters (something like general guidelines) for it to work to.

Going back to the telephone system earlier, the parameters selected might require the system to operate so that for example, no incoming outside call can be refused (even if it means cutting off an internal conversation to free an extension) and assume that extensions 1-20 must take priority between 10 and 12 o'clock. As it runs, the system will collect statistics such as we saw earlier and could present these as management information.

Later on, we will look at large communications networks in a wide geographical area. They contain hardware units for switching calls between users and making the connections between them. This kind of equipment is called a network *node.*

Voice and/or data messages are passed through the network from one node to another and when the traffic intensity rises (ie, when things get busy), there will be lots of competition for node access because everyone wants their call to go ahead of everyone else's. A particular node may have to contact all those nearest to it, to find out what their loads are at present and what they are likely to be in the next few seconds.

The node may then need to look at the likely demand for its services for the near future and make a decision whether to close its queue, get some priority from other units or whatever.

If the system keeps records (ie, logs its own performance), a human can at any time, examine the records and look to see if the comms traffic is being handled in the most efficient manner and if not, alter the operating parameters.

This will continue, almost on a trial-and-error basis until the system achieves a satisfactory level of performance (or we decide that this is impossible and say, install more telephone lines or restrict the number of calls out).

This constant monitoring process by the system itself and by humans is supremely important for the successful operation of any network.

Part of the control process concerns itself with the detection of faults and errors and it looks for answers to questions such as:

- which hardware units are giving regular trouble?
- which need servicing and which need replacing?
- if one unit goes out of action, how should we reschedule the other units to minimise the shock to the system as a whole?

Types of computerised system

Firstly let us introduce the *operating system* as the directing mechanism and the two techniques *multiprogramming* and *time-sharing* as fundamental bases for the internal operation of computerised systems. We can then introduce the two major approaches to data processing systems, namely *batch processing* and *transaction processing*.

Operating systems

In DP, the word **system** is used more specifically than we have done so far. A computerised system is usually a means of achieving some sort of business objective and will involve:

- clerical (manual) procedures
- computer procedures (usually called *programs*)
- input data
- output data
- file and/or databases.

The heart of a computer is its processor which can only operate efficiently (ie, run the required programs) if it is 'managed' and the operating system is a very complex piece of software that can monitor the hardware and carry out jobs (run programs) efficiently as required by the user.

Multiprogramming

A program is a set of instructions that are given to the computer to make it carry out a series of operations to achieve some objective. Some of these operations will involve:

- moving data around within the memory
- calculations on data held in memory
- changing the form of data in memory.

The processor carries out operations such as these, incredibly quickly because they only involve electronic circuitry. Even a cheap PC will carry out tens of thousands of instructions per second.

Another set of operations involves:

- transferring data into memory from outside the computer (input)
- transferring data from memory out of the computer (output).

These are much slower than the first set because as well as the circuitry, they involve moving parts - readers, printers etc. A typical input or output operation might take anywhere between 1 millisecond and 1 second (ie, tens of thousands of times slower).

Once the computer has initiated an input or output operation, there may be a long delay while it waits for the operation to be completed. This time delay can be used very effectively to carry out other operations. In other words, while the computer is waiting for a data record to be read in or printed out (resulting from the execution of an instruction in one program), it could carry out a further instruction which is part of another program.

In practice this means that several programs appear to be running at the same time, the whole sequence of operations being managed by the operating system.

Figure 1.7 shows a time snapshot of three jobs in multiprogramming execution.

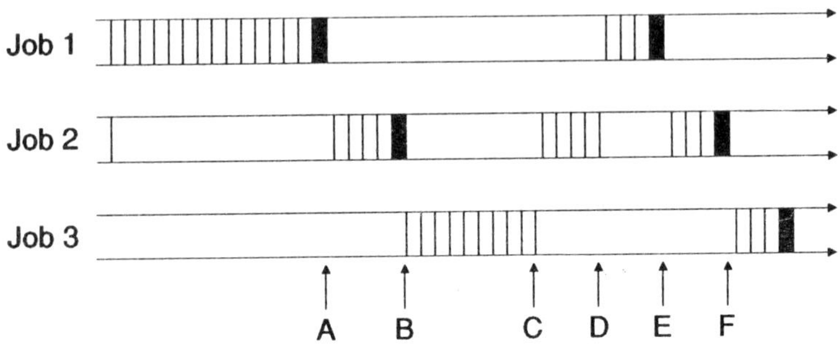

Figure 1.7 Multiprogramming 3 separate jobs

Job 1 has been running for a while and at point A, has just initiated an output instruction. It tells the operating system it is idle and the system can then pass control to Job 2. It runs for a while, until point B, where it starts a wait for an input. Job 3 can then carry on until point C, where job 2 has finished waiting. At point D, job 1 has finished its wait so jobs 2 and 3 have to wait until it releases the processor again at point E, and so on.

Although only 1 instruction at a time is actually being executed, it seems to the observer that all three jobs are running simultaneously. In general, a program will run until it needs to wait for input or output. Once it is waiting, say for a disk record to be read, or a line to be printed, another program can be run for a while, and so on until either an earlier program is no longer waiting, or all the running programs are waiting for data transfer.

To make this kind of operation possible, the programs being run should be those that involve a lot of input and output in comparison with their need for the processor, otherwise one processor-hogging program will prevent the others from running. Also, there is a limit to the number of programs that can be run simultaneously, largely due to computer memory restrictions. We are usually limited to a small number of jobs, perhaps three or four at a time, each of which will require minutes to complete.

Time-sharing

With on-line systems, we might have hundreds of users wanting the computer for a very short time. The actual computer time needed to look up one stock balance or date of last payment from a particular customer, might be a few thousandths of a second once the command has reached the computer.

The operating system now needs to handle hundreds or thousands of users wanting short bursts of computer time at any time of the day, with the minimum *response time*. Users will not want to wait long for a reply to their enquiry or a confirmation that their transaction has been received and understood. In this kind of operating environment, there is little point in carrying out the multiprogramming that we illustrated before and we use a modification called *time-sharing*.

In this, each user's command (which actually represents a request for a program to be found on a library and run) is put into a queue held on a magnetic disk. The operating system scans the queue regularly, giving each user who wants it a *slice* of computer time in turn. During this short slice a job can run once it has been loaded into the memory.

If this is enough, OK, and the results of the processing are sent back to the user. If not sufficient, the job is taken out of the memory in its current state (ie, partially complete) and put into the queue, where it waits until other users have all been given their slice. Then it is dropped back into the memory and run for a further slice. This will continue until the job is completed. Fig 1.8 shows time-sharing in operation.

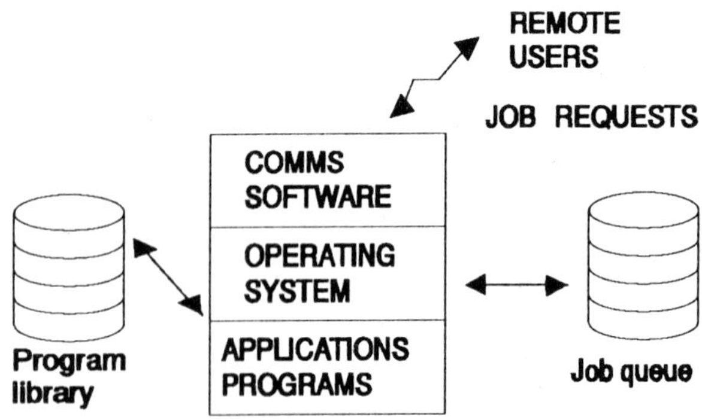

Figure 1.8 Time-sharing operations

Not all on-line systems make use of time-slicing - there are variations, but it is one of the most common techniques for time-sharing.

Communication with the operating system

Human operators must communicate with the operating system to tell the computer what it is to do (which programs it is to run) and this is accomplished using what is called *job control*. This is a very complicated set of instructions that can look something like a programming language and requires the user or creator of the job control to be experienced, and to understand quite a lot about the workings of the computer and the operating system.

For on-line use, the operating system is handled by means of commands which are a form of very simplified job control designed for the non-expert user. These commands are often given implicitly - the user does not even realise that he is giving job control commands in his dialogue.

Of course, the operating system itself is not simple. It must be able to handle simple commands to do complex jobs particularly in support of on-line users. Systems designers take a lot of care over the design of the dialogue associated with an application to make man-machine communication as *user friendly* as possible. This dialogue allows a typical on-line user to log on to a remote computer and at some stage, tell the computer what job it is to carry out ie, which program it is to run.

Pause for thought

Refer to Figure 1.4 for an example of the VDU screen that might be presented to the user.

Note that the *icons* (meaningful shapes) in the diagram are not the only basis for selection from a menu. Similarly, menus are not the only basic dialogue structure. For information on alternatives, see chapter 7 of this book and the case studies in my 'Systems Analysis and Design - Case studies for Business Students', published in 1989 by Heinemann Newnes.

We can broadly classify systems into two main types depending on the operating environment in which they operate. Once we have introduced these, you will appreciate why we have talked about operating systems, job control and dialogue.

Batch processing

This is where input data is entered as a group and the identity of the group is maintained throughout all the processing stages. The following example is typical of batch processing.

1. A batch of cheques is received in payment from our various customers
2. Payment data is keyed to magnetic disk (say 300 records)
3. This file is then passed into a validation program to see if there are any mistakes in the data. Some of the records will be in error and will require correction
4. After correction, the file has to be re-validated. Processes 3/4 continue until no further errors are detected

5. Valid records are sorted into customer sequence. The original batch might have been in sequence, but with all the messing about with error correction we cannot be sure that they are still in order. This matters, because after the sort, we will need to update the customer ledger so that afterwards, the customer balances will reflect the latest payments.
   As the number of customer records to be updated is likely to be fairly high in comparison with the total number of customers on the file, (a *high hit rate*), it is efficient to process the two files sequentially. Hence the need for the sort.
6. Receipts are produced - a whole batch, corresponding to a whole batch of payments.
7. A batch of overdue reminders (a selection print) is produced for customers who have not paid for quite a long time.

The essential feature of batch processing is that the various jobs (programs or groups of programs) are carried out from within the computer room, where operators load input data, tapes, magnetic discs, printer paper etc, and tell the computer which jobs to run.

With modern operating systems, this does not necessarily mean that the operator has to tell the computer which program to run after a previous one has finished. He can stack up job requests so that the computer has a complete set of instructions for say, the next 24 hours and it will tell the operator when to carry out any necessary tasks, such as changing disk or tapes.

Obviously, this kind of processing is fully centralised in that all operations (except perhaps for the collection and preparation of input data) are carried out at the *computer centre*, the site where the computer is situated.

Referring back to what we said about multiprogramming, a batch process is very wasteful of computer processing power, because so much time is spent waiting for input/output. The obvious answer is to instruct the operating system to run jobs in multiprogramming mode, so that the computer is used fairly efficiently.

On-line processing

This requires a completely different approach. The term implies that input, output and/or processing might not be entirely within the computer centre.

It may be necessary for users of the system sited many miles from head office, to have immediate access to enquiry data, such as stock levels or customer balances, in order to carry out their daily work. On the other hand, it may be necessary for some of the data to support the enquiries to be entered into the system by the user for transfer to the computer centre, rather than it being collected manually and entered by batch processing at the centre.

In both of these situations, we need a means of accessing the computer from a *remote* (distant) location and this is where data comms comes in.

With batch processing, we are concerned with fairly large quantities of data, probably being processed in a simple way in the sense that processing will be largely a matter of data manipulation and filing. The on-line situation is usually very different. We are dealing with many users connected to the computer indirectly, not in the computer room, but perhaps many yards or even thousands of miles from the computer which is to process their requests.

The on-line user will be largely concerned with small quantities of data, perhaps one transaction (and we often refer to on-line processing under the name *transaction processing*).

In addition, no operator is involved to tell the computer which programs to run and the user himself must do this via the computer dialogue designed for his application.

The user sits at a keyboard with certain **application requirements**, which he has **serviced** by the computer which runs **jobs** consisting of **programs**, backed up by the comms network. He does not know about operating systems, time-sharing or job control and the dialogue represents his contact with the computer that carries out his application servicing.

Common applications in on-line processing

Whether you look at what the user enters, or what the computer does with the data entered, almost all on-line DP applications fall into one of the following:

- *enquiry* - an on-line user wants to interrogate a file ie, to refer to the contents of a particular record(s). For example a store may need to carry out a credit balance or 'stolen' check on a customer's credit card before completing the sale of goods

- *enquiry/update* - the user wishes to enquire, and if the enquiry is satisfactory, he may want to change (update) the file being interrogated. For example, 'are there enough seats available for tomorrow night's performance? If so, I will book four first-class tickets'
- *low-volume* data entry - the user wishes to enter a small number of transactions, perhaps dozens. He does not necessarily want the processing performed immediately, but he does not want to send the source documents to a computer centre to enter the data for him. He needs a system which will allow him to enter his data, in his own time, in his own way, and then to be able to tell the operating system to run the validation, update etc, when he is ready.

This latter is often referred to as *remote job entry* (RJE). In effect, once the user has decided that his batch is big enough, he 'fools' the operating system into thinking that he wants to run a batch job consisting of validation, update, print etc. In other words, the remote user sends a command which is the equivalent of the job control from an in-house operator

- *high-volume data entry* - something like RJE but now we have large quantities of data to enter and we make use of high-speed devices such as document readers or magnetic disk drives. So, we tell the computer (actually we are telling the operating system) that there is a big batch of data coming, and then we connect up the document reader or disk drive and transmit the data to the computer centre.

The data is received by the mainframe computer and stored as a batch. Then, as with RJE, we tell the computer to carry out a batch job. This is often called *remote batch processing*.

Pause for thought

Before going on to developments in on-line systems, this is a good point to look at a summary of the differences between batch and on-line processing. In the following table, the column headed 'batch processing' has been completed. Have a look at the details and see if you can complete the right-hand side, showing how on-line processing differs.

BATCH PROCESSING	ON-LINE PROCESSING
There is usually a delay between the collection of data, or the request for output and the actual processing	
Source documents are usually grouped into batches	
An error report is produced on the whole batch and correction/re-entry is for the whole batch	
There is usually a batch update of files/database	
Typical printed reports relate to a whole batch	

When you have some answers, compare them with these:

	ON-LINE PROCESSING
	Usually immediate processing to give immediate results
	Single transaction input
	Error reporting is usually immediate; correction/re-entry is line-by-line/field-by-field
	Immediate update/report usually occurs on entry of valid transaction
	Single or limited VDU output

The trend to on-line and distributed systems

As soon as we allow for the possibility of remote users, we can see that there may be a need for *decentralisation*.

Years ago, before the mid-1960s, when data comms was in its infancy, many companies had quite powerful and sophisticated computers, with all operations being carried out at a computer centre. If a company had a strong need for computing remote from the main computer, it had to buy machines for the site.

If these computers needed to share files, there was little alternative but to ship a disk pack from one site to another. This was the only practical way to transmit data. (A desperation measure might have been to print out the file and then enter it as a telex and send it off, but the cost would be ridiculous.)

It had been realised before this time that data could be sent along telephone lines using modems (as will be explained in later chapters) but there was only a limited number of companies that could afford this. At this time data transmission rates were quite low, there was little requirement for hardware research and development so costs stayed high. Several factors changed all this and contributed to the explosion in data comms that has continued during this decade.

The growth of remote processing

About 1980 saw the introduction and adoption of microcomputers. This meant that the user now had access to computing power from his desk-top and started to become 'computer-wise', realising what computers could be used for. This was particularly significant with spreadsheets, where the user could for example carry out financial and other calculations with ease and then display the results as nice coloured graphs.

Word processors and 'electronic office' packages all helped to add to this computer wisdom and users started to demand access to the central company computer for even more sophisticated computing power. If they could not get it, they could connect their micro to a company that was prepared to provide the service.

This caused a dramatic increase in demand for data comms hardware and services and as more micros were sold, unit production costs fell, until now it is possible to buy a microcomputer for under £2000 that has similar power to a system that might have cost £30,000 less than 10 years ago.

In addition to very powerful processing chips, these micros now come with large disks which hold large files and can be used for *local processing* ie, carrying out DP work that a less powerful terminal would have to initiate at the host computer.

As the electronics industry started to invest profits in R&D, smaller and more sophisticated 'chips' started to appear and were used increasingly in data comms hardware. The *liberalisation* that occurred after the Telecommunications Act of 1984 meant that users could now buy modems from any supplier instead of what was the case before - having to rent them from the GPO.

While all this has been going on, wide-area technology and application have been expanding and the public network suppliers have put in wide-ranging, fast and fairly error-free connection paths.

Two other factors in the explosion of data comms to support DP have been the increasing demand for sophisticated telephone facilities (which require the same supporting facilities and services as DP) and the increasing requirement for using comms facilities to send text and image. Both will be referred to again.

Decentralisation

A further impetus was provided by the massive take-up in *POS (point-of-service or point-of-sale) systems* particularly with bar-code and plastic card readers connected to central computer facilities.

To support this, the use of data comms equipment has continued to snowball. As suppliers made more sales, they put more efforts into the design of more and more error-free equipment making data comms even more cost-effective.

Now that computing and communications hardware and software are reasonably cheap, users rely increasingly on their PC or computer terminal for servicing their DP applications.

In addition, companies have been forced to spread out geographically, largely because of operating costs in large cities and business and industry have gone along the road of decentralisation, with increasingly more processing carried out and more decisions being made at region, area or branch level.

This means that management responsibility has become decentralised and to support decisions, companies must be prepared to install *distributed systems,* which demand a hierarchy of computing power and of data.

Most organisations have all their separate sites connected, sharing data where necessary. A computer at one site can assist one at another site if it is overloaded. Back-up copies of databases can be sent to other sites for security purposes. If one processor breaks down, data can be switched to another.

Choice of system type

Let us look at some of the questions that need to be answered before a systems designer can make a choice as to the level of decentralisation (distribution) of DP facilities for an organisation or part of an organisation.

- what is the ratio of on-line to batch processing?
- for on-line users, what is the balance of data entry (low and/or high volume), enquiry and update?
- will sites (separate divisions, branches etc) need access to their own local software or versions of common software?
- are there several users at a particular site that can be grouped together as a local area network, acting in isolation except for regular sending or receiving of bulked data?
- what are the distances between sites and how will this affect to costs of data transmission?
- will central data stores need to be updated or can regional or local stores cope, leaving just overall figures to be passed to head office as needed?
- is there a requirement to make regular security copies of data stores and if so, should the copy be transmitted to another site?
- if major data stores need access from all sites, should all access to it be on-line or is it cheaper to send a copy of the whole file (or large parts of it) to the sites and then send updating data as needed?
- how much scope is there for automatic terminals, such as bar-code or badge-readers in warehouses and production lines?
- what printing facilities are needed - can a small local printer handle most of what is needed or must we have high-speed printers at central sites and send large printouts to the sites that need them?
- are there any possibilities for sharing network facilities with other organisations?
- What are the time factors? For example:
  what response times from terminals will be acceptable to users?
  will other users at the site (or in other sites) be affected by a particular transaction (eg, airline or theatre seat booking)?

can input or updating data be held at a site and sent overnight (at cheaper rates)?

This list is nowhere near complete, but you will begin to appreciate why the on-line systems designer needs a knowledge of comms. Chapter 10 provides a rather more detailed examination of on-line systems design thinking.

A classification of comms applications

A classification of applications and techniques, shown in Figure 1.9, will help you to think about what the user is going to do with all these comms facilities.

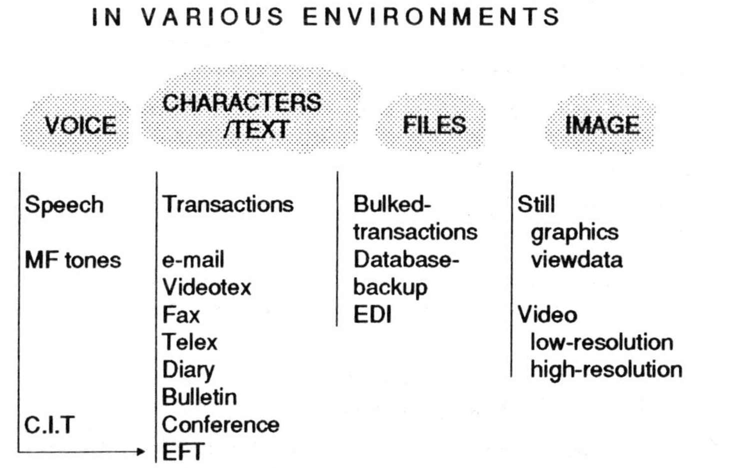

Figure 1.9 Communications applications

Note that not all of them are necessarily anything to do with DP. As we have said already and will continue to find, data comms and DP are now so closely linked that it is almost impossible to consider them in isolation.

We will finish with a short explanation of each:

- voice - not just making phone calls - there are many ways that computers can assist the telephone user such a providing dialling from stored directories - called *computer-integrated telephony (CIT)*
- sound - using the **telephone dialling tones themselves** as a code with which to send data

- characters - in particular, single transactions, such as order entry, airline flight enquiry etc. A particularly important application here is *electronic funds transfer (EFT)* associated with banking and shopping
- text - the sending or exchanging of textual material including telex and electronic mail *(e-mail)*, whether provided within an organisation, or by an outside supplier and extensions to e-mail, such as computer conferencing and electronic diary
- videotex - text displayed in a form something like Teletext or Prestel
- fax (facsimile transmission)
- files - the transfer of whole files between sites for security purposes, as part of a normal DP application or when associated with *electronic data interchange (EDI)* where for example, one company sends a whole file of cash or credit transactions to another.
- image - a single picture such as a diagram, technical drawing or even a moving image, with the definition usually associated with TV. There is also the future possibility of very high-resolution videotex - perhaps you could do home-shopping, say, book a holiday by viewing holiday resort moving scenes and ordering the one you want.

The main fault with this classification (which should be taken as no more than a rough guide), is that many of the items overlap:

- a transaction usually consists of characters, but a file could consist of transactions. How many transactions must we have before we switch from low- volume input to file transfer?
- telex and e-mail were originally designed for sending messages like letters - they are often used to send transactions as well
- fax was originally designed for sending drawings and diagrams. These days many people use it for letters and copies of business transactions. Is it a text transaction or is it still image?

Hopefully the rest of the book will help you to resolve some of these questions and give you an overall view of on-line applications.

Recap

- the bulk of this book is concerned with the transmission of data within a computer system, how it can be captured from outside the company and how it can be passed to the outside
- a typical system consists of a grouping of input, output, stores and processes all acting together to try and attain some objectives
- any system needs control mechanisms to ensure that it works and looking at a typical business system, control is exercised by managers. They will want information from the system to help them in their decisions as to what to do if things are going wrong
- computerised systems can involve several different approaches,depending on what they are used for and how. Batch-processing systems tend to rely on one or more centralised large computers. A system is usually designed around centralised files or data bases
- these systems are used for jobs involving the processing of large amounts of data collected over a period of time and whose running does not usually involve the user except for the correction of errors in data entered
- on-line systems usually have some batch processing aspects but the processing tends to be oriented to the user who may carry out local processing and who may access local data
- cheap electronics and consumer demand have led to an increasing use of on-line systems and there is now a wide range of services available that complement traditional DP functions and in some cases replace them. Companies making use of them can reduce the amount of programming needed and the amount of data to be collected and stored.

Typical questions

Question 1.1

Explain the following terms and give examples:-

- remote process
- local process
- computer centre
- intelligent terminal

- point-of-service processing
- distributed data base.

Question 1.2

For a typical high-street clearing bank, make up a table showing the main activities it will carry out with the aid of computers. Pay particular attention to those processing activities that might be distributed throughout its network as opposed to that carried out at the head office.

Assume that the logical structure of the bank is:

Head Office<——>Regional office<——>Branch<——>Terminal

Question 1.3

Now, do the same thing for a supermarket chain, the structure being:

Warehouse/Factory<——>Head Office<——>Store

Question 1.4

A sales manager has a computer terminal with a link to his company mainframe and to a range of external services. Write a sentence on each of seven external services he might make use of, with a brief explanation of why he might use each one.

2: Who 'talks' and what is 'said'

Objectives

After reading this chapter, you should:-

- appreciate the significance of the term *conversation* to be used throughout the book
- understand why two or more parties need to 'talk' to each other ie, have conversations
- understand why rules are needed to permit the conversation
- be aware of the different kinds of terminal that are used to link into a network
- understand various modes and methods of transmitting data
- understand several differing meanings of the term *network*
- understand the difference between data transfer and data transmission
- appreciate the forms in which data and information are stored and transmitted
- understand the sources of some problems that arise in data communications
- appreciate the importance of time and timing in data transmission.

Chapter 1 has given you a general introduction to the computing environment and where data communications fits in to this. We can now look in a fairly detailed (but hopefully simplified) way at **what** is transmitted and **how** - you already have some idea of **why**.

(If you already know something about the subject, you will probably spot many 'hooks' - areas where I have sneaked in something as the basis for development later on, without a full explanation. Don't worry! All will be revealed).

Conversation

In it widest sense a conversation involves the transfer of information from a *sender* to a *receiver*.

In this book, we will use the term *message* to mean whatever is transferred from sender to receiver:

- regardless of the 'identity' of the sender or receiver (computer-computer, person-person, network-network)
- irrespective of the form that it takes (voice, text, image)
- whatever the method used to transfer it (broadcast, telephone network, wire).

Figure 2.1 Sending a message

We will also use the term *talk* to mean 'sending any kind of message' as summarised in Figure 2.1.

Can we actually have a one-sided conversation like this, where only one side talks? You may think that some of your friends can do this when they phone you up and you cant get a word in edgeways. But, you must have said something, even if it was only 'hello' and 'goodbye'. Perhaps you managed the occasional 'yes', 'can you say that again' or 'rubbish'.

In other words, during the conversation, the sender sends and the receiver receives, but at some point there must be a switchover when the original sender becomes the receiver and vice versa as shown in Figure 2.2.

In an attempt to get round these potentially confusing definitions (sender and receiver), people in data comms use the terms *primary* and *secondary*. These recognise the fact that for a conversation, both 'send' and 'listen' are needed and at any point

Figure 2.2 Did I get through?

in time, the primary is the one sending while the secondary is listening.

In fact, this is not strictly correct. The term 'primary' is really used in a situation that does not occur in voice conversation over the telephone - it is common in data comms to have a primary *broadcasting* to several secondaries spending most of their time listening.

Then, any one of the secondaries might at the same time be broadcasting to its own set of secondaries; so it also acts as a primary.

What is needed for conversation

For conversation (summarised in Figure 2.3) to be possible, there must be:

- a sender (primary) - me wanting to phone you!
- a means of creating the message - my brain thinking out what to say!
- a machine for sending the message - computer terminal!
- a medium for linking the two ends - a telephone line or the air!
- a receiver (secondary) to interpret the message - you waiting to get a letter!
- a machine to receive the message - your adapted TV set for a Ceefax weather report!

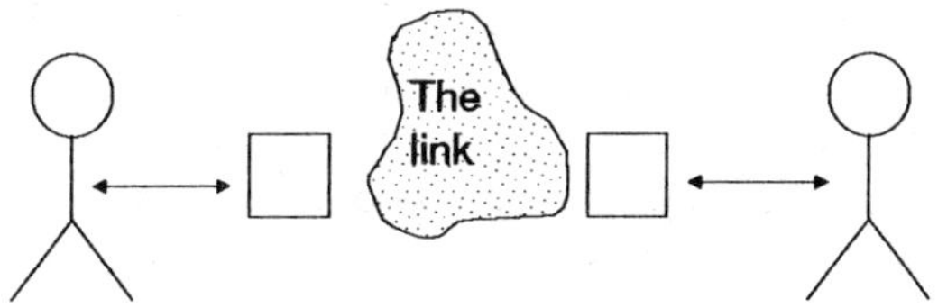

Figure 2.3 A conversation

- a set of rules to enable the conversation to proceed - I will keep talking until I hear you say 'hang on'!

The historical development of conversation

Primitive man probably started off 'speaking' with just a few grunts and his conversations were very limited, although he could probably bellow for quite a long distance. His grunts were probably reinforced by body movements such as shaking a fist or baring the teeth.

Then, speech gradually developed and it eventually became possible to have nice little chats over a reasonable distance, but only as far as was polite at the time, or as strong as the voice of the sender. Since sender and receiver can be thought of here as face-to-face, we say that we have a *line-of-sight* connection, illustrated in Figure 2.4.

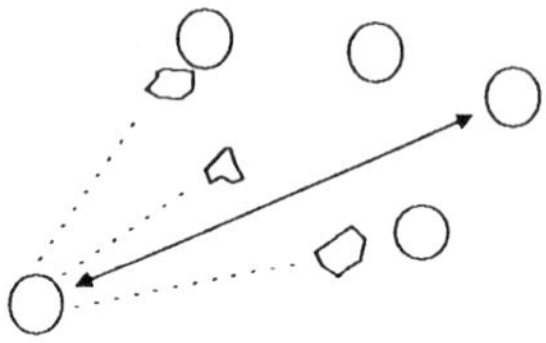

Figure 2.4 Line-of-sight

Man then found that he needed a means of communication over greater distances and perhaps not in line-of-sight. Amongst other techniques developed was the *heliograph* in which messages can be sent in a code made up from flashes of the sun reflected from a mirror.

Another technique is *semaphore* where (in the British navy version) two flags held in various positions, like the hands of a clock, are used to represent letters. (Other possibilities include firing an arrow with a message tied to it and sending a carrier pigeon.)

All of these methods suffer from the disadvantage that you cant direct your message to a particular person - you cant guarantee that it will be received only by him/her. You are *broadcasting* to anyone wanting to listen.

This does not necessarily mean that others will **understand**, but they can **hear** you if they want to.

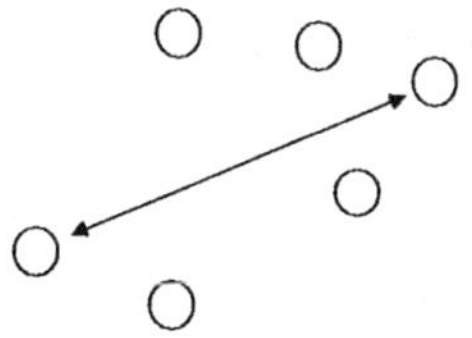

Figure 2.5 Point-to-point link

If one person talks to just one other, we say that there exists a *point-to-point* link (Figure 2.5). Where several senders and receivers are involved, we refer to a *multi-point* link (Figure 2.6).

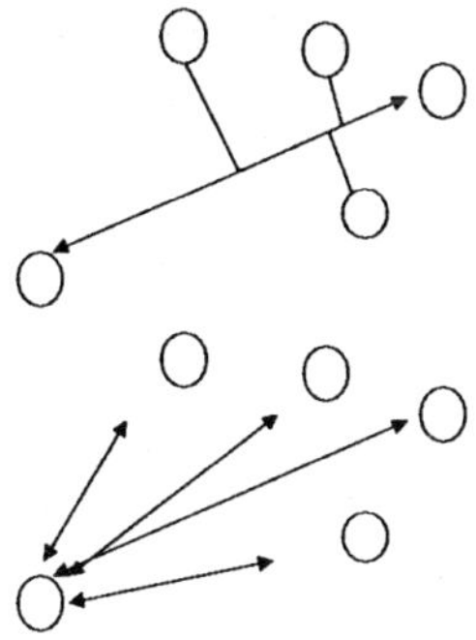

Figure 2.6 Multi-point links

Partly because of the need for 'privacy' and need for long distance transmission, *telegraphy* was developed (the Greek 'tele' means 'distance' and 'graph' means 'write'). Telegraphy uses the making and breaking of an electrical circuit over a transmission wire, to produce short and long sounds (dots and dashes). These can be used to send messages in what is called *Morse code* where for example, an 'A' is dot/dash (usually represented by .__). The letter 'R' is dot/dash/dot (.__.) and 'E' is just a dot. Telegraph allows us the means for a true point-to-point link.

The next two developments in distance messaging (*telecommunications*) were *telephone* (the Greek 'phone' means 'speak') and telegraphy without a wire ie, *wireless (radio)*. Radio is obviously broadcast through the air, while a telegraph or telephone wire is a *directed medium* which acts as a point-to-point link (later on, you will find that even telephone calls are not always point-to-point).

The link

Today, we have computers talking to computers, users broadcasting to users and many other variations. In many respects, the link itself is as important as what and who we are linking.

Although we said that it was impossible to have a one-way conversation, in practice, there are situations where once the initial contact has been made between the two ends, almost all the messages go in one direction. For example, think of a bar-code reader in a warehouse, recording deliveries of stock and 'informing' the head office computer. The link only allows messages in one direction and is called a *simplex* link, shown in Figure 2.7.

Figure 2.7 A simplex link

It is more likely though, that both ends will want to speak although not necessarily at the same time:

- I send a line
- you say whether you like it or not
- I then resend the line or send the next one
- and so on ....

This is called a *half-duplex* link, illustrated in Figure 2.8. A more sophisticated name is *two-way alternate* (or *switched simplex*) - for part of the conversation, the line is simplex in one direction. Then it is switched to simplex in the other direction.

A more complex link is needed when we want simultaneous message transfer in both directions say, a user at a workstation is sending sales transactions to head office and at the same time the boss is sending electronic mail to his *in-tray* for him to look at later on.

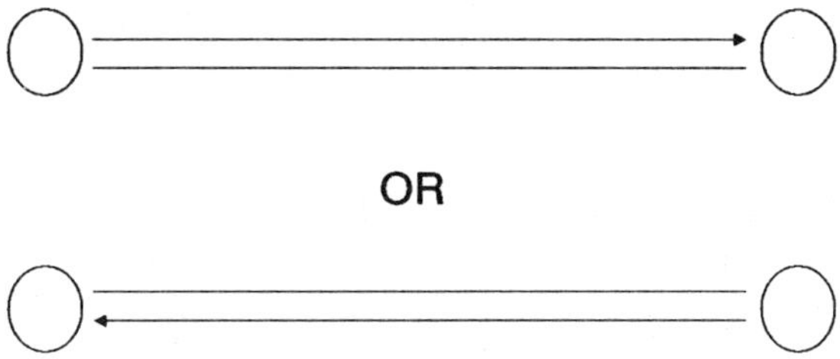

Figure 2.8 A half-duplex link

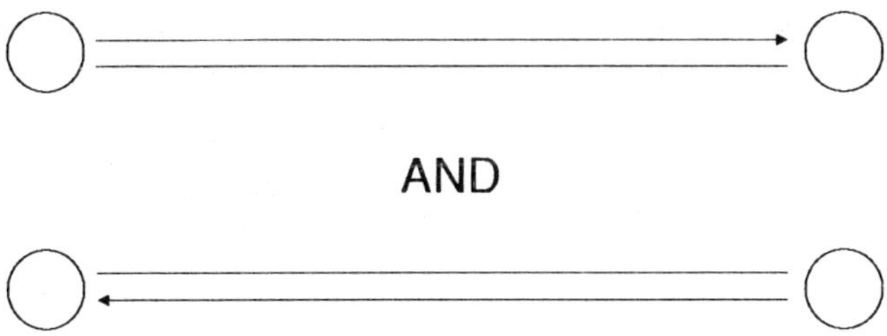

Figure 2.9 A full-duplex link

We refer to this as a *duplex* link (*full-duplex, two-way simultaneous*), shown in Figure 2.9.

The typical voice conversation usually implies that both ends 'send' at the same rate, but in computer conversations, the rate of data transfer in the two directions does not have to be the same. We might be employing an *asymmetric* link - perhaps one direction is for simple requests, while the return is for large quantities of reply and needs a high transfer rate to avoid excessively long transmission times (Figure 2.10).

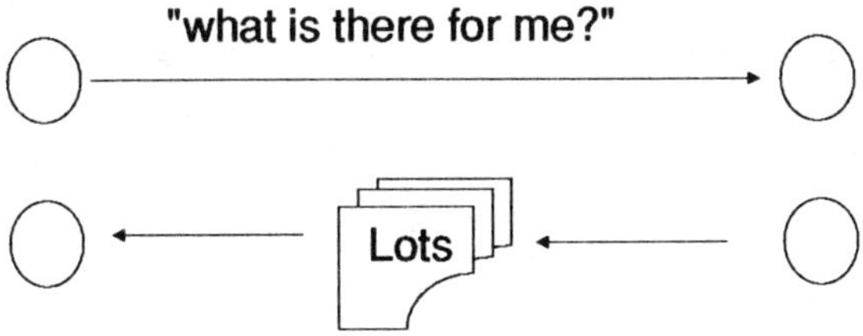

Figure 2.10 An 'asymetric' conversation

Pause for thought

Before we introduce the hardware and techniques of data transmission, we must touch on the rules of a conversation. You may not have experience of dealing with computer terminals, but you must have made lots of phone calls. Have you ever actually thought about the rules you follow unconsciously?

Think about the following:

- who and what are the two ends of the conversation
- the conversation might be confidential
- why is the conversation necessary?

Now see how many factors you can identify that might form the basis of a set of rules. Then look at this suggested list:

- can anyone listen in?
- who will speak first?
- how do I know its him talking?
- does he speak English?
- does it matter?
- I am talking about the exam. Is he talking about the same one, on the same day?
- will I allow him to interrupt me?
- how?
- did he understand my last sentence?
- what happens if we are cut off. Do we restart at the beginning or carry on from a *checkpoint*?

The need for rules

You can probably think of many other problems that require resolution before the conversation can be carried out successfully. Fortunately, common sense sorts most of these out in voice conversations. On the other hand, it definitely does not when we deal with conversations when one or both ends are not human and if there are no rules there can be no proper conversation.

In an ideal world we would have *standards*, ie, generally-known and generally-accepted procedures. Both sides would accept them and there would be no need for rules:

- this is 123-4567, Joe speaking, can I talk to Fred?
- after a cut-off, when we go back *on line*, I say 'Now, where was I...'
- to ask for a repeat, you say 'Sorry I didn't catch that'
- to interrupt, you say 'Hey, just a minute, ...'

Unfortunately, everyone may choose not to use your standards - they might prefer their own or not have any at all. This is why we need rules - to overcome the lack of, or difference between the standards applied at each end of the conversation. As we will see in chapter 3, the set of rules applying to a conversation is called a *protocol* and protocols are responsible for some of the biggest and knottiest problems in data communications today.

In this chapter so far, we have taken many of our illustrations from voice conversations and to remind you that we are as much concerned with data transfers not involving voice, go back and re-read the final section of chapter 1.

We are dealing with a subject that has many practical applications and to help you appreciate the 'human' end of the very common man-machine conversation, we will now look at some of the 'machines' that enable data communication in a variety of application areas.

Types of terminal

A basic classification of terminals

Here, we introduce a number of 'devices' that are used to send or receive data:

- *dumb (unintelligent) terminal.* This has no processing power (it cannot compute) so is only used for input and output.

  The simplest kind is an *output terminal*, such as a VDU in an airline concourse showing flight arrival times, or a printer to receive telex messages.

  Similarly, some terminals are used for input only, such as for automatic *data collection* - we have already mentioned the bar-code reader in the warehouse. (A similar bar-code reader is used at a supermarket check-out.)

Another common data collection terminal is a *magnetic card reader* such is used in a garage or shop for credit card sales or in a cash point. (Note that the cash point itself is often referred to as a terminal but is in fact a combination - keyboard, magnetic card reader, VDU and printer!)

The other kinds of terminal all involve a keyboard and vary from the very simple to the extremely complicated:

- *semi-intelligent terminal.* This has a certain amount of processing power, but is not fully programmable, ie, it does not have the flexibility of a computer in its own right).

  The power of the semi-intelligent terminal will be used just to support the communications. This could involve forming up data for transmission or changing its code, doing a little bit to support the software at the other end of the link or counting the number of transactions sent so that the other end will know if one gets lost

- *fully intelligent terminal* - programmable (the programs usually being stored until wanted on floppy or hard disk).

The user will often select an application from a menu and this causes a program to be loaded from disk and then run. In contrast, the semi-intelligent terminal program is not usually on disk but in *ROM*, a special kind of electronic memory that cannot be altered once set by the manufacturer.

A basic classification of intelligent terminals

Although these are given different names, it is often the case that a particular terminal can act as one of several types depending on the software driving it:

- *character terminal* - used to send characters one at a time rather than in groups. This method of transmission is called *asynchronous* and will be explained at the end of this chapter. The basic set of characters supported is covered by American National Standards Institute recommendation 3.64, equivalent to European Computer Manufacturers Association 48

- *forms (page) terminal* - sends and/or receivers whole pages (or forms). It is designed for the *synchronous* transmission of blocks of characters (see later in the chapter)

- *packet terminal* - a special kind of synchronous terminal used to link via the *public data network (PDN)*. This terminal will be discussed in chapter 8
- *graphics terminal* - which can display more than just alphabetic and numeric characters.

Different manufacturers supply terminals to different specifications (one of the reasons why protocols are needed) and the extra characters supported, may differ between different makes. This becomes a bit of a problem if your terminal is linked to a mainframe sending non-standard characters that yours cannot recognise. It may send a character meaning that it wants your VDU screen to be blanked off; your terminal might interpret this as the command to 'beep'.

Once a terminal has the capacity for more than just simple text, it really should be called an *image terminal*. Such terminals can often show and manipulate very detailed displays, perhaps even those that are moving. Remember, what you see on the screen is made up from dots and with higher quality electronics and more sophisticated control, we can attain higher and higher grades of resolution (the clarity and precision of the image with which we are presented). Often, the increased performance from a terminal can be selected by putting the relevant 'card' (printed-circuit electronics board) into the computer.

The way that terminal and data comms technology is developing, it wont be very long before full TV-like video is possible on the same VDU that is used for DP.

Figure 2.11 shows a piece of output from a word processor (*Wordstar 5 by Micropro*). You can see two pages from the draft of this chapter on the screen simultaneously and at the top left, a 'pull-down' menu.

So, we know a little about particular conversations and where/how they occur, but we have as yet said nothing about connection and inter-connection. There are lots of people who want a conversation and some kind of network is needed to enable one or more users to link up with one or more 'other' users.

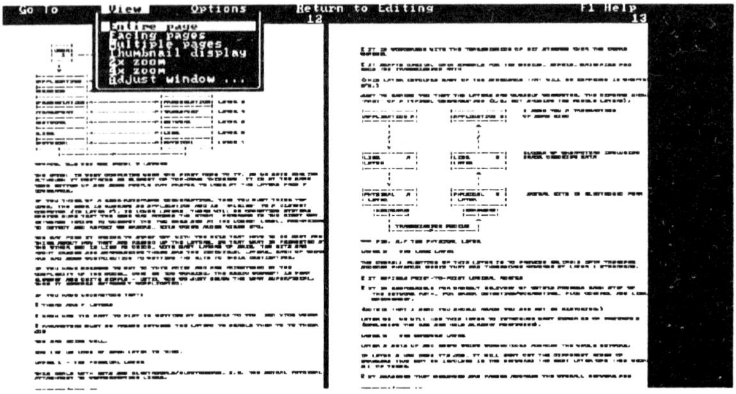

Figure 2.11 A high-resolution VDU report

Networks

So let us return to the link for a conversation. With a point-to-point link, all we need to worry about is the rules being kept to at each end, but when we consider multi-point links, we introduce the possibility of *contention*.

When more than just a few points exist, all may be struggling for a communications service and may want to talk to one person (or everyone) and we must utilise methods of *contention resolution* to control this struggle and ensure that there is a reasonably fair allocation of resources available.

We need to design much more complex and sophisticated sets of rules for this kind of communications environment. One possibility is to give everyone a fixed slot of time each and then they must shut up until it is their turn again. Another is to give priority to the user with the most urgent work or perhaps the one paying most for the service).

The real-life situation is complicated because we have the problem not only of the protocols relating to **who** will get service and **when** they will get it, but the added consideration of **how to connect** the various people involved. Remember, this is a multi-point situation and as soon as we introduce more than one sender and one receiver, we are dealing with a *network*.

This term is perhaps one of the most confusing and ill-understood terms used, so let's see if we can sort it out.

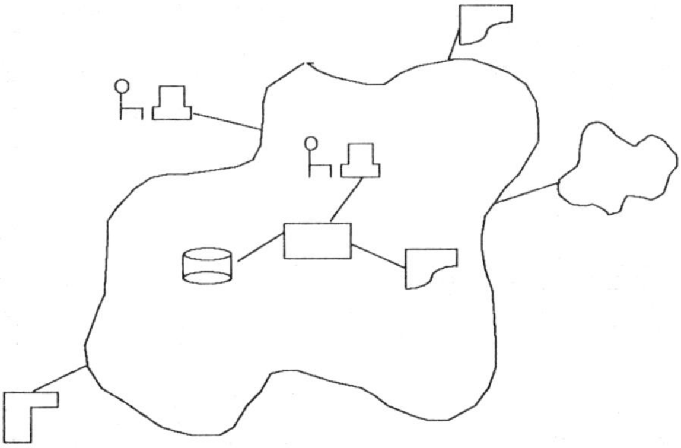

Figure 2.12 The 'A' Network

A very rough definition might include some or all of the following:

- a collection of entities wanting to have conversations
- resources or facilities that make the conversations necessary
- the means whereby the parties know they are being called, can be linked up and can have messages transferred between them.

This is a very messy 'definition' and although fairly complete, is not very practical, so let us try to simplify the concept by taking parts of it.

I have invented the terms *A Network* and *B Network* which students have found of some use. (Note that they are **my** definitions and are not in general use.)

Looking at an organisation, the A Network is the complex of users, terminals, computers, files, programs and procedures needed to carry out the DP to support its activities (Figure 2.12). To do their DP, users need to be linked with resources such as computers, files, printers and other users, within the company and outside.

The wires, switches and other pieces of equipment needed, together with everything from the companies that supply the connection and data transmission services, make up the 'B Network', needed to 'carry' the A Network (Figure 2.13).

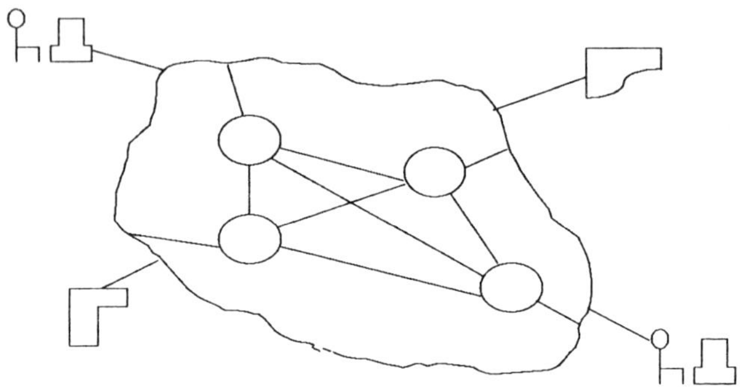

Figure 2.13 The 'B' Network

There are many different kinds of hardware device making up the network. Some of these will be involved with routing calls, some with making transmission more efficient and some with just sending or receiving messages. We use the term *node* to cover any component that is involved with the running of the network itself rather than being there to send or receive messages. (This term will often crop up in the book.)

Before going on with our classification, bear in mind that there are many different kinds of network and people even use different names for the same network, so let us build on the 'A/B networks' concept to differentiate between different kinds of network. Note that a network may fall into more than one category).

Physical network

A physical network has a real existence and is mainly related to the hardware and the connection/transmission service it provides. Examples include:

- the British Telecom telephone network
- the Mercury Communications Ltd data network
- the Thames Valley College network.

For all of these, since they actually exist, you could look at the hardware involved and work out its cost or perhaps arrange a maintenance schedule.

Logical network

A logical network is what people think of as a network because you can link up to it and use its services or facilities. Most developed countries have a public data network which will link to others because they all recognise internationally-agreed protocols and standards. Users can access networks in other countries giving the appearance of an international data network although nobody actually set out to create such a network initially.

If you subscribe to the service provided from 'G. Mandoff financial services' network, you can use your computer to link up and obtain information about the stock exchange or you can get the system to carry out financial calculations on your data.

But all that G. Mandoff is really providing is some of the spare time on the small mainframe computer which he uses to run his other businesses. All he needs is a couple of telephone lines piped into his computer rented from BT, Mercury or one of the other telephone network suppliers and a bit of electronics to handle several calls at the same time to his computer.

To link up, you dial the number of his computer and 'talk' to it through your *modem* (coming up soon). Hardly a network is it.

The next consideration in our classification is to examine who owns, or who provides the network.

Private network

A *private network* is one which is bought and controlled by the company that is to use it. Depending on what services it offers, the owner company may be allowed to offer its use to the general public (ie, other companies) but in general, a private network is for private use.

For example, Thomas Cooke, Thompsons Holidays and most of the other large travel companies make use of their own private viewdata networks to make life easier for their agency staff in booking holidays and answering customer queries about flight times, hotels etc. British Rail has its own private telephone system as do the major banks.

Public network
A *public network* is provided by a *network supplier* and is intended for general use. Note that it is becoming common for some of the public network to be rented out for private use.

Our classification must also pay some regard to the size of the network.

Local area network
If it covers one room, floor, building or a smallish site, it may be appropriate to refer to it as a *local area network (LAN).*

The main difference between a LAN and other networks is usually the very much higher data transmission rates that are possible with LANs because they employ higher-quality electronics and more sophisticated transmission techniques.

Metropolitan area network
If it is somewhat larger, it could be just a private network covering a limited area, such as a factory site or a college campus. But if it spreads perhaps across a whole city, it may be called a *metropolitan area network (MAN).*

The MAN is often a logical network - it might consist of several large private networks linked by fast private lines supplied by the public telephone companies, ie, it doesn't exist completely as a private network because part of it is not totally owned by the company that runs it.

Wide area network
Anything larger is almost certainly a *wide area network (WAN),* most of these being for public use (except say, British Rail, regional hospitals and the banks, who have their own).

Public networks

The public network suppliers
The official suppliers of public telephone or data networks are called *Public Telephone Operators (PTOs).*

The UK Telecommunications Act of 1981 in effect gave permission in the form of a PTO licence to the following companies to enable them to compete and provide voice and/or data networks for public use:

- British Telecom plc (formerly part of the GPO - General Post Office)

- Mercury Communications Ltd (MCL, owned by the British company Cable & Wireless)
- Kingston Communications (Hull) plc (once called Hull City Telephone Corporation)
- Telecom Securicor Cellular Radio Ltd (Cellnet - owned by British Telecom and Securicor)
- Racal-Vodafone (Vodafone - Owned by the Racal Corporation).

Quite recently, a number of *cable companies* (organisations that started off in cable TV), have been given licences to provide *local loop* networks that link into other PTO networks. *Cable Telecom,* provides a telephone network in the Slough area, based on optical fibre connections that can service all local calls and which links into the MCL network for non-local calls.

The Public Switched Telephone Network

As a former part of the General Post Office, British Telecom was responsible for putting in and developing the telephone network that covered the whole country, except in the region of Kingston-upon-Hull Corporation which was allowed to offer its own service in this area.

This network was called the *public switched telephone network (PSTN),* usually just called the *PTN* these days. It consisted of a massive amount of equipment, wires, cables, switching exchanges, switchboards, telephones etc, all supplied by the then GPO. Since the early 1960s, with the development of micro-miniaturisation in electronics and other technical advances, the company has gradually updated and improved its equipment, but as a telephone network, like many other things, it is as strong as its weakest link.

Today, most of the BT network consists of very modern computerised equipment but still has some of the old-fashioned kit, some of which is quite old and not very reliable. This means that in certain aspects, the best you can get from the telephone network is no better than it was 30 years ago. However, in most cases, especially when we look at data networks (which is more the subject of this book), the BT network is extremely modern and as good as any other.

The main problem with the BT voice network, and to a lesser extent with the others is that its current performance suffers from historical limitations imposed on it. During the birth and development of the telephone service, a decision had to be made as to the quality of service that would be offered, partly based on technology as it existed, the economics of running the service and what the customer would put up with. In the event, it turned out that the electrics and electronics that make up the voice network are such that voice calls quality is somewhat limited.

You will get clicks, screeches and dropped lines and you will also hear very squeaky voices (no high and no low notes). If you listen to music through a standard telephone handset, you certainly won't think that it's hi-fi.

One of the consequences of the limitations is that the network is not particularly good for sending data - the most recent hardware developments allowing for transmission up to about 2000 characters per second, which is slow in computing terms. It is actually too fast really for applications like electronic mail and entering sales orders, but is not good enough for large-scale operations such as transferring whole files between regional offices.

The trouble is that, by law, the other PTOs must provide a service that links in with BT so if BT can only provide a certain quality, there is no incentive for the others to do any better in many cases. The result is that we have a PTN made up of equipment and lines from all five PTOs (there are several more that might be coming along as well) with a fair amount of nearly obsolete equipment co-existing with very modern equipment, the overall network (illustrated in Figure 2.14) being not bad for voice, but nothing special for data.

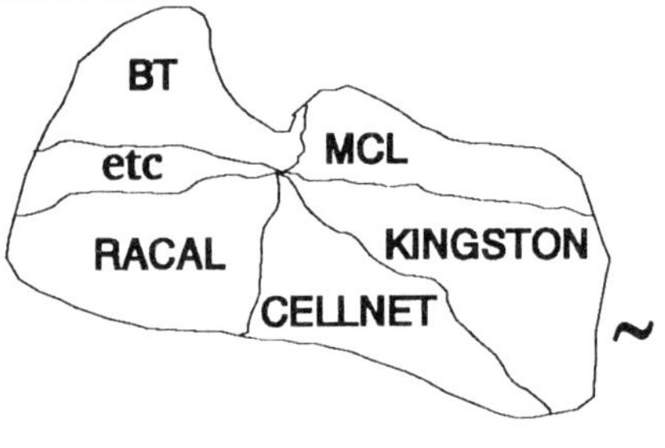

Figure 2.14 The Public Telephone Network

The public data network

The public data network (Figure 2.15) is at present provided largely by BT and MCL based on extremely high quality and expensive equipment including some enormous controlling computers. It is designed to carry data, at rates up to 100,000s of characters per second.

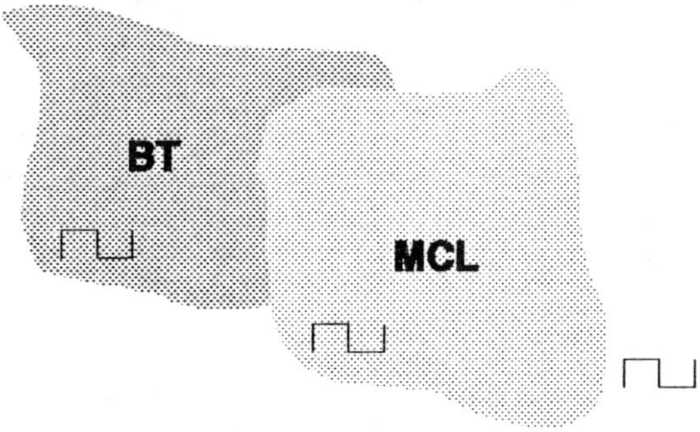

Figure 2.15 The Public Data Network

An interesting thing is that as the PDN suppliers have brought out new equipment and techniques to handle data, they apply them to voice as well. This means the PTN uses some of the same equipment and transmission paths as the PDN. In practice, voice and data are completely mixed together for, or during transmission and carried along the same transmission media allowing us two views of the overall public network (Figure 2.16).

We keep loosely referring to 'conversation' and the applications of communications in data. Before we go much further however, we need to examine exactly in what forms the computer sends data down the line into the network - in the next section we look at information, data and data storage codes.

Information and the represention of data

Information must inform

Information is 'that which informs', ie, conveys some ideas or concepts **that have meaning to the person it is intended for**. This means that, strictly speaking computers cannot store information nor can they transmit it.

Rubbish? We know for example, that:

- Ceefax and Oracle are controlled by computers and the basis for weather forecasts, sports reports and so on is held in computer store
- a word processor is a computer program that can be used to produce letters, labels and so on
- a spreadsheet program can produce a sales forecast, informing you that you need to consider increasing production.

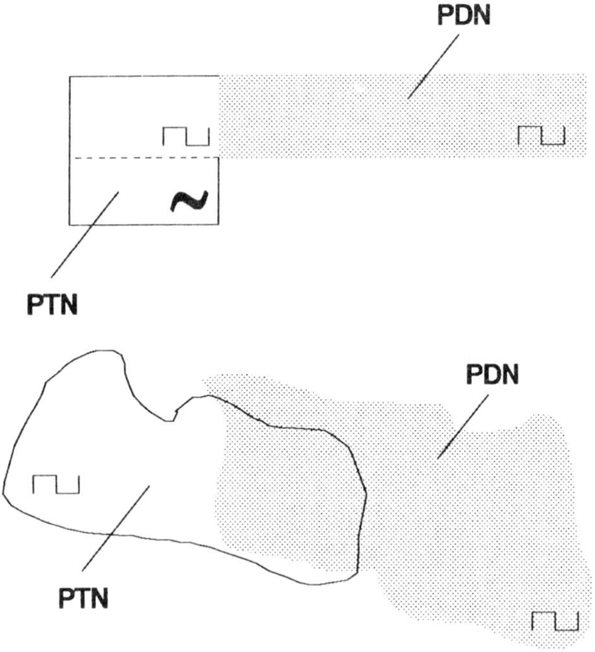

Figure 2.16 Two views of 'The' Public Network

In all of these, the end-product is information **produced by computer manipulation of data**. In order to convey this information it is necessary to consider the form in which it is conveyed. If the cave man shakes his fist, his enemy knows that he is being threatened. If I send you an electronic mail message, you can read my invitation to lunch next week. But, what actually goes through the link is **data**.

When a heliograph or semaphore flags are used, information is conveyed **only to someone who can understand it**. Anyone could take down a note of what was sent - 2 short flashes, pause, 1 long flash, pause, ... but unless you know the **code**, it wont have any **meaning**.

Data

I think of data as being **information without any meaning** and when we examine data, either it must have an inherent meaning (the data supplies its own information), or we must have some rule that allows us to work out the meaning, ie, *decode* it. For example '210789' could be:

- the date 21st October 1989 (you would know for certain if it was shown as 21/10/89 or perhaps 21.10.89)
- the 21st record in the 078th track of disk 9
- a product code (where 2 means 'metal', 10 means 'sheet', 7 means 'round' and 8 means 'contains vegetable' - perhaps its a tin of beans).

As well as items such as 'CAT', '12345', 'pi', 'zero' etc, information could also include instructions like 'be careful', 'shut up' and 'say again'. When we consider exactly what is transmitted in data comms, we need to appreciate how data codes are used to carry meaning.

As you can work out (by considering the application of comms to DP), data can be, or contain of one or more of the following:

- *alphabetic* - the upper case (capital) letters 'A' to 'Z'
- *numeric* - the digits '0' to '9' (and conventionally including a decimal point and perhaps a + or - sign)
- *alphanumeric* (alphabetic and/or numeric)
- *special characters* - such as '!', '$', '%',and '^' (and sometimes the lower case letters 'a' to 'z'
- *image* - 'pictures' made up from straight lines, curved lines or dots
- *control characters* (commands) - 'skip to a new page', 'blank off the screen', 'stop', 'start your timer'.

To examine how data is handled in transmission, we must know what code systems are used and how these codes are represented during the conversation. To start with, we need to know something about *binary* numbers. The point of looking at binary is to lead in to a number of data storage codes used in DP and comms. If you are not concerned with the details, skip on to 'data storage codes'.

Number systems and codes
A number is a short-hand way of representing what is called in mathematics, a *series*. 2145 is actually:

$$2000 + 100 + 40 + 5 \quad \textbf{or} \quad 2 \times 10^3 + 1 \times 10^2 + 4 \times 10^1 + 5 \times 10^0$$

Strictly speaking, we should show the original number as:

2145_{10} or 2145 *base* 10.

The base might have been 8, in which case 2145_8 would mean:

$$2 \times 8^3 + 1 \times 8^2 + 4 \times 8^1 + 5 \times 8^0$$

which of course, is not the same as 2145_{10}.

Being very mathematical, if the base is 10, it contains *decimal* digits (they can take one of 10 different values) and the number is said to be a *denary* number. Similarly for 8, the words are *octal* and *octenary*.

Base	*Name of number system*	*lowest digit*	*highest digit*
10	denary	0	9
8	octenary	0	7
4	quaternary	0	3
2	binary	0	1

A binary number can only contain the digits '0' and '1', for example;

10011011_2 is (1 x 128) + (1 x 16) + (1 x 8) + (1 x 2) + (1 x 1)

= 155_{10}.

Just for completeness, the base 16 is quite often useful but brings a slight problem because the highest digit is '15' - except that this is not a digit but 2 digits. In practice we use 'A' to 'F' to represent the 'digits' 10 to 15.

For example, $FACE_{16}$ is:

$$(15 \times 16^3) + (10 \times 16^2) + (12 \times 16^1) + (14 \times 16^0)$$

(you can convert this to denary yourself).

For DP and comms considerations, binary is most important because all commercially-used computers and much comms equipment is *digital* in nature. This means that the 0s and 1s of data and instructions can be represented as a series of pulses, equivalent to 'on and off', '+ and -', 'small voltage and large voltage' etc. The data or instructions involved are said to be digital in nature and can be represented as a kind of bar-chart indicating on/off or whatever.

Figure 2.17 shows a waveform which can represent digital binary data. Engineers refer to this pattern as a *square wave*.

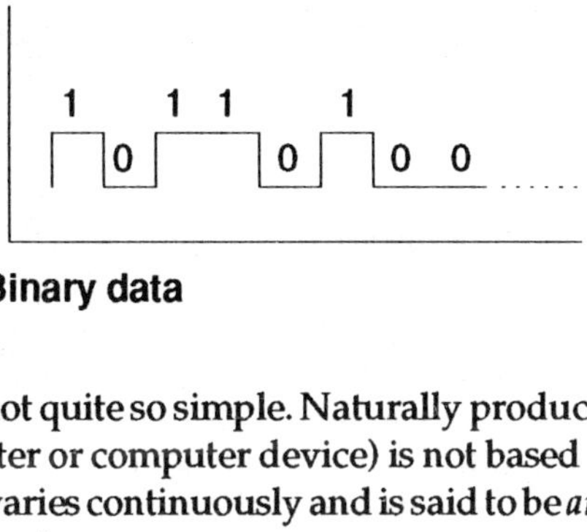

Figure 2.17 Binary data

Real life is not quite so simple. Naturally produced data (ie, not from a computer or computer device) is not based on 1/0, on/off etc. Instead it varies continuously and is said to be *analogue* in form (coming up soon).

With electrical or electronic equipment, it is fairly easy to arrange for this 1/0 or on/off significance and we can use this as the basis of code systems to hold data or instructions/commands.

Remember the binary number above, consisting of 0/1s only. We can use the 0/1 in a different way and a group of commonly-used code systems (called *data storage codes*) that have as their basis a 4-digit binary number together with some others.

Data storage codes

There is a technique called *binary coded decimal (bcd),* where we use 4 *bits* (*b*inary dig*its*) to represent a decimal digit in the range 0 to 9. For example, 0110 is 6, 1001 is 9 an so on.

So, if I send you the time of day as 0010 0100 0000 0000, you might be able to work out that it is midnight (24.00).

It is no use for non-numeric data of course and has been extended, by the addition of two extra bits to make up the 6-bit code called *expanded binary coded decimal (EBCD)* which enables four ranges of characters to be represented for storage and transmission.

With EBCD, the bcd part indicates where, in a particular range, a character falls, and the other two bits specify which range, illustrated in Figure 2.18.

1234	5	6	
bcd	x	y	range
0–9	0	0	0 – 9
1–9	1	1	A – I
1–9	1	0	J – R
2–9	0	1	S – Z

Figure 2.18 EBCD

The code allows for some other characters which are not important for this discussion, but note that with six bits, the maximum number of different characters possible is 64, ie, 000000 to 111111. This is not really enough. If you are sending me a letter, you need 'A-Z', 'a-z', '0-9' and some punctuation characters. This is more than 64, so EBCD is really too limited.

The code in use for telex is called *Baudot code* and is based on five bits. This would seem to have only 32 combinations (00000 to 11111) but they are extended by using the idea of a *shift character* like the shift key on a typewriter. The significance of a particular combination of bits changes depending on a 'shift up' or 'shift down' character received earlier.

The range of characters is: A-Z 0-9 ? : $! &' ( )' : / ' =

The next two developments use more than six bits. The first is an extension of EBCD developed by IBM and is called *EBCD*

Interchange Code (*EBCDIC*). This uses two extra bits, allowing more ranges and up to 256 different combinations altogether. For data comms, it only has importance when we are connecting to IBM mainframe computers.

However, the code you will meet most often for representing characters was formalised by the American National Standards Institute (*ANSI*) and is called *American Standard Code for Information Interchange (ASCII)*. The full range of ASCII representations is shown in Figure 2.19, characters and 'non-characters' (ie, control combinations) since some of the latter will be referred to in chapter 6.

7	0	0	0	0	1	1	1	1
6	0	0	1	1	0	0	1	1
5	0	1	0	1	0	1	0	1
4321								
0000	NUI	DLE	SP	0	@	P	\	p
0001	SOH	DC1	!	1	A	Q	a	q
0010	STX	DC2	▪	2	B	R	b	r
0011	ETX	DC3	?	3	C	S	c	s
0100	EOT	DC4	$	4	D	T	d	t
0101	ENQ	NAK	%	5	E	U	e	u
0110	ACK	SYN	&	6	F	V	f	v
0111	BEL	ETB	'	7	G	W	g	w
1000	BS	CAN	(	8	H	X	h	x
1001	HT	EM	)	9	I	Y	i	y
1010	LF	SUB	*	:	J	Z	j	z
1011	VT	ESC	+	;	K	[	k	{
1100	FF	FS	,	<	L	\	l	:
1101	CD	GS	_	=	M	]	m	}
1110	SO	RS	.	>	N	^	n	▪
1111	SI	US	/	?	O	_	o	DEL

Figure 2.19 ASCII combinations

The code is essentially based on seven bits, giving 128 combinations (0000000 to 1111111). In practice an extra bit called the *parity bit* is added for error-detection purposes making eight bits in all, but since this extra bit can be optionally ignored, we will leave it out of the table until we have explained its use (when we look at the handling of errors).

The bits of a character are usually numbered 1 to 7 from the right and the table is arranged so that the left-hand three bits (bits 7 to 5) are shown along the top row of the table and the right-hand four (bits 4 to 1) are at the side. Picking a few examples from the table, we have:

'A' in ASCII is 1000001, '+' is 0101001, 'BEL' the command which makes a VDU 'beep' is 0000111 and 'ACK', used to ACKnowledge a message is 0000110.

Later, we will use the term *octet* to mean eight bits as any kind of group, while *byte* means a groups of eight bits that represent a character. It is important to distinguish between the two.

Pause for thought

A typical computer or comms unit can generate a character representing it as a set of electrical pulses, perhaps voltages, typically where a voltage between +3 and +15 volts is taken as a '0' and -3 to -15 volts is taken as a '1'.

When the machine generates the sequence 'AaBb.....' or

.......1100010	1000010	1100001	1000001
b	B	a	A

the bits and the characters are sent from right to left and typically, we might see a pattern of positive and negative voltages to represent this, as illustrated in Figure 2.20.

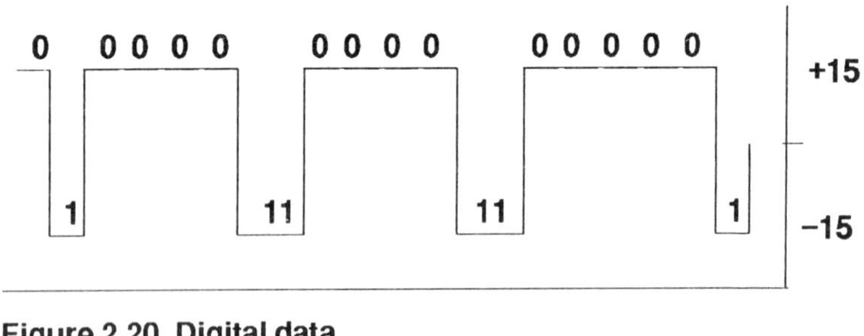

Figure 2.20 Digital data

Don't forget that in real life, we don't usually want to send single characters. The human application is far more likely to be concerned with documents, pages or lines. Its all very nice to have codes for characters, but we also need some way to tell the receiver where the breaks are between characters when we send a whole string - such as a line of text. We will return to this when we look at how characters are 'transmitted' ie, passed to and along the transmission medium, rather than the form in which they are generated by a device.

Data transfer and data transmission

Serial and parallel transfer

Computers are expensive items, built mainly from high-quality components and are very reliable. Data has to be moved around in memory, into it from input devices and out of it, to output devices. The actual distances involved are fairly short, probably not much more than 10-15 metres between central processor and peripheral.

You may have seen pictures of the massive computer installations used by national and international organisations. Although these computer rooms may seem enormous, there are almost certainly many processors and their peripheral devices are usually quite close by.

As long as we are dealing with fast, reliable electronic circuits and good-quality wires and cables, we can send data by *parallel transfer*. This means that for a given ASCII character, each of the seven bits is represented by a voltage **along its own wire**. Figure 2.21 shows the parallel transfer of the character 'b' in ASCII.

Figure 2.21 Parallel transfer of the ASCII character 'b'

Computer-peripheral data interchange usually occurs in bursts. A typical 'block' of data sent to/from magnetic tape/disk might be up to 10,000 characters long. Then, there will then be a short pause, while the mechanism locates the start position of the next block. This data exchange is based electrically on *direct current (DC)* pulses, where for example a burst of a particular voltage means '1' and a burst of another voltage is for a '0'.

Provided we are dealing with bursts, with high-quality equipment over short distances, we can achieve very high speeds (hundreds of thousands of characters per second) with a very low error rate. If these restrictions are satisfied, we are carrying out *data transfer*. If not, we are probably dealing with *data transmission*.

Once we are dealing with data comms, distances involved are longer and we are usually involved with much cheaper equipment. (We don't mind paying £3.00 per metre for high-quality connection cable for a distance of 5-10 metres, but suppose we want to link a terminal to a mainframe, 500 metres away!) In addition, as distance increases, there is more chance of finding imperfections in the cable, hence more errors.

Parallel transmission is particularly troublesome because of this and the individual bits can 'get out of step' so that one may 'creep forward' and get there before the others.

This leads to errors since the receiver does not get a proper character and it becomes necessary to send all the bits along one wire, one after another in time. This is called *serial transmission* illustrated in Figure 2.22, again for 'b' in ASCII. For short distances

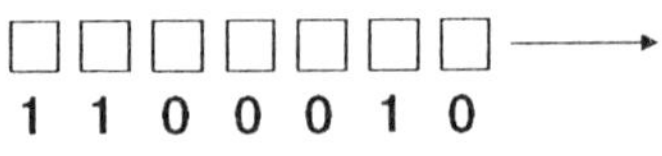

Figure 2.22 Serial transfer of the ASCII character 'b'

and high-quality equipment, the idea of sending '0' and '1' as DC pulses, such as quick bursts of voltage, is fine, but for much longer distances, real life is hard. Without going into the physics of the problem, please accept that generating an instantaneous pulse is difficult and the DC 'square wave' that we are hoping for actually takes a short time to build up and to die away - the square wave is slightly curved which means that the receiver may get confused (Figure 2.23).

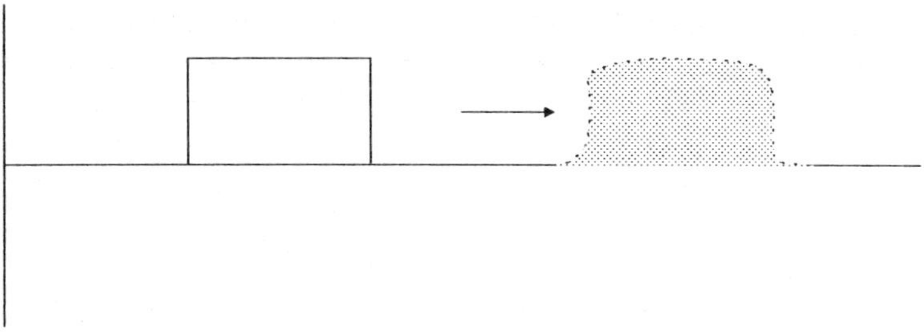

Figure 2.23 Distortion to a square wave

Since it is going to become relevant fairly soon, please accept another piece of science. Again, you can skip it if you want to.

Sine waves and their significance in comms

Strictly speaking, there is no such thing as an electrically generated square wave. It is actually a combination of many curves.

A *sine wave* is the mathematical representation of a number of naturally occurring phenomena such as a pure, steady musical note. The mathematical way of showing that some variable Y (eg, 'power') can have its value determined because it varies as the trigonometrical sine of X (eg, 'time') is:

Y = SIN(X)

It can be shown mathematically that a square wave is formed from the series:

SIN(X) + SIN(2X) + SIN(3X) + ... to infinity.

All sounds, noise, and electrical signals too are made up from combinations of sine waves. To understand the significance of this in data comms, we need some definitions.

A sine wave (Figure 2.24) has certain characteristics. The greatest height of the wave is called the *amplitude* (bigness). The wave repeats itself after a certain length of time called the *period*. One individual element of the wave (the bit that repeats) is called a *cycle*. The rate at which the cycle is repeated in time is called the

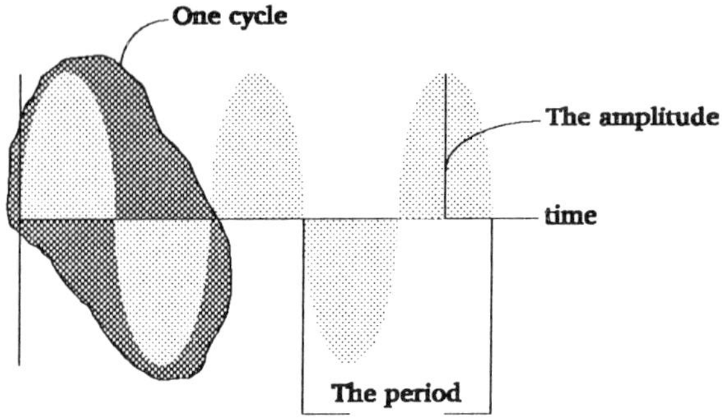

Figure 2.24 A sine wave

frequency (measured in cycles per second). The name *Hertz* (Hz) is given to the unit 'one cycle per second', after a famous physicist.

Middle C on a piano has a frequency of 256 Hz. BBC Radio 3 broadcasts on a frequency of 1,215,000 Hz (1215 kHz - *kiloHertz*) and on FM at 90.2 MHz (*megaHertz*).

A typical medium used as a conversation link will be able to handle a certain range of frequencies. Your ear if you are say, below the age of about 20, can handle frequencies between about 100 and 20,000 Hz. As you get older, you cannot hear the high notes and your upper limit comes down by several thousand Hz.

The difference between the lower and upper limits of a medium is called its *bandwidth* - we say that transmission is over a *band* of frequencies. We can also use the term *frequency response*. Electric wires and cables will have differing bandwidths depending on how they are made but they will not be able to handle an infinite range of frequencies, so, if we try to send a square wave down the line, some of the higher-valued sines will be lost and the receiver will only get the lower ones. The effect is that the receiver will not see a square wave but one that is distorted because it has lost some of its components (illustrated in Figure 2.25).

Pause for thought

We must be able to overcome the problem of not being able to send pure square waves if we are to use the PTN for sending data.

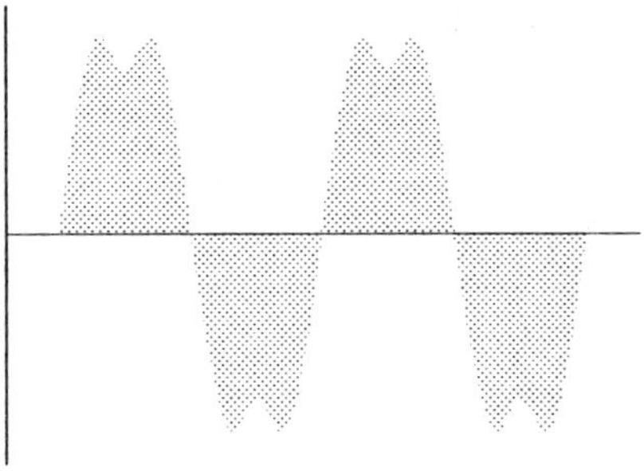

Figure 2.25 A distorted sine wave

We said earlier that the network was designed to give a certain quality and has what you now know is a limited frequency response (actually about 300 to 3300Hz) and this is hopeless for transmission of decent square waves. (We will look shortly however, at the way we can 'fool' the network into transmitting square waves so that we can send data through what is essentially a voice network).

One of the laws of physics shows that even if there are no distortions or interruptions, the speed with which you can send data is related to the frequency response of the medium - as the bandwidth is restricted, so is the data rate. A practical analogy of this is to think of traffic going along a road. If the width of the road gets less (the road narrows), the rate of traffic flow will fall.

So, we now have the double problem that the low bandwidth helps to produce errors **and** reduce data rates. It doesn't sound very hopeful does it? Despite all this, many people use the PTN for all their data transmission purposes as well as voice, and provided a lot of care is taken to reduce errors and detect them when they arise, data transmission via the PTN is acceptable and reasonably cheap.

Analogue and digital data

In order to appreciate the different methods whereby a user can gain access to a network and its services, we must look at modems and to lead into this, we must look at the two main ways that data is transmitted.

We talked about the sending of 1s and 0s as square waves. If we consider a serial device (one that handles data as serial bit-strings rather than in parallel) such as a terminal keyboard, or a printer, a particular character will be sent or received as a series of pulses, perhaps represented in time as bursts of voltages (refer back to Figure 2.20).

Almost all devices associated with computers are digital in nature - data is represented as a series of 1s and 0s. However, there are many other places where data is not digital in nature. Consider the following problems:

- write a program that examines the accesses to a high street ATM and produces a print-out showing how it was used during the day and whether there was a peak time for failures
- write a program that examines the noise due to traffic next to the ATM and produces a report showing when the level was too noisy for the user to concentrate properly.

The first of these is straightforward - it will probably count the number of successful and unsuccessful accesses for each hour and produce a histogram or bar-chart to summarise the data. The second program is not too difficult to write **once you can determine what 'too noisy' means**. The problem lies in the actual measurement of noise levels.

The need for the ATM to transmit data is intermittent. Sometimes no-one wants to use it. During use, there will be periods when the user is thinking.But, when transmission is necessary, just 0s and 1s will go down the line. However, noise is continuous. This does not just mean that it goes on all the time. It is continuous in the statistics sense (continuous as opposed to discrete). There is never silence - just a varying noise level. No matter how accurately you measure it, an exact value is not possible.

Noise is a combination of the continuous sine waves which we have already met and we refer to this kind of data as *analogue* in form. This difference between computer-generated (digital) data and voice is a big problem for us when we want to use the PTN to send data because:

- the PTN was designed to handle speech of a certain quality (controlled noise and hence analogue in form)

- we now know that the square waves representing digital data cannot be transmitted without an unacceptable error level.

So, we must find a way to resolve these two apparently irreconcileable facts and find a way of using the analogue circuits of the PTN to 'carry' our digital signals.

Speech is actually carried through part of the network with a *carrier wave*. Once a connection between called and caller has been made, a continuous signal (a sine wave) is generated and the speech waveform is electrically 'attached' to the carrier and then 'unattached' at the other end. (The carrier is changed and 'de-changed' during this process.)

We say that the speech wave *modulates* the carrier which then has to be *demodulated* so that the speech can be received by the called party.

Digital data is modulated and demodulated in a similar way (shown in Figure 2.26), except that the data is much simpler to start with and a 1 or 0 modulates **one cycle** of the carrier.

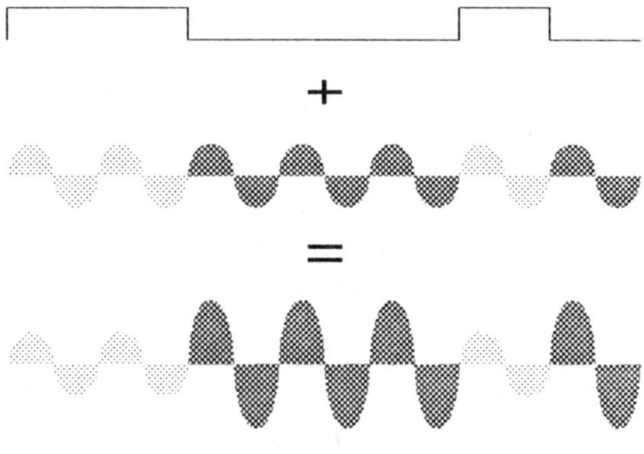

Figure 2.26 Digital data modulation

How this is actually carried out is covered in more detail in chapter 5 but for the time being, you should appreciate that the PTN can carry data, fairly slowly and with a fairly high level of errors. The PDN actually carries digital data, without modulation, is much faster and produces far fewer errors (but is more expensive to set up).

To understand how a user can connect up to the various networks, requires some basic knowledge of connection techniques, transmission media (wires and the like) and also some familiarity with how errors occur and what we must do to handle them.

Switching

The term *switching* has several different meanings, particularly for the manner in which connections are made in a network and there are three alternatives for this.

Circuit switching

Circuit switching was the original method and is still in use today, largely for voice. It implies that an electrical link must be set up (a circuit formed) between the ends of the conversation for the duration of the 'call'.

It takes time to set up this connection and is wasteful of the network facilities because they must be employed in maintaining the link even if there are pauses in the conversation. Once the link has been set up, it stays open until cleared down, even if neither end is talking. In addition, if one of the parties is 'engaged - busy', no other contact is possible.

In the early days of telecommunications, the link would actually be a wire circuit. These days, the circuit could be a combination of wire, optical fibre and microwave link, depending on how the PTN routes the call.

Message-switching

Message switching was developed to overcome the need for a dedicated link. Instead of passing along a fixed circuit, a message is passed from node to node within the network along a predetermined route. Obviously these nodes need to have some storage capacity and in practice, a node will 'store' a message until it gets a signal from another node that it can 'forward' the message for farther down the line. It is for this reason that message-switching is often called a *store-and-forward* technique.

With circuit switching, if there is no circuit available, you just have to try later. With message switching, even if the network is busy, provided you are prepared to wait for your message to be passed through the system (as nodes become free to accept the message for passing on) you should always be able to send.

Obviously, store-and-forward is not much good for normal voice conversations because of the time delay, but it is very suitable for applications such as centralised voice message libraries. It finds one of its best applications in electronic mail, particularly when a message is to be delivered to several destinations.

Packet switching

The third and most sophisticated method is called *packet-switching.* A data message is divided into small units called *packets* containing the sender and receiver addresses. These pass from node to node but not along a predetermined route. It will be up to the network to break messages up and reassemble them when they 'get to the other end'. (We will have more to say about this in chapter 8.)

Because of the complexity of packet-switched networks and the wide variety of terminals and host computers that make use of it, such a network must support users sending at different rates and will itself adjust rates to cope with the level of traffic.

At the beginning of this chapter, we touched on the possibilities for conversation via a 'directed medium' and through the air. Until we deal with the very high data rates in the highest levels of the PTN and PDN, you will find that most data and voice transmission is carried out along solid media.

We will shortly take a brief look at the commonest media in use but before doing so, we must introduce the second main meaning of the word 'switching' in the concept of *line status switching.*

Line switching and baud rate

As you are aware, we can represent '1' and '0' by two different electrical states and the speed with which we can send data down a line will depend on the rate at which it can **switch** (change state) from whatever is a '1' to whatever is a '0' and back again, as necessary. This not a property of the line itself but is dependent on the electric and electronic circuitry sending the data.

To specify the switching rate, we use the term *baud* which is defined as one state change per second; hence a 1200 baud connection is one that can switch 1200 times per second.

In theory, if each state change is associated with a 1 or a 0, this should be equivalent to a data transmission rate of 1200 bits per second *(bps)*. **It almost never is.** The reasons why it will often be much **less** are to be found later in this chapter and in chapters 6 and 7, but we can touch on why the transmission rate might be **greater** than the baud rate.

With the increasingly complex modulation techniques being developed, it is possible to arrange for more than two states to be represented by the circuit. If we have only two states, corresponding to '1' and '0', they can only represent bits.

If we could have **four** different states, they could be arranged to correspond to '00,' '01', '10,' '11'(called *dibits*), **eight** could be '000', '001', '010', '011', '100', '101', '110', '111' (called *tribits*) and so on. Such multi-state possibilities are represented in Figure 2.27.

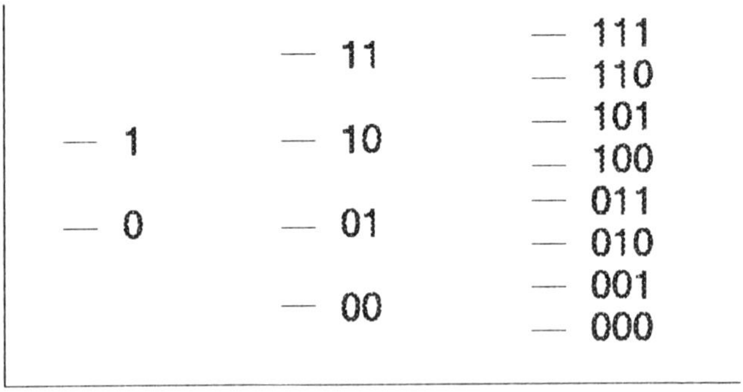

Figure 2.27 Multi-state possibilities

For a circuit with a given baud rate, each state change can be associated with whatever choice is specified. Thus, for two states, each 'baud' means **one** bit. For four states, each 'baud' means **two** bits which means that the data rate is twice that for a two-state circuit. Similarly, with eight states, each can in effect carry **three** bits, thereby trebling the data rate. (The most sophisticated modulation techniques currently available allow for 32 different states.)

Transmission media

Firstly some definitions:

- *line* - a general term used to describe any kind of physical link. (Also used to refer to the wires in a multi-wire cable)
- *circuit* - similar to line but used by more technical people such as hardware manufacturers and comms suppliers
- *channel* - a more theoretical concept - a line may carry, or be able to hold, several simultaneous conversations. For example, a TV aerial, is actually carrying many different radio and TV channels at the same time down the coaxial cable. The tuning circuit in your TV picks out the particular one you want.

When we look at RS232 in chapter 5, you will find that individual wires are connected to various electrical circuits with particular functions. One standard calls these **wires** or **lines**, another calls them **circuits**.

Similarly, when we look at public networks, you may say telephone **line**, but the network supplier is more likely to say telephone **circuit**. You could even hear that the **channels** are busy.

A list of media

Now a quick list of the main media used in communications (fuller details in chapter 5):

- twisted wire - usually used in one- or two-pair form
- coaxial cable - of varying thicknesses
- special 'cables' (such as RS232)
- optical fibre, which carries flashing light
- various forms of radio transmission.

So, we now know a bit about communication and the lines that connect up to networks and who provides networks. But, real life again. There will be many errors that can affect a conversation. Let us now look at why.

An introduction to error handling

First of all, we can define an error as something that has 'gone wrong' and a general diagram can be used to show what we try to do about them (Figure 2.28).

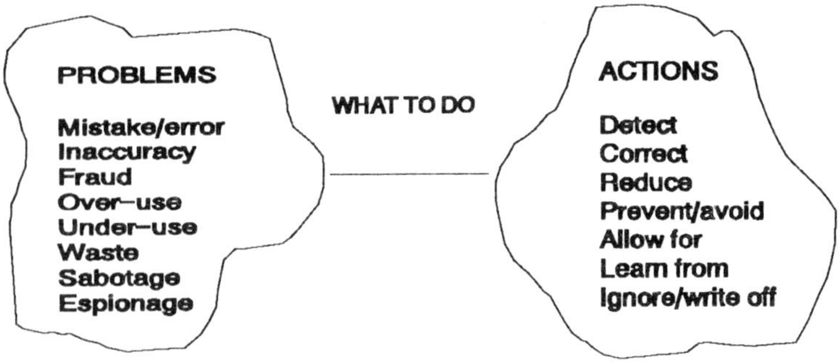

Figure 2.28 'Handling' errors

Sources of errors

In communications, an 'error' could be caused by a break in the line, outside interference, failure to pay your phone bill, a computer breakdown and many other reasons. It is almost impossible to classify all the errors that can arise, so for the time being, let us just look at those caused by hardware. These include:

- equipment failure - obviously, if your telephone is broken, you cannot make a phone call. Similarly, if your computer terminal is out of action, you cannot send data.

  But it could be a more insidious than this. Perhaps your output connection is supposed to be switching at 1200 baud and because of a slight electrical malfunction, it is actually going at 600 or 2400 baud or perhaps the keyboard has developed a fault and sends 'a' instead of 'A'. A user will not be aware of this, but the equipment at the receiver's will certainly know and unless it can detect that there is a difference it will not be able to pick up the data correctly

- line failure - rats seem to like chewing up coaxial cable. They use it to make nests (no-one seems to know if they like the taste) and are particularly good at doing so when it is buried deep inside a building (say in a lift shaft or under the floor). This might cause problems.

  When you use the PTN for sending data, it will be subject to the same problems as for voice. You will get crossed lines (- a computer cant tell another one to get off the line) and even complete line drops, where your connection breaks off for no apparent reason. You could also get bursts of interference and noise so great that you have to ring off mainly due to the general quality of the PTN circuitry and equipment. (We can only hope that the PTOs will eventually eradicate this kind of problem.)

Problems with the PTN and with direct links arise from inconsistencies in the line leading to power dissipation. If this is the case, you must either buy more expensive hardware or just accept that errors will occur and try to do something about them

- 'external' factors - people in the business say that the environment in which data comms is carried out is very **hostile** - the typical user linking a character terminal to the PTN via a modem has a very high risk of errors. Not only is the basic connection to the network of fairly low quality, but we also have to battle with interference from electric motors, thunderstorms and other sources of electrical energy. As we will see later, such problems become even more severe when we try to communicate using mobile terminals, something becoming very popular.

Electronic equipment does not have the reasoning ability of human beings who may be able to make judgments about what has gone wrong and what to do about it. To enable it to deal with problems, we must take special measures to try and cope with the many different errors that can occur.

What can we do to detect errors

The most well-known technique is that of *parity checking*. With this, we introduce an extra bit to those that are to be transmitted and arrange that the setting of this 'parity bit' is such that the number of bits that make up the message altogether is even (or odd). Figure 2.29 shows this applied to one character.

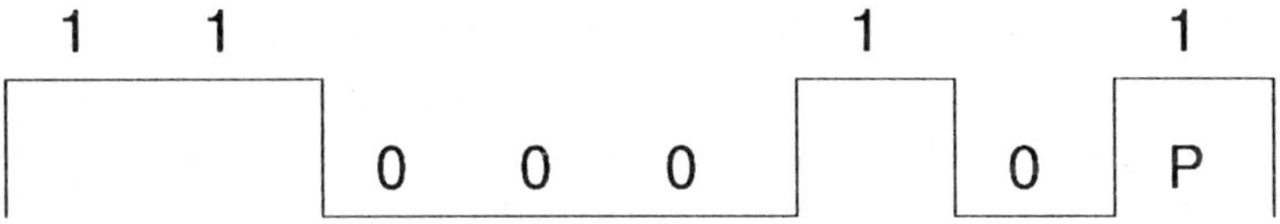

Figure 2.29 'b' in ASCII with even parity bit

The problem with parity checking is that it is only of use in detecting an odd number of errors (especially one) in an octet - an even number will restore the parity. This is not a lot of use in practice because external errors occur in bursts - outside interference or internal noise could last for a relatively long time and destroy several octets of data.

An extension is to arrange for parity to be set across a group of octets as well as within the octet. This is called *horizontal (lateral) parity checking,* illustrated in Figure 2.30.

L	E	T	T	E	R	S	
1	1	1	1	1	1	1	0
0	0	0	0	0	0	0	1
0	0	1	1	0	1	1	1
1	0	0	0	0	0	0	0
1	1	1	1	1	0	0	0
0	0	0	0	0	1	1	1
0	1	0	0	1	0	1	0
0	0	0	0	0	0	1	0
1	2	3	4	5	6	7	

Figure 2.30 Horizontal odd parity across ASCII 'LETTERS'

Redundancy

Error-detection and correction are the subject of chapter 4, but before then, we need to introduce the concept of *data redundancy.*

Most of the more common error-handling techniques require extra bits to be sent along with the data. We say that 'data redundancy' has been added and it consists of the bits (or octets) that are added to assist in error detection and correction. The parity bit in an 8-bit ASCII character is redundant in the sense that it is additional to the seven bits actually required to represent the character. The same applies to a horizontal parity checking byte formed from the corresponding bits of 8 data bytes.

This redundancy is unfortunate but it does demonstrate the trade-off that often applies in comms - the more chance of errors, the more redundancy and hence the less actual data that is transmitted.

Although we can use each circuit state switch to carry a bit, in practice the effective data transmission rate (the number of data bits transmitted per second) may be considerably less that the baud rate.

Not only must we allow for redundant bits, but even more wasteful of the circuit's switching capability, we must allow for **resending the message,** once an error has been detected. Data is not always sent in single characters and it could easily be the case that a whole line of text (or even a screenful) may need to be retransmitted when an error is detected.

If we allow 10% for redundancy and 10% for retransmission, assuming we are using a simple modulation technique, a 2400 baud circuit will have an effective data rate of 2400 x 0.9 x 0.9, ie, about 1900 bits per second.

Now we know a little more about the storage of characters and the form in which they are generated, we must look at how we deal with the time interval between successive bit and bytes.

Timing and data transmission

When two parties converse, one has no idea of what the other is doing. With voice, we can use our intelligence and fairly quickly sort out any confusion that arises over people talking at the same time, or long pauses where both are waiting for the other.

With data comms, we need ways of ensuring that the receiver knows exactly when data is about to arrive. The problem is that of separating bits and bytes in time and there are two basic methods of organising data to achieve this separation.

Asynchronous transmission

The first method, called *asynchronous transmission,* is where each character is delineated by markers. The receiver listens all the time and the sender's hardware generates the marked characters as and when it is ready to send them. As soon as the receiver detects a beginning marker, his hardware starts a clock and 'ticks in' each of the character bits until it reaches the end marker. At this point, if it has not received the correct number of data bits, it knows that an error has occurred.

The start marker is called a *start bit* and the end marker a *stop bit*. (At one time asynchronous transmission was called *stop-start* transmission.) Figure 2.31 shows the ASCII code for the character 'b', with odd parity, ready for asynchronous transmission.

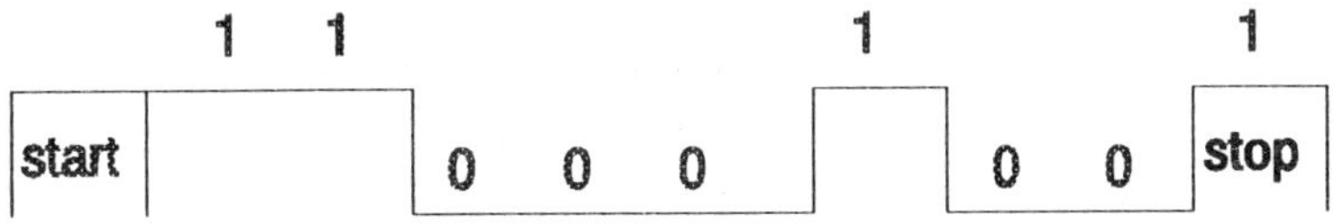

Figure 2.31 ASCII 'b' (odd parity) ready for asynchronous

A choice can often be made between 1, 1.5 or 2 stop bits to terminate a character. We say that the start and stop bits *frame* the character. The reason for the name 'asynchronous', meaning 'not in step' is that there is no need for sender and receiver to be in step with each other in time.

Provided the receiver:

- is always listening
- knows that the sender is transmitting asynchronously
- knows the baud rate of the sender's hardware
- knows the number of stop bits
- knows the kind of parity associated with each character,

and a few other things, all his hardware has to do is wait for the start bit, clock in the data bits, detect the stop bit(s) and then wait for the next start bit, whenever it arrives.

If the conversation is one between low-volume and intermittent users, asynchronous transmission is very useful and is very common eg, where a user is interrogating a distant mainframe using a menu-driven form of dialogue. The user makes a selection and his terminal perhaps sends a single digit corresponding to the selection. The mainframe receives it and sends back a whole screenful containing further selections. The user then stops and thinks for a while and then sends another choice. The mainframe then replies with another screenful, and so on (See Figure 2.10).

At no time during this session is there a continuous interchange of data, nor is a very high data rate needed. The mainframe may be able to pick up data from its database at hundreds of thousands of characters per second but there is no point in sending it this fast - the user's PC screen can only handle about 20 characters per second (or less if it is producing fancy graphics).

Synchronous transmission

If we are involved with situations where we need continuous and reasonably fast data exchange, asynchronous transmission is inefficient and not fast enough. We look to the alternative method, where characters are grouped together and framed. This is called *synchronous transmission* and implies that the sender and receiver at some point must be in step in time.

We can trivialise the two methods with two examples and then explain the latter method in more detail:

- *an asynchronous conversation:*

  I am going to talk to you. I will 'bleep' before and after each character. Are you ready?

  __bleepAbleep_____bleepBbleep__bleepCbleep________blee pDbleep_________ _ _ _ _ _

- *a synchronous conversation:*

  I am going to talk to you.

  On your marks____get set___here they comeABCDEFGHbleep _____________on your marks____get set____here they comeIJKLMNOPQRbleep____

The group of characters is initiated by the sender issuing one or more bytes containing signals that the receiver detects as *synchronisation bytes*. They enable his hardware to line up in time so that they are ready to 'clock in' bytes at the rate at which they are sent.

The two ends must be in step while the data block is being transmitted. Figure 2.32 shows how synchronisation bytes (*SYN*) are located at the beginning of a synchronous block of data. The end-marker (*EOB*) indicates that the block has been transmitted.

SYN	length	....data bytes....	EOB

Figure 2.32 A 'synchronous' block

The receiver can determine the actual block length when it receives the EOB marker, or if there is a count of the number of characters in the block itself, or by arranging that sender and receiver negotiate the number of characters in the block to be sent. (We will see examples of this variation in chapter 6).

Connecting distant users

Finally, for this chapter, you will find it helpful to see a summary of the six main options available for the 'connection routes' between sender and receiver (shown in Figure 2.33).

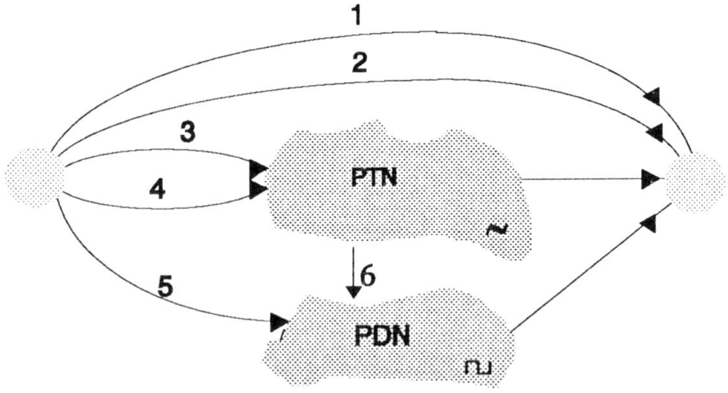

Figure 2.33 User 'connection routes'

1 Direct link

This is fairly slow and is often based on wire (twisted pair, co-ax etc). It is susceptible to error over distances more than say 30-100 metres for reasons that will be expanded in chapter 5.

2 LAN

LANs uses direct linkage based on wire, but of much higher data rates. Nevertheless, distances are still limited to, say a maximum of 1000 metres.

3 Public telephone network - dial-up

You have to dial the number you want, them switch from voice to data so that the terminal can send/receive via a modem. The link is provided at connection time.

4 Public telephone network - private line

This is a higher quality, more expensive circuit provided by the PTO. Connection to the other end is permanent and is made as soon as both ends are switched on.

5 Public data network - direct

Your special terminal (*packet terminal*) is designed to link directly through a *terminator* to the data network. The link to the PDN from an appropriate packet terminal is a special link called a *dataline* by British Telecom.

6 Public data network - via the PTN

For users who do not have a packet terminal, a link may be provided from the PTN through a device acting as a *gateway* between the PTN and the PDN. This gateway will be explained in chapter 8 and for the time being can be referred to as a *packet assembler-disassembler (PAD)* although it should really be called a *network protocol conversion unit (NPU)*. Figure 2.34 illustrates PDN access.

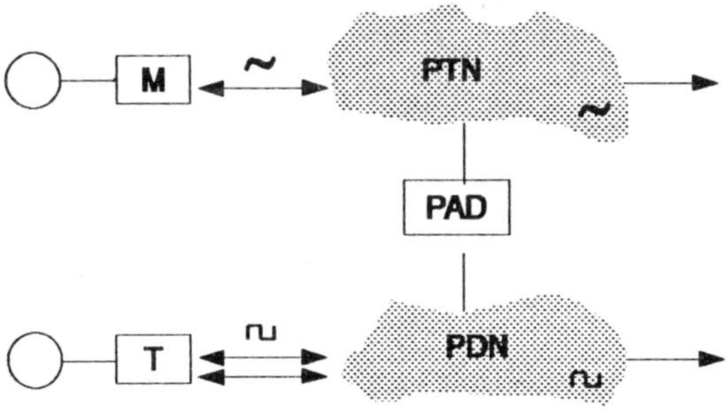

Figure 2.34 PDN access

Recap

- a conversation is more than people talking - it represents all the reasons why data comms needs to be implemented.
- we met the terms primary/secondary, line-of-sight, simplex/duplex
- for data communications, many different types of terminal are in use to send and receive data and information in different forms

- conversations do not occur in isolation - many users and computers may be involved as a logical network. This must be supported by a physical communications network
- we tried to define a number of different kinds of network and who provides them was considered
- as a basis for the physical aspects of comms, we must have some idea of how data can be represented and transferred between devices and users. For the same reason, we need an idea of how data is transferred in networks. We tried to lay a basis for the data storage codes used and in particular, introduced ASCII as one of the most important of these
- an introduction to network mechanisms, transmission media and errors will help for later chapters and we met the various switching techniques, how errors arise and how they can be detected
- timing mechanisms are essential in data transmission. Asynchronous transmission of single characters and synchronous transmission of logical blocks of characters are important
- the chapter finished with a review of methods for connecting users to other users, computers and external services.

Typical questions

Question 2.1
Identify 4 differences between data transfer and data transmission

Question 2.2.
Discuss the following terms giving examples where appropriate: private network, PTN, data storage code, carrier wave, bandwidth, modulation, stop bit, synchronous data transmission

Question 2.3
I want to send electronic mail messages from my PC to people in my office and to friend who lives in another town. Suggest ways by which the necessary connections might be made.

Question 2.4
Suggest four business applications where a dumb terminal might be employed, two for *input only* and two for *output only*.

3: Open systems interconnection

Objectives

After reading this chapter, you should:

- understand the need for 'top-down' or 'layered' thinking
- appreciate the importance of *open systems interconnection*
- appreciate the significance of the ISO 7-layer model
- understand the main functions of each of the seven layers and how services exist to link them
- be aware of three important groups of protocols which are especially relevant for OSI
- have some appreciation of how OSI is being developed

Chapter 2 has thrown a large number of concepts, ideas and techniques at you, the intention being to introduce as many of them as possible and provide you with an overall picture of data comms and how it 'operates'.

Our route now is to expand on these ideas and in particular, say a lot more about hardware and the techniques involved with the fast, error-free transmission of data in its various forms. Then we can look at specific applications.

Unfortunately, we can't go straight into a description of the various bits of electrical and electronic equipment without knowing a lot about how errors occur and how we try to deal with them. Furthermore, we cant really deal with errors without getting involved with standards, since one of the main considerations in standards is how to deal with errors.

The handling of standards and a standard approach to system development and operation requires an integrated approach and it is this which is the subject of this and the next chapter.

The most important development in comms in the last 20 years has been the *OSI 7-layer model* and we will now lay down some background in order for you to appreciate its significance.

Structured thinking and working

Top-down working

When starting a task, anyone with a milligram of intelligence will plan the work and it is usual to break it up into a set of subsidary tasks to be carried out in a sensible order. The list that we make up is in effect a model or scheme that will determine how the work should be done for maximum efficiency or convenience. Once the list and the order are finalised, we can expand the items in the list to any desired degree. Here is an example involving the preparation of a lecture:

- decide on subject matter
- prepare any visual back-up
- decide on validation of knowledge/skills gained
- arrange room and resources.
- etc.

This kind of thinking, starting at the highest level and then expanding downwards as needed, is called *top-down development* or *stepwise refinement*. It is characterised by a step-wise approach in which we plan at the highest level, then take each of these main elements and do the same thing again - break each down into a lower level set of steps and so on until we reach the lowest, or atomic level (as illustrated in Figure 3.1). A diagram such as this is referred to as a hierarchical diagram.

The lecture preparation step 1 can now be expanded by perhaps looking at a syllabus or course program, or a similar lecture given on a different course. Step 2 follows on and requires the selection of handouts, OHP foils, videos and so on.

Step 3 will require the selection of tests, homework and so on, while step 4 will mean checking with the rooms coordinator and

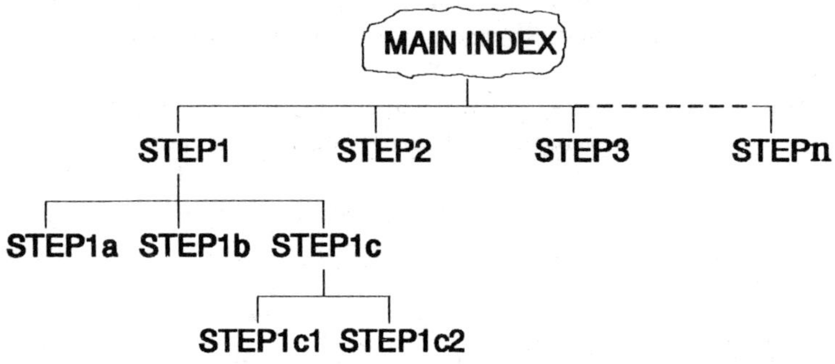

Figure 3.1 A top-down structure

perhaps the resources coordinator (perhaps the lecture will need a microcomputer with a large display VDU).

It would seem that step 1 comes first and step 2 next, although step 4 could be the most important since without the room etc, the lecture cannot proceed.

When we look at step 3, it is possible that the organisation might have a standard approach to tests, with a procedure already worked out. Similarly, there may be a fixed procedure for booking rooms and equipment.

Bottom-up development

Sometimes, we can look at an overall job and identify low-level tasks that are likely to be needed in other jobs, or have already be done for other jobs. This is the opposite of top-down thinking and is called *bottom-up development*. Obviously when a particular job is part of a larger project, it makes sense to do some bottom-up work as soon as the higher 'top-down' levels have been identified.

Top-down or bottom-up?

A top-down approach should always be adopted at the start of a system design, network implementation, etc. You define the major tasks, decide in which order they will be carried out, take each one in turn and see if it breaks down further, and so on is really the only way to carry out a complex job, but it is surprising just how many people do not plan their work this way. They identify a particular task and then get on with it. When it is finished, they pick another one.

Eventually they have a whole set of separate 'products' which are brought together. This is OK provided detailed notes are kept so that you know what as been done and what is to be done. But, if a change occurs during development, it is very difficult to sort out just what the effects of the change are. Perhaps the biggest advantage of top-down development is that the resulting structure makes changes and extensions easier than would otherwise be the case. Nevertheless, there are plenty of times when a bottom-up approach can be of value. For example, suppose I am designing an on-line computerised sales support system and the user has insisted that VDU screens are to be very user-friendly. I can start straight away on broad designs for the screens even before I think in detail about the data that will be input and stored, or the processing that will be required.

Similarly, I know that I am going to need some comms software to send files. Again, I can investigate the software on the market before I really know the exact details of the application in which I will use it.

I could even start looking at the modems I could use for transmission (provided I am sure that analogue transmission through the PTN will be able to support the expected data rates).

A layered approach

The next chapter will go into details regarding standards, why they arise, where they come from and how they are upheld. If you have had any experience or training in DP, whether from programming or systems, you will know something about standards (or the lack of them) in a particular area.

The subject of communications is absolutely riddled with standards, put down by people with different objectives, for different reasons and applied differently by different people. Over the years, most people have realised that this situation is totally unsatisfactory and from different sources, there has started to evolve an extension to the top-down approach where we try to think about any problem at a series of separate levels. We apply this to the development of systems, networks, and applications.

It is often referred to as a *layered approach* in the sense that it considers a problem area and tries to isolate the various aspects so that each one is a separate and self-contained *layer,* in such a way that **a standard approach can be laid down for each aspect, without having to think about the others.**

The aim of this is to enable communication between people, machines, systems or applications, in different situations but which can be considered as being on the same level or layer. The concept is called *Open Systems Interconnection.*

Peer-to-peer and layers

In a conversation, there are several layers to be considered and each element involved in the various layers of the conversation, whether modem, network, user or whatever, is referred to as an *entity.* An entity at a particular layer will need rules to enable it to 'talk' to another entity in a different system but at the same layer.

Let us look at some typical conversations (such as those introduced in chapters 1 and 2):

- *between a remote computer user and a head office mainframe computer.* We may know all about the modem, the telephone network, how errors are handled and so on, but surely the most important aspect is the fact that a human user is using a computer to carry out his job, perhaps doing a stock level enquiry.

  In this sense, the user is at the same level as the computer in that both are only concerned with the application, ie, the stock enquiry.

  Obviously factors affecting other levels of the conversation are important. Such factors might include: measures taken to reduce errors, there is a guaranteed minimum response time to enquiries, line failure should only occur with a certain maximum probability.

  Note that these are **not** the concern of the application itself, nor of the parties involved in the application

- *at the end of a day's business, between the head office mainframe and the one in the regional office: the latest version of the company stock file is to be copied across for security reasons*

  Now we are talking about computer-to-computer conversation in its strictest terms

- *the U.K. digital network passing a whole bunch of international comms traffic over to the French digital network.*

  Obviously the 'network layer' is the only one of interest to the networks

- *my modem telling your modem to 'go slower' because the line is noisy*
  Here the consideration is a the electrical or 'physical' layer - neither modem is the slightest bit interested in what actual data is being transmitted - only in the transmission speed.

Comms people use the term *peer-to-peer* to describe conversation between equals such as:

- person-to-person
- computer-to-computer
- network-to-network
- modem-to-modem,

ie, communication is between 'peers' (a rather old-fashioned English word meaning 'an equal') and we say that a particular set of peers are at the same level, or more often now, that they are entities concerned at the same layer.

Communication obviously goes on at different levels and rules are needed to ensure that messages get through as sent, whether voice, data, text or image. As technology has advanced, comms has become more sophisticated, both in what is sent and how. Hence the need for more rules and standards.

Layers in practice

Let us look at some problem areas in typical conversations that should demonstrate the need for standardisation.

- the two parties might be in different countries and several public (and private) networks could be involved
- receiver and sender may be using quite different terminals and modems and the receiver's kit will need to know the sender's data codes and the difference between data and control signals (end-of-block, end-of-text etc)
- outside factors (weather, nearby power supplies and so on) and electronic and electrical imperfections and malfunctions will cause interference and distortion. It will be necessary to detect (and possibly correct) these and certain procedures (such as parity checking) will be needed.
- requests to repeat whole blocks or whole transactions might arise because of electronic failure, line failure, software error, processor break-down etc

- rates of flow might need to be adjusted at either end of the conversation, or throughout the passage of the message through the various nodes of the network.

However, is the user to be bothered with these problems? Consider these examples:

- my character terminal talking to your character terminal does not want to know how the intermediate packet-switching system might convert characters to packets and route them through the network
- when I send an electronic mail message from my workstation to your terminal in a LAN, I am not concerned with how the LAN works, where the mail server is sited, what mechanism it uses to ensure fair access to facilities for all users and so on
- but, if I log on to an external service in another country, I need to know rules relating to a session (phone number, times, user number/password). I also need to know about the application, eg, how do I select a particular application/function.
- I don't want to know about multiplexers, optical fibre etc. I have a standard slow modem attached to my PC. I know that the service I am accessing can handle 1200/75 even parity, and that's all I am concerned with
- however, the modem manufacturer **is** concerned, since his machine must be able to take my digital signals with certain electrical characteristics and convert them so that the network can carry them to the other end and then allow the receiver's modem to convert them back again. He is not in the slightest interested in my application other than that I want to send bytes at a certain speed, with a specified number of bits per character, parity setting etc
- the network supplier has to find the most economical way to get the message from me to the receiver within a given quality of service
- the provider of a mainframe enquiry service has to be sure that a proper level of authorisation exists so that only the right people can get at files and programs.

Layer separation

In each of these examples, you should be able to see the idea of separating problems into layers to which individual attention can be paid and standardised procedures adopted. Unfortunately, manufacturers, computer companies, trade organisations and governments have been heavily involved with data/voice comms for years and have developed their own standards, rules and procedures.

What we need is the development of hardware, software, networks, techniques and rules to support communications at all levels in such a way that for a given environment, what goes on at a particular level is standardised and is independent of all other levels. In this way, we can proceed towards an agreed and acceptable environment for working and for future progress. Let us develop this idea by starting with the original stock enquiry conversation.

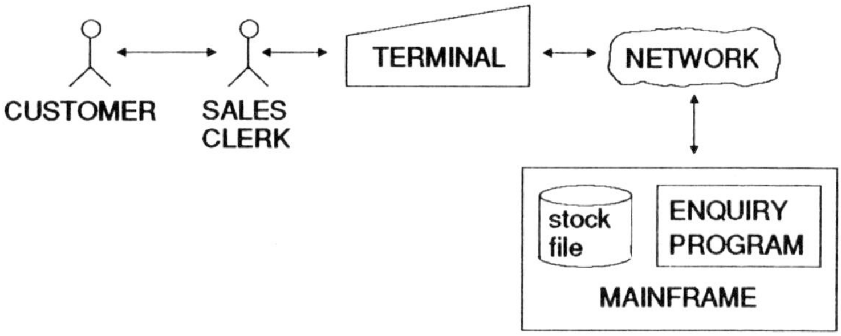

Figure 3.2 Elements of a stock enquiry

From the early part of chapter 2, we can think of the conversation as in Figure 3.2. The layers involved could be thought of as:

- A *customer* <—> *company sales catalogue*. He wants a price, or delivery date. He doesn't care that there is a computer involved
- B *sales clerk* <—> *stock enquiry program*. He knows that if he selects say option 3 from the menu and enters the stock code, the computer will give him the description, price and delivery date. He has no interest in what kind of mainframe nor where it is in the network
- C *terminal* <—> *mainframe*. A program, activated by the terminal or the mainframe, will cause characters to be read from the clerk's workstation keyboard and transferred to the memory of the mainframe. It doesn't care who the user is or what stock he wants
- D *terminal comms device* <—> *mainframe comms device*. The comms device is not concerned with the significance of the data, only

that it is to be sent and received with a certain baud rate and parity. The mainframe end has similar objectives

- E *sub-network <—> sub-network*. Perhaps the clerk has a character terminal while mainframe access is through the PDN. The PDN is only concerned with ensuring that blocks of data are received from the PTN and sent with the maximum efficiency to the mainframe site.

Inter-layer service

If you look at any of the above layers, there is a lot going on beneath the surface. The phrase '...does not care...' appears several times. Well, someone has to care and to enable each of the layers 'not to care', varying degrees of *service* are needed.

For layer A, the clerk will have to be provided with the exact stock code from the customer and then will need to know how to operate the keyboard to send off the request. He will also need to know how to interpret the reply from the computer. It might indicate that the item is out of stock, or that there is a very long delivery period. His further instructions might then be to try and persuade the customer to look at an alternative.

In layer B, the clerk may hit trouble; perhaps the telephone line fails, or is badly scrambled. What does he say to the customer?

One layer C problem might be that the mainframe has hit a snag and can't service the enquiry for a while.

From these, you can see that the layers are not separate at all. Aspects of the conversation are actually continuous across the layers, but it is still convenient to think of layers as being self-contained.

Another point that people find difficult to grasp is that although the thinking is top-down, it is rather different from the more conventional examples of top-down thinking given at the beginning of this chapter. It is not absolutely necessary to start at the top and work down. There is no reason why you cant start in the middle and then work up and down.

Taking layer A of the stock enquiry example again, the inter-layer service is the application of the procedures that enable the clerk to deal with the customer in order to set up the enquiry and deal with the reply from the computer.

If we look at layer B, there is no reason why we can't we start here and design the dialogue associated with the stock enquiry, perhaps as part of a more complex set of enquiries and other options. Figure 3.3 shows some possible menus.

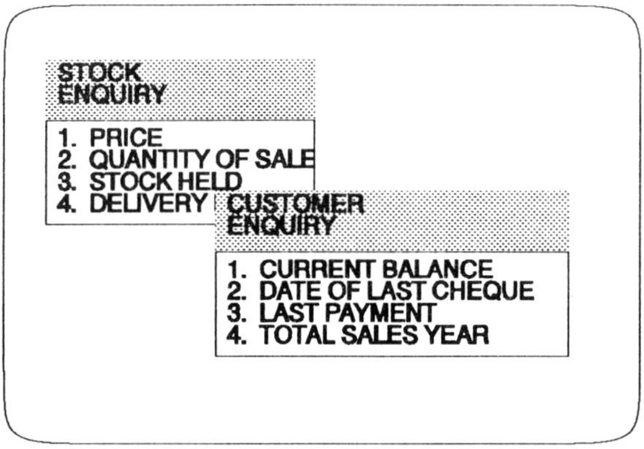

Figure 3.3 Sales clerk enquiry menus

Before the system goes live, someone will have to sort out the service to link layers A and B. Similarly we will need to service B/C - someone must decide on the communications profile and the comms software that will need to be run from the terminal in order to send enquiries to the mainframe and collect the replies.

To make this possible, the work done between the layers, ie, the service that is provided must be subject to rules and as we have seen, a set of rules and the data that is needed to follow them is called a protocol.

So, we are looking at an approach to communication to enable one *open system* to link with another. An open system can be described as one which is structured in such a way that it takes full notice of a layered approach

What would make the sales clerk and his environment an open system would be for the work at the layers and the inter-layer services to be carried out according to known standards. In this way, layer A would not be affected if a different approach was adopted to layer B, provided that the inter-layer service was changed accordingly.

Another clerk in a different sales office could have his layer A work changed and still be able to work at layer B.

Yet another possibility would be to change the mainframe programs or even the mainframe itself (layer C) with no apparent change at layers A and B.

Network models

From our definition of a network in chapter 2, we can see that the customer- clerk-computer set-up is a kind of network and we have been looking at a layered model of the network.

A layered model is useful for several reasons:

- it provides a theoretical or conceptual view of what will eventually be put into practice
- it enables thinking and development to be concentrated on particular aspects of the network, independently of others
- it provides a way of concentrating thinking on the services needed and the standards that need to be applied **or need to be developed.**

Various layered models are in use, most of which correspond more or less to the one that we are coming to now.

The OSI 7 layer model

Everything so far in this chapter has been used to lay the basis for what is now a well-documented approach to open systems interconnection. The overall subject of the OSI model is so wide as to make several books of this size and we cannot do much more here than scratch its surface to prepare you for further studies. In this chapter, we will go through some of the most fundamental concepts of the seven layers.

The lowest layer will be expanded in chapters 4 and 5 and we will spend more time on layers 2 and 3 in chapters 6 to 9. In this chapter, the treatment of layers 4 to 7 will be very superficial. They are extremely important but at the present time, as there are so many standards still being worked on and many areas where agreement has to be reached, it was felt that a detailed discussion should not be included in a book of this level.

In the mid-1970s, it started to become obvious that computer networking and inter-networking were going to snowball as the costs of hardware started to fall and industry started to realise the potential of WANs and LANs. As there are so many different people and organisations involved in comms development and practice, it has become essential to organise a rationalised approach

A number of bodies are concerned with the development of standards, in particular, the *CCITT (Comité Consultatif Internationale de Telegraphie et Telephonique)* and *ISO (the International Standards Organisation)* started to think very seriously about recommendations for international standards that would support data comms networking.

The CCITT put forward its recommendation for *X25,* a three-level standard for a public packet-switched network, in particular relating to the interface between the terminal end and the digital network.

A year or two later, ISO put forward its framework for open systems thinking, the 7-layer model as specified in its standard ISO7498 and later confirmed by CCITT in standard X200 (also British Standard BS6568).

One of the problems of open systems working is the fact that X25 predated the OSI model and its three levels do not exactly correspond to layers 1-3 of OSI. (Note that X25 will be covered in chapter 8 and although its main aim is OSI layer 3, it is logical to summarise X25 later in **this** chapter.)

The seven layers of the ISO model are something like the layers A to E, invented by me in the stock enquiry example earlier.

The specification defines why the layers are chosen but in particular, the model identifies the entities that exist within a particular layer. For each layer, there is a *service* specification defining the facilities that a layer must provide. The model requires that each layer builds on the facilities provided by the layer immediately below it to provide better or more enhanced facilities to the layer immediately above it. Facilities are to be provided so that **what** they achieve is independent of the mechanics of **how** they are achieved.

Associated with a particular service, there will be one or more protocols. Their objective is to provide control information that must be passed to the next layer and the procedures that will need to be followed so that the service can be carried out successfully.

At any particular level, an entity is only concerned with ensuring that the higher level provides the service, not with the protocols that support it. In effect, entities at the same layer (in different systems) can communicate via the protocols.

In practice, we are really talking about passing parameters from one piece of software to another and each layer will gather the necessary data into what is called a *protocol data unit (pdu)* illustrated in Figure 3.4. This pdu is passed to the next layer

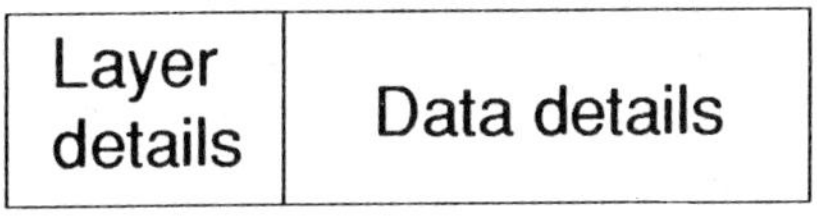

Figure 3.4 A protocol data unit

software which surrounds the pdu and data of lower layers with data and control information necessary for it to communicate with the next layer up. The pdu is built up in the manner shown in Figure 3.5.

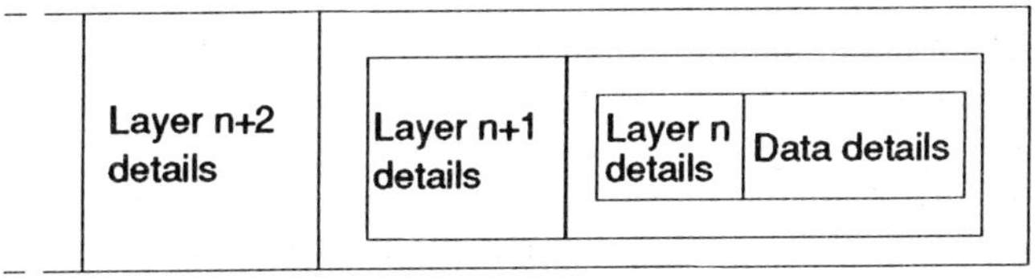

Figure 3.5 The layers within a pdu

Before we go on, we must recap on the significance of the term protocol. This was touched on in chapter 2 but we need to consider it in a bit more depth.

There are several concepts that need to be clarified in order to develop what we have started in this chapter - in particular the difference between **the data associated with the protocol** and **the protocol itself**. You must also be aware of the difference between the terms **protocol**, **standard** and **recommendation**.

Protocol

A protocol is a set of rules that **must** be followed and will usually imply in addition, the format and content of data that is associated with the protocol. Casual reference to a particular protocol, via the index of a book, is often likely to draw your attention to the data rather than the rules. For example, BSC (see chapter 6) is a typical protocol. The data frame associated with BSC is well-defined and is similar in form to Figure 2.33. But, it is not the **whole** protocol. This must also include the rules and data formats for replies to a message, such as 'OK I got it', or 'what was that rubbish'. This kind of protocol will specify how to reply to messages received OK, received garbled and not received at all. It can also allow for the actions to be taken by the primary after receiving a reply from the secondary.

Standard

A standard specifies (or defines) a way of doing something or the end-result of the doing. Originally a standard was intended to define and formalise current practice, ie, make sure that everyone knows what everyone else ought to do in order to get things right.

The more modern trend is for standards to lead on research and development since they point to future developments. This particularly applies to OSI.

Recommendation

A recommendation from one of the main standards bodies is something like a suggestion as to what should be done. In general, it is designed to be the basis for a standard or group of standards. Bodies like CCITT and ISO make their recommendations which manufacturers and service suppliers then try to implement. The recommendation usually indicates **what** and does not attempt to say **how** this should be implemented in practice.

The OSI 7-layer model is a recommended framework for open system interconnection and many companies and organisations have been working ever since its introduction to produce implementations of different aspects of OSI.

In theory, any model for open systems interconnection could be called OSI but in this book, when referring to an OSI, we mean the OSI 7-layer model.

Pause for thought

The seven layers of the model are next identified and very briefly explained (bearing in mind what was said earlier about the need to simplify the treatment).

The functions of some of the layers will make sense to you immediately, while others will not really mean anything until you are more familiar with chapters 5 to 8 and some of chapter 9.

You might say that this is surely a case for putting this chapter after these. Now you have been introduced to structured development and know what is meant by the term layer, please accept that the layered approach of OSI is fundamental to data comms and it was felt that it had to be introduced as early as possible.

You will need to keep referring back to this chapter as you go through later ones - there is no alternative if you are to put OSI into perspective.

The seven layers

In general the layers can be summarised thus:

- layers 1 to 4 are designed for error reduction. They provide for the inter-connection of and data transfer between the ends of a conversation
- layers 5 to 7 are designed to improve services to the user
- layers 5 to 6 provide functions supporting the exchange of information.

Figure 3.6 simplifies things by imagining that we are looking at the transfer of data from User 1 to User 2. This does not of course deny that data could flow in the reverse direction or even in both directions at the same time.

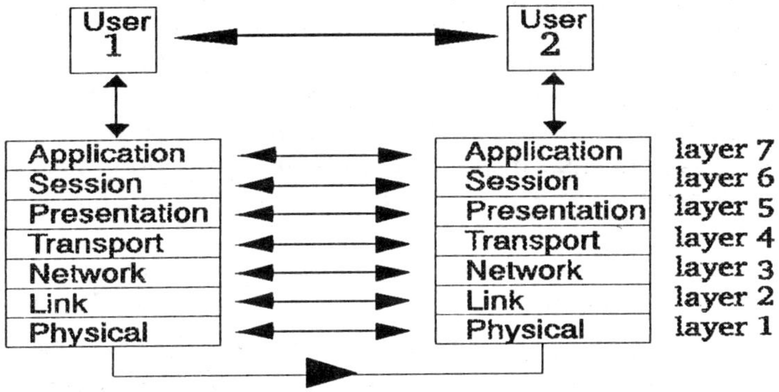

Figure 3.6 The OSI 7 layer model

It also tries to show that although the data passes down to the lowest layer and hence back 'up the other side', each layer corresponds to a kind of theoretical entity which can communicate with the corresponding entity associated with and supporting the other end of the conversation.

Note that in spite of what we said about data flowing from User 1 to User 2, between the different layers, the diagram shows a double-headed arrow between all layers. This not a mistake. Remember that the layers provide various services and this must allow for the possibility of two-way communication between peers. For example, it could easily happen that an error is detected, say at the network layer applying to User 2 and it needs to signal the network layer of User 1 for a retransmission of the offending data.

Similarly, User 2's link layer may need to tell User 1's to slow down a bit (illustrating what is called *flow control* - covered in chapter 6).

The model is very confusing when you first come to it. As we said earlier, although it contains an element of top-down thinking, it is at the same time bottom-up and some people may prefer to look at the layers from 7 downwards (or upwards?).

If you think of a user-mainframe conversation, then you must think top down. The user is running an application and is 'talking' to a distant computer (in layer 7). In lower layers, there will be operating systems making sure that the user can access the right programs in the right way, networks trying to connect the two ends and at the lowest level, mechanisms to detect and report on errors, bits going along wires and so on.

You may find it easier to start off with the bits that have to be sent and think about how they are passed up the layers, so that what is presented at the other end is like an onion, with many layers of skin. The bits are right inside and surrounding these are the individual layers, each of which has made some contribution to getting the bits to their destination.

If you have managed to get to this point and are frightened by the complexity of the model, don't be too worried. The basic concept is very elegant and quite simple - until you go just below the very superficial. Then it becomes extremely complicated. If you have understood that:

- there are seven layers
- each has its part to play in getting my messages to you and vice versa
- parameters must be passed between the layers to enable them to do their job,

you are doing well. Now let us look at each layer in turn.

Layer 1 - the physical layer
This deals with bits, electronics and electrical connections, ie, the actual physical attachment to communication lines. The layer:

- is concerned with the transmission of bit streams over the comms channel
- adapts digital data signals for the medium, starts, maintains and ends the transmission path

(This layer involves many of the standards that will be expanded in chapters 5 and 6.) Just to remind you that the layers are closely connected, Figure 3.7 shows 'part' of a typical conversation (ie, not showing the middle layers).

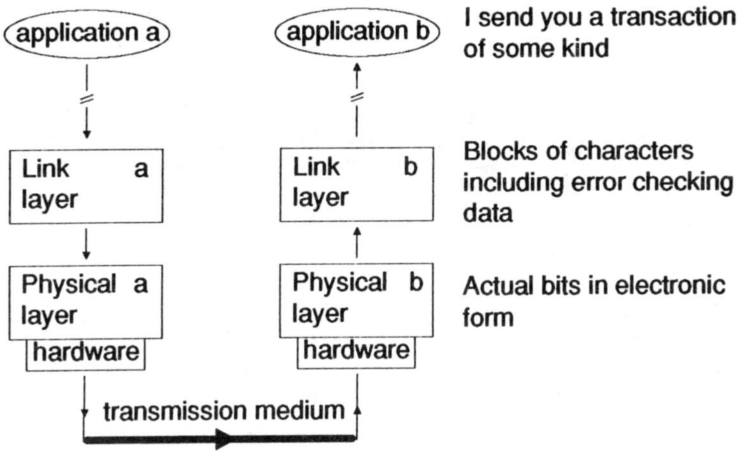

Figure 3.7 The physical layer

Layer 2 - the link layer

The overall function of the link layer is to provide reliable data transfer across physical media that are themselves covered by layer 1 standards. This layer:

- defines point-to-point logical routes
- is responsible for orderly delivery of octets across each step of the network path, for error detection/correction, flow control and link management. (Octets that I send you should reach you and not be distorted.)

Later on, we will use this layer to introduce many examples of protocols (including the BSC and HDLC already mentioned).

Layer 3 - the network layer

The network layer sets up and keeps going connections across the whole network. If it has done its job, it will sort out the different kinds of hardware that may be involved in the network: the next layer can then ignore all of these. The network layer:

- arranges that messages are passed across the overall network and that the network performs properly
- it is concerned with the routing of messages between the various components of the network and internetworking across similar networks
- relates user addresses to network addresses
- arranges for the breaking up and reforming (segmentation/ reassembly) of messages in transit through the network.

Layer 2 protocols may have framed data octets into blocks which may be too long for efficient transfer (perhaps we want to send lines, VDU screens or whole records from files). Layer 3 will arranges to change these blocks to a convenient size, as determined by the conditions that prevail at a particular time.

Layer 4 - the transport layer

The function of the transport layer is to ensure that layers 5 to 7 can ignore network reliability and cost-effectiveness and concentrate on servicing the user's applications. The transport layer:

- ensures that all errors not picked up in the lower 3 layers or those actually created by the network are handled. Further levels of error control are negotiated (the software at each end exchanges parameter information as part of the protocol to agree on what will be done)
- optimises transmission resources by further measures such as enhanced flow control
- ensures that network quality-of-service is maintained by improving that of layer 3, for example allowing for changes in the maximum block size permitted within layer 3.

Layer 5 - the session layer

The session layer manages the break-up of dialogues into the different activities handled in one session. A *session* to the user is all that happens between the start of a job and its end. During this user session, the system may have been involved with several set-ups and clear-downs.

For example, to provide optimal network performance, the layer may decide that it might be worthwhile to shut down the connection to the user terminal for a while, perhaps while the user goes into 'thinking' mode. It would then start a new session when he is ready. The session layer:

- is responsible for the coordination and synchronisation or resynchronisation of dialogue between different systems, ie, who actually will 'speak' next. Part of the layer protocol allows for the passing of a 'token' as a kind of permission to speak next
- manages connections and provides recovery mechanisms such as the recovery of an entire transaction at session layer from some convenient point (checkpoint), eg, what happens if there is a line failure in the middle of sending a financial transaction (or a whole block of them)
- introduces levels of checkpoint by negotiation at the start of the session depending on the level of service reliability required and numbers these checkpoints for reference and later action
- resolves differences between the allowed direction at any time for half-duplex and full-duplex users.

Layer 6 - the presentation layer

The presentation layer can be considered as a set of facilities that are made use of to support a range of different styles in a particular application and these act on the data to make it more usable and useful, ie, its resolves data representation differences in different users applications. The presentation layer:

- receives bit strings and convert them into a format suitable for processing. A simple example is where one end is sending say ASCII characters, while the other end wants EBCDIC
- by negotiation, resolves differences of data representation and format between different systems, ie, it arranges for the presentation of data in a format appropriate to the application. The term *abstract syntax* is used to describe the logical structure for data exchange: the corresponding *transfer syntax* allows for agreement on the format/coding of exchanged data
- arranges to compress data into a more compact form and encrypt it (as a kind of private syntax) into an non-comprehensible form. (This can be considered in a lower layer - see chapter 5.)

Layer 7 - the application layer

The application layer is the 'front-end' to a system which makes the applications provided within the 7-layer framework available to the user in the manner most useful to him. The application layer:

- is concerned entirely with the user interface and how the user can select actual functions/programs etc
- allows for common DP activities to be shared by different systems, ie, it relates a user service request to the network function(s) that can support the request.

(Note that the term 'application' here means the activity that the human user expects to carry out - electronic mail, database enquiry, airline booking or whatever.)

Pause for thought

Hopefully, you have gained some idea of the layer concept and to help you to think about them a little more, the following tries to explain the OSI model by relating it to some rules that might apply to a lecture:

- at the **application layer** we have the actual subject matter of the lecture The arrangement might be that the lecturer hands out next week's lecture at the end of this and when the next lecture has started, the protocol requires students to ask if there are any problems relating to the previous subject and whether they want more explanation or examples

- at the **presentation layer**, we include items such as the size of the room, number of desks, whether the lighting is OK, whether a particular subject is best delivered as a lecture, a class exercise, video etc. It could also involve adjusting the coverage of the subject to allow for classes of differing ability or syllabus requirements
- **session layer** rules can be illustrated by perhaps a bell ringing throughout the college to sound the hour and start/end of a session. In addition, the lecturer asks the students to cough 5 minutes before the end of the lecture session. The lecturer gets the students' attention at the beginning by shuffling his papers
- the **transport layer** could relate to mechanisms that enable a particular piece of material to be used in different courses and/or by different lecturers perhaps transferring it to a different context. Similarly, it could indicate alternative sources for the material. It could also be concerned with ensuring that lectures are delivered in the correct sequence
- the **network layer** might ensure that originals are properly extracted from the library, enough photocopies are produced for students, the original is returned and the copies given to the lecturer for the students. All of these would involve confirmations at each stage
- the **data link layer** could be represented by rules relating to clear handwriting so that typists/wp clerks can correctly transcribe written material (crossing zero, line through 7 and so on). It could also involve the rules relating to whether a particular piece of material was below the minimum quality for reproduction
- at the **physical level** we might need to specify the ink used in the production of diagrams since clear copies can only be made from certain inks on certain papers. Similarly, all writing may need double-spacing so that corrections or recommendations can be inserted. Yet another possibility might be rules requiring characters or diagrams to be above a minimum or below a maximum size.

Application layer services

As the layer directly of concern with the application, rather than the network or anything else to do with the actual transmission of messages, the functions of this layer are not too difficult to understand, although we will not be concerned with how they are implemented.

The various services necessary are supported by functional building blocks called *common application service elements* which are concerned:

- with the integration and management of services for a particular application
- with ensuring that applications in quite different networks can communicate in terms of the application itself.

We can identify the most important of these services, which at the same time are the ones on which most standardisation efforts are being made.

Messaging standards

These determine the operation of a store-and-forward *messaging service* and enable access to it. CCITT recommendation *X400* is of particular relevance here and will be covered shortly.

Virtual terminal

The *virtual terminal (VT)* is a concept involving an idealised or hypothetical terminal, which aims to resolve the differences between different types and makes of terminal. It would be nice if everyone could standardise on the type of terminal to be used. Unfortunately there are at least eight terminal types in very wide use, which have widely differing characteristics.

Chapter 2 discussed the main types of terminal from the functional point of view and chapter 7 says a little more about particular makes. The problem is that they have differences in how they cope with number of lines per screen, characters per line, code representations for reverse, flash, colour and so on. As there is no possibility for agreement on one particular make, the VT makes use of a hypothetical terminal with certain characteristics and arranges that the system can convert (or map) the functions of the real terminal in use to that of the virtual one. The concept is illustrated in Figure 3.8.

FTAM

File transfer, access and management (FTAM) allows a user at one end of a link to access and manipulate files stored at the other end.

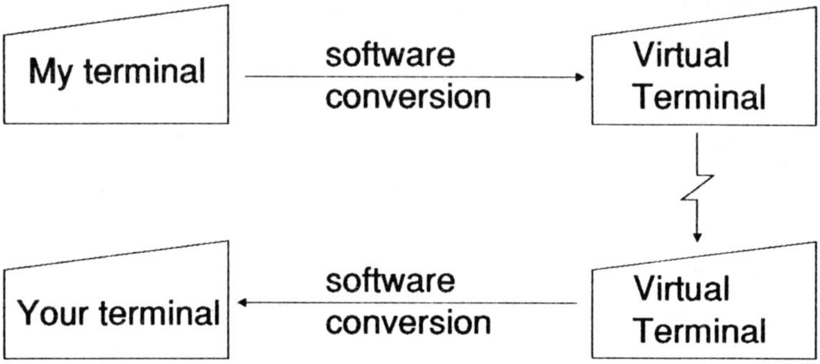

Figure 3.8 Virtual terminal

Remote file manipulation, creation, amendment and deletion and the setting and changing of file or record access levels are typical FTAM tasks.

In effect, FTAM provides a kind of conceptual or 'virtual' file store and provides access to files right down to individual records. Software to implement this must take account of and resolve the totally different methods of file organisation and access that apply between different computers and each application will need to

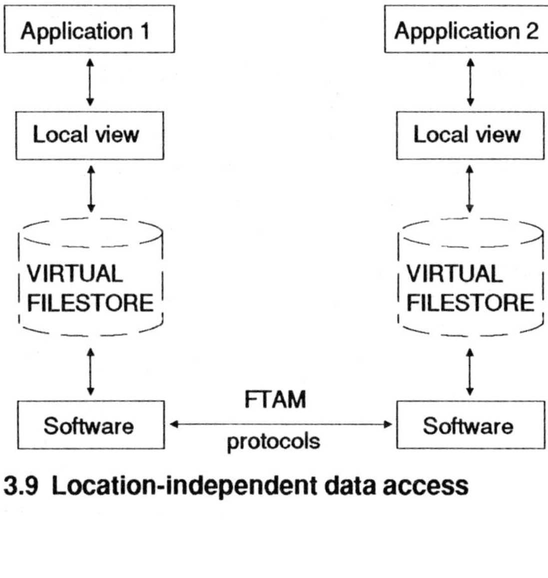

Figure 3.9 Location-independent data access

map standardised FTAM commands to local commands to local file-handling software. Figure 3.9 shows a view of this.

JTM

Job transfer and manipulation (JTM) aims for a distributed approach whereby users and/or user processes can operate, independent of their locations. In this way, one site can request 'work' and supply the necessary data. Then, another can carry out the necessary processing in response to a *job initiation* which initiates a *work specification*. A third site can then ask to receive the results.

The protocol prefers to use the term *document* to refer to input data and output results. It defines a number of *agencies* including:

- *initiation agency* - the 'person' that starts off the whole process
- *source agency* - responsible for the collection and entry of the source 'documents'
- *sink agency* - responsible for the output 'documents'
- *execution agency* - carrying out the various application processes on the documents.

Note that chapter 1 pointed out in detail, that an application has inputs, processes, outputs and data stores - the first three of these are the responsibility of one of the above agents.

Hopefully, you can see that JTM must be supported by FTAM if it is to be truly **open** (as in open system interconnection) because all applications will involve files in some way.

Some important protocols

Various protocols will be discussed throughout the book but there are three that need special mention.

X25

This is not really the place for a detailed discussion of X25 (it is considered in more detail in chapter 8), but any mention of OSI must contain at least a reference to it because it is perhaps one of the most important of all protocols.

Several years before the OSI 7-layer model was proposed in its initial form, a number of organisations realised that a new standard was needed for digital networks and the CCITT eventually rationalised this into recommendation X25. It is a

3-level model, which corresponds roughly to the first three OSI layers and includes the physical connection to a digital network, the link protocols and the handling of data in the most efficient way at what is approximately OSI layer 3.

Since most networking is going fully digital, any serious implementer of OSI has almost no choice in adopting X25 these days.

X400

This book deals with various methods of data communication. *X400* is particularly important in relation to the transfer of 'documentary' data and information.

Until X400, all the various hardware and network suppliers providing telex, electronic mail, viewdata, fax (and digitised voice) had developed standards, procedures and techniques on their own, leading to a high level of incompatibility.

From about 1980, the CCITT started looking at electronic messaging with a view to defining some 'rules', based on OSI, that would help to integrate all the various forms of messaging and X400, covering *message handling standards* was published in detail in 1984. It is a set of protocols/standards that tries to define:

- the general content and format of a message
- an addressing and delivery mechanism.

It attempts to provide a model for the universal interconnection of mail and messaging systems that are independent of the 'method' the user employs (eg, telex, fax, e-mail) and which at the same time supports the existing international telex standards.

Although it relies on OSI 7-layer thinking, the current recommendation relates mainly to layer 7, with a tiny bit of layer 6.

One of the problems of setting out any kind of standard is the necessity to state it in unambiguous terms - this often leads to the creation of new words or the new use of old words - 'jargon' or 'buzz-words'. DP and comms are full of these and X400 'conforms' to this. Terms include:

- *user agent (UA)* - the means whereby the user gets his message into the system. The UA will attach the global address to a message, send it off and receive messages for pick-up by the receiver

- *message transfer agent (MTA)* - the 'store-and-forward' message exchange that sends the message on to receiving message exchanges. MTAs are responsible for connecting one UA with another
- *message transfer system (MTS)* - a group of MTAs.

Even this model has been extended recently. The original recommendation was for a mailing system - a mechanism whereby messages can be sent to a receiver. Notice that this is not quite the same as one that allows for the use of a *mailbox*, where there is indirect message delivery, the user collecting messages from his mailbox when convenient.

This involves the extra concept of a *message store (MS)* where messages can be held for delivery. The service will also provide some management facilities such as the ability to delete messages, transfer them to permanent store and of course be able to determine charges for all the services.

The overall complex of UA's, the MTS and the associated MS is given the name *message handling service (MHS).* Figure 3.10 shows an overall MHS where many users link to many user

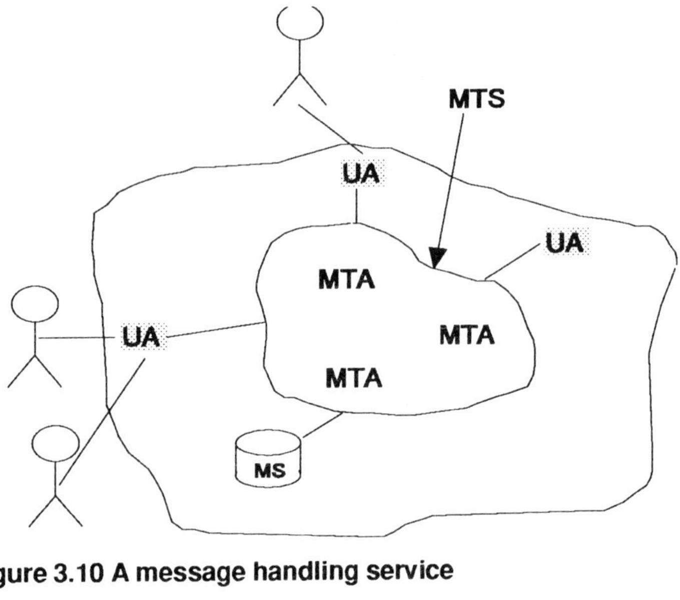

Figure 3.10 A message handling service

agents, each of which links into a message transfer system, the whole system making use of the message store. The UA allow access to other networks for example, providing the facility to be able to receive an e-mail message, modify it and then send it out as a telex.

X400 recommends a basic structure whereby a message is placed in a 'envelope' that contains delivery information such as time sent, send and receive addresses and a 'text' part containing a header and the body of the message which can allow for all the various different formats.

The actual protocols associated with messages are as follows:

- *P1* which covers linkage between MTAs within an MHS and to other MHSs ie, it relates to the envelope
- *P2* which covers the format of the message header body
- *P3* relates to transmission of the envelope from UA to associated MTA.

British Telecom about 3 years ago, introduced their public MHS which supports such complex activities as allowing user to broadcast a fax message of publicity material to a group of customers. If a particular customer has a fax terminal, the message will be received as sent. If another customer has a PC as a terminal, the system will convert the faxed data into characters for display on the PC screen. Yet another customer may only have a telex terminal, which supports a very limited set of characters, The system will have to convert the original fax text into the form that the telex terminal can display or print.

Access to BTs MHS is from dial-up or leased lines, private circuits, the telex network or the packet (digital) network.

Many other organisations, both public and private have introduced X400-based MHS and a real approach to multi-medium communications is just round the corner - before long, you should be able to do such complex things as send an e-mail message with a request for it to be faxed to the receiver from your mailbox.

Another development that will have a major effect is the application of X400 is EDI, (the electronic interchange of data that will be discussed in chapter 10).

MAP/TOP

These are two protocol groups that are often considered together because they are both based on OSI thinking and are both in common use in the engineering industry. *Manufacturing automation protocol (MAP)* was developed by the US General Motors Corporation in 1980 for use in process-based industry and manufacturing to try and overcome the lack of standards that existed in automated car production lines, where robotics feature quite heavily.

Different manufacturers' equipment needs to interface with each other and with mainframe computers for the management and control of production, so GM decided that MAP would be the standard whereby all new robotic and other devices would communicate.

The current specification includes standards and options for all seven layers (except the presentation layer) although layer 7 includes a *manufacturing message format standard (MMFS)* that is unique to MAP.

The Ford Motor Company has been making extensive use of MAP-based networks in the UK and in Spain.

Another American organisation, Boeing Computer Services (the software division of the Boeing aircraft manufacturer) quickly took up MAP, but soon started to apply it to office side of the business where it realised that a similar set of standards was needed for an open connection of general workstations, CAD (computer-aided design) graphics terminals, a range of printers and mainframes. It also needs to cater for e-mail, database access and management and the transfer of documents and images (such as are used in aircraft design). They devised the *technical and office protocols (TOP)* as a subset of MAP.

Other organisations and suppliers got together to form a MAP users group and a similar one for TOP. In 1985 they joined forces to form the MAP/TOP users group. A number of large computer manufacturers have invested heavily in the development of MAP and TOP and now there exist many standards for their implementation in local area networks.

TOP is actually more extensive than MAP because it has to cater for a wider range of user organisations and applications and a wider range of terminals; in layer 7, it specifies some concepts and usage standards that are very similar to those in X400.

Where OSI is going

Once you have completed the remaining chapters of this book, you will be in a good position to understand how DP and communications are coming together and where they appear to be going. This hopefully will also finally convince you that standards must be developed and kept to.

OSI in the UK and Europe is now firmly established and most major private and public network suppliers follow at least some of the OSI philosophy.

The USA is in some respects, different from Europe, partly because IBM has its own approach to OSI, called *systems network architecture (SNA)*, which is a 6-layer model. Obviously, such a large supplier of hardware and software can carry a large number of users and other suppliers along with it, so SNA and its derivatives are strongly supported.

However, the ISO model as we have said, is very strongly supported in Europe and a lot of work is being done to arrange for ISO-OSI and SNA-OSI systems to talk to each other.

The UK Government has set up a number of national organisations to develop and monitor standards including those relating to OSI.

There is also the *Government OSI Profile (GOSIP)* which is under the control of the *Central Communications and Telecommunications Agency (CCTA)*. This, in conjunction with a number of suppliers, acts as an advisory body to the Government in all issues on information technology and comms hardware relating to the application of functional standards for government systems.

In the UK, the Department of Trade and Industry (DTI) has its *Information Technology Standards Unit (ITSU)* which is designed to assist companies and other organisations in finding out what needs to be known about standards and OSI. The address of this unit is:

DTI IT Standards Unit
Room 634, Department of Trade and Industry
29 Bressenden Place
London SW1E 5DT.

They will supply a vast range of documents and assistance on matters relating to OSI and in particular, they have set up what are called *DTI Implementer Groups (IGs)*. These are groups of people who have already experienced and resolved problems and whose knowledge and ideas can be made available to others.

In preparation for 1992 and the hoped-for trend towards international open systems, several European governments have accepted the UK GOSIP and the USA also has a GOSIP.

Other bodies helping towards this goal are:

- the *Standards Promotion and Application Group*, an association of European IT suppliers that acts as a guide to the use of OSI standards
- the *European Working Group on Open Systems (EWOS)*
- the *European Telecommunications Standards Association (ETSI).*

Within the last two years the EEC has issued a directive that requires the development of all comms systems above a certain size to conform to international standards especially OSI.

With the progress hoped for, particularly in layer 7 (FTAM, JTM etc) we may be able to look forward to *open distributed processing*, an approach to open systems data processing as an extension to OSI in communications.

Finally, a rather newer development has been a lot of thought to the concept of *layered open system management*. This will involve extending open systems thinking and protocols to include a model that is oriented to the problems of running a network and allow for a system-independent approach to the control and progress reporting of network operation.

In spite of all the work already carries out, OSI has a long way to go - I am not going to make any predictions as to its progress!

Recap

- the chapter started with an introduction to a top-down or structured approach to work and related a layered structure to a particular problem environment. It brought out the ideas layer, peer-to-peer and open interconnection

- it then introduced the concept of an open network model and discussed the origins of the ISO 7-layer model for OSI, the idea of layer services and the need for protocol data units as parameters passed between service elements in different layers
- it then gave an overview of each of the ISO seven layer showing the main functions that the layers support
- next we looked at some ideas for conceptual OSI services and showed their importance in network development
- it then went on to introduce three important groups of protocols. These included X25, a 3-level standard which is crucial in modern networks, X.400 the basis of many electronic messaging systems and MAP/TOP, a pair of protocol groups which are becoming widely used in industry
- the chapter ended with a brief look at who is developing OSI ideas and monitoring their progress.

Typical questions

Question 3.1

Bake me a cake please!

a Make up a list of 5 headings which could provide the top-layer specification for this job

b Discuss five tasks that you could complete before you even know what kind of cake, or what ingredients to use

Question 3.2

Having completed the baking of the cake, you find out that I have gone abroad. You write a letter explaining what you have done and post it to me.

Using the example 'preparing and giving a lecture' in the chapter above, see if you can relate the communication problems involved to some of the seven layers of OSI

Question 3.3

a Why is there a need for a virtual terminal standard?

b Explain with examples what is meant by a 'multi-medium' messaging system

c Taking examples from your answer to question 3.2, explain the difference between a standard and a protocol.

4: OSI layer 1 - standards and errors

Objectives

After reading this chapter, you should:

- appreciate the need for standards at all levels
- know the main sources of standards
- appreciate how and why standards must be maintained
- understand the more common methods of error detection and correction
- understand the need for forward error correction
- appreciate that data reduction techniques can reduce errors
- appreciate some measures that can be taken to reduce unauthorised access

---

Introduction

We have actually covered, or at least touched on quite a few standards and now you have a feel for the OSI layered approach, we can look in more detail at standards, why they are needed and how they arise.

What is a standard

Let us start with a review of some comms problems:

- we are trying to get users with different requirements to talk to each other and to different computers. They may be connected through different networks using different terminals that generate different codes, making use of different software

- suppliers and users of comms facilities and services have differing methods of working and in particular, may have adopted differing solutions to commonly occurring problems
- the OSI model has pointed out the need to converse with others on different levels and if we all had the same approach to normal and abnormal conditions, there would be no problem.

These all point to the need for standards. A standard can be a number of different things:

- an approach to work or a method of working
- the procedure for a technique or process
- the specification of an end-product.

In all cases, what makes these standards is that they are generally recognised, recommended, defined and documented for general use.

Standards evolve because of the need to communicate. If I want you to carry out some work, you need some guidelines as to how to carry out the task and we both need some in order to estimate the amount of effort (and cost) involved and to measure the quality of the final product - **did it come up to standard?.**

A particular standard could be said to define and formalise what most people would have considered as 'the best way to do things' but with so many different standards setters and users around this is no longer really true.

Quite often, as technology advances, people in research and development make advances and come up with a technique or product which then has to be tested in real life. The more standards that are laid down (provided they are followed), the more chance there is of the innovation being successful and fitting into the existing framework.

There has also been an increasing adoption of the *de facto standard* - something that has become a standard because:

- someone has set it and can put a lot of weight behind it
- everyone uses/applies it because they can see the benefits (or they cannot afford not to follow it because everyone else does).

Examples of standards

To remind you of the kind of thing we are talking about, let us detail four different standards that you have met or will meet later:

- CCITT IA5 (also called ASCII code) - a set of bit combinations that can be used to represent a wide range of printable characters and control commands
- Electronic Industries Association EA-232-D (more commonly known as RS232) - one of the most widely-used interfaces between PC and modem and PC and peripheral devices
- BSC - a set of rules and accompanying data structure, introduced by IBM, that assists in the remote transmission of characters (chapter 6)
- DEC VT52 terminal - a basic terminal developed by Digital Equipment Corp, that can accept a particular set of printable characters and commands and carry out particular functions
- *Pseudocode* - although not really a standard, a standard approach to the specification of system or program logic as a kind of formalised 'English'.

Sources of standards/protocols

There are four main categories of standards setters - people or companies that initiate or define standards:

- trade and professional organisations such as the *European Computer Manufacturers Association (ECMA),* the USA *Electrical Industries Association (EIA)* and *Institute of Electrical and Electronic Engineers (IEEE)*
- government bodies such as the *British Standards Institute (BSI),* the *Department of Trade and Industry (DTI),* the *British Approvals Board for Telecommunications (BABT)* and the *American National Standards Institute (ANSI)*
- international bodies, in particular the *Comité Consultatif Internationale de Telegraphie et Telephonie (CCITT)* and the International Standards Organisation *(ISO).*
- manufacturers and suppliers - a wide range of organisations; the ones you may already know include Digital Equipment Corp (DEC), IBM, British Telecom and modem suppliers such as Microcom and Hayes.

Development of standards

As a result of working experience with different work approaches and new developments, organisations are anxious to 'be standard' or have their say in the standards that are evolving and they make their views known either by publishing their standards to customers of their products and services, or by getting them across through representation at the various trade and professional bodies, such as ECMA and IEEE.

These organisations may decide that an idea looks good and put forward drafts which are turned into draft proposals. These can then be submitted to ISO and be voted on by each national standards representative country within ISO and eventually an international standard is thrashed out.

ISO and CCITT put forward their recommendations, 'others' adopt them and standards start to evolve.With experience, modifications become obvious and if adopted, recommendations are altered and standards changed and reissued.

Many standards and recommendations are not necessarily complete. It is their function to specify **what** but not always **how**. Users and manufacturers implement them if they wish to be standard, but there is often scope for development within a standard. If it has been decided to adopt MS-DOS as the operating system for your PC, this means it will accept all the MS-DOS commands you enter and will handle hardware in a standard manner.

However, there is nothing to stop you having a different operating system underneath MS-DOS. This could mean that your PC actually is working in a completely non-standard way but you as a user will not know, because the machine appears to be standard. In practice, the operating system that you are using will have to simulate MS-DOS.

When we look at networking and internetworking, there are standards applying to message routing, packet-switching, quality of network service etc. How one organisation decides to implement a particular standard is not important, provided it connects as per the standard.

For example, the mode of operation of a PAD (that acts as an interface between an asynchronous terminal and a public data network) is defined by CCITT recommendation X3. If my character terminal is to link via my PDN to your PDN overseas and hence to your character terminal, neither of us knows who actually supplied the PAD. The manufacturers of the two PADs might have chosen quite different electronics techniques and could have produced very different equipment. However, provided they both perform according to X3, there is no problem.

CCITT

Much of this book is concerned with CCITT recommendations and standards and this is a good time to make some introductory remarks about them. For our purposes, any standard beginning with a *V* or *X* may be of interest. The *V series* relate to analogue transmission and in particular, the range *V21* to *V33* relates to modems allowing data transmission in the range 300 bps to 14.4 kbps.

V24 describes the way that a terminal links to a modem.

V25bis is a specification for a set of commands to a programmable modem.

V41 defines an algorithm that is used in a particular error-detection technique (CRC - coming up in this chapter).

V.54 defines a procedure for testing linkage between terminal, modem and network.

The *X series* is concerned with digital interfaces and transmission, that is, it applies to digital networks and the connection between analogue and digital networks (which will be covered in more detail in chapter 8).

X1 to *X96* relate to international user facilities, packet switching standards and higher speed, synchronous standards

X3 defines a set of negotiable options applying to a PAD ie, the facilities that the PAD must provide if it is to act as a link between a character terminal and a digital network.

X21 is the digital network equivalent of *V24*

X25 provides the specification for sending packets from PAD to remote host computer (see chapter 8).

X28 and *X29* relate to the exchange of control information between terminals and PAD.

X72 and *X75* are concerned with internetworking specifications

X200 to *X225* constitute the actual specification for the ISO 7-layer model

X400 relates to electronic messaging systems (see chapter 3)

CCITT recommendations also include the *I series* which relates to ISDN (see chapter 8), the *Q series* that deal with signalling within networks and the *G series* that relate to network trunks ie, the 'main lines' that make up a public network. (For example G703 relates to the BT Megastream service discussed in chapter 8).

Note that it is very easy to confuse **standard** with **protocol** - people use the terms very loosely. For example, *RS232* is a standard that specifies the plugs, cable, pin connections and voltage levels for the interface between PC and peripheral - nothing to do with modems. CCITT recommendation *V24* is a protocol specifying the exchange of signals, along an RS232 interface, between data terminal equipment (computer, intelligent or dumb terminal) and data circuit-terminating equipment (usually the modem, but could be a network node).

Once we have looked at errors and layers 1 and 2 of OSI, you will be in a much better position to appreciate standards.

Error detection

Chapter 2 said that an error was 'something going wrong'. In this chapter, we are going to look primarily at the detection and possible correction of errors where the receiver cannot actually receive a message, or having received one, cannot make proper sense because the message is in some way garbled. We will also have a little to say about methods that try to prevent unauthorised access to data and services.

The environment in which we carry out comms is very hostile. We have already seen that:

- electrical and electronic circuits are prone to failure
- electrical inconsistencies cause the dissipation of power over distance
- outside interference can disturb transmitted signals
- background circuit noise (hiss, Gaussian noise or white noise) is usually present and reinforces other errors.

These add up to a produce a situation in which the sender cannot ever guarantee that what is sent will be received at all, nor that what is received will be the same as what was sent, and we are forced to implement measures that try to detect errors and in some cases, actually locate them (and hence make corrections).

There are two main aspects to consider. We need to detect that an error may have occurred and then decide on what action to take. Looking back to chapter 2, Figure 2.29 implies that we should do everything we can to reduce errors. For a certain price, we can aim for a certain level of errors, but they will always occur and it is most important to detect them and/or reduce their effects.

Parity checking and its derivatives

The commonest detection techniques involve data redundancy ie, sending more data than is actually needed for the message, the redundant data being used for error detection.

We introduced parity-checking in chapter 2 because you needed it to appreciate the difference between baud rate and data transfer rate and now we can say more about it.

Parity checking across one octet is more properly called *vertical parity checking*. It takes its name from the early days of comms, when punched paper tape was a common input medium. Characters were held along the length of the tape reel as a set of small holes across the tape, so one character can be thought of as having 'height'. The technique will detect an odd number of bit errors. To expand on this, suppose we send ASCII 'N', odd parity and the left-hand three bits are flipped the other way during transmission as shown in Figure 4.1.

100 1110	1	garbled →	011 1110	1
- data -	p	transmission	- data -	p

Figure 4.1 A Multiple bit transmission error

The received octet is no longer in odd parity (there are six bits set to '1') and the receiver can pick this up. Of course, there is no way of knowing what the error actually is. For simple character-by-character data transmission, this form of parity checking is quite good if we assume that single-bit errors or bursts involving three, five or seven bits occur.

But, these days, sophisticated transmission techniques mean that a piece of quite short-lived interference affecting one cycle may actually disturb several bits (remember a circuit switch may be associated with a dibit, tribit etc).

Furthermore, outside interference may result in longish bursts of error - not much good having a method of detecting a bit error in one octet if the error has meant the wrecking of whole octets or groups of octets.

The extension to simple parity checking called longitudinal redundancy checking or *block check character (BCC)* involves an extra 'character' and associates seven data octets with an extra octet formed from the bit 1's, bit 2's and so on, of each of the seven data bits in each octet (see figure 2.30).

A variation on this is to form one BCC from the even characters in a group and another from the odd characters, the idea being that if a burst occurs and wrecks two adjacent octets, having two BCCs will reduce the chance of an error being missed.

Yet another variation is in effect, to 'turn the octets on their side' before forming the parity bits. It is called *interleaving* and works as follows.

Initially, the ASCII character string 'LETTERS' is shown as a set of vertical columns (without the parity bits) in Figure 4.2

L	E	T	T	E	R	S	
1	1	1	1	1	1	1	
0	0	0	0	0	0	0	
0	0	1	1	0	1	1	
1	0	0	0	0	0	0	
1	1	1	1	1	0	0	
0	0	0	0	0	1	1	
0	1	0	0	1	0	1	
0	0	0	0	0	0	1	
1	2	3	4	5	6	7	– octet number

Figur 4.2 ASCII 'LETTERS'

Interleaving would then produce a new set of columns. Figure 4.3 shows the result after interleaving and with an odd parity bit attached to each of the seven new 'characters' and a BCC attached. The big advantage is that even if a whole octet is destroyed, so that we have lost all of the 2 bits or the 5 bits of all seven characters, we can still detect a parity failure in each of the original characters.

L -	1	0	0	1	1	0	0	0	
E -	1	0	0	0	1	0	1	0	
T -	1	0	1	0	1	0	0	0	
T -	1	0	1	0	1	0	0	0	
E -	1	0	0	0	1	0	1	0	
R -	1	0	1	0	0	1	0	0	
S -	1	0	1	0	0	1	1	1	
Parity -	0	1	1	0	0	1	0	0	
	1	2	3	4	5	6	7	8	- octet number
								BCC	

Figure 4.3 The same characters after interleaving

This technique helps when there are several sources of error which add up to produce compensations that ruin the effect of redundancy checking. It has been employed in a protocol called *CDLC* developed by Racal, which is dealt with in chapter 6. The protocol employs interleaving with a method of locating the error, so although a whole burst has occurred, we can find which bits were wrecked and set them back to their original state.

Before looking at techniques for locating errors, we must deal with one of the most important detection methods. This is called a *cyclic redundancy check (CRC)* and is used in most layer 2 protocols (including CDLC) where blocks of characters are sent.

Although only of use in detecting errors, the method is almost infallible and relies on a kind of mathematical operation being carried out on the bits that make up the message to be transmitted. Using the right procedure it is possible to achieve a probability of failing to pick up an error as low as 1 in 10^{14}. CCITT recommendation *V41* suggests the use of the mathematical function:-

$x^{16} + x^{12} + x^5 + 1$

or 10001000000100001_2.

(For comparison, another mathematical function employed is $x^{16} + x^{15} + x^2 + 1$. This is called *CRC-16*.)

The theoretical basis for the method and the choice of function is beyond this book: a simplified explanation follows.

The sending hardware treats the bits of the message as a binary number and multiplies it by the chosen mathematical function, collecting the remainder after division, as the CRC, which is then attached to the end of the message bits sent.

The receiving hardware receives message bits and CRC. It carries out the same operation on the message bits and if the remainder is not the CRC, something has gone wrong.

The calculation is done these days in a special chip inside the modem as the messages is transmitted. As bits are sent off, a copy is sent to the chip and at the end of a block, the chip regurgitates the CRC which goes down to the receiver. His chip is doing the same thing (as shown in Figure 4.4).

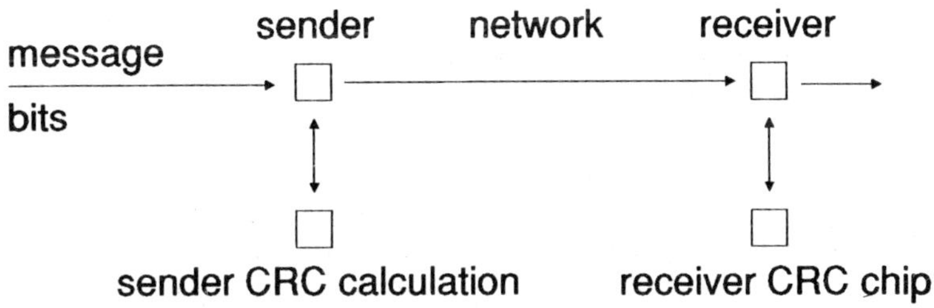

Figure 4.4 CRC calculation

A simplified CRC is called a *checksum,* formed by finding the sum of all the octels in a block (treating each as a binary number) and holding the last 8 (or 16) bits of the sum as the *checksum.*

How nice it would be if the receiver, having detected an error, did not have to go back to the sender so that the correct message could be retransmitted. We will now see how this can be arranged.

Forward error correction

We now look at *forward error correction (FEC),* methods that detect, locate (find) and hence enable the receiver to correct errors in data received ie, protocols and procedures once errors are detected.

Why is forward error correction needed

One possibility for error-handling is to rely on *echo-checking,* where what is received is sent back, so that the sender can look for any corruption by comparing original with what came back.

A much more common method is to rely on some kind of acknowledgement ie, a reply confirming that redundancy checks were OK (or not OK) and its implied request to retransmit some or all of the message. (This is covered in detail in chapter 6.)

Unfortunately retransmission uses up some of the available line capacity, which is already not being used **just** for data, because of the redundancy added in order to detect errors. Methods of forward error correction involve trading off **even more redundancy** against the reduced requirement to retransmit. We will look at just one of these and mention another.

Note that FEC is not easy to understand and provided you appreciate why the technique is needed, you can skip it and go on to the next section that deals with data compression.

Hamming code

This is an extension of parity checking based on the principle that if we build in enough redundancy, we can **always** be sure to **detect and locate** any single-bit error that has occurred and detect multiple bit errors. It relies on inserting one or more extra parity bits in pre-defined locations in the message bit stream.

We can look at an example of a 4-bit code applied to a 7-bit ASCII character such as 'T' (1011001). To see how these bits are inserted, it is better to look at the 'T' showing the bit numbers as illustrated in Figure 4.5.

```
1 0 1   1 0 0   1
7 6 5   4 3 2   1
```

Figure 4.5 ASCII 'T'

The theory shows that we need four extra bits which are inserted into the original bit string and placed in the bit positions which are powers of 2 (including 1, which is 2^0).

The inserted bits appear as an 'h' in Figure 4.6

```
 1  0 1 h 1 0 0 h 1 h h
11 10 9 8 7 6 5 4 3 2 1
```

Figure 4.6 ASCII 'T' with 8 Hamming bits

Next, we identify the locations of all bits containing a '1', here 11, 9, 7 and 3. We then form the sum (in binary) of the numbers of these positions ignoring all carries (modulus 1 arithmetic). The four bits that make up the sum now become the four 'h' bits needed for the code. This 11-bit pattern is sent as a new Hamming-encoded character (shown in Figure 4.7).

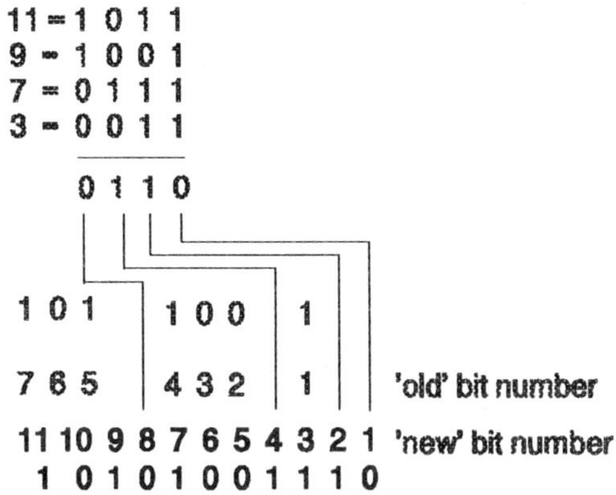

Figure 4.7 ASCII 'T' fully Hamming-coded

As we are producing an 11-bit Hamming 'character' for each 7-bit ASCII character, we say that the encoding mechanism is generating an (11,7) code.

The receiver examines the character and forms the sum in binary of the positions of all the bits set to '1' (again to modulus 1), in this case:

```
11 = 1 0 1 1 +
 9 = 1 0 0 1
 7 = 0 1 1 1
 4 = 0 1 0 0
 3 = 0 0 1 1
 2 = 0 0 1 0
    ________
     0 0 0 0
```

If the sum is not zero, an error has occurred and the non-zero value tells us where the bit was flipped.

Suppose bit 8 had been flipped during transmission. The sum for the receiver becomes:

```
11 = 1 0 1 1 +
 9 = 1 0 0 1
 7 = 0 1 1 1
 4 = 0 1 0 0
 3 = 0 0 1 1
 2 = 0 0 1 0   plus the new position set to 1
 8 = 1 0 0 0
     ---------
     1 0 0 0
```

As the sum is now 8, it indicates that the 8th bit was flipped.

If further Hamming bits are added and if a combination of vertical and longitudinal checking is employed, it is possible to detect and correct as many errors as you like - provided you are prepared to put up with all the extra redundancy.

Now you can see that, as the technique can detect a single-bit error in a received string, with interleaving, even if we were to lose the whole of an octet, it represents the loss of only one bit in each of the original characters. Hence full recovery is possible.

Trellis code

The details of this and several other methods of FEC are way beyond the scope of this book, but we must say a little about Trellis coding because it is related to a very sophisticated modulation technique that is starting to play an important part in modern modems.

The code has as its basis a kind of sliding window - a group of bits that can be shifted to the right, dropping off right-hand bits and adding extra bits on the left. The main feature of the code is that redundancy is attached as the window changes and depends on what has been previously transmitted, allowing the receiver to detect and correct an error.

Accepting that errors will occur and that measures can be taken to detect them, some lateral thinking might indicate another possibility for reducing the effects of errors - **find a way of sending less data.**

Data compression

We can accomplish this by using *data compression* techniques.

Repetition factor

The simplest form is to use a repetition factor - instead of sending 'n' characters, we send the 'n', followed by the character of which we want to send n.

This is very useful in text-oriented transmission, where in particular, one of the more common characters transmitted (unfortunately) is the blank.

One layer 2 protocol handles a string of 10 ASCII blanks as:

- the character ~ (called the *tilde*)
- the binary for 10
- just one ASCII blank.

Another possibility which is useful for numeric characters (denary digits), is to convert their value to binary and send this. A single octet can hold a binary value up to 255 and a pair of octets will hold up to 65535.

So for '1234', instead of sending the four ASCII octets (odd parity):

01100010 (1) 01100100 (2) 01100111 (3) 01101000 (4)

we would send it as $1234_{10} = 1024_{10} + 128_{10} + 64_{10} + 16_{10} + 2_{10}$

$$= 2^{10} + 2^7 + 2^6 + 2^4 + 2^1$$

$$= 0000010011010010_2$$

we can send two octets containing 00000100 and 11010010 achieving a 50% reduction in the data to be sent.

Tokenising

Another group of techniques represents common occurring bit patterns by *tokens.* If we relate this to the text that makes up this book, for example, 'communications' could be represented by 'cm' and 'error' might be 'rr'.

Taking this a little further, we could tokenise part of a word say, 'refer' as 'rr'. Then 'referral, reference, referring' would become 'rrrel, rrence, rrring'.

This can be extended to data transmission and made more sophisticated (hence more efficient). Short bit sequences are used to replace the more commonly occurring characters and longer ones for the less common ones.

The basis for a particular coding (called *Huffman coding*) that employs this, involves a decision being made as to the probability of occurrence of any character to be encoded. From this, the method can determine unique and varying length representations of each character and minimise the number of bits to be sent.

Combinations of compression of reduction techniques can lead to significant lowerings in the actual volume of data transmitted, particularly if the transmitter is adaptive ie, can select the best technique depending on circumstances and change as the data changes.

Archiving

One more possibility exists - reduce the volume of data **before it is sent** by using *archiving software.* A number of people have written programs that use techniques similar to those described above.

The US company PKware Inc supplies two utilities called *PKARC* and *PKXARC* which compress and then decompress PC files (up to 70%). PKARC reads in the file, applies several compression techniques and produces the archived file as a result. On some later occasion, PKXARC can be used to reproduce the original, uncompressed file.

These days, even though a typical PC will have a 20- or 40MB hard disk, modern software takes up a lot of space and by the time you have stored a few files, you can easily fill up a disk.

Similarly, when you want to load software, it is very inconvenient to have to load it from perhaps 10 floppy disks - archiving programs could reduce this to perhaps four floppies.

Security/secrecy measures

Identification

The prevention of unauthorised access to services or data is not unique to comms. It is appropriate to mention it here because this book is obviously concerned with on-line applications and you should be aware that the designer of on-line systems must ensure that remote users are only allowed access to what they are entitled to (or are paying for).

An unauthorised person accessing your data is another kind of error and measures are adopted, often in combination, to control access to data or services. They include:

- user number - usually a first-off method of ensuring that only registered users can access a basic service (ie, 'log on' to it). Generally the user will be given several tries before being shut down
- password - having gained basic access, the user is then asked for a confirmation or authentication. It could be that a group of people can gain access to a general service with the same user number. They must then identify themselves with a password in order to access particular facilities within the service.

A cash-point as operated by banks and building societies will read the user account number from the magnetic strip on the cash card and then ask the user to enter a password as his *Personal Identification Number (PIN)* through the keyboard.

Unfortunately, many companies are extremely naive in their selection of passwords and it is often easy to guess how to get in. (I have heard of 'sales' being the **security password** to access sales information and even 'password' as the password).

Hackers can take advantage of this by writing and running programs that generate a massive range of random number and letter combinations, each of which can be sent to the remote service until one 'breaks through'.

Levels of privilege

This implies different users having different levels of access to facilities, possibly in different modes, carrying out different jobs within the same system. Having sorted out their identification, certain users will only be given certain possibilities for doing things in relation to files and services. For example:

- any authorised user can read files A to D but only those with a password beginning with X can access files E to G
- anyone can read files A to G, but only with those with a password beginning with Y can add to or change files A to E and only password SPECIAL can amend file G
- all users can access files and programs relating to sales and stock but only payroll staff can get at the wages data
- Only the office manager can access the telex gateway.

At the end of chapter 9, we will look at practical examples of these in the local area network called *Tapestry*.

Variations exist on these basic security measures:

- the identification could tag a user to a particular terminal - Hey!, you are not at your own terminal so you are obviously trying to get someone else's privilege. Get off!
- there is a particular adventure game going the rounds which employs a kind of 'knowledge-based' password, before you can get in.

  It assumes that you are a knowledgeable adult (!) and asks you at least 10 questions to prove this and you must get them all correct. If you try to learn the questions and give different answers, it fools you because the answers are randomly selected from a very wide range
- personal back-up to identification can be made almost bullet-proof by extending it with voice or thumb-printing (or even signature verification), using some modern digitisation techniques.

Data encryption

Although we will take measures to prevent unauthorised access, additionally making the data itself difficult or impossible to read seems a good idea and this is what *data encryption* tries to do. This involves in principle, the same objectives as those of secret service agents and spies when they send messages in code.

The idea is to scramble the data in such a way that its meaning cannot be discovered. This book is not the place for a detailed discussion of encryption but a few points are worth making.

You may already know about substitution codes where for example, we slide letters so that A becomes N, B becomes O etc. Even complex derivatives of this can fail because, it is known that in a normal piece of text, E is the most common letter, T is next, then A,N, and so on.

You can fool someone and get round this letter frequency quite easily by inserting rubbish characters or words before you apply the encryption procedure:

'The yyenemyyy is klunk going, to grkattack, nurdle on Saturday'

However, more useful techniques may depend on the generation of random numbers from a particular key word or number. Unless you know it, you cannot decipher the message.

Real-life, 'unburstable' encryption must be employed by banks and financial institutions as well as by military and defence organisations and methods may depend on shifting around the bits that make up the character in a particular data storage code (see chapter 2). The processing logic to carry out the necessary encryption is often built into a chip, which can be placed in the user terminal or at a control node higher up in the network.

More recent encryption standards employ the use of two encryption keys, one at each end of the conversation. The user sends on his key to the receiving end (itself dangerous because it could possibly be intercepted) followed by the message. The receiver can then use his key to unlock the meaning.

Banks have very sophisticated encryption methods - I have not been able to find out anything - and a good thing too!

The need for encryption becomes even more important when you appreciate that a recent hacking development has enabled the potential thief to use 'listen-in' hardware and software. It allows him to cut in to the transmission and make a list of passwords as people log on. Then, at his leisure, the hacker can log on to whatever he wants using the passwords he has collected.

There are many hardware measures that can be taken to reduce errors so that they do not need to be detected. They will be covered in chapter 5 when we look at layer 1.

Recap

- we started off by looking at the significance of the term standard and showed some examples. This tried to explain why, with so many different people making hardware, developing software and supplying networks and network facilities, it is essential to agree on a very wide standards range of standards

- then we looked at organisations and companies that set standards and the procedures whereby standards evolve and are developed to make them of use
- we then make a serious start on the application of certain standard techniques for the handling of errors. These will keep coming back in the next few chapters because you must constantly bear in mind that the communications environment is hostile - if something can go wrong to wreck a conversation, it will
- then we looked at the idea of reducing the amount of data to be transmitted by making it smaller. If the amount of data is reduced by 30%, for a constant probability of error, we should reduce the number of errors by 30% as well
- the chapter finished by looking at some measures that try to reduce the possibility of the wrong person getting at on-line services or data and the need in certain circumstances, to make data unreadable except to authorised 'accessors'.

Typical questions

Question 4.1

How does the adherence of an organisation assist in the training of new staff and training existing staff in new procedures?

Question 4.2

What is *forward error correction* and what are its advantages and disadvantages?

Question 4.3

An organisation has an office correspondence pool consisting of four word-processing clerks and a supervisor in a 5-station LAN that links to the company mainframe so that users can send requests for typing and data (such as spreadsheet and fax output) by electronic mail, for inclusion in reports etc.

The pool is involved in the production of many manuals, documents and letters, some very confidential. Making any assumptions you feel are justified, give a list of recommendations for access restrictions you feel are needed.

5: OSI layer 1 - physical considerations

Objectives

After reading this chapter, you should:

- have a working knowledge of the main methods whereby users can connect to services and other users
- appreciate some of the practical problems of using transmission media
- understand the major difference between analogue and digital transmission
- understand the need for and methods of modulation
- appreciate the main facilities required from a modem
- have an awareness of some important standards

If you look back at chapter 2, you will find that a large part of it was concerned with the transmission of bits - exactly the subject of OSI layer 1. This chapter extends the knowledge you have hopefully gained so far and says a lot more about communications techniques, in particular, it deals with 'matters of concern' at OSI layer 1.

Data transmission media

For transmission purposes, there must always be at least two connections, one for send and one for receive. The earliest form of telegraph used one wire, making use of the earth itself for the other connection. The problem with this over longish distances is that the earth is not completely uniform as an electrical conductor and in addition, the transmission is very susceptible to the electrical atmosphere (especially lightning) and it was quickly realised that a pair of wires was needed. If both of the wires are 'balanced to ground' ie, connected to the earth, many noise sources will have no effect.

The media that are used for transmission are basically of two types. *Directed media* are those for which signals pass along the medium unidirectionally, ie, in the direction in which it is sited. With *broadcast media*, we are usually dealing with the air. Signals are transmitted in all directions and anyone with an appropriate receiver within broadcasting range can pick up the signal. Send and receive can be at different frequencies - equivalent to two wires.

Twisted wire

This is the least expensive transmission medium and is usually used in the form of a pair of plastic-coated copper wires twisted together although it can be obtained in groups of two, four or many more (multicore). Until relatively recently, public telephone systems made use of massive 3000 pair cables. It is also used in ribbon (flat) form.

Twisted wire pair is used to connect a telephone handset to the telephone exchange in the street. It is also used with a typical PABX, the switchboard used to connect extensions in a company. Since it can be used for data as well as voice, it may already be in place for future data comms use.

The twisting of the two wires reduces some electrical interference problems (such as *crosstalk*) but even if the pair of wires are sheathed it is very susceptible to local electric noise such as from office machinery and even fluorescent lamps. For short distances, with some sophisticated LANs, it is possible to transfer data at up to 4Mbps but losses very quickly increase with distance and 64Kbps is the figure usually quoted. It is essential to allow for losses for distances much more than 20 metres by amplifying the signals or regenerating them (coming up soon).

Its limited bandwidth (1MHz) means that it is normally used for baseband transmission, ie, just one channel.

Coaxial cable (coax)

This is also based on a pair of wires but not as a twisted pair. Standard TV aerial cable is the form you are most likely to have seen. *Coaxial cable* consists of a central, usually solid, copper core surrounded by a plastic electrical insulator, this being surrounded with the other 'wire' as a copper mesh or braid wrapped round it. The whole thing is then covered with a plastic sheath.

Separating the two conductors has important advantages over twisted pair. In particular, crosstalk is largely eliminated. With normal wire, the combined electrical and magnetic effects of the transmitted signal cause a signal in one wire to 'induce' a signal in the other. Coax is designed so that the two wires are coaxial and this diminishes the induced effect.

The other problem with twisted pair is the higher frequency components of a signal go to the outside surface of a conductor rather than straight through it. This *skin effect* would otherwise mean that the received bits (1/0s) are distorted. Coaxial cable overcomes this effect.

A variety of coax cables are marketed with varying thicknesses of inner core, separating insulator and strength of outer sheathing. The commonest coax for baseband usage is thinner than standard TV cable and is referred to as *thin coax*. A common cable used with *Ethernet LANs*, is often called *thick coax*.

Coax has a much higher frequency response than twisted wire (up to 400MHz) and can support transmission rates of millions of bits per second. It is used in the PTN although is gradually being replaced by optical fibre. One advantage of coax is that it is widely used in broadcast and cable TV and in LANs, so the wire is fairly cheap and many accessories are available such as connector/extender plugs and cable taps.

Optical fibre

Optical fibre is based on fine cylindrical glass tubing that is specially coated so that light is passed in one end is internally reflected along its length and emerges with little loss of energy.

Data is transmitted along the fibre by modulating the light itself so that it flashes the 0s and 1s, rather than by sending electrical signals. This means that the fibre is not subject to electrical disturbance. Further, as light has an enormous bandwidth it can carry enormously high data rates over long distances (a single fibre can in theory, carry up to 560Kbps).

The wide bandwidth also allows for the overall band to be divided into many sub-channels.

Digital or analogue data signals to be transmitted can be converted into light by a *photodiode (light-emitting diode).* For more sophisticated applications, a laser can be used. The transmitted signals are received by a *photodetector.*

The U.K. company *Plessey Opto-Electronics* produce devices that can handle well over 500 Kbps and has supplied them for use in the public network.

As we have already said, the higher levels of the PTN/PDN are largely based on microwave and optical fibre; there are several thousand miles of fibre in place installed by BT, MCL and the cable operators.

Optical fibre can also be used in LANs and in any other situation where high data rates are needed and electrical disturbance and interference may be a problem.

British Telecom has recently announced (May 1989) the commencement of pilot experiments, whereby telephone services from the local exchange will be provided via optical fibre right to customer premises ie, in what is called the *local loop.*

There are two possibilities:

- *telephony over private networks) (TEPN)* where the lines are split off to individual customers
- *broadband integrated distributed star (BIDS)* which involves switching customers to particular services.

Cable Telecom has a fibre-based local loop in the planning stage in Langley (Berks), expected to be offered throughout the area next year.

Now we must look not just at the actual medium but some of the control problems associated with interfacing PCs and related equipment.

Special-purpose interfaces

In addition to the various media, there are circumstances that call for particular connectors and interfaces between devices. They originate from a particular requirement and often represent de facto standards themselves. Examples include Centronics, IEEE488 and the most well-known, the EIA standard usually called *RS232*. This was first published in 1969 and you will usually see this referred to as *RS-232-D*, the 'D' referring to the latest version of the specification. In fact, the correct name is *EIA232*, but we will continue to call it 'RS232'.

Almost every book written on comms has some coverage of RS232 and we cannot miss it out. The interface is very important, firstly because it is very widely used in Europe and the USA and secondly because a full knowledge of the standard and its application is needed in order to understand the more complex standards associated with high-speed analogue and digital interfaces.

However, our coverage gives a general overview of the circuits involved, with a little more detail on those that are under the control of the PC programmer. (As you will see in Chapter 7, it is possible to write comms software in BASIC and examples will be shown where a program can 'talk' to a modem and test some of the circuits.)

RS232

People get confused about the difference between RS232 and CCITT recommendations *V24/28; the proper description of RS232 is for a 25-wire:*

interface between data terminal equipment (DTE) and data communication equipment employing serial binary data interchange.

It was originally intended to apply to connections such as computer-to-printer but nowadays it is often applied to PC-modem links. In such a link, the PC is the DTE and the modem is the DCE. (Note that the modem is more properly called *data circuit-terminating equipment.*)

The DCE is essentially the link between the user and the network and could be for example a network protocol converter such as a PAD.

Although we are looking at a 25-wire cable (or a 25-pin connecting plug and socket), the RS232-C interface, as stated above, is for **serial** data and only **two** of the wires actually carry data - for send and receive. The others are all for control purposes.

The DTE is taken to be the terminal device connected to the modem, usually a PC, but could be say, a data collection terminal such as a bar-code reader or perhaps a dumb output device such as a teleprinter.

V24 and V28 are the specific CCITT recommendations for the interface between DTE and DCE normally taken in Europe to be the equivalent of RS232. V24 relates to the function of the circuits while V28 relates to the electrical signals associated with the circuits.

The electrical D-shaped connector plug and socket and the associated pins are defined by ISO specification ISO2110.

The main circuits

The various circuits are referred to by number (100-200) in V24 (often called the *100 series*) and by names (such as BA and CC) in RS232, as shown in Figure 5.1.

EIA Ref.	V.24 Ref.	'D' pin	Ref	Description / comments
AA		1		protective earth (screen) – DTE only
AB	102	7		signal earth/common return (must be connected)
CE	125	22		ring indicator
BA	103	2	TD	transmitted data (data goes out on this line)
BB	104	3	RD	received data (data comes in on this line)
CA	105	4	RTS	request to send
CB	106	5	CTS	clear to send (or ready for sending)
CC	107	6	DSR	data set ready
CD	108	20	DTR	data terminal ready
CF	109	8	CD	carrier detect
CH	111	23		data signal rate selection (DTS)
CI	111	23		data signal rate selection (DTS)
DA	113	24		transmitter signal element timing (DTE)
DB	114	15		transmit data timing (DCE source)
SBB	119	16		transmit data timing (DTE source)
DD	115	17		receive data timing (DCE)

Figure 5.1 RS232/V24 circuits

The headings in this table need some explanation. **EIA Ref.** is the reference code used for the circuit in RS232. **V24 Ref.** is the circuit number reference as used in recommendation V24. **'D' pin** is the pin number on the D plug. **Ref** is the name commonly used for an important circuit

Note that although there are 25 pins in the plug and socket, not all are necessarily used and in particular, the PC sends data only on pin 2 (circuit 103) and receives data only on pin 3 (circuit 104), all other lines either being earths or for control.

We will not cover all the circuits, but the ones with a reference under the Ref heading in Figure 5.1 need expansion and we will do this by considering the interchange of data between a PC running a comms program and the modem that is connected to the telephone line.

Where we say **send** for a signal, it means **send a 1 down the circuit.** Conversely, **turn off** means **send a 0**. Where we use a **Ref,** it will be followed by the circuit number. (You will find this helpful if you look in other books for an alternative explanation).

The transfer of signals is as follows:

- the modem sends CD (109) to show that a carrier signal is present on the telephone line
- the modem sends DSR (107) as long as it is powered up and connected
- when the program wants data to go out, the PC software will signal this with an RTS (105) and if OK, the modem will prepare for modulation and send back CTS (106) and as long as the PC sends RTS, the modem if it is in a fit state, will always send CTS
- once data has been sent (perhaps the PC is now waiting for a reply), it turns off RTS (105)
- if the modem picks up a reply from the telephone line, it sends CD (109) and DSR (107).

If you think about it, data can only flow if RTS, CTS, DSR DTR and CD are all on.

Other circuits

Timing by the modem is provided from a combination of circuits 114 and 115 if it has an internal clock. If the PC is to provide timing (referred to as an external clock), it sends the timing signal as circuits 113 and 115.

In sophisticated modems, circuits 111 and 112 may be used to select the baud rate for transmission. Other circuits are used to test the quality of the line and for secondary timing.

Although V24, V28, ISO2110 and RS232 provide a complete and unambiguous specification for the DTE-DCE interface, **the situation is often complicated because computer and modem suppliers sometimes choose not to follow the standards, using incorrect pin numbers to connect circuits and even incorrect connectors altogether.**

Limitations of RS232 and V24

For general use, it is recommended that the interface cable is reliable only up to about 16 metres eg, between PC and printer or PC and modem. Any greater distance than this is likely to result in corruptions to data caused mainly by electrical inconsistencies, which in shorter lengths would be insignificant.

The maximum effective data transfer rate is about 20Kbps. This does not mean that your PC can talk to a modem at this rate. The IBM PC and its compatibles for comms are fitted with a port (asynchronous comms adaptor) that can only switch at a maximum of 9600 baud and can only handle asynchronous transmission.

Pause for thought

Suppose we want to link two PCs together. Should we use a modem for an application like this?

Remember that the modem is used when we know that DC pulses will be so corrupted that a conversation is not possible, such as for connection via the PTN. As we are inside the distance limit for the interface, we can send data asynchronously along the cable with a fairly low error rate, so no modem is needed. However, we need to do some juggling with the connections as is explained next.

Null modem

Attempting to use a standard interface cable causes a problem for PC-PC linkage. The circuit specification requires RTS to be received before CTS can be sent to the modem. For the situation here, neither PC has a modem attached, so which one acts as the 'modem' ie, which one sends CTS to show that it is ready for the other one to send? The answer is **neither of them.**

To provide a link between the two we use a *null modem.* In its simplest form it consists of a cable modified to 'fool' the PCs into thinking that they are each connected to a modem (and hence to an outside line).

You can't just connect the transmit data and receive data circuits together however - both PCs are waiting for a CTS - neither end would get it so neither end would start sending!

The simplest null modem is set up by connecting the two PCs as shown in Figure 5.2.

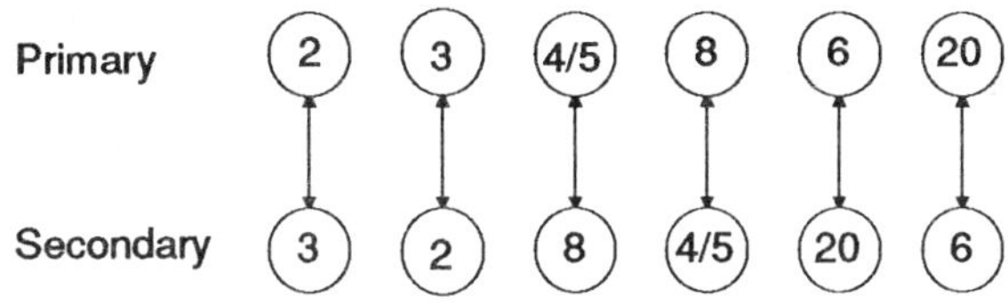

Figure 5.2 A 'null' modem

If you refer back to Figure 5.1 and think carefully about the significance of these lines, you should be able to suss how the null modem works. This is left to you as the best way to understand the most important aspects of the interface.

If the null modem is extended to include an internal clock, it can carry out timing synchronisation and is then called a *modem eliminator.* (Chapter 7 will have more to say about how a PC program can test some of the RS232 circuits.)

The V24/RS232 interface has been around quite a long time and there are now a number of newer standards. An in-depth analysis is beyond this book, but we must at least mention three other interface specifications.

More sophisticated interfaces

RS-449

This can be thought of as a 'super extension' to RS232 and is a synchronous interface using 37-pin plug, with a distance maximum of about 1 kilometre and a maximum data rate of over 1Mbps.

X21 and X21 bis

These interfaces are very important for digital transmission. *X21* has a 15-pin connection (*ISO4903*) providing a synchronous DTC/DCE interface to a public (digital) data network based on CCITT X25 packet-switching (chapter 8).

The standard allows more complex operations than V24/RS232, such as the ability to test the progress of a call. It makes use of control changes (transitions) and coded data patterns rather than separate signal lines.

X21 is not popular in the USA and *X21 bis* was introduced as a modification to RS232 for digital use with analogue networks. This allows for the initial preparation and development of digital transmission on analogue telephone networks.

Having dealt mainly with various 'wires' we now look at the 'air' as a transmission medium.

Broadcasting methods

Now, we can introduce broadcasting as it applies to comms. The essential difference between broadcasting and other methods of transmission is that we are dealing with an *undirected* mechanism ie, signals radiate out from a transmitter and if the receiver is within reach, contact can be made.

Radio is a form of energy and you need to have some idea of where data by radio fits into the overall spectrum of energy frequencies. Figure 5.3 gives approximate frequency values. Note

Signal	*Frequency range*	
Medium wave radio (AM)	540–1600	KHz
FM radio	88–108	GHz
Commercial TV	200–300	MHz
Cellular telephone	840–950	GHz *
Microwave transmission	18–23	GHz
Infra red	1000+	GHz
Visible light	600,000+	GHz

* Recent developments in the 300–400GHz range

Figure 5.3 Frequency table

that *mega(M)* means 'millions of' and *giga(G)* means 'thousand millions of'.

One point to remember is that there are many users of the various frequency bands and the Government has to regulate their use in the UK so that certain bands are allocated to certain users, such as the police, fire services, the army etc.

Radio data

Pure radio transmission is already used for data but only in limited ways so far. Note however that teletext services such as *Ceefax* and *Oracle* in the UK, provided by the BBC and ITV respectively, are actually data by radio (even if they broadcast on TV frequencies).

There is a little-known development of teletext, called *datacast*. It is more properly called *subscriber user group teletext*. Unlike teletext, which is broadcast universally to anyone who wants to buy the special TV set adaptor and pick it up, datacast is offered to specific users by the BBC and ITV. (Of course, this is for one-way data transmission only.) Companies making use of the system include the *Financial Times* and the *Stock Exchange*. Several banks, department stores and radio-cab companies are said to be experimenting with the service.

Recently (April/May 1989), Racal and Cable & Wireless have announced a cooperative effort called *Merec* which is an experimental radio data network operating at 1.6 GHz expected to go into operation in 1990.

A number of companies are developing quite small radio-modems and it is believed that before long, people will be using mobile terminals based on radio data networks as well as on the cellular networks (coming up next).

For pure radio, there are several protocols in use, including *A25* which is similar in many respects to the X25 that applies in public data networks, but data by radio is quite slow and obviously subject to much interference. Radio transmission is used in a number of modified forms both for data and for voice.

One of the big problems with any kind of broadcast is that there are only a limited number of frequency bands available for new applications, most of the spectrum being used by the armed forces and organisations such as the police and fire services, commercial broadcasting (radio and TV), fishing fleets and taxis as well as many amateurs.

For short distances, broadcasting, particularly in a straight line (line- of-sight) can be very effective, provided we appreciate that power is needed to broadcast and that a typical receiver will need to be very selective if it is not to pick up signals from different sources, sent at the same time.

Incidentally, when we look at local area networks in chapter 9, we will meet certain techniques for resolving contention (everyone wanting service at the same time) that were developed for use in radio data transmission.

We can now review a number of other broadcasting applications.

Cellular telephone

This was originally developed for voice use and is based on a *cellular network,* as provided currently by the two cellular PTN suppliers Cellnet and Racal-Vodafone (introduced in chapter 2).

The network consists of a series of radio transmitter/receivers (or *transceivers.* A transceiver (known as *base station*) is located in an area called a *cell* and the network suppliers have provided cells which cover most of the populated area of the country.

A cellular user can have a completely portable phone kit or mounted in a car. When a call is made, the transmitter in the user's set sends the message by radio to the nearest base station which is then passed by the network operator into the main PTN. Similarly, when a call comes in, the base station nearest to the called party will broadcast a message to his kit.

As the user moves around, the transceiver in his terminal may detect that a base station signal is becoming weak and automatically adjusts to the frequency of one that is stronger. This allows for *roaming* between cells as a call progresses.

The distance between base stations (and so the size of a cell) varies depending on the amount of expected use in a particular area and could be between hundreds of metres and tens of kilometres. The signal strength of base stations is such that a particular frequency used in one cell can be used again in another cell a small distance away without interference. This means that only a few frequencies are needed to cover a large cellular network.

Figure 5.4 gives a conceptual view of a cellular network, showing how a frequency can be reused.

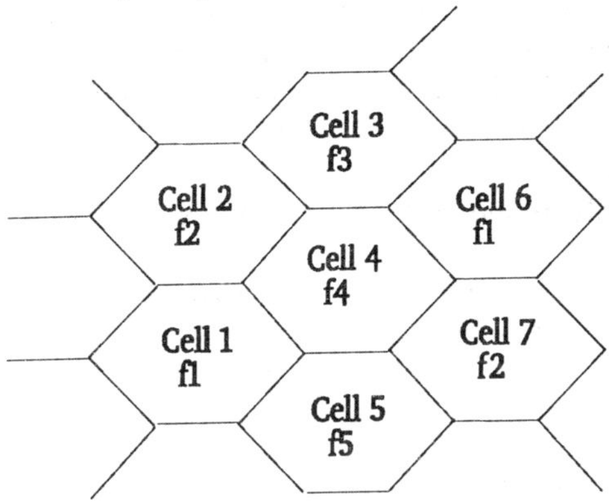

Figure 5.4 A group of cells

Even so, the original *total access communication system (TACS)* used for cellular telephone (which allows 40 channels per base station frequency) has been unable to cope with the current number of cellular telephone users (over half a million). *Extended total access communication system (ETACS)*, with 60 channels per base station frequency, has been developed for used in heavily populated areas such as in Manchester, Central London and around the M25 motorway.

The hope is that with most users moving around and automatically switching to other cells as the distance from the current base station becomes too great, there should be a spread over all the cells, so that there is not too much congestion.

Of particular interest for this book, is the use of the cellular networks for data transmission. Racal have made great strides in developing mechanisms to help overcome the extreme hostility of the cellular network for data transmission.

The basic problems of data transmission over a cellular network are as follows:-

- hand-over from one station to the next results in a short delay. This is irrelevant for voice, but at 2400 bps, a delay of 1/300th of a second could result in a burst error affecting 2400/300 or eight bits ie, the loss of a complete octet

- reflections from buildings and other vehicles which could cancel out bits transmitted
- general interference from other transmitters in similar frequency bands
- complete signal cut-off where the vehicle goes into a tunnel or is blocked off from the base station by a large building.

The latter two problems can cause delays of many seconds and for data purposes, the protocols need a means of detecting that a complete breakdown has occurred and some kind of checkpoint is needed so that a retry, once successful, can continue from the point where transmission stopped. This is further complicated by the fact that break-down can occur completely at random and with no warning, particularly in built-up areas such as in London and its outskirts - areas where cellular transmission is at its most dense.

Nevertheless, Racal has recently implemented a linkage from its cellular network to the PDN which means that the mobile user now has access to a wider range of services (chapter 8).

An important cellular data application these days is vehicle control. A large computer manufacturer is piloting a system whereby all servicing engineers are equipped with a mobile terminal. This can direct them to the next customer to be called on and even suggest the best route. Once on site, the terminal can record time spent by the engineer and any components replaced. If an urgent component is not carried, a message can be sent to the nearest 'mobile warehouse' vehicle, which can get over there as soon as possible.

With this kind of system, customer service can be dramatically improved and the company has almost immediate update of its customer and stock files.

CT2

This is a very new development and uses 864-868 MHz base stations sited in shopping centres, hotels, railway stations and other heavily populated areas or sites where people are likely to stop to make a call. The CT2 user will have a pocket-sized telephone transceiver and when he wants to make a call, he will go near to a base station and then dial out. The base station will pick up the call and relay it into the PTN.

There are four differences between CT2 and cellular telephone:

- a user can only call out - it is for send-only, so a CT2 call can only be received by a user with a conventional or cellular telephone
- base stations will only be sited in city areas or those where demand is to be expected
- there is no hand over from one base station to another - a CT2 call is from a stationary user
- the maximum distance of coverage from the caller to the base station will be about 200 metres.

CT2 should be well in by the Summer of 1990.

Radiopaging

Radiopaging has been around for several years and although of little interest for data purposes, is very widely used. It seems likely that it will before long, be linked with CT2 so that they together, constitute a two-way service. (Mobile paging services are offered by BT, MCL and Racal.)

The technique of paging is such that a person with a pager can be contacted by radio, the user's attention drawn by a bleep from the pager, with several different tones being possible - one could mean say, 'call the office' and another perhaps 'call home'.

More sophisticated pagers have an LCD display, memory and even a little printer so that a printed record of calls can be made.

Other broadcasting developments

When linked in use with phone messaging systems, mobile communication has become very clever indeed. When not in the office, the user can have calls diverted to his messager and later on, dial in from a remote location to find out what there is for him. This could be extended to let him know that there was some e-mail or fax waiting for his attention.

It is expected that there will be an increase in the number of external services available to the mobile user, such as weather forecasts and voice access to certain information - or databases provided as value-added data network services (such as will be covered in chapter 10.)

There is talk of a European CT2 facility and an even more exciting possibility of a satellite-linked international network for CT2 and paging.

Other ideas for the future include the possibility of having a single piece of telephone kit that can be used in the office via the normal PTN and switched automatically to the cellular or CT2 network as soon as it is disconnected from the office PBX.

We will have to wait for a year or two before we find out what impact all this will have on data communications.

Microwave

Microwave is rather different from the other broadcasting methods discussed, in that signals are directed. The transmitting aerial (dish) is designed to send out an almost parallel radio beam and the receiving dish picks up a nice strong signal. Transmission is effectively line-of-sight, so to allow for the curvature of the earth, the greater the distance for transmission, the higher up must the dishes be placed. Major microwave retransmission centres are usually sited on high ground, many being hundreds of feet above sea level.

Line-of-sight distances are usually limited by the nature of the terrain (hills etc) to about 20 km or so but by having a fair number of centres, a large part of the country can be covered. (There is also be the possibility of using repeaters to boost signals.)

Microwave is particularly useful where a fibre cable would be too expensive to install, or perhaps where the supplier cannot get right-of- way to the land where a cable would need to be installed.

The massive bandwidth of microwave allows for many thousands of voice and data channels to be multiplexed onto a single microwave link (see *multiplexing* later in this chapter) and a large part of the PTN/PDN is carried by microwave. In particular, the MCL network in the City of London although based on fibre, has many points where what are called *local access microwave hops*, are made from the main network fibre 'trunk' to the customer's site.

Satellites for data transmission

Microwave transmission is also used in conjunction with *earth satellites*.

Where communication has to be sent over great distances, the curvature of the earth means that line-of-sight is out of the question. The satellite has a microwave transceiver on board and an *earth station*, consisting of a microwave transceiver and a dish aerial, can send microwave signals to and receive them from a satellite. These communications satellites are usually placed in a *Geosynchronous orbit*, ie, they rotate at a constant height above the Earth (about 36,000Km) which means that to a particular earth station, a particular satellite appears to be stationary.

There are many satellites in orbit and it is possible to send voice and/or data almost from anywhere to anywhere else using one or more satellites, even from mobile sites - it is possible to mount the dish on a vehicle such as a van or Land Rover and use it as a mobile telephone or data communications centre.

UK satellite users go through BT or MCL who are both members of the *Intelstat* satellite consortium. There is also a *Eutelsat* satellite consortium which has governments represented on it. There are plans for a series of satellites *(Eutelsat II)* that will have the capacity for 20,000 telephone channels. They will also be used for TV.

The main problem, apart from booking space/time on the satellite (assuming that there is one spare for you to use or you are rich enough to buy your own rocket) is the *round-trip delay* that occurs. Electrical signals travel at 3 million metres per second. Over the distance of a LAN, or even a PTN in one country, the time taken from A to B is negligible for voice (although it could be a problem in a very fast LAN).

But, if you want to go from say Northern Canada to Southern India, the actual distance travelled from Canada up to a satellite over the central Pacific, then to another over the Pacific and then to India, might be 25,000 miles (45,000 Kilometres) and the signal could take perhaps 100ths of a second. Even in a voice conversation, this delay might be noticed.

Figure 5.5 shows a conceptual view of a signal passing along a satellite link.

Another problem with satellite transmission is the major disturbance that can be caused by Sun spot activity. When this is high, the satellite may be unable to handle traffic without a high error level for minutes or even hours at a time.

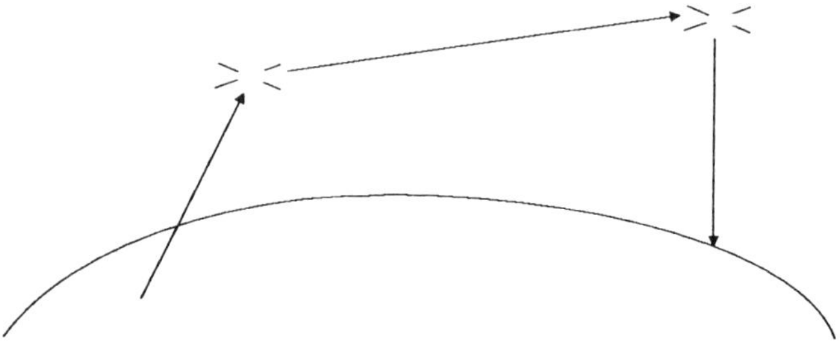

Figure 5.5 Microwave transmission across the Earth

The very high-volume international user has to be extremely careful in times like this because the only alternative is undersea cables and these are very heavily booked (which is why so many people use satellite links).

There are conflicting reports and forecasts of future transatlantic satellite usage and it is difficult to say how things are likely to go.

Some organisations have predicted a 600% increase in facilities to be made available with 120% increase in their use. On the other hand, Cable & Wireless (who own MCL) are planning to introduce a new, massive-capacity transatlantic cable, so they obviously expect a large increase in traffic which they will service in competition with satellites. Who knows?

Fairly recently, 6 organisations were granted local satellite licences intended for one-way transmission in the UK, mainly for TV and video.

Perhaps this will be extended for two-way use and make high-speed data transmission even more available.

Now we know a bit more about the main transmission media and methods, we must come back to some more basic aspects of OSI layer 1 particularly in relation to how errors occur and what we need to do about them.

The previous chapter looked at methods of detecting errors and a few ways of avoiding them. Some of these will be expanded later in this chapter when we look at modems, but first we introduce a number of specific pieces of hardware or hardware measures that can be used in various situations, to reduce errors so that time and effort can be saved in their detection and correction.

Error reduction hardware

Amplifier

An *amplifier* is designed to boost signals that have become weakened because of the physical and electrical inconsistencies in the transmission medium over the total transmission path. In an earlier chapter, we saw that local lines from user to local exchanges are usually two-wire. From the local exchange however, four wires are used for send and two for receive. For electronic reasons, amplification on a four-wire circuit is fairly simple, but two-wire amplification causes some problems.

For data purposes, there are several other devices similar to an amplifier, that can extend the operation of a V24/RS232 interface from its basic 16m up to thousands of metres. They have names such as *baseband modem, short-haul modem, local modem* and *line driver*.

Signal regenerator

With any kind of amplifier, there is always the problem that amplification of the signal will also amplify any noise on the line. A *signal regenerator* or *line driver* does not boost the signal. In fact, it looks at each bit of the weakened signal (look back to figure 2.25), works out whether it is looking at a 1 or 0 and then actually recreates the digit in a nice, clear form and passes it on. In this way, noise is removed completely.

Equalisation

We have said that distance causes a loss of signal. Remember that a signal is made up of a wide range of frequencies, In practice, the higher frequency components of the signal may be reduced more than the lower frequency components and this will lead to a distorted signal. Better quality lines are *equalised* (or *conditioned*). This means that at some stage, the high frequencies are amplified more than the low, resulting in a much longer transmission path being possible before losses need further compensation.

Echo-suppression

There are times when *echo-suppression* becomes necessary. Electrical signals travel at very high speeds in wires and data sent earlier may reach the end of the circuit and echo (bounce back) thereby interfering with further data being sent. This echo disturbance is particularly important in LANs with transmission distances of many dozens of metres and steps may need to be taken to reduce its effect.

One possibility is to detect the echo of the sent signal in the return channel and switch off the channel for a short time, so losing the echo. Another is to generate a copy of the echo and send its mathematical inverse to cancel it out. CCITT recommendations V26 and V33 require this from the modem (see figure 5.21). This echo-cancellation is usually carried out by a special-purpose chip (integrated circuit).

Unloading

The transmission characteristics of long, voice-grade telephone lines can often be improved by the addition of what are called *loading coils* (or *speech coils*) about every 2000 metres. Their presence however, may reduce the data transmission rate over a modem link. The supplier of the line may charge for *unloading* the line (ie, removing the speech coils before the line is installed for data transmission use).

Telephone lines

The PTOs provide an analogue telephone network, based on twisted pair and some coax at the lower levels and microwave and optical fibre at the highest. (Remember that direct links such as LAN and PC-host, may also be based on wire and optical fibre.)

Dial-up and leased lines

PTN lines (telephone channels) are either *dial-up* or *leased.* A dial-up channel is one for which the call is made as for a voice call and is switched through the network. It is based on two-wire and incurs charges only while a call is actually in progress.

A leased line on the other hand, is a dedicated four-wire, point-to-point link - the connection is made as soon as both parties 'switch on' and is charged on a rental basis, irrespective of how much it is used.

Leased lines can be conditioned and echo-suppressed and more easily amplified but their biggest advantage is the fact that the four wires are, in effect, two independent pairs and can be used for independent send/receive. (With a single pair, time is wasted while the modem is switched from send to receive - *modem turnaround time.*)

BT offer cheap *within-exchange-area* leased lines (BT ref. EPS8/9) based on twisted pairs of fairly wide bandwidth, or ordinary voice-grade lines with 3KHz bandwidth.

Now for multiplexing, signalling and modulation, three very important techniques in comms.

Multiplexing

Accepting that we have decided on a particular transmission line for our voice and/or data comms needs, there still remains the problem of how to make the best use of it. But, assuming you have selected a line, have decided that your data transmission will be at say 1200 baud and have purchased the appropriate modem, can you make full use of it?

Remember that many data applications involve low-volume, intermittent transmission and for much of the connect time, the line is idle.

With voice transmission, one of the two parties involved is talking almost all the time, but with data, the line is not sending or receiving data until the terminal makes a request. For perhaps 90% of the time, a typical user is looking at what is on the screen or keying in data lines - both of these processes occurring at say 3-6 characters per second (20-70 bps!).

At 1200 baud, even after allowing a 50% reduction for redundancy and error-retransmission (to 600 baud), the line could still carry about 75 characters per second. (Remember we are probably dealing with asynchronous transmission and characters per second can be calculated by dividing the 600 by 11 - 7 data + 1 parity + 1 start + 2 stop). This is obviously a waste of potential transmission capacity and ideally, the single link should be shared between a number of users, whose combined data transmission requirements add up to somewhere near the maximum for the link.

This is possible with the technique of *multiplexing* which is carried out in two main ways. We can either chop up the signals, so that they are interleaved in time - *time-division multiplexing*, or we can send the separate signals at different frequencies - *frequency-division multiplexing*.

Time division multiplexing (TDM)

With TDM, the *mux* (multiplexer) goes round to each terminal in turn and collects/sends a byte to/from each in turn as they are ready (Figure 5.6). If there is nothing to do for a particular terminal, the mux inserts a 'null' to show this.

start	term 1	term 2	....	term n–1	term n	start	term 1	......

Figure 5.6 Time division multiplexing

The technique appears to be effective but can only be used to advantage if a fair number of terminals are involved - even with several, each individual terminal is used intermittently and the overall data transmission requirement may still be far less than the link can handle.

When multiplexing is in operation, the link is now supporting several channels, in the sense that the physical line is carrying more than one message, in effect at the same time. In practice, it is better to think of each user occupying a slice of time, say, I have the first 1/10th of each second, you have the next 1/10th, he has the next and so on.

Statistical multiplexers

The *statistical multiplexer* sometimes called a *statmux)* has buffering facilities (in the form of digital storage), so can pick up bytes and store them until a reasonable block has been collected and send them as one.

There are many different types of statmux. Some buffer data from each terminal and send single blocks, others buffer characters plus a terminal identifier for each terminal and send these as a block. Some can act on a **bit** rather than a **character** basis, interleaving individual bits rather than characters.

A normal multiplexer connects to each of the users in a specific order, whether it is ready to receive/transmit or not. The statmux can attach an identifier (address) to the data for each user, so it can ignore one if necessary - this means that the order does not need to be maintained and the receiver can work out which item of data is for which end-user.

Other techniques are employed to make line usage more efficient, in particular using statistical probability to decide whether a particular terminal can be ignored for a while (because it has been idle, or not idle). Similarly, flow control can be used, so that the statmux can signal the sending terminal to hang on for a while if it is busy.

Modern statmuxes can handle blocks in synchronous transfer as well the characters in asynchronous transfer. This is obviously much trickier but there are machines which can pack 16 users into a 19.2Kbps stream.

Statmuxes become even more important in taking advantage of the 64Kbps links available from digital networks. Some are available that employ error handling and recovery techniques similar to sophisticated modems (later on in the chapter).

Frequency division multiplexing (FDM)

This is the basis of broadband transmission. The available transmission bandwidth of the line is divided into several channels separated by *guard bands* to prevent interference between channels (Figure 5.7).

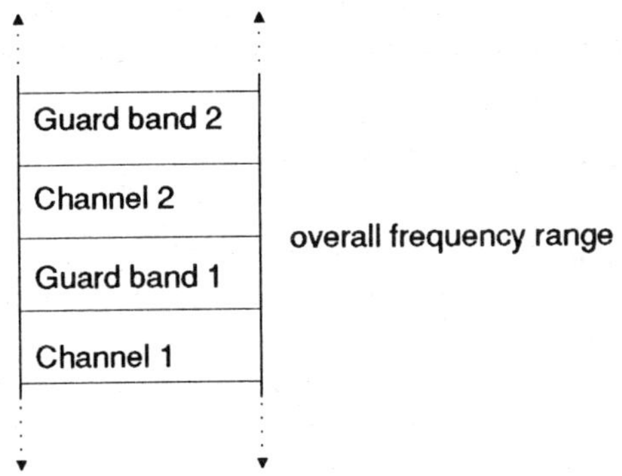

Figure 5.7 Frequency division multiplexing

The overall frequency range of the transmission medium must be sufficiently wide to allow a reasonable bandwidth for each of the channels otherwise there will be the same distortions that occur with baseband transmission along, say, a voice-grade line with its limited bandwidth.

With voice multiplexing, to prevent interference between different channels, *guard bands* are inserted in the original 4KHz baseband, ie, 300-3300Hz for the signal and the bottom 300 and top 400 for guarding.

A big advantage of FDM over TDM is that full-duplex operation becomes much simpler because send / receive will be on different channels.

Multiplexing of telephone channels in the PTN takes place progressively. Each conversation is allocated an individual channel bandwidth of 4kHz (300Hz to 3.4kHz, the remainder forming the guard band). Carrier waves, with frequencies ranging from 64kHz to 108kHz, at 4kHz intervals, are modulated by 12 individual telephone conversations (channels), forming a *group* (4 x 4kHz giving 48kHz).

Five groups modulate further carriers in steps of 48kHz, from 420kHz to 612kHz, to form a *supergroup*. Finally, 15 or 16 supergroups modulate carriers to form a *hypergroup*. This is all summarised in Figure 5.8. (What we have just been through, may help you to appreciate why high-capacity links require the extremely high band-widths available with microwave and optical fibre.)

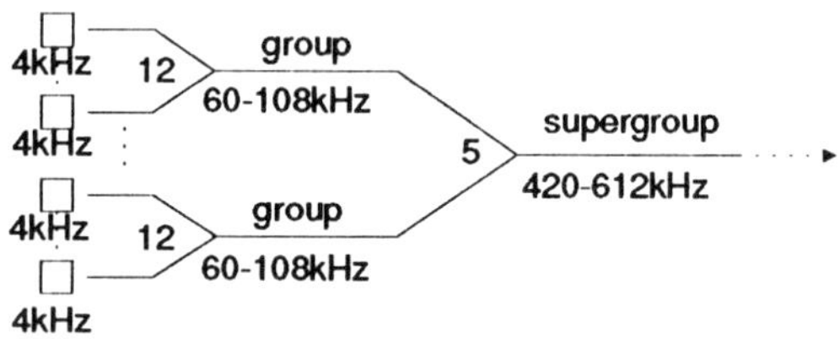

Figure 5.8 Levels of multiplexing

Dialling and signalling methods

Two signalling methods between telephone and local exchange are use. They correspond directly to the type of exchange and the telephone used. Older telephones have a dial which when turned to a particular digit, returns and generates a number of clicks corresponding to the digit dialled: so a '1' is one click and a '5' is 5 clicks ('0' incidentally, is 10 clicks). This signalling method is called *loop disconnect (LD)* or *pulse-code dialling.*

With the introduction of digital exchanges an alternative method of signalling has been introduced known as *dual-tone multi-frequency (DTMF, MF),* also called just *tone dialling.*

A digit is selected by pressing a button on this push-button type of phone and an internal circuit generates a pair of tones (musical notes) whose frequencies are unique for each digit. In Europe, the CCITT dial tones are used. In the USA a different set is employed. Figure 5.9 lists in Hertz, the two sets of dual tones.

Digit	*CCITT*	*Bell*
1	700/ 900	697/1209
2	700/1100	697/1336
3	900/1100	697/1447
4	700/1300	770/1209
5	900/1300	770/1336
6	1100/1300	770/1447
7	700/1500	852/1209
8	900/1500	852/1336
9	1100/1500	852/1447
0	1300/1500	941/1336

Figure 5.9 DTMF dual tone frequencies

One of the advantages of DTMF over loop-disconnect is that it takes less time to dial the number so the route for the call can be set up more quickly.

Some push-button phones have a switch option to generate DTMF signals or LD. Note that some push-button phones do not support DTMF - although you may hear a pair of tones, the circuit in the phone handset actually sends LD signals.

Now we must look at the techniques of modulation and how they are employed in modern modems.

Modulation and modems

Although digital networks are becoming increasingly more used, a vast amount of data comms is carried out along analogue lines, dial-up or leased. Much is asynchronous although synchronous communication is needed because some applications require the higher speed provided.

Until fairly recently, a good modem would be expected to handle 2400 bps, but in the last year or two, with falling microelectronics costs, we have seen the adoption of more sophisticated modulation and error-handling techniques and there are now modems that can handle well over 10,000 bps. Quite a few of the many modem suppliers would even say that users of digital services might do well to consider using their analogue modems with the low-cost analogue network in preference to the PDN, particularly for data rates below 64Kbps.

There are two main sources of standards for modem specifications, the CCITT and the *Bell Telephone Company* in the USA. Many of their modem specifications are similar although not always equivalent and as the subject is quite difficult enough without this complication, we will only consider CCITT recommendations in detail.

However, some individual companies must be mentioned here, because they have been prime movers in setting standards, in particular the modem manufacturers *Hayes Corporation* and the *Microcom Corporation,* both of the USA. In the UK, *Racal* also supplies modems, but they are of particular interest because of their level 2 protocol CDLC (mentioned earlier).

All of these companies (and others) have developed either techniques or standards which have lead to increasingly faster and more error-free modem performance.

Pause for thought

Before we have a look at the 6 methods of modulation that you could meet, a reminder of why modems are needed:

- the DTE is digital in nature (it generates DC pulses)
- the V24 interface is for binary digital transfer to the DCE

- the PTN used as the transmission network, is analogue in nature (it can't cope with DC)
- data signals are passed along the PTN by means of an AC carrier signal of some form.

So we must find a way of using the carrier to hold DC signals.

The modem does just this by 'arranging' that the two binary states '1' and '0' affect cycles of the carrier differently.

We can now look at how this is achieved.

Amplitude modulation

Amplitude modulation (AM) as a single method is never used these days but it is always the one shown first in books, because is the easiest to understand and the one that provides a nice easy mechanical representation.

The two states are arranged by changing the height (amplitude) of the carrier differently for 0 and 1, corresponding to two different power levels (as shown in Figure 5.10).

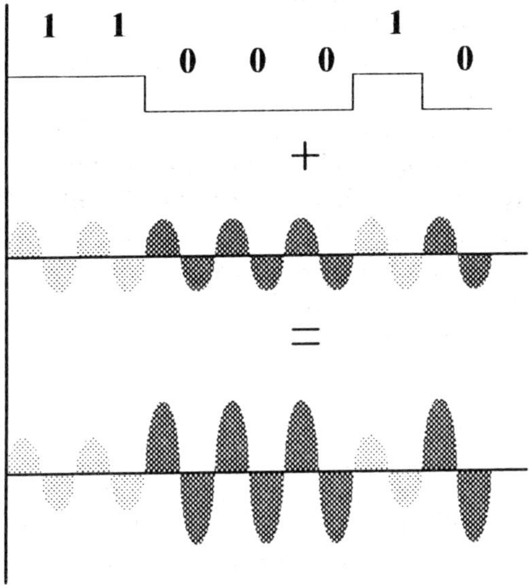

Figure 5.10 Amplitude modulation

The mechanical analogy for this is 'loud' for 0 and 'not so loud' for 1.

The major problem with AM is that it is badly affected by noise, which has an effect on the amplitude of the carrier while it occurs (it is however used in one of the more complex modulation methods covered shortly).

Frequency modulation

Frequency modulation (FM) arranges that the two states are represented by two different frequencies as shown in Figure 5.11.

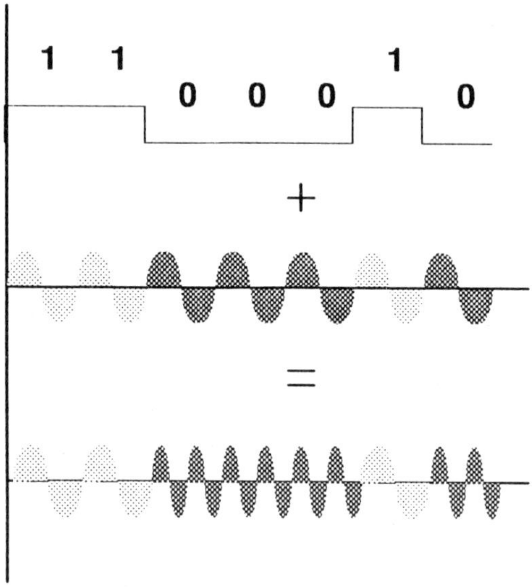

Figure 5.11 Frequency modulation

The mechanical analogy for FM is 'low note' for 0 and 'high note' for 1.

In the slowest CCITT modem specification, 1 and 0 are sent at 980 and 1180Hz and received at 1650 and 1850Hz. This allows for full duplex operation. One modem can send data at 980/1180 at the same time as the other is sending at 1650/1850. Note that the modem contains a modulator/demodulator for **each** pair of frequencies.

The next highest modem specification uses the frequencies shown (in Hertz) in Figure 5.12:

Baud rate	Freq. for 1 (Hz)	Freq. for 1 (Hz)
600	1300	1700
1200	1300	2100

Figure 5.12 FM multifrequencies

Generally, for voice-grade lines, a frequency separation (gap between the different frequency levels) of at least 300Hz is needed and at higher data rates, this separation must be increased. Without an adequate separation, it is difficult for a modem to detect the different frequencies.

Pause for thought

This is a good time to introduce a little experiment to explain this point about frequency separation. We have said that data transmission rate is limited by bandwidth and you can demonstrate this for yourself with a little help from a friend.

Select an ASCII character, say '1001001' and get someone to sing or whistle two different notes to represent 0 and 1. Make sure that the two notes selected are a fair way apart in frequency (say one octave).

Then get the friend to do it faster and faster. Provided he can whistle that fast, you should be able to detect the difference between 0 and 1 because the frequency difference is quite wide.

Now repeat the experiment, but this time select two notes that are much closer together. As it gets faster, you will find it increasingly difficult to separate a 0 from a 1 ie, errors are introduced.

This should show you that the narrower the bandwidth of the medium, the lower the data transfer rate.

Phase modulation

I have always found this difficult to teach, because there is no really satisfactory mechanical analogy to represent it. The best I can come up with is to think of the alternating current as being something like a 'push' for the first half-cycle and then a 'pull' for the other.

For a practical demonstration you will need:

- one bath, half-full of water
- one volunteer to sit in the bath, with a belt round his/her waist
- one large towel

Place person in bath. Grip belt and get into a rythmn of pushing and pulling, ie, push down until they hit the bottom, then pull up till they are partly out of the water, and so on. This is the equivalent of the push/pull for each half-cycle and you are transmitting say 0, all the time.

Now, the next time you are about to push down, pull instead. This shows you are sending a 1. You have just carried out a *phase change* equivalent to that shown in Figure 5.13.

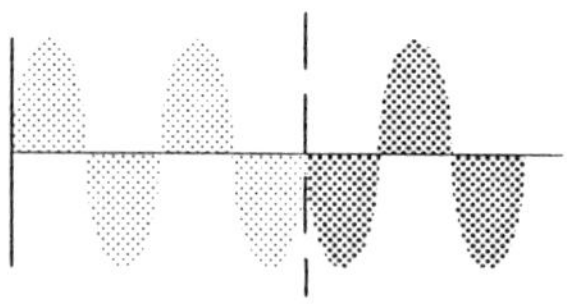

Figure 5.13 A half-cycle phase change

This is the basis of *phase modulation (PM)*. By changing the phase, we can show a change say from 0 to 1 and a later phase change will show a change from 1 to 0.

This is actually very much simplified. The first problem to tackle is how the receiving modem detects a phase change. It does this because a reference signal containing no phase changes at all is sent with the modulated signal, so that the receiver can compare the two to see where phase changes occur. Fine, but we must ensure that the two modems start exactly in phase as far as the reference signal is concerned and this is not easy to do electronically. Furthermore, noise and other effects can cause phase jitter which can make things worse.

The answer is to use a slightly different method of modulation called *differential phase modulation (DPM)* which relies for the detection of the state changes, not just on a phase change but the actual **amount** of phase change. As each new bit is associated with a phase change, there is no need for a reference signal.

As described here, DPM has only two phase changes (push/pull change in the bath above). WIth more than two phase changes, it becomes possible to represent more than one bit per phase change and so increase the bit rate without increasing the modulation rate. In effect, dibits, tribits or even larger groups can be coded (see chapter 2) as long as the corresponding phase change can be detected. Figure 5.14 shows dibit values for V22 and V26 phase changes.

Binary value	Phase change (A)	Phase change (B)
00	0	+ 45
01	+90	+135
10	+180	+225
11	+270	+315

Figure 5.14 Dibit values

Figure 5.15 shows a graphical representation of phase changes. On the left are shown four pairs of sine waves out of phase by 270, 180, 90 and 45 degrees respectively, and on the right we show complementary phase changes.

Quadrature amplitude modulation

An extension of DPM, called *quadrature amplitude modulation (QAM),* uses eight phase state changes and two levels of amplitude, giving 16 states (8 x 2) in all, leading to the possibility of tetrabits (0000 to 1111). Another possibility is to have 12 phase states and 3 amplitude levels making 36 in all, of which however, only 16 combinations are actually used.

It is most common in explanations of QAM to use a circular diagram to show the range of states possible, as illustrated in Figure 5.16 for V22bis modems.

Notice that the dots look a little like a pattern of stars and manufacturers often refer to their modem's *state constellation.*

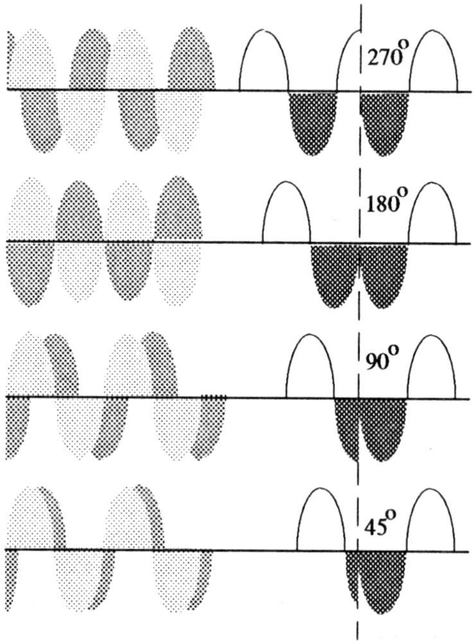

Figure 5.15 Multiple phase changes

Each manufacturer will decide on how to represent the 16 different states, by certain phase and amplitude levels while considering the difficulty of detecting the difference at the other end.

The next method is quite advanced and not easy to understand. Feel free to skip it altogether.

Trellis code modulation

The basis of *Trellis code modulation (TCM)* is to try and improve on one of the problems of QAM. If you look at Figure 5.16, the more different values we want to represent, the closer together do the points of the constellation become. The modem receives the signal and separates out the AM and PM components to produce what are in effect, two map references. It uses these to look up a two-dimensional table in order to find the value represented. But as the required bit throughput rate increases, so does line noise

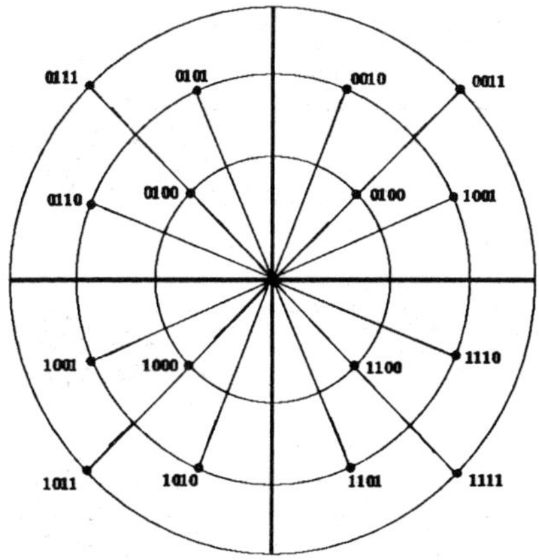

Figure 5.16 CCITT QAM (V22bis)

and it becomes very difficult for the receiving modem to distinguish between different points.

TCM modems send a redundancy bit along with the seven data bits, so with the resultant error detection and the possibility of 256 different constellation points, much better results are obtained. Even more complex derivatives of basic TCM are possible and far too difficult for us.

Most of our discussion of layers 1/2 was concerned with analogue techniques and before we look at other aspects of modems, we should introduce some ideas on digital techniques.

Digital transmission

As we have been discussing modulation, let us start with a look at the main technique used in digital transmission.

Pulse code modulation

The technique is called *pulse code modulation (PCM)* and is intended mainly to carry voice messages after digitisation for sending through digital networks.

Instead of a continuous, analogue carrier, PCM makes use of a *pulse carrier* signal as shown in Figure 5.17.

Different digital values can change peaks on the carrier differently depending on the value to be sent (001, 010, 011 etc).

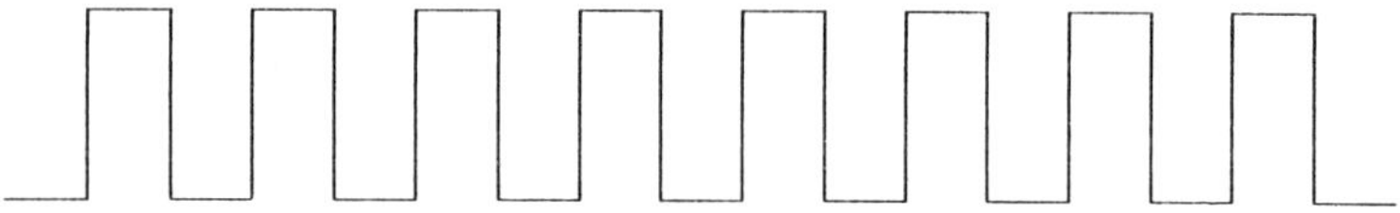

Figure 5.17 Pulse carrier

The carrier can be modulated according to one of three main methods. Modulating data can affect:

- the **height** of a peak *(pulse amplitude modulation - PAM)*
- its **width** *(pulse duration modulation - PDM)*
- its **position** *(pulse position modulation - PPM).*

These are shown in Figure 5.18.

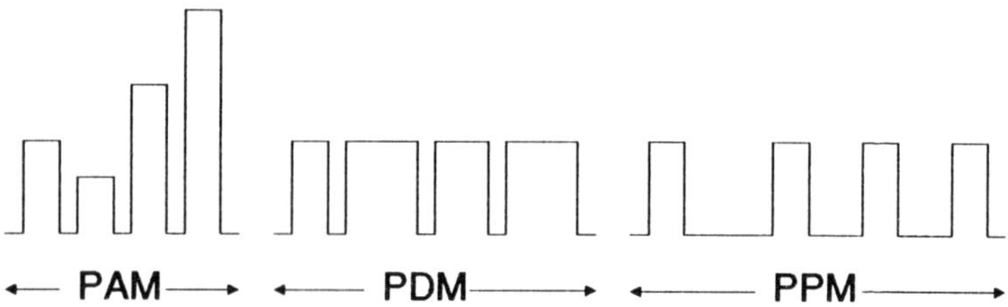

Figure 5.18 Pulse modulation techniques

Digitisation

With the introduction of computer-controlled digital networks, there has been a corresponding demand for voice to be transmitted in digital form. A few years ago, people were predicting a massive increase in data transmission to the state where by 1990, it was expected that over 50% of the full capacity of public networks would be for data traffic. However, it now seems likely that by 1992, only about 10% will be for data and there is talk of **data goes free** - so much investment in voice will mean that data transmission becomes almost a by-product of voice.

Voice is analogue in nature and must be *digitised* ie, converted to digital pulses, if it is to be carried along a digital network. A very commonly-used procedure involves *sampling* by measuring the analogue amplitude of the speech waveform, at regular time intervals.

Basic physics shows that to recreate the analogue signal after digitisation, we must sample at a minimum of **twice** the highest frequency likely. If we are dealing with existing, voice-grade channels with 4kHz bandwidth, this means a sampling frequency of 8000Hz ie, an inter-sample time of 8 microseconds. (If we were prepared to upgrade the electronics and sample at a much higher rate, we could have much higher quality speech over the telephone.)

The method takes each sample and converts it to the nearest digital value on a scale of 0 to 255 (held as an eight-bit binary number). These binary values can then be transmitted to the receiver where they are reformed into what is nearly the original speech waveform (the human ear cannot tell the difference anyway).

Figure 5.19 shows a simplified view of sampling (with a reduced vertical scale).

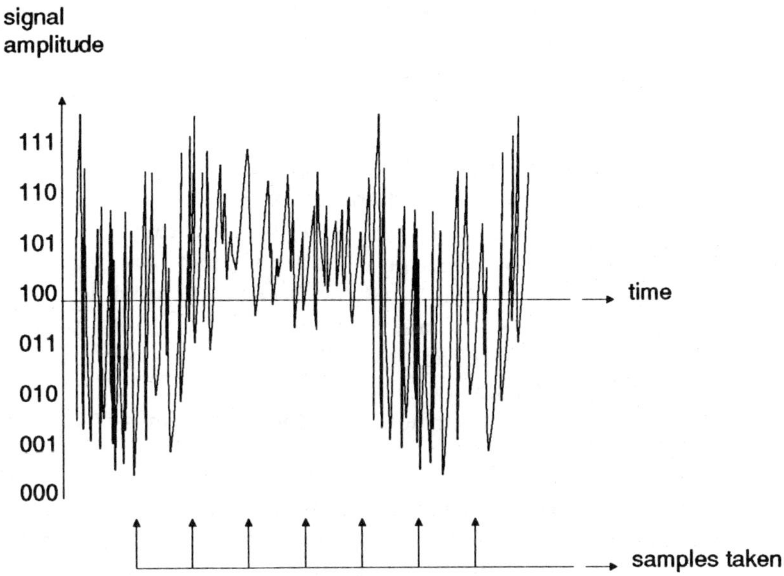

Figure 5.19 Digitisation by sampling

Apart from a slight digression into digital transmission, this chapter has been mainly concerned with the actual techniques for converting digital data into analogue form for PTN transmission. Chapter 7 will discuss the comms software that enables you to link your terminal through a modem to the outside world. To prepare for this and to remind you what the modem does (and what it actually receives and sends) we need to say a little about what the software has to be told.

Communications profiles

What is a comms profile

In order to set up a conversation via a modem link, it is necessary to determine the *communications profile* ie, the parameters that will have to be passed to enable the conversation to be set up and maintained.

The parameters are as follows:

- the telephone number to be dialled
- the method of dialling - pulse or tone
- the bit rate at which the conversation will be conducted
- the number of data bits
- the number of stop bits that end the asynchronous character frame
- the setting and checking of the parity bit in the octet.

Note by the way, that ASCII characters are seven bits long and the parity setting can be *odd, even, none, mark* (always 1) or *space* (always 0). With EBCDIC, characters are 8 bits and parity must be none. Similarly, when sending data whose type is unknown to the communications software, (binary, floating point, packed decimal etc) parity setting has no significance and we must set 'data bits' to 8 and 'parity' to none.

This is discussed further in chapter 6, when we look at protocols.

Other aspects of the profile

There are two other sets of parameters that need to be set for successful conversation:

- the terminal being emulated - if you are not using that particular terminal, your comms software needs to include *terminal emulation* facilities that can make your terminal behave as if it were one of another type

- the file transfer protocol in use - relating to the structure of the data sent and the rules for message confirmation and how errors are handled (see chapter 6).

Each external link you want to set up may have its own comms profile and it is often possible to keep a file of common profiles, either on disk or in the modem.

Now we look at how the modem links to the telephone line.

Dialling and answering calls

Simple modems are manually connected to the PTN after the user has dialled the receiving modem or after the user has received a call from a sending modem.

V25

Sometimes, an *autocall* feature is added to the simple modem with an *automatic call unit (ACU)*, a black-box arrangement which couples the DTE and modem on the V24 interface (using circuits other than those discussed earlier in this chapter).

A separate interface is specified by CCITT recommendation *V25*, specifically for autocall modems. It defines a different set of circuits (the 200 series) to V24.

The rest of this section introduces 'automatic' modems and shows how they can be 'instructed' to change their settings.

Smart modems

The typical modem user until fairly recently would have been content with a basic modem with a fixed bit rate and simple switch settings for parity, stop bits and so on. Now, there is an increasing trend for multiple speed modems, able to change parameters automatically as the application is changed. From the same workstation, a user may want to link to viewdata (at 1200/75 baud), a private service (at 2400) and perhaps an amateur bulletin board (at 300)

This kind of user needs a modem that is in effect, programmable, so that on command, it will adjust to one of many required comms profiles, then dial out.

The US Hayes company was one of the first to develop and market such a programmable modem (the *Smartmodem*) and the name **smart** is now generally used for any programmable modem.

Commands used to set up a modem follow two different sets of standards. The first and more common is that used by Hayes, which has now become a de facto standard for asynchronous comms. (A large amount of PC comms software supports the Hayes set.)

The other is the *CCITT V25bis* set which is aimed at high-speed, synchronous modems especially when linked to the X25 switches that enable connection to a PDN via the PTN.

Hayes commands

The Hayes commands are all preceded by the characters *AT* and as such, are universally referred to as the Hayes *AT* set of commands. 'AT' is simply a command to the modem to respond if properly connected. Further parameters set up aspects of the profile with specific meanings, such as:

- *AT /* - causes the modem to accept a repeat of the last command issued
- *AT SO=N* - set the modem so that it answers a call after N rings

This latter is very useful if the modem is connected to a dial-up line. If N is set to say 3 or 4, it gives you a chance to pick up the phone and check to see if it is a voice call before the modem automatically picks it up.

To make a Hayes-compatible modem dial out, you send it the command:-

- *AT D M (9) pn* - where M specifies the dialling method (P = pulse, T = tone), 9 is **get an outside line**, if going through a switchboard and pn is the telephone number you want to connect to (see Fig 7.30).
- *AT I* - causes the modem to send its product identity code
- *AT I1* - causes the modem to carry out internal checking
- *AT I2* - causes the modem to conduct internal memory testing.

V25bis

This is the CCITT recommendation for an autocall/autoanswer modem, (specifically **automatic calling and/or answering**

equipment on the General Switched Telephone Network using the 100-series interchange circuits) and it defines the interface between the terminal (DTE) and the autocall/autoanswer modem (DCE).

Like the Hayes modem, the V25bis modem is programmable (although with very different commands). Messages to and from the terminal and modem are preceded by a three-character identifier, followed by a ';'. For example:

- *CRN; "phone number"* - means dial the number
- *PRN; "address"; "phone number"* - means store a phone number in modem memory
- *RLN;* - means send a list of stored numbers to the terminal
- *LSN; "memory address"; "list of numbers"* - a message from modem to terminal, telling the terminal that the modem is sending a list of numbers from its memory.

V25bis is particularly useful for high-speed, synchronous operation and although it supports character transmission (one start bit, one stop bit, seven data bits, even parity), it can also send frames corresponding to the layer 2 protocols BSC and HDLC (see chapter 6). Hayes on the other hand, is mainly for asynchronous use.

Pause for thought

So far in the book and particularly in this chapter, there have been many references to CCITT V series recommendations and by now, most books would have given more details. I feel that it is important to have a good feel for what the modem can do over and above the speed at which it operates, the modulation technique employed and whether 2- or 4-wire.

Without knowing something about these, the 'V' series will not mean much - in particular, the methods employed for handling errors have a lot to do with the specification. So, before the 'V' series table, let us look at general error handling techniques and then the recent V42 recommendation and its ramifications.

Error reduction

The modern modem is a very clever piece of kit and can carry out many different tricks. You will recall that for a given baud rate of 2400, because of the various problems (hostility), without taking special measures, you will not get 2400 bits in every second (even if your terminal can actually send 2400 bits in each second) - bits will be lost and retransmission is bound to occur.

Newer modems are designed specifically to perform two main tasks:

- reduce errors
- increase the data transmission rate.

These tasks are, technically very different, but are nevertheless complementary. Some of the procedures involved require a modem to make a decision based on line quality and detected errors, then inform the modem at the other end what it is going to do. This is quite independent of the comms software that is passing data to the modem. (We use the term *adaptive* to describe the ability of an intelligent body to change the way it operates depending on the prevailing conditions.)

CCITT and other specifications will recommend which of the various possible procedures are to be supported by a particular modem. They include:

- *fallback* - a technique in which a modem changes its data transmission rate to a lower one in order to ensure a lower error rate. Generally this is undertaken after a modem detects a line with too much noise to support the higher data rate, usually by switching to a simpler modulation scheme (eg, from 16 states to 2, such as from QAM to FM). Since the electronics associated with FM is simpler, it is more tolerant of the noise - in simple terms, the receiving modem is less likely to confuse a 0 with a 1
- *error detection* - although comms software often carries out error detection, if the modem introduces its own CRC, the need for the DTE to carry out error detection is reduced
- *synchronous transmission* - although the DTE transmits data asynchronously (from the PC asynchronous comms port to the modem), there is nothing to prevent the two modems in a link from transmitting synchronously. Generally, this will involve take each framed character, stripping off the start and stop bits, then forming a

suitable block of characters for synchronous transmission. The receiving modem recreates the original characters by adding the start and stop bits

- *adaptive block sizing* - the advantage of sending synchronously, as explained in chapter 2, is that synchronisation time is saved by synchronising on the start of a block rather than on each character frame and the longer the block, the greater the saving.

  On the other hand, if there is an error that the receiver detects but cannot correct, the block will have to be retransmitted. There is therefore, a trade-off depending on the noise level - the longer the block, the less bits to be transmitted but the more to be retransmitted if there is a problem. With adaptive block sizing, the modems adjust the block size to meet the current conditions. (Note. In other literature, this technique is sometimes called adaptive **packet** sizing. I have used the term **block**, preferring to retain the use of **packet** for OSI level 3 - in this chapter we are looking at layers 1/2.)

- *adaptive sub-channelling* - in which a modem monitors line noise throughout the 3KHz line bandwidth, with the aim of locating part of the bandwidth (a *sub-channel*) with lower noise. When noise is excessive in one sub-channel, the modem automatically transmits in another. Some modems are capable of dividing the overall line band into many sub-channels, each of which is perhaps just a couple of hundred Hertz wide. The procedure is also called *statistical duplexing*

- *data phase optimisation* - a synchronous transfer procedure which involves a more efficient block header. It relies on the fact that the header contains control information relating to the block and if many similar blocks are transmitted, it is inefficient to have to repeat this for each block sent. The method arranges that control information is only sent when there is a change, so less overhead data is carried and the transfer rate goes up

- *compression* - although introduced earlier, worth mentioning again here. The method can be made adaptive, in that it alters the compression basis to suit the data that is being transmitted by sampling and recreating the coded table. Also, 'local rules' can be implemented, such as 'u' will probably follow 'q' and after this will probably come 'i' or 'e'. (See MNP class 7 later in this chapter.) Major companies such as BT, are researching new data compression algorithms all the time

- *predictive compression* is a development in which the next character to arrive can be predicted on the basis of the table built up and the frequencies of which characters have actually been sent so far

- *retransmission* - if the receiving modem detects an error which it cannot locate, it will ask the sending modem to resend the block. This requires the sending modem to hold at least one block in a buffer, while it is setting up the next one
- *bit interleaving* (introduced in chapter 4)
- *forward error correction (FEC)* - while it is forming up blocks, the modem can generate FEC codes and the receiving modem can correct errors. *Cellular data link control (CDLC)* for example, as developed by the Racal Corporation, makes use of an extra eight bits for each character transmitted (see chapter 6). FEC can then be used in conjunction with byte interleaving. In this way, if an error burst occurs, even if a whole byte has been lost, FEC can recover from it.

Other modem features

Several modem suppliers provide a number of other features that are more for operating convenience that for error handling.

Hayes/V25 bis compatibility

Some of the more sophisticated modems can be set either to Hayes AT or CCITT V25bis commands. This is very useful in view of the unclear future of the two different sets (the USA seems to have standardised on Hayes.)

Dial-up backup

A particular V series modem may be used on a leased line for a given bit rate. However, if the leased line goes down or is hopelessly noisy, *dial-up backup* is a useful facility whereby the modem can automatically fallback and dial up a link to the PTN through a normal voice line.

Universal link negotiation

Universal link negotiation involves intelligence in the modem that allows it to talk 'down' or 'to' another modem. The sending modem will 'find out' what is the most sophisticated conversation the receiver can hold and proceed with this (see MNP class 6 later).

Line indication

It is often useful to see what is happening while the modem operates and many companies provide lamp or LED displays that flash to indicate signals going down some of the interface circuits (such as RTS, CTS, DSR and DTR).

Testing

Some suppliers provide circuits within the modem to carry out hardware testing. Sometimes, signals consisting of test patterns can be generated and sent to examine the line performance. Results can be observed with the line indicators. CCITT recommendation V54 defines a *loop-back test* which many manufacturers use.

Card/rack

Until a few years ago, the modem was a separate unit, connected to the terminal with a cable. Now, suppliers often offer the modem on a single board or *card* that can be dropped into one of the PC expansion slots. Examples of such single-card modems include the Dowty *Quattro* and Hayes *Smartmodem.*

Multi-port

Situations arise where a host may be contacted by many users and instead of having one modem for each user, a *multi-port* modem can be employed. This is in effect a modem containing a bit multiplexer to combine all data to the host.

For example, a 14,4 Kbps synchronous modem may be configured to have four 2400 bps ports and one 4800 bps port.

Profile store

Some modems provide a battery-backed store of perhaps 20 telephone numbers and associated communications profiles. Then, a particular profile can be selected without the need to store it in the PC.

V42

To allow for the need for clever modems that will cope with error handling and reduction, CCITT have put forward general recommendation *V42*.

Developments in error reduction

There are two different general developments in the approach to errors, *MNP* in the USA (coming up shortly) and an asynchronous derivative of *link access protocol(LAP)* called *LAP-M*. We will meet LAP-M in chapter 6, so let us look at the alternative.

MNP

The Microcom Corporation is a US company that is up with the leaders in modem development. Their representative company in the UK is *Tricom Communications plc* (who very recently have bought up *Micom-Borer* another UK modem supplier).

They have patented a recommended set of standards for modem performance called *Microcom networking protocol (MNP)* which is being adopted, under licence, by other modem suppliers. MNP recommends several classes of service, which encompass various of the procedures discussed earlier.

At present, classes 1 to 4 are in the public domain - anyone can implement them. On the other hand, Microcom require a royalty fee for the use of classes 5 and above. Figure 5.20 lists the main classes of MNP.

Class	Details
1	based on asynchronous framing, half-duplex byte protocols for data exchange. About 70% efficient
2	full-duplex. About 80% efficient
3	bit-oriented, synchronous. About 110% efficient
4	uses adaptive block sizing and data phase optimisation. 120-130% efficient
5	data compression at up to 1.5:1. Up to 200% efficient
6	uses universal link negotiation (300 to 9600 bps). Also uses statistical duplexing. Up to 400% efficient
7	uses more complex compression including 'local' character frequency tables for codes. Up to 400% efficiency
9	uses prediction methods based on pairs of characters. Also uses faster error-handling methods - selective retransmission if packet confirmation fails

Figure 5.20 MNP classes

In figure 5.20, 'efficiency' means roughly, the actual data transfer for a given V series recommendation. For example, at a nominal 2400 bps, 110% efficiency means that the data is actually transferred at 2640 (2400 x 1.1) bits per second. The efficiency quoted for each class implies that it employs techniques of the lower classes and the figure is an overall figure in each case, not one to be added to lower classes.

It should be noted that some modems feature LAP-M/MNP compatibility ie, the modem can be switched to MNP or LAP-M error handling.

1989 has seen much controversy over the future of MNP and LAP-M. V42 actually allows for both and although it seemed initially that MNP would become standard, there is now an increasing demand for the alternative and at present, it is difficult to see where things will go.

Having left it right to the end, we can now look at the CCITT recommendations for modems. Remember that CCITT recommendations relating to analogue circuits are prefixed with a V. It is unfortunate that the V series numbers cover modems and other aspects of analogue circuits. People tend to think of them in relation to modems, but you already know about V24/28, V25 and V25bis, which are recommendations that do not.

CCITT V series modem specifications

If you are to talk professionally about modems, you need to understand Figure 5.21 which lists those recommendations in the V series that defines modems, together with various parameters.

To understand this table fully, you must have an appreciation of much of what has gone before in this chapter.

- The parameters and abbreviations of Figure 5.21 need explanation:

Rec no.	Basic mode	Basic rate	Fall-back1	Fall-back2	2-wire	4-wire	Modul-ation
V.21	A	300	-	-	duplex	-	FM
V.22	A/S	1200			duplex	-	FM
V.22 bis	A/S	2400	1200		duplex	-	QAM
V.23	A	1200	600		half	duplex	FM
V.26	S	2400		600	-	duplex	DPM
V.26 bis	S	2400			half	duplex	DPM
V.26 ter	S	2400	1200		duplex	-	DPM
V.27	S	4800				duplex	DPM
V.27 bis	S	4800	2400		half		DPM
V.27 ter	S	4800	2400		half		DPM
V.29	S	9600	7200	4800		duplex	QAM
V.32	S	9600	4800	2400	duplex		QAM/TCM
V.33	S	14400				duplex	QAM/TCM

Figure 5.21 The CCITT V series of modem specifications

- recommendation number is self-explanatory
- basic mode is either Synchronous or Asynchronous
- basic rate is the nominal speed at which the modem will transmit

- fall-back 1 and 2 specify the first and second fall-back rates (V29 has a third)
- two- and four-wire show how the modem is to be applied on dial-up and leased lines
- modulation method will be frequency modulation, differential phase modulation, quadrature amplitude modulation or quadrature + trellis code modulation.

Just a little point to finish this chapter. IBM PCs and compatibles support two asynchronous comms adaptors (ports), numbered 1 and 2. Industry standards for areas such as computer memory addresses, time scheduling etc, cover PC port numbers 1 to 4, for which 1 and 2 coincide with the IBM PC ports. But the newer PS/2 range of IBM computers can support serial ports 1 to 8 and in particular, the parameters of port 3 and 4 are not the same as industry standards. This means that in more sophisticated applications, the PS2 user needs to be sure that standard comms software can be used.

Recap

- data transmission is carried out using widely differing transmission media including directed and broadcast methods

  For PC-to-PC or PC-to-peripheral data transfer, V24/RS232 is a very important interface although extensions and derivatives are becoming more important with the increase in digital transmission
- to overcome some of the problems caused by unavoidable errors, certain hardware units and techniques are employed
- to achieve optimal use of transmission lines, multiplexing techniques are used which enable a number of channels to be employed in one connection
- as computers send/receive digital data and the PTN is initially analogue in nature, we need modems to effect the digital-to-analogue conversion and vice versa.

  Several modulation techniques are used, some of which can lead to increased data rates over what should be obtainable from the basic network baud rate

- to enable connection via a modem, it is necessary to make use of communications software - to inform the modem what to connect to and the hardware and software parameters of the connection
- because the PTN and the general transmission environment are so hostile, modem suppliers provide a wide range of techniques and facilities to reduce errors, generally overcome their effects and dramatically improve data rates
- modem suppliers also provide the user with a number of options to make modem use operationally convenient
- CCITT has specified very detailed recommendations for modem performance which are almost universally recognised.

Typical questions

Question 5.1
Explain why a null modem is needed to connect PCs

Question 5.2
What is the difference between V24 and RS232?

Question 5.3
What are the essential features of a mobile data terminal and for what applications might one be employed?

Question 5.4
Explain how several slow-speed terminals could be connected to a host computer along one telephone line

Question 5.5
Why does 1200 baud rarely mean 1200 bits per second?

Question 5.6
What are the main parameters that must be defined to enable connection via a modem?

6: OSI layer 2

Objectives

After reading this chapter, you should:-

- have a further appreciation of the concept of a protocol
- appreciate the need for link control mechanisms
- appreciate the need for flow control mechanisms
- understand in context, the problems of error detection and correction introduced earlier
- be able to design simple protocols for different situations
- be aware of some byte-oriented protocols
- understand the basics of HDLC
- appreciate some practical aspects of level 2 protocols.

Layer 2 is entirely concerned with the logical link between the two ends of a conversation and as such, assumes that layer 1 will 'take care of itself'.

We now develop the concept of a protocol both in theory and in practice, by examining some of the functions of the layer.

What layer 2 is about

To understand this layer, consider that we are dealing with different kinds of conversation - where primaries are linking to one or more secondaries, sending and receiving data. Also bear in mind what we have said in chapters 3 and 4, about a protocol being a set of rules and a definition of the data that is need to support the rules. Figure 6.1 summarises the need for protocols. In the working of protocols in this layer:

- we look at the rules to maintain a conversation

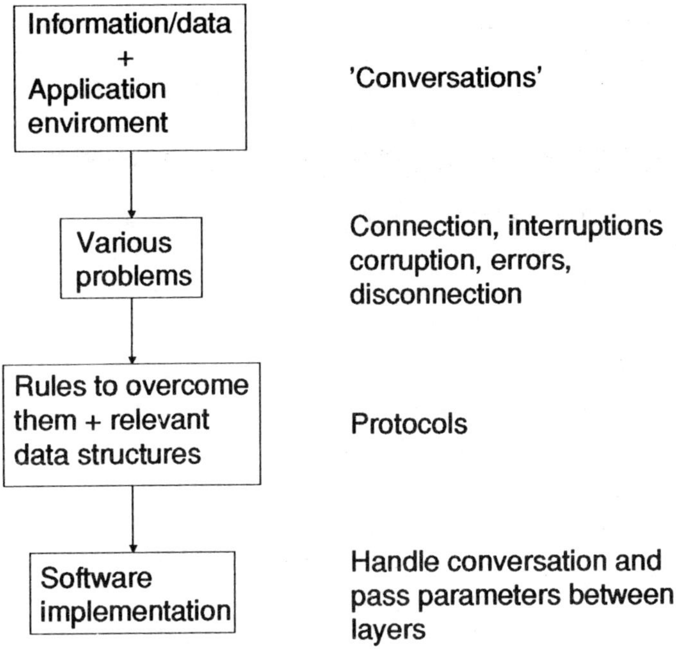

Figure 6.1 The need for a protocol

- we examine the data framing needed to assist the rules
- we consider how to know when to retransmit if one end doesn't hear
- we look at ways to avoid overflow if one end is slower than the other
- we reconsider some of the error detection/correction techniques that are applied in layer 1.

These can be summarised in the **three main layer 2 objectives**: *link_management, flow control* and *error control.*

Link management
We must be able to:

- start off the connection/conversation
- try to keep the conversation going when there are interruptions
- end the connection normally or abnormally.

We are primarily concerned with a simple point-to-point link, but we must also consider multi-point links.

There are two main types of multi-point link defined by the access mechanism employed; with both there may be several terminals, all waiting to establish a link with the host and/or needing to be contacted by it.

With the mechanism known as *polling*, the host looks at each terminal in turn, sending a 'you are being polled now' signal. The terminal if ready, sends its data or receives some from the host, the host acknowledges, and so on round the cycle.

With the *select* mechanism, the host makes a decision as to which terminal it will talk to and sends 'you have been selected', the terminal replies 'OK, hit me', the host sends the message and the terminal confirms receipt.

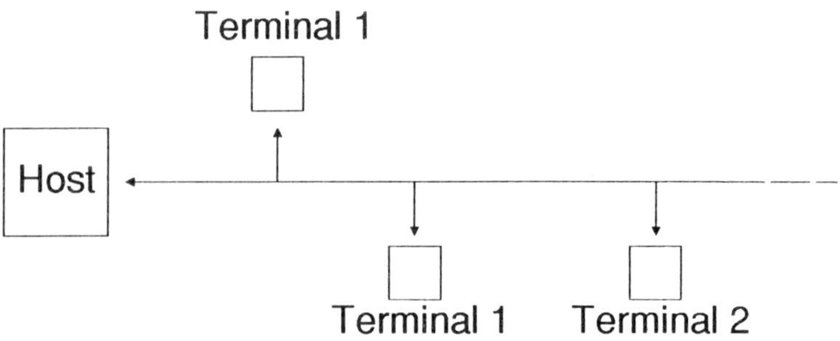

Figure 6.2 A multi-point connection (poll/select)

Flow control

Flow control addresses the problem of trying to prevent transmission at a rate faster than that which the receiver can handle while still keeping up as high a transmission rate as possible. This is accomplished in effect, by 'throttling' the sender to regulate the transmission rate. For example, sometimes the receiver may be temporarily too busy to cope with the incoming data stream. We may need to 'slow down' the sender or even arrange to suspend his transmission for a while.

Data transmission may have to be interrupted because:

- the receiver could be writing blocks to disk at intervals and while doing so, cannot receive at the same time
- the receiver could be linked to several 'other ends' and be too busy *(processor flooding)* to cope with the demand for its services.

When either of these happens, the receiver needs a signal saying in effect 'hang on for a while, I am pushed at the moment; I will get back to you soon'. Once it has sorted things out, It can send an 'OK, carry on' signal.

The generally-accepted way to accomplish flow control is with the use of two ASCII control combinations:

X-OFF (0010011) equivalent to 'stop sending'
X-ON (0010001) equivalent to 'carry on'.

Error control

As we have seen, there are many possibilities for errors that can disturb a conversation and we need to try and detect them and recover from their effects. The main concern of error control at layer 2 is a series of mechanisms that enable data to be retransmitted when necessary. They go under the general name of *repeat request (RQ)*.

Repeat request mechanisms

Consider the asynchronous transfer of the characters of a message. I send you a character: either your receive it or you don't. If you receive it with a parity error, you know that there is something wrong. If you don't get it at all, there is not much you can do since you have no way of knowing I sent anything at all.

Pause for thought

The following is a piece of *pseudocode* that represents the logic of a hypothetical protocol for sending and receiving characters. The pseudocode is introduced because we will meet it again in chapter 7, where we develop some program logic for comms situations. Many programmers use this method to work out the logic of programs they write and although it looks complicated, it makes use of three basic *structured programming* building blocks. They consist of:

- a *sequence* of operations
- a *selection* where a choice of what to do is made, characterised by *if*, *end if* and appropriate combinations of *then* and *else*
- an *iteration* or *repetition* of a set of operations, usually characterised by *while* and *end while*.

Sender

1. While 'characters to send'
2. Send character
3. If 'no reply' or
   reply is 'I cant understand',
   send again until 'fed up', then stop
4. End if
5. End while
6. Send final character
7. Stop

Receiver

1. While not final character
2. Listen for next character
3. If received
   If 'character makes sense', send normal reply else
   send 'I don't understand'
   end if
   else
   keep trying until 'fed up', then 'give up'
4. End if
5. End while
5. Stop

This protocol requires a lot of time confirming or denying and becomes very complicated if the conversation is in full duplex. (Do I send my next character or reply to yours first?) It is even more complicated if the primary is linked to several secondaries and has to poll between them (or select on some priority basis).

This kind of procedure is not adopted for character transfer but we can extend it to the situation where we are sending synchronously and we can introduce the concept of *repeat-request*

(RQ), a set of rules that govern what to do if the sender doesn't get a message, or if the receiver does not get a reply.

Unless we make use of a trivial protocol called *send-and-hope* (which means sending, in the hope that the receiver can hear), we need some rules so that one or both ends can be sure that their message has been received.

It is possible in theory to use echo-checking whereby, whatever is sent is returned so that the sender can carry out a character-by-character check that nothing has gone wrong. However, there is no guarantee that the echo itself has not been corrupted. Also, we are doubling the amount of data to be sent overall.

More important, in practical situations the application may be more concerned with blocks of data than single characters, ie, logical blocks of data (irrespective of the fact that characters actually leave the comms port). Examples include whole records during file transfer, whole print lines or even whole pages. Protocols must be developed need to be able to handle these.

Automatic repeat request (ARQ) is the name for a series of techniques that require the receiver to make a reply at each stage.

Idle RQ

Its simplest form is *idle RQ* or *send-and-wait* and with this, in a half-duplex situation, the primary sends a frame and then waits for an acknowledgement of receipt. This could be an 'OK' or 'not OK' but at least it says that something got there.

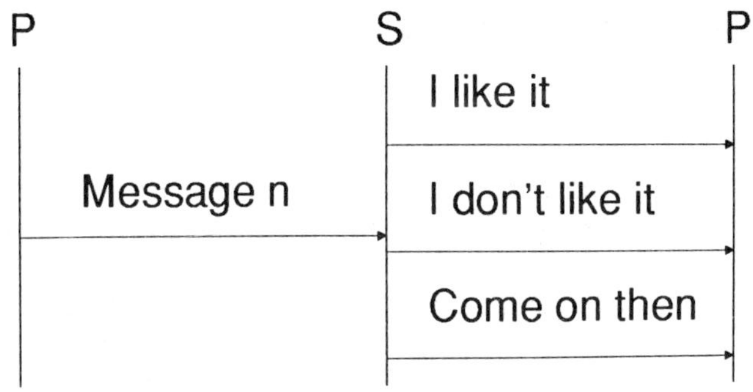

Figure 6.3 Basic ARQ

From the point of view of the primary, having sent a block, there are three possible replies from the secondary. (Figure 6.3)

- confirmed as OK
- confirmed as not OK
- what about sending me something then (message not received).

If 'OK', the next frame can be sent. If 'not OK' the frame can be resent (presumably there was a parity error, CRC failure. Alternatively, the receiver was temporarily 'otherwise engaged'). To cope with the third possible reply ('fed up' in the earlier pseudocode), there are two approaches:

- one or both ends restart a clock as each block is sent (or received) and after a suitably long interval, either end can give up and shut down
- decide how many times the sender will retransmit a corrupted block or how many times the receiver will keep telling the sender that a particular block was corrupted.

This idea of 'always replying' is called *positive acknowledgement* and conventionally, a confirmation is called an *ACK* (ASCII 0000110) and a denial is called a *NAK* (ASCII 0010101).

Basic ARQ needs extension to cope with other than the simplest situations:

- what about the possibility of an ACK or NAK being corrupted?
- what about the rules for a full-duplex connection, where both ends may be sending data frames and ACK/NAKs?
- what if an ACK is distorted into a NAK and the sender retransmits the frame?

Extensions involve numbering all frames sent, both data frames and replies. In this way both ends can check to see that a frame has not been lost.

Continuous RQ

The disadvantage of idle RQ is that **transmission capacity** is used up sending confirmations and is used up waiting for confirmations. With the alternative procedure, called *continuous RQ*, we send a frame and keep sending, frames ignoring any time-out, until a NAK is received. This is referred to as *negative acknowledgement*.

There are two approaches to frame retransmission, depending on what is transferred and what the other end will do with it:

- *selective retransmission* - with this, the sender sends frames and the receiver tells the sender which frame(s) to retransmit. This implies that the sender must store a minimum number of frames already sent and we often refer to this as a *window* - a window size of eight would imply that the sender keeps a store of the most recent eight frames sent. When the next is transmitted, the oldest frame is discarded
- *go-back-N* - slightly different and used where frames are received but not processed until a certain number have been checked out. (Perhaps we are sending a sales order consisting of 10 lines, one frame for each and we don't check frames received until we get the line that contains the total for the order.) When an error is detected, the receiver, instructs the sender to **go back N** frames and retransmit all from this point.

Layer 2 protocol thinking

- a protocol is a set of rules designed to enable a conversation to start, proceed and terminate
- for a given conversation in a given environment, there will be the need for a set of conditions to enable this
- when we design a protocol, we look at all these conditions and try to set up a group of rules that will cover any 'situation' that may disturb the conversation
- once the rules have been set up and tested, they become a protocol and can be implemented in software (we can write programs that will cope with either or both ends of the conversation).

Students get very confused when they first meet protocols because books tend not to draw a clear distinction between the rules that make up the protocol and the data that is an integral part of the protocol.

I think of the protocol rules as a **program** and the data framing and content as the **parameters** that must be passed to/from the software that allows the rules to be followed.

We will look shortly at different types of basic protocol, but to give you an idea of what is meant by a protocol, we can look at an example to show why a protocol is needed and then anticipate appendix 3 and look at a question taken from a recent Thames Valley College examination in *data communications.*

A simple protocol example

Consider a PC being used as a message centre for several other enquiry terminals and the problems that might arise. The PC has two functions:

- a file server - either terminal may request the reading of any record from a particular file (we will assume just one file to simplify matters)
- A print server - terminals will use data from the record read (perhaps product prices) together with that input from keyboard (customer order quantities) to generate printed reports (customer quotations). The terminals do not have printers and will need to pass the print lines to the message centre so that the quotations can be printed there. As one terminal may request printing while the main PC is printing a report from the other one, it needs to be able to *spool* output, ie, store printlines on disk and output them to the printer when it is available (as shown in Figure 6.4).

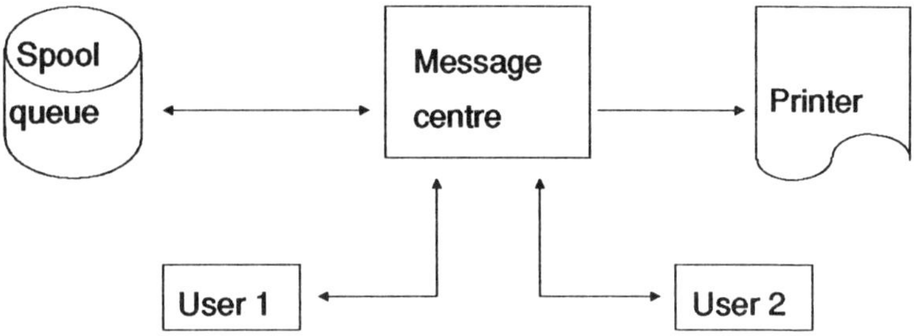

Figure 6.4 An application 'message centre'

We can learn from this just by looking at what needs to go in each direction, ignoring the actual structure of the data sent. We will simplify as much as possible (eg, we ignore a missing 'last print line' from a terminal and an invalid frame sent in either direction). What frames does a terminal need to send in order to start, continue and eventually terminate a conversation?

Connection:

- I want to start: is that OK?

- I am shutting down for now: goodbye.

Enquiry:

- get me that record (say XXX)

Print request:

- print the following lines
- here is the next one
- here is the last one.

Looking at the server, what must it send?

Connection:

- OK, start sending
- OK, goodbye.

Message confirmation:

- I have received the last message OK! Here is your record
- I have received the last message OK and am printing.

Flow control:

- hang on, I am busy at present
- OK, carry on.

Error handling

- you are off, I am fed up waiting (no reply after time t)
- stop mumbling! (corrupted message)
- XXX - no such record, try again, old boy.

Pause for thought

Note that this is a very elementary set-up with just two users accessing one file. In chapter 9, we will look at situations where there are many users, with different files and several printers. This kind of situation occurs in many LANs and because of the wide range of user requirements, will need a more complex set of protocols to ensure that everyone gets a fair share and that errors are handled.

Now let us look at a slightly different environment and develop the actual frames needed in more detail. You are not really expected to be able to do this on your own yet, but if you work through it, you should learn a lot about layer 2.

An examination question

This is taken from the three-hour examination that was set at TVC this year (and which is given in full in appendix 3). The exam consisted of five compulsory questions, this one being worth 20% of the marks.

We will not produce a complete model answer, but use the environment to demonstrate the kind of thinking involved at layer 2. (In the last year or so, a number of my students have attempted assignments similar to this, including the actual coding in BASIC. They almost invariably found it very difficult to think out the rules, but once they had done so, they could see the value of going through the agony.

A high-street ATM

Problem statement

A high-street bank ATM provides the following services for its customers:

- accepting requests for a statement or a new cheque book
- issuing up to £100 cash, provided the account has sufficient credit, this is the first withdrawal of the day or the user's card is not stolen.

The ATM is permanently on-line to the bank's centre (unless out of service). You can assume that all validation/verification is carried out in real-time, irrespective of the number of cash points in use.

What you have to do

A. suggest and give reasons for a suitable format for the data frames that might be sent from a particular terminal (10 marks)

B. From these, develop a set of rules for the conversation, setting out the logic in any convenient form (diagram, pseudocode etc) to represent the protocols associated with all aspects of transaction processing. (10 marks)

This question is designed to see if students can apply knowledge of layer 2 link management and flow control, to a specific communication situation. Part of the answer should demonstrate design skills in the structure of the frames sent and the remainder should show that you can work out what might happen to disturb communication and how to handle it.

Assumptions

- the actual user menu structure has already been designed
- the machine gives you one more try if you muck up the account number/PIN.
- the machine logs off when you take your cash, or hit cancel after using the machine for something other than cash withdrawal
- the head office computer logs you off if there is a delay of more than two minutes
- transmission to head office could be corrupted but to make life easier, no garbled frames are received by the ATM
- head office gives up if a garbled frame is re-garbled more than three times
- the cash point knows exactly what cash it holds and in what notes
- it will sort out for itself using local intelligence (without reference to head office) when it cannot dispense an exact amount asked for and tell the user (eg, 'only able to dispense 10 notes').

Approach to the solution

We will not put the rules into words, partly because we would need to know exactly how an ATM operates and this would be unfair in a comms examination. More important, if you spend time looking at the frames suggested, you should be able to work out for yourself what should go on. Instead, we will show the data and control frames in each direction.

Note that some frames will cause actions transparent to the ATM user, for example, the NAK frame (5/1) from head office causes the ATM to retry (say 10 times) before it informs the user. The user will not know about a frame 4 from the ATM. However,if head office sends a frame 7 (with A=1, ie, busy) the user will be told to wait for a while.

The numbering chosen for the frames is entirely arbitrary and has no significance except in this problem. The figures under each frame item indicate the length in characters.

Note that we will not have anything to say about that actual physical make-up of the frames, such as the actual representation for a frame start-marker, (we will do this later on in the chapter). As far as the comms hardware is concerned it is just sending strings of characters one by one.

The frames

- frames on the left are sent from the ATM
- frames on the right are from head office
- the first byte of each frame is an identifier that tells the receiver what kind of frame has been received
- the figure under each field of each frame is the length in bytes.

ATM *Head office*

Log-on | 1 | A/c number | PIN | (lengths 1, 8, 4) — | 1 | A | (lengths 1, 1)

A=0=OK
A=1=one more try
A=2=log user off
(Doesn't know PIN or stolen card)

The ATM software will read the account number from the card and ask the user for his PIN (personal identification number). It will then form up a type 1 frame and send it off. The head office machine replies accordingly.

Request | 2 | A | (lengths 1, 1)
A=1=C/B
A=2=Stmnt
A=3=balance

| 2 | A | (lengths 1, 7)
A=balance
A=-1=confirmed

A frame 2 from the ATM is a request. Head office will send a type 2 with 'A' containing a -1 to confirm a request or with the actual cash balance requested (the -1 allows for a zero balance to be sent back if the user is so unfortunate!).

Withdrawal | 3 | Amount |
1 2

| 3 | A | A=0=OK
1 1
A=1=> current balance
A=2=>1 withdrawal today

To save space, the ATM sends (amount-1). The reply is self-explanatory.

No cash | 4 | A | A=1=£5
A=2=£10
1 1 A=3=empty

| 4 | Noted for action
1

After telling the user what is going on, a type 4 tells head office to get some more cash down quick.

| 5 | T | garbled frame
T=type
1 1

This is the reply to any frame that the head office computer cannot recognise (see frame 6, A = 2).

| 6 | A | Logoff A=1=timeout 2 minutes
1 1
A=2=4 garbled frames

Head office gets impatient and sends a type 6, A=1 if it does not hear from the ATM for two minutes. Also, if it gets four successive garbled frames, it gets fed up and shuts down the ATM.

| 7 | A | A=1=busy
A=2=continue
1 1

Here we demonstrate flow control. There are going to be times when the head office computer is flooded or the transmission network has some problems. Frame 7, A=1 is a 'hang on for a while, I'll get back to you' (equivalent to X-OFF) and frame 7, A=2 is 'OK, carry on then' (equivalent to X-ON).

Log-off | 9 | A/c number |
1 8

| 9 | log-off accepted
1

Once the user takes his card and/or his cash, the ATM informs head office that the business is finished and it gets a confirmation.

This latter is not absolutely necessary here, but it is nice to finish off in a tidy, controlled way!)

Pause for thought

Apologies to the banks if this is nothing like what really happens. It doesn't matter anyway as long as you can see the thinking involved.

Try to work through this problem, without bothering about the physical side - wires, networks etc - just think about data sent and received or not received. Hopefully, you will then see why it is important to consider the frame content and the rules when designing a protocol.

Real-life protocols

We will look at several protocols in common use, starting with those that are used to send characters and then introducing one that can be used to send anything and which is important in layer 3 as well as layer 2.

Before we do so, we must present some of the ASCII combinations again, because they are of extreme importance in framing. We will state almost all of them here and introduce them when necessary in protocol examples.

ASCII control characters

The American National Standards Institute definition of a control character is something like:

any bit combination that initiates, modifies or stops any action affecting the recording, processing, transmission or the interpretation of data.

We will see how these control characters are used in particular protocols shortly, so let us present a complete set of all the ASCII combinations that represent control characters (as shown in Figure 6.5).

Binary code	Name	Function/notes
Logical control characters		
0000001	SOH	start of heading
0000010	STX	start of text
0000011	ETX	end of text
0000100	EOT	end of transmission
0000101	ENQ	enquiry - used in call set-up and link protocols
0000110	ACK	acknowledge - received ok
0010101	NAK	negative acknowledge - not received ok
0010000	DLE	data link escape - with next octet = control combination
0010110	SYN	synchronous idle - used in synchronous framing
0010111	ETB	end transmission block
Device control characters		
0010001	DC1	device control 1 primary flow control - start (X-ON)
0010010	DC2	device control 2 - secondary flow control - start
0010011	DC3	device control 3 - primary flow control - stop (X-OFF)
0010100	DC4	device control 4 - primary flow control - stop
(Secondary and primary flow control characters are used where we have a setup such as host-terminal-printer and we want the host to have the option to apply flow control to the terminal or through the terminal to the printer.)		
Format effecters (for physical control)		
0001000	BS	backspace
0001001	HT	horizontal tab
0001010	LF	line feed - can be 'new line' (= CR/LF) by agreement
0001011	VT	vertical tab
0001100	FF	form feed
0001101	CR	carriage return
Separators		
0011001	EM	end of medium - paper tape
0011100	FS	file separator
0011101	GS	group separator
0011110	RS	record separator
0011111	US	unit separator
(All of these except EM are used only in IBM protocols.)		
Miscellaneous		
0000000	NUL	null character
0000111	BEL	bell - ring bell/bleep - audible signal
0011011	ESC	escape - with next octet = escape combination
0001110	SO	shift out
0001111	SI	shift in
0011000	CAN	cancel - cancel previous block or message
0011010	SUB	substitute
1111111	DEL	delete/rubout - ignore

Figure 6.5 ASCII control characters

Further possibilities exist based on combinations of characters, such as for VDU cursor control, erase field and space fill.

Now we must look at some protocols in common use. The simpler ones are intended for character transmission, the more complex are for any kind of data.

Byte-oriented protocols

Very common comms situations occur where:

- we are linking a primary to one or more secondaries
- half-duplex conversation is needed (not full duplex even if we are using a modem that supports it)
- data is character in nature eg, text or business transactions
- data volumes are not high
- data volumes are high but data origination is intermittent, so asynchronous transmission would be inefficient.

Remember that for asynchronous (character-by-character) transmission, each character is framed and there is a minimum of 20% overhead to carry the stop and start bits (one start bit, one stop bit + eight data bits). Where this is the case, we can make use of *byte-oriented protocols*.

As you know, everything goes through as bytes, both data and control information (frame delimiters, error detection blocks etc). So what? How else can they go except in the form of bytes?

Pause for thought

This is a good time to remind you about the difference between byte and octet. It is a pity that this difference is not made very much in practice.

Strictly speaking, a byte is a group of bits representing a character in some code or other, while an octet is just eight bits.

An octet could hold a printable character or a control character, or could be part of a group of octets, perhaps part of a binary or floating point number.

This is the importance of the distinction - with byte-oriented protocols, we are dealing with bytes (as just defined). If we are not sending just characters, this kind of protocol falls down.

In byte-oriented protocols, we make use of some kind of idle RQ and there will always be the condition that one end is more important than the other eg, as the half-duplex 'I will send and you will confirm'. Data and control frames are always separated, even if a data frame has to contain some control characters.

More complex protocols are needed:

- for duplex use where a sender might want to acknowledge a received frame while at the same time sending a data or control frame
- where the data being transmitted is not just text characters but could include any kind of data format (as explained above).

The protocol that follows forms the basis of many others in use.

Binary synchronous communications (Bisynch, BSC)

BSC is actually a group of character-oriented half-duplex protocols. The original was developed by IBM but appears in several variations.

The basic data frame format is fairly standard. It has a series of SYN octets at the start, a variable length data portion and an ETX at the end as illustrated in Figure 6.6.

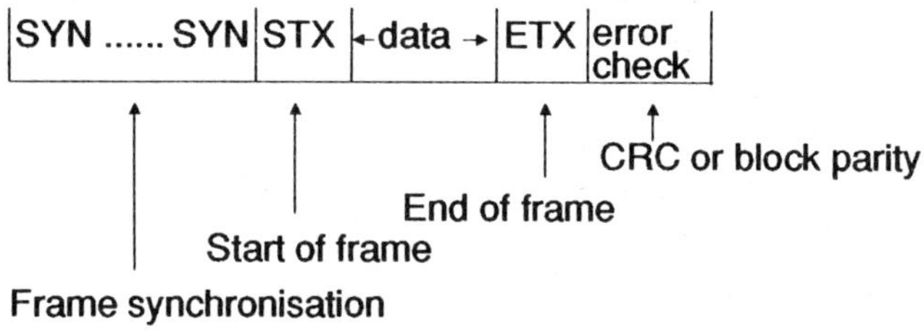

Figure 6.6 The basic BSC frame

The SYNs are synchronisation octets to allow the receiver to get into step in time with the sender (refer back to chapter 2 for details). STX is the 'start of text' marker and ETX is 'end of text'.

The error check is either a pair of horizontal and vertical parity check blocks or a CRC block.

Where we are dealing with a multi-secondary situation, the frame must allow for an address as shown in Figure 6.7, where SOH is a 'start of header' marker (the address being a special part of the frame acting as a kind of header for the rest) and can also be used

SYN ...... SYN	SOH	←address→	STX	←data →	ETX	error check

Figure 6.7 BSC frame with addressing

where a frame is to be sub-divided. This might be the case for two main reasons:

- where blocks to be sent are too long (remember the balance between the data efficiency of a large block and the danger of having to resend a large block)
- where there is a practical reason for sub-dividing a block, such as where it represents say, an order with a set of detail lines and a total line, or a series of line/paragraphs making up a whole page.

In this case, each sub-division is held in a frame, only the first starting with SOH and all but the last ending with ETB instead of ETX as shown in Figure 6.8.

SYN ...... SYN	SOH	header info	STX	←data →	ETB	error check

First frame

SYN ...... SYN	STX	←data →	ETB	error check

'Middle' frame

SYN ...... SYN	STX	←data →	ETX	error check

Final frame

Figure 6.8 BSC multi-line framing

Some of the other control characters referred to earlier (Figure 6.5), can be used with page terminals, to delimit fields etc, where the chunk of data to be sent is a whole screenful of data and each subsidiary frame is an area of the screen (a window).

Acknowledgement and 'end of transmission' are signalled by special frames. These frames are called *supervisory frames* to distinguish them from data frames (Figure 6.9).

SYN	SYN	ACK

Positive acknowledgement

SYN	SYN	NAK

Negative acknowledgement

SYN	SYN	EOT

End of session

Figure 6.9 BSC supervisory frames

The octet ENQ is also used to signal an enquiry, when we are dealing with multi-secondary sessions. (We will not go into this except to state that the primary is usually either polling a group of secondaries or selecting a particular one, and the receiver needs to know what the primary wants).

Data transparency

What happens if we send a data frame that happens to contain a control character? This could be due either to an error, or because say, we are sending a binary number which by bad luck happens to have the same bit pattern as a control character. For example, take the binary equivalent of 260_{10} which is 0000000100000100_2.

If we happened to send this as 16-bit binary number, the second octet in fact would be read in as EOT (refer to Figure 6.5), a signal for end of session.)

To overcome this kind of problem, protocols often employ *data transparency*. This means taking some measure to ensure that a control character is ignored **unless it is intended to be there.**

BSC in action

We have not shown it in earlier figures, but in BSC, data transparency is maintained by inserting DLE (ASCII 0010000) in front of each control character, so a typical frame becomes as shown in Figure 6.10.

SYN	SYN	DLE	STX	....	DLE	ETX	CRC

Figure 6.10 Data transparent BSC frame

Also note that DLE/SYN is used as a 'filler', where one end wants to ensure that the other can catch up. DLE/STX as well as frame start, can be used as an 'abort frame' message when some problem is detected by the sender during transmission.

As we have said, BSC is based on idle RQ or send-and-wait. The receiver confirms negatively with a NAK and actually confirms positive receipt with a numbered DLE. (It alternately sends DLE 1 and DLE 0 to accepted frames.)

Figure 6.11 shows a possible series of frames representing a particular session (SYN bytes and error blocks are not shown). The order of the conversation illustrated, is as follows:

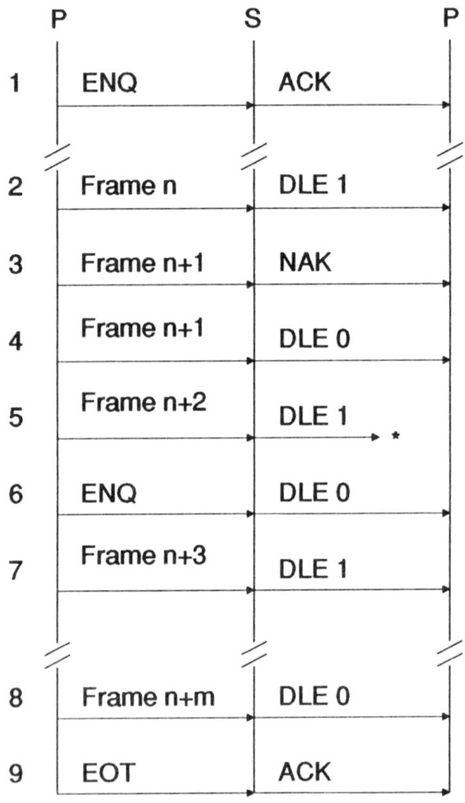

Figure 6.11 A BSC 'conversation'

1	P (primary) asks S (secondary) if ready to start.	S confirms
2	P sends next data frame	S confirms receipt
3	P sends next data frame	S confirms receipt garbled
4	P resends the frame	S confirms
5	P sends next data frame	S confirms but reply is lost
6	P asks 'what is going on'	S says 'carry on'
7/8	P sends remaining frames	S confirms
9	P says 'that's it'	S says 'right'

As a basis for simple communication, BSC is quite good, especially in situations where a primary is linked to a number of secondaries, grouped into *clusters*, each group being managed by a *cluster controller*. As we have seen, addressing is possible and the basic ENQ frame can be extended so that poll or select can be specified.

The main problem with BSC is that no frame length is transmitted and there is always the possibility of one of the separator characters being corrupted during transmission.

A number of byte-oriented *file transfer protocols* have been devised which attempt to overcome problems such as these. Proprietary software includes names such as *X-modem*, *Y-modem*, *Y-modem-g*, *SEElink*, *Blast* and *X-PC* and we will look at some of these.

Note that all these protocols except Y-modem-g and Blast are designed for half-duplex use (based on idle RQ).

File transfer protocols

X-modem

X-modem uses a frame containing a fixed 128 byte data block, as shown in Figure 6.12, where the checksum is the remainder

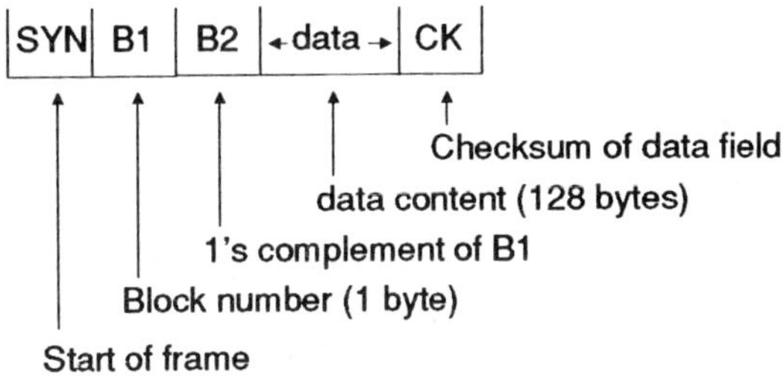

Figure 6.12 X-modem frame structure

formed from the addition of the ASCII value of each character in the data block (treated as 128 binary numbers) and dividing by 256.

The conversation is actually controlled by the receiver in that the sender will always wait for acknowledgement or a shut-down request. After receiving a frame, the receiver can check for errors:

- is there an SOH at the beginning?
- is the block number one more than the previous?
- is the block number still the same as the 1's complement of the next byte?
- is the checksum still correct?

If any of these is not the case, the receiver returns a *CAN*(cel) (ASCII 0011000). The sender will try up to 10 times before giving up.

X-modem is designed so that only one file is sent in one session although extensions allow it to handle several.

Kermit

This is a more sophisticated protocol where the frame can be of different types. As with X-modem, the secondary always returns a single character response.

Conversation starts with the secondary sending NAK. The primary then sends data frames and the secondary responds with ACK/NAK or CAN.

Unless a CAN has been returned, the primary will keep sending new frames (on ACK) or resending (on NAK) until endfile. Then it sends EOT, which should get a NAK. The Kermit frame structure is shown in Figure 6.13.

This protocol is particularly useful for file transfer since the frame type field can be used to hold a file name or an endfile marker, as well as a file record. This means that in one session, several files can be transmitted.

It can also be used to specify the maximum frame size that the receiver wants and for a slow sender network, can be used to indicate the maximum length of time to wait for a message.

The check block can either be a CRC (split up and stored in three bytes) or one of two different checksums.

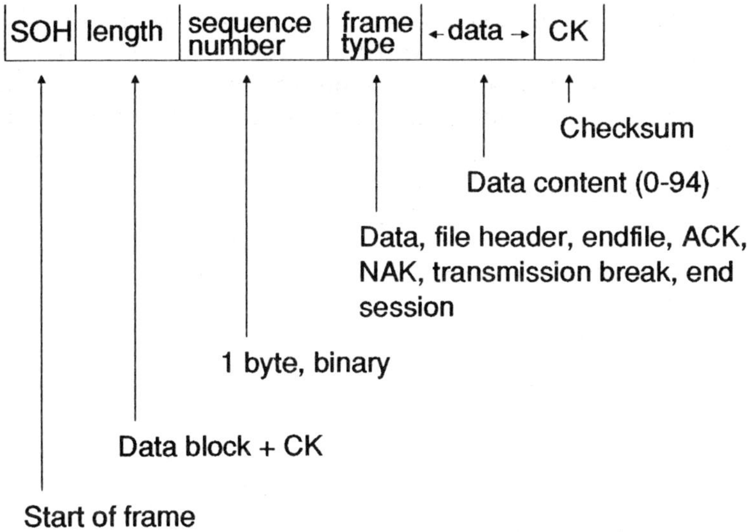

Figure 6.13 Kermit frame structure

Other file-transfer protocols
Y-modem (or *X-modem-k*) is a variation on X-modem that allows for multiple files and can block to 128 or 1024 bytes. *Z-modem* is another multi-file protocol that maintains the exact file size. *Y-modem-g* (or *X-modem-k-g*) employs continuous RQ and requires a high quality connection to be successful.

Bit-oriented protocols

The byte-oriented protocols recognise that some data to be transferred will not necessarily consist of just characters and they have various approaches to transparency, such as a prefix for any non-ASCII character and other tricks such as the use of the ESC and DLE.

Blast (*bl*ocked *as*ynchronous *t*ransmission) and Y-modem-g by contrast, have features that allow for files to be transferred without send-and-wait - up to 16 data blocks can be transmitted before acknowledgement (continuous RQ). They also allow frames from each end to be interleaved so that one frame can be acknowledged while fresh data is being sent (ie, in full-duplex operation).

Another convenience is that after error correction, the sender can continue sending records from the recovery point unlike X-Modem, where you have to start again from the beginning of the file.

However, perhaps the most important modern protocol is the true bit-oriented protocol originally developed by IBM called *synchronous data link control (SDLC)*. The ISO variation goes under the name *high-level data link control (HDLC)*.

HDLC

HDLC is extremely important because it is designed for the synchronous, full-duplex transfer of anything - all forms of data and control information, but it also forms the basis of the layer 2/layer 3 logical interface adopted in CCITT recommendation X25. (We touched on X21 in chapter 5 and since X25 approximately spans OSI layers 1/3 rather than just layer 2, we will leave it now and cover it in chapter 8.)

We cannot go into the intricate details of HDLC, but you need an overview in order to understand some of the layer 3 network protocols. In particular packet-switching networks rely heavily on it.

HDLC is a general name in that there are different possible implementations depending on the environment in which it is to operate. The most common are *normal response mode (NRM - or LAP) and asynchronous balanced mode (ABM - LAP-B)*.

In HDLC, the term balanced means that each end is of equal importance while normal implies that there is some kind of 'master-slave' relationship. This is not just as simple as it sounds, especially in layer 3. Figure 6.14 shows a host of some kind surrounded by 'terminals'.

We might be looking at a mainframe computer connected to some smaller 'front- end processors' or cluster controllers, or it could be a central network exchange linked to subsidiary exchanges.

To the host, the subsidiaries are slaves and they regard it as the host, but each subsidiary processor is looking after several terminals which it regards as slaves. Each of the terminals shown could be a further subsidiary processor and in a real-life situation

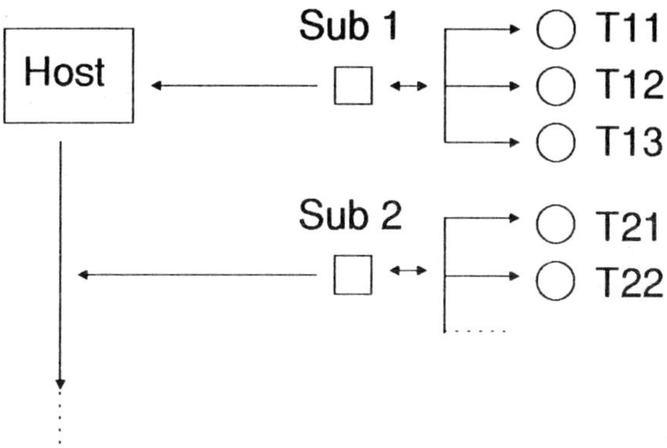

Figure 6.14 Subsidiary link management

(especially in the network and transport layers), we will need to handle link management, flow and error control at all levels.

The following are the most important alternative modes in which HDLC can be employed:

- NRM (LAP) - this is designed for a main primary and many secondaries which transmit on request from the primary (ie, not balanced) such as in terminal-host situations where the host is considered the master and the only primary. The terminals are considered to be slaves and of lesser importance and as half-duplex operation applies, a secondary can only transmit if given permission
- ABM (LAP-B) - this is a full-duplex procedure intended for user at higher network levels such as host-to-host communication or where two network nodes are passing packets (layer 3 frames) around the network. As it is a full-duplex procedure, either end can send at any time and a balanced approach is needed. ABM is employed in the link layer of X25.

The main characteristic that makes HDLC different from other protocols is that there is more that one type of frame, frames may have different functions and their content varies with the type of frame (Figure 6.15).

We will look in some detail at the basic frame format. In this, 'Data' is the part that varies for the different types of frame and 'Control' is the part that varies depending on what is wanted such as call set-up, flow control, data/information etc:

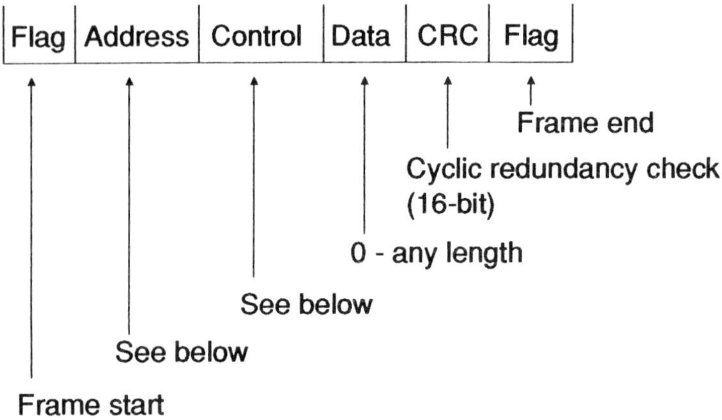

Figure 6.15 HDLC basic frame structure

- a frame sent by a primary is called a *command frame*
- a frame returned to a primary is called a *response frame.*

  (Note that there is no length field in the frame. Can you see why?

  If you look back to Figure 6.14, at any particular time, a subsidiary is receiving data and passing it on. It doesn't necessarily know how long the frame is that it is sending (it hasn't received all of it yet)
- the frame start and end marker is called the *flag* byte (01111110).

  (This is the equivalent of the SYNs/STX of BSC.) As we are dealing with a bit-oriented protocol, there is always the possibility that this particular bit pattern might occur within the data itself so to protect transparent-mode operation, a technique known as *redundant zero insertion* or *bit-stuffing* is used. During transmission, as each string of five bits is being sent, an extra 0 is inserted which is removed at the receiving end
- address (one byte) is use to specify the destination and could relate to a specific secondary, a group of stations or if set to all 1s, every secondary (ie, broadcasting). In ABM (see above) the address can be extended to two bytes to allow for subsidiary addressing
- control is complicated and provides the basis of duplex operation and different functions are indicated by its first bit.

The various formats of the HDLC control byte are shown in Figure 6.16.

	1	2	3	4	5	6	7	8
Data frame (I-frame)	0	N(S)			P/F	N(R)		
Supervisory frame (S-frame)	1	0	S		P/F	N(R)		
Unnumbered frame	1	1	M		P/F	M		

Figure 6.16 HDLC control byte formats

The bits involved are:

- P/F - this is the *poll/final* bit that allows for confirmation request and its acknowledgement
- N(R) - is always the number of the next frame expected by the secondary (except for unnumbered frames)
- N(S) - in a data frame, is the number of the frame being sent.

Note that there are only three bits available for these counts allowing 1-8 ie, 000_2 to 111_2. The frame count is in fact held modulo 8 - when it reaches 8, it goes back to one, equivalent to a 'window' of eight frames. For a supervisory frame, S is used to indicate the status of the receiver to the primary (ready/not ready for flow control, reject last/selective reject ie, retransmission requests).

Unnumbered frames are used in sending and acknowledging basic frames, to restart transmission if there is a serious loss of synchronisation (e.g. frames right out of sequence) and to allow for switching between ABM and NRM.

Working of the protocol is beyond our scope, but if you look at the frames, you will get some inkling of how things work. We will look at the matter again in chapter 8. Note that since HDLC supports full duplex, both ends need a timing mechanism to enable them to initiate synchronisation.

CDLC

This has been referred to before as the *c*ellular *d*ata *l*ink *c*ontrol of Racal Vodafone. It was developed for mobile data terminal use in their cellular network which as you know has special problems, in particular, a bit corruption rate of up to 2% - 2 bits in every 100 sent are wrecked.

The protocol is derived from HDLC but the frame structure is altered slightly. The main extensions are:

- eight FEC bits are added to each character (BCH code)
- byte interleaving is employed across groups of eight characters
- a frame length field is included
- an enhanced frame synchronisation procedure is introduced (to prevent slippage and retransmission)
- selective retransmission based on windowing.

The protocol is applied transparently to the user and Racal claim that transmission is almost entirely error-free with recommended V26 modems.

Having dealt with the theory behind some common layer 2 protocols, we will finish with some more practical techniques.

Practical aspects

Protocol chips

Although most protocol logic forms part of communications software, it is often very convenient to implement such logic in a chip and many chips are on the market for incorporation in terminals and network hardware.

One class includes the *Universal synchronous,asynchronous receiver/transmitter (USART).* It can accept parallel data streams and convert to serial for transfer. It allows for data from five to eight bits with all parities and can operate in half- or full-duplex. The transfer rate is also selectable, from 75 to very high values.

More sophisticated chips (sometimes called *multi-protocol chips*) allow even more options including:

- byte- or bit-oriented protocols
- generation of frames and the type detection of frames received
- a range of CRC types
- data transparency options (zero-insertion or DLE doubling).

Chips such as these are built in to modems to give some of the facilities detailed in chapter 5.

Link protocol chips can also be obtained, for example a full HDLC-based X25 chip. A hardware supplier or network builder would take the basic chip and build it into the hardware to enable full protocol handling to be implemented.

Testing

Facilities for network fault isolation and testing are part of a very large subject, but the real-life network manager must be able to implement techniques and procedures for testing out hardware set-ups and tracing and clearing up any faults.

Equally important, **he will want to compare different protocols in action** and to do this, he needs help in deciding which protocols might be needed in different operating situations. It may not always be convenient to use live data and several tricks are used, including *pattern sequence generators*.

One type is the *foxbox* which produces strings of random characters ('the quick brown fox...'). Other types will produce customised strings. Note that we may want an option to produce a repeatable stream or a totally different one each time.

We may also want to get clever and include a time or probabilistic element, sending byte streams at different (irregular) intervals, or according to some predefined frequency distribution as to length or inter-departure time.

An extended piece of kit is called a *multi-protocol line tester* and will allow for:

- analysis - examine the incoming messages and determine the protocol being applied
- send and receive within many different protocols
- generate patterns to send
- handle different character codes and different data rates
- be able to collect data received for later analysis
- be able to analyse data collected, such as statistical print-outs, scanning/searching for particular strings etc
- act as a range of different interfaces, such as CCITT V24 and X21, EIA (see chapter 5), military specifications and so on

- be able to act as a terminal or a DCE (such as modem, multiplexer or digital interface).

Information gathered will be useful in estimating performance and indicating for example, where a particular protocol is falling short of estimates.

Protocol conversion
Again a big subject. All we can really say is that when we are implementing a network component, if it is to be useful in a multi-functional environment where it will link to different networks, mainframes, terminals and so on, it needs to be able to convert from one protocol to another. To enable this, protocol conversion hardware/software will be employed when data is received into the network. It will often be able to determine the particular protocol in use and convert to its own if necessary.

Similarly, when sending data out it will be able to convert to other protocols so that different networks can interface with it. Sophisticated protocol conversion will also include testing capabilities. (We will return to this subject when we look at *internetworking* in chapter 8.)

Recap

- the chapter starts out by explaining the function of layer 2 protocols, introducing the concept of RQ and its extensions. In particular it shows the difference between idle and continuous RQ
- byte- and bit-oriented protocols are discussed showing how link management, flow control and error handling are accomplished
- several file-transfer protocols, derived from BSC, are introduced
- HDLC, perhaps one of the most important protocols in the network layer, is introduced
- some of the hardware needed to analyse and check out protocols is looked at and the need to be able to convert from one protocol to another is considered.

Typical questions

Question 6.1

Two sportsmen want to have a conversation about the merits of the yellow ball in tennis. Assuming that you know absolutely nothing about the two sportsman, draw up a set of rules to enable the conversation to take place. Allow for different languages, the actual medium for the conversation and flow control.

Question 6.2

A conversation is in progress employing ARQ. I have just sent you the next message and there is no reply.

A why?

B what should I do?

Question 6.3

In the level 2 protocols discussed, why is it often necessary to precede control characters with DLE?

7: Comms software, external services and PCs

Objectives

After reading this chapter, you should:

- be aware of how to access external services with a PC and modem
- have an appreciation of what is required from communications software
- appreciate how simple communications software can be set up using BASIC
- have an overview of the facilities for communications provided by some general-purpose and specialised software packages
- have some knowledge of two particular communications packages.

Now we know something about the errors that can occur throughout the total connection path involved with a data conversation, we can look at a typical PC user who needs communications software to link to companies and services outside his own organisation. We must appreciate that typical user might be linked to his mainframe with software proprietary to the manufacturer/supplier of the mainframe or he could have a single PC running applications but also wanting to gain access to external services.

For simplification, we will mainly restrict ourselves to this latter user so that we can cover fairly simply, most of what is needed. (Dont forget however, that even this simple PC user may be part of a LAN which has a gateway server for all the PCs in the network).

The early part of this chapter overlaps with chapter 10, so we will not go into great detail in explaining facilities such as viewdata. For the time being it is enough to appreciate that there are services or facilities needed by the user and that comms software must be provided by someone to enable them to be accessed.

Why is comms software needed

What does the typical user want to do with his PC? Basically, he wants to establish a link with one or more companies or services offered by these companies and we can identify six main possibilities for this.

Other users

This could be for simple electronic mail text message or perhaps something more complicated. The software for a simple mail system could reside in each user's PC and developed by the user in a suitable programming language such as BASIC or C, but anything complicated is likely to be bought in as a special package or as part of a general package, again resident in each user's PC. Packages such as Symphony, Smart and similar integrated packages usually have a module that can be used to set up remote communications.

If the requirements of e-mail are very complicated, either it will be handled on the company mainframe (for private e-mail) or through an external e-mail provider such as British Telecom *Gold* (now supplied with *Prestel* under the name *Dialcom*) or MCLs *Link7500*. In such cases, the e-mail management software is not in the user's PC. All he will need is some simple software to link to the external e-mail service.

The company mainframe

Electronic mail is all very well, but it it is not the main reason for communication. For the user, perhaps the most likely application is in some form of *transaction processing* such as the entry of customer orders, purchase requirements or perhaps timesheet or performance data.

Note that as mentioned in chapter 5 there is an increasing trend towards the use of mobile data terminals so in this catagory we might have a salesman with a customer order, entering the details into his carphone-based terminal so that the head office computer can organise delivery of goods.

Another possibility is use of a mainframe in a general enquiry. In the commercial world, many people use their terminal to access mainframe data so that they can give customers immediate, on-line quotations and estimates, or indications as to resource availability (cars, rooms, theatre seats and so on).

External services

As well as e-mail, there are a number of very important facilities that can be lumped together as *external services*. Broadly, they provide:

- general information/electronic conversation
- text-based information
- graphics-formatted information.

Bulletin board

Exactly what it says. Someone (usually an amateur enthusiast) offers an electronic noticeboard that has dial-up access. Anyone interested, can look at the noticeboard to see what is for sale, get hints and tips and generally find out what is going on. The user can often put in enquiries and questions, especially about hardware/software problems and scan the bulletin board later on to see what has come up.

A more sophisticated version of this is called *computer conferencing* and is being increasingly used in companies. It means that anyone with a problem can post it into the system (just like a more conventional written memo) and examine the replies later. Other people may poke their nose in and add their comments and further questions - the overall effect is that of having a conference without having to get everyone together at the same time.

(A by-product of conferencing is that management can arrange for the software to keep a record of who puts questions, who does and does not provide answers etc.)

Data base access

Perhaps one of the largest uses of terminals is in collecting information. For example, an engineering company may employ an estimator, whose job might be to produce cost and deliver date quotations for work to give to potential customers. Typical databases he may need include:

- a labour database so that he can see when people are on holiday or committed to other contracts. He can also look at the machinery and equipment data base for similar reasons
- applications, perhaps something to do with the effect of hot water on a particular plastic, or the effect of -20 degrees on a paint
- weather conditions in a foreign country if the contract is for overseas
- currency exchange rates, so that he can make quotations in the customer' own currency, at the best exchange rate
- customs and excise regulations as to the export of certain products
- other companies that offer similar services.

A very large organisation might be prepared to provide much of this information to its employees, but there are many companies who have already invested resources in the provision of databases containing such information for sale to anyone who wants it.

These databases could be for general (or public) use - anyone paying a subscription and who owns a terminal with the appropriate modem/comms software can access them. Others are more specific in what they offer and who can access them. They are provided by companies like British Telecom and institutions like the Stock Exchange and the Financial Times. Still others might be from a trade organisation or some other interest group.

The information provided can be literally 'encyclopedic' - covering a very wide range of subjects such as news sport, cooking, hobbies, history and so on. Alternatively it might be more specialised and be specifically oriented to commercial, financial or technical users. (Subjects might include agriculture, pharmacy, medicine, chemical engineering, carpet manufacture, insurance and estate agency.)

Data processing services

The final possibility is where the host computer provides actual data processing, rather than just supplying information. There are two main areas in which this applies. The first is in technical applications where users need access to large, complex software, which their company machines do not support, either because they need very powerful processors or massive disk space, or they are expensive and not used often enough to justify buying the software.

Companies such as Boeing Computer Services and GEISCO (Honeywell) will make engineering calculation and design software available from a user's terminal. The user sends in data and after processing, the results can be sent back along the wire or by post.

A similar kind of service is supplied for commercial organisations and includes such processing as payroll, credit checking, home-shopping and home-banking. (Chapter 10 gives examples of mortgage and insurance calculations that are provided by associations of insurance conpanies.)

For the rest of this chapter we will look at the software needed to get at some of these services and we will expand on the services themselves in chapter 10.

Communications profiles

Terminal, modem and link

To make the connection to another computer, a certain amount of information must be provided so that the comms software can do its job properly. All of the following will need to be covered:

- baud rate - usually between 300 and 2400 for most applications
- number of data bits - seven for ASCII, eight for EBCDIC and when sending non-character data
- parity setting - generally even (none for 8 data bits)
- telephone number of the required service and the dialling method needed
- terminal type expected.

All of these except the last have been covered in earlier chapters.

Most comms packages recognise that different terminals have different characteristics, in particular what features they support (including colour, range of characters, varying character height and width, differing line width and so on). Generally, the software allows the user to make the terminal emulate (act like) a number of common terminals. (Among other functions, the software often changes the effect of keyboard keys selected.) The most common terminals that can be emulated are:

- TTY (Teletype)
- DEC VT52 and VT102
- viewdata
- IBM 3270.

The TTY is the simplest kind of terminal and generally displays all the ASCII combinations it receives. (There is a derivative used in the USA called *ANSI-BBS* which can send and receive combinations to provide slightly more interesting effects.)

The VT52 and VT102 terminals are from a range of terminals produced by DEC and have a large number of functions.

A viewdata terminal must be able to handle the graphics that support the viewdata frames produced by public and private viewdata suppliers.

The IBM 3270 is a range of IBM mainframe-compatible terminals which are designed as full page- or forms terminals. A number of functions relating to the screen as a whole page are needed, (not supported by the usual PC keyboard). In addition, IBM-format file transfer is supported, as is multiple-window processing.

An interesting product of the US company DCA, marketed by Computer Marketing of Camberley is called *IRMA* and is a PC card containing an on-board processor to enable a PC or PS/2 micro to emulate a range of IBM mainframe terminals and handle IBM file-transfer protocols and applications software.

File transfer protocols

Generally, whatever the terminal type, file transfer protocols are required. We have covered most of the well-known of these in chapter 6. Figure 7.1 shows the protocol selection screen from the comms package called *Telix*, marketed by the Canadian PTel Inc.

Log-on dialogue

Often, once connected to the external service, there may be a need for some questions and answers between the sender and the service. This could be just the entry of a user identity and password, but it might be more sophisticated. Figure 7.2 shows a hypothetical log-on dialogue between mainframe and terminal.

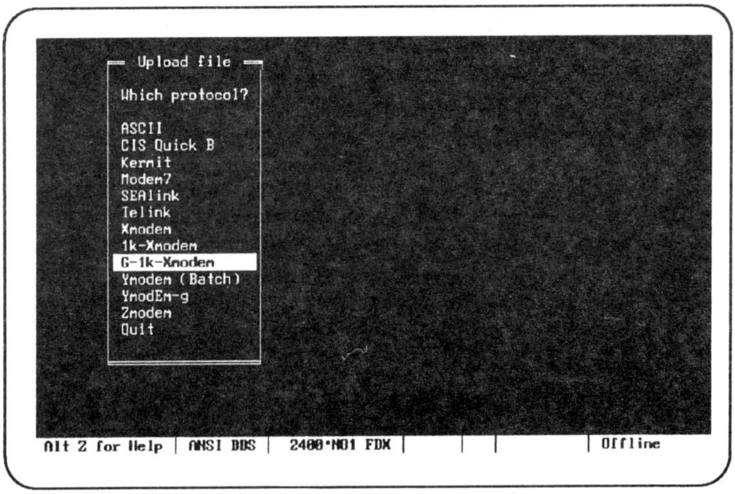

Figure 7.1 Protocol selection in 'Telix'

It is often useful to be able to store all the answers to the questions put by the service when you log on - the user can then initiate all of it from a single keystroke or menu selection. (Further examples will be shown later in this chapter when we look at *Mass Breakout*.)

Mainframe			*Terminal*
Please enter user identity			User enters identity
Please enter your password			User enters password
Enter your priority class, A/B?			User enters A
Select main option	A	e-Mail	
	B	viewdata	
	C	telex	User enters A
Select sub-option	A	create mail	
	B	inspect in-mail	
	C	prepare list	
	D	send mail	User enters B

Figure 7.2 Log-on dialogue

BASIC for PC-PC data transmission

This section discusses how comms can be implemented in BASIC. You can skip it altogether if:

- you know BASIC already
- you are familiar with any other language that can be employed for comms
- The is no chance of your ever wanting to write comms software.

However, to reinforce some of the knowledge gained in chapter 5, you are advised to try and understand this section which shows how the communications port on a PC can be 'programmed'. (You are also advised to look at Appendix 1 which gives a broad introduction to BASIC as a programming language, in particular, showing you how to carry out input and output and how to manipulate non-numeric data.)

OPEN COM

BASIC on a PC supports two comms ports or *asynchronous communications adaptors* (assuming that both cards have been inserted into the machine), both of which are designed for duplex operation. In effect, BASIC treats a port like a file and conventional file operations, such as GET, PUT, PRINT etc can be applied.

Each port must be activated just like any file and this is carried out with the *OPEN COM* statement. It has the form shown in Figure 7.3 where the parameters are as follows:

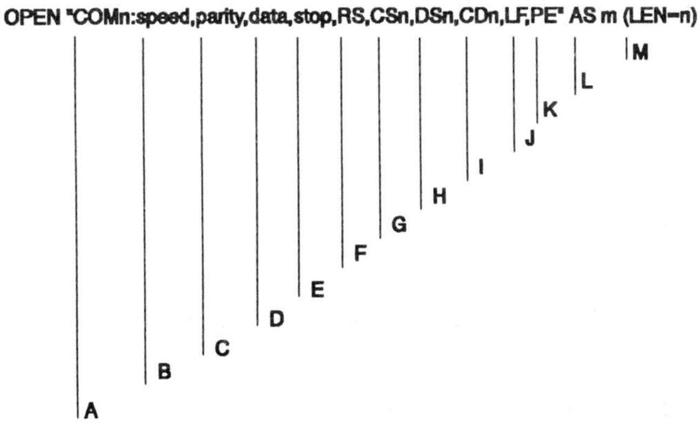

Figure 7.3 BASIC OPEN "COM"

A - COM tells BASIC that we are setting up a comms port and *n* is either 1 or 2 (for two ports, we need two OPEN statements)

B - this specifies the data transfer rate in bits per second, possible values are: 75, 110, 150, 300, 600, 1200, 1800, 2400, 4800, 9600, the default value (if you dont specify anything at all) is 300. (Note that for a modem-to-PTN link, the maximum baud rate allowed is 2400)

C - this parameter specifies the parity checking to be used on characters transmitted and is closely linked with parameters D and K. If parameter K is not included, no parity checking is carried out at all

D - parameter D can take values 5, 6, 7 (default) and 8 and if set to 8 (all eight bits make up the character, such as for EBCDIC), no parity checking is carried out at all. If D is not 8, checking is carried out on the leftmost bit as shown in Figure 7.4

Parity

parameter	*setting / checking*
O	ODD
E	EVEN (default)
S	always a 0
M	always a 1
N	not checked

Figure 7.4 OPEN "COM" parity checking

E - this specifies the number of stop bits that frame a character. The default is 1 for all speeds above 110.

The next 4 parameters relate to V24/RS232 circuits and except for parameter F, include a time option (in milliseconds) after which an error occurs if a signal is not received. (Refer to chapter 5.)

F - *RS*, if present turns off the *request to send* signal. The default (ie, not specified) leaves the signal enabled

G - *CSn* controls the *clear to send* line and an error will occur after n milliseconds (default 0 or 1000 if RS is specified)

H - DSn controls the *data set ready* signal (compare this with parameter G)

I - CDn should only be used for a modem-to-PTN connection since it is used to detect the presence/absence of the carrier signal. An error occurs if the carrier drops (fails) for more than n milliseconds. The default is 0. When transmitting along a null modem, parameter H should be omitted

J - LF if specified causes a *line feed (0001000)* to be sent after each *carriage return (0001100)*. This will normally only be used in association with a printer and is usually omitted. The default is *no LF*

K - already discussed under parameter D. Default value is *no checking*

L -this is the file number that BASIC will need with input and output statements so that it knows which file to associate with the port specified with parameter A. The value of m is any integer (or integer expression) within the maximum supported by the version of BASIC in use

M - to understand this parameter, you need to know how BASIC sends and receives characters. Imagine PCs A and B (Figure 7.5) are communicating. When A sends characters and B is switched on and receiving, characters are passed into the buffer (communications storage area) of B. If B is not receiving, then the characters fly off into the air and are lost to the receiver.

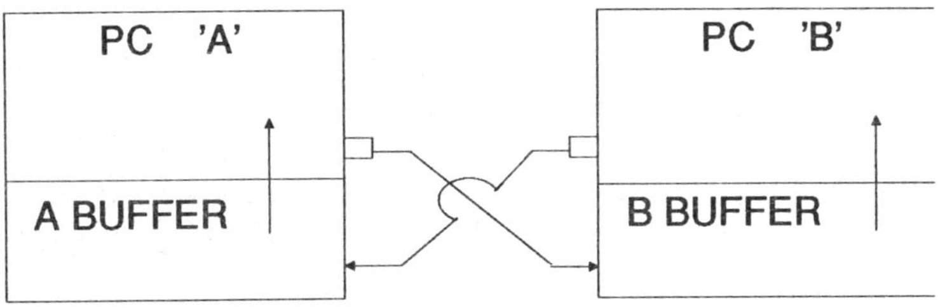

Figure 7.5 Data flow between PCs

Perhaps more difficult to appreciate is that the characters are removed from B's buffer **only when B reads them.** (Parameter M specifies the length of the buffer in characters, the default being 128.)

Pause for thought

It would take several chapters to discuss in detail, the problems of setting up comms programs in BASIC. It is hoped that you will try and work through the programs presented to give you a working knowledge. For now, we can cover a few general areas which will help you when and if you try to write your own program.

Time

Remember that the big difference between comms software and most other forms is that the sender **never knows what the proposed receiver is doing at any instant in time** (because a different program is running at each end). This is why we need layer 2 protocols.

Even if the connection to the receiver is good, and even if it has been established that the receiver is awake and ready to receive, there is still the question of whether he is capable of receiving the data as fast as the sender can transmit.

One way to get round this is always to use a positive acknowledgement approach and always making sure:

- the LEN option (ie, length of largest block to be sent) is specified in both programs
- that the first frame (representing *are you there and ready for me?*) is fairly small in comparison with the maximum
- frames are never sent until an acceptance of the previous one has been received.

Next, what about flow control? Suppose you have sent me a frame. I have received it and now go away and do some time-consuming processing such as reading disk records. Unless I have a multitasking computer (most PCs are not), I can't carry out application processing and at the same time request the transfer of data from my comms buffer - I may need to tell you to shut up for a while.

Unless a receiver is able to signal to a sender to stop transmitting, its buffer may overflow. The buffer is set up as a *FIFO (first-in, first-out queue)* which means that as the sender transmits bytes to the receiver's buffer, it may gradually fill up unless the receiving program takes bytes out. Figure 7.6 illustrates this concept, showing how the buffer fills and is emptied.

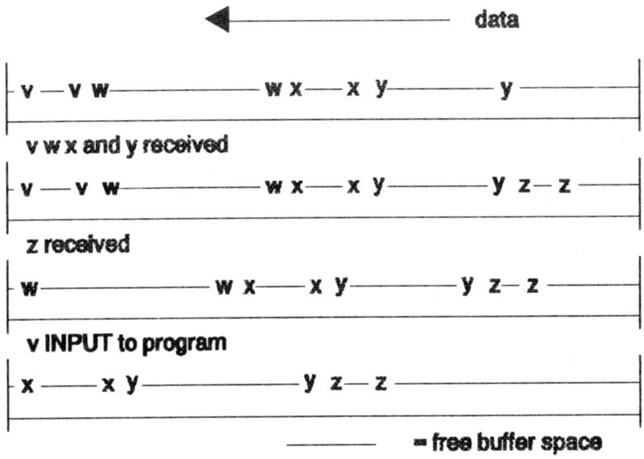

Figure 7.6 BASIC comms buffer usage

Data enters from the right and the receiver's program *INPUTs* or *READs* it from the left.

The buffer should be monitored to determine how full it is and there are two BASIC functions that allow this. *LOF(m)*, where m is the file number (see parameter *L* in the OPEN statement), returns the amount of space left in the buffer and *LOC(m)* returns the location in the buffer of the next byte to be read.

Perhaps the most useful application of these is to test for *LOC(m) = 0* which if true, means that the buffer is empty. If the buffer is getting full, you can then send *001011*, the ASCII for X-OFF with:

PRINT #m,CHR$(19)

When you are ready to receive, you send X-ON (*0010001*), with: PRINT #m ,CHR$(17).

Error handling

Device timeout and *device error* are the main error messages and what causes them and how you handle them is very much dependent on the version of BASIC and the machine you are using so we will not go into these, except to say that when an error occurs, it can be trapped with *ON ERROR*. It is usually possible to access a set of error flags that will give you an idea as to the cause.

Pause for thought

This not a book on communications programming, nor does it attempt to make you an expert in BASIC. The aim of this part of the chapter is to give you an insight into some of the problems of comms software development and prepare you for student assignments in the appendixes.

The approach is simply to show layer 2 thinking and for this purpose, the major simplifications made are:

- *idle RQ* (positive acknowledgement) will be used - the buffer should never overflow
- a null modem link is always used (to avoid having to worry about *CD* and *DS)*
- *RS* is always suppressed.

This means that the *OPEN COM* statement is of the form:
OPEN "COMn,B,C,D,E,PE" AS m# LEN='some convenient number'

Which end speaks first?

There is one practical problem to be pointed out, with a method for overcoming it. You will be writing two programs, one for the sender and one for the receiver. Assuming you have writen and tested the two programs and have two PCs available and connected, which program do you get going first? If the sender does not get a response to his initial frame, he will give up.

Conversely, the receiver will not know you are tying to make contact. Let us illustrate this with a simple example.

Suppose the sending PC program is acting for a user, wanting to contact a mainframe for say e-mail and the receiving PC is acting as the mainframe. In real life, the mainframe will be polling users all the time and cannot be expected to sit there waiting just for one user.

Your receiving program is not actually polling, because for simplicity it assumes just one user (the PC has only two ports anyway). Figure 7.7 indicates some logic (in pseudocode) for overcoming the problem.

Sending program

```
Set reply = none
While reply = none
  note: when mainframe replies, reply will no longer be none
  Send initial log-on frame
  Wait for a short while
End while
Continue with main logic eg,
display opening menu to user .....
```

Receiving program

```
While nothing in buffer
  Test if anything in buffer
  Wait for a short while
End while
Continue and eg,
check validity of user number .....
```

Figure 7.7 Initial log-on pseudocode

Using this logic, the sender will keep trying until an ackkowledgement is received and the 'mainframe' will keep listening until the sender logs on.

Starting a simple program

Anyone involved with programming, with any training at all will realise that writing a program does not mean poking fingers at keys and producing lines of BASIC code - you must **design** the program first. This means that you should work out what the program is to do and how it will do it **before** you start coding, so:

- select the options available to the user and design the dialogue
- decide on the basic protocol and what to do if a frame is not received or the return is garbled
- define the format of the data frames to be sent and received (see the ATM exam question in chapter 6)
- decide on the need for and the mechanism to be employed for flow control
- decide on the line profile.

Then you can do some BASIC.

The short program illustrated in Figure 7.8 should help you to see how BASIC can be applied. It logs on according to the logic of Figure 7.7 and then sends capital letters, randomly generated, until the mainframe tells it to stop.

```
01 REM Program to send bytes to a mainframe.
10 INPUT "PLEASE ENTER USER NUMBER";UN$
20 OPEN "COM1:9600,PE" AS #1
30 WHILE LOC(1) = 0
40   PRINT #1,UN$
50   INPUT "I AM TRYING";X$
51   REM The machine will wait for a keystroke/return key,
52   REM equivalent to a random wait, before trying again.
60 END WHILE
61 REM So the mainframe has now woken up.
62 REM
63 REM Note. We assume that the mainframe will not be busy
64 REM until after we have sent the first data frame.
65 REM
70 FRAMECOUNT = 0
80 XON$ = CHR$(17)
90 XOFF$ = CHR$(19)
97 REM**************************
```

```
98  REM Main logic starts here *
99  REM *************************
100  WHILE MAINFRAME$  "LOG OFF PLEASE"
101  REM We will keep sending data frames until the
102  REM mainframe gets fed up.
103  REM Mainframe sends "OK", "X-OFF", "X-ON" or
104  REM  "LOG OFF   PLEASE".
110  IF LOC(1) = 0 THEN 190
111  REM We must not send until we have dealt with what
112  the mainframe might have sent us.
113  REM
120  INPUT #1,MAINFRAME$
121  REM Find out what it has sent.
130  IF MAINFRAME$ = XON$ THEN 190
131  REM Mainframe is now free.
140  IF MAINFRAME$ = "LOG OFF PLEASE" GO TO 300
141  REM So, MAINFRAME$ = XOFF$,
142  REM showing that mainframe is busy
143  REM
150  WHILE LOC(1) = 0
160    INPUT "I AM WAITING";X$
161    REM Compare this with line 50.
170  END WHILE
171  REM
180  GO TO 120
190  LETTER = INT(26*RND) + 1
200  LETTER$ = CHR$(LETTER)
201  REM This logic randomly generates a letter
210  FRAMECOUNT = FRAMECOUNT + 1
220  PRINT #1,FRAMECOUNT,LETTER$
221  REM Now we must listen for the acknowledgement.
230  IF LOC(1) = 0 THEN GOSUB 400
231  REM We must decide how long to keep sending since
232  REM there is no reply.
240  IF REPLY$ = "GIVE UP" THEN GO TO 310
250  INPUT #1,MAINFRAME$
251  REM Get a byte from the mainframe.
260  IF MAINFRAME$ = XOFF$ THEN GOSUB 400
270  IF REPLY$ = "GIVE UP" THEN GO TO 310
```

```
280  INPUT #1,MAINFRAME$
290  END WHILE
291  REM**********************
292  REM End of main logic.*
293  REM**********************
300  GO TO 310
310   PRINT "RUN ABORTED"
320  CLOSE #1
330  PRINT "END OF SESSION"
340  GO TO 999
397  REM*****************************************
399  REM Subroutine to waste time and retry*
399  REM*****************************************
400  WHILE LOC(1) = 0
410    INPUT "FED UP, Y/N?"; REPLY$
420    IF REPLY$ = "Y" REPLY$ = "GIVE UP": GO TO 430
420  END WHILE
430  RETURN
998  REM
999  END
```

Figure 7.8 A sample BASIC comms program

The mainframe program is left to you as an exercise. Note that 'mainframe busy' will need to be forced - you could arrange perhaps that it sends X-OFF whenever it receives the letter Z. For simplicity, the sending program assumes that all data frames are acknowledged as received and correct. You might care to amend it so that the acknowledgement is *OK* or *BAD* (corresponding to *ACK* and *NACK*). If *BAD*, the program will have to re-send the frame.

Hayes commands

If you are talking to a Hayes modem, you send the commands as suggested in chapter 5, so to dial a number:

```
100  OPEN "COM1:............
200  INPUT "ENTER PHONE NUMBER ";NO$
210  INPUT "ENTER T FOR TONE P FOR PULSE";P$
220  PRINT #1,"AT";"D";P$;"9";NO$ .........
```

(Remember the 9 is to get an outside line from the switchboard if you have one.)

We will now say just a little about viewdata - how it is supplied and who provides the information will be covered in detail in chapter 10. For this chapter, we will only look at the special aspects of comms software aspects as it applies to viewdata.

Viewdata

Viewdata (or videotex as it is often called) is basically any on-line service that presents text in a particular stylised form. It is not just database acceess through a stylised screen though. Companies have adopted the screen format because it is familiar through Prestel and TV-based teletext services such as Ceefax and Oracle. The general viewdata format is used for many applications where menu selection is needed either for information/data access or for data entry.

The main characteristics of UK viewdata are:

- *CCITT V23 transmission* ie, send at 75 and receive it at 1200 baud
- *viewdata-unique file transfer protocols* such as that recommended by CEPT (the protocols are something like Y-modem)
- *secure printing*, in particular *STREAMA* and *CEPT*. These provide extra validation and error detection measures for the numeric data that is particularly important in business and financial applications (such as insurance quotations)
- *enhanced error handling* such as *VASSCOM* which at one level includes a checksum or CRC at the end of each block sent. Because of this block checking, you can see the data arrives on the screen in groups with short gaps in time between each, as the error-checking is done.

Pause for thought

A startling demonstration of enhanced error-handling was provided by JCC Ltd, while producing many of the VDU screens used in this book. As we were picking up a particular on-line viewdata screen, a telephone was plugged into the modem and we continually tapped the mouthpiece making some interference to simulate severe noise on the line.

All that happended was that blocks arrived *slightly more slowly on the screen* ie, with longer gaps in time. This very clearly showed the success of the error-handling procedure in an 'extremely hostile environment'.

Sophisticated package facilities

Many users will want access to a number of services and will make use of one or more of the many comms packages on the market such as Procomm, Kermit, Telix and Chit-Chat.

Others may in addition utilise the comms options provided with integrated packages such as Symphony and Smart. Figure 7.9 shows a comms profile screen from one of these packages.

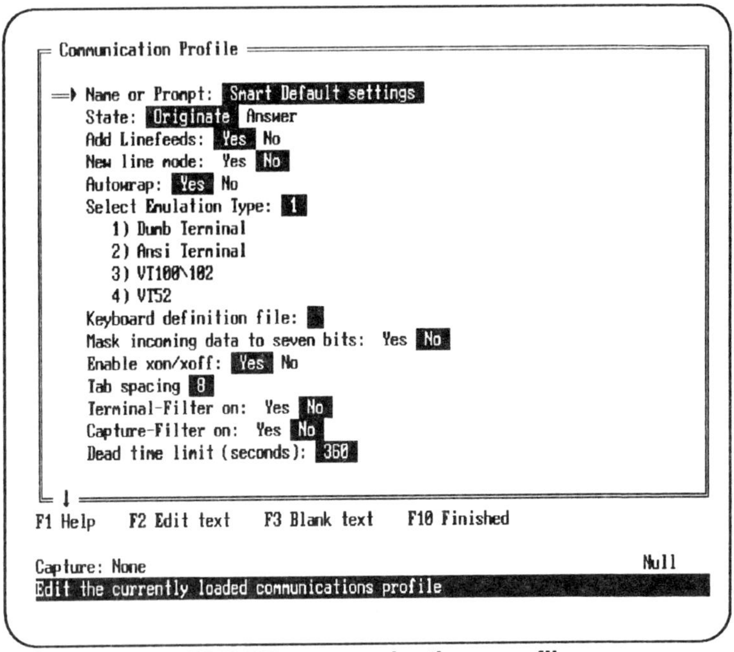

Figure 7.9 The SMART communications profile screen

All of these packages give options for profile selection and they allow for a wide range of modems, emulation of a range of terminals a wide range of file transfer protocols, directory dialling etc. (See the two packages discussed at the end of this chapter and the review of Tapestry in chapter 9).

But even more facilities may be wanted and the following is a selection of some of the facilities that the user can apply.

Screen capture

Having accessed an information/data service, it may be useful to be able to capture a screen, either as an image (in a form that can be passed into a DTP package) or as straight data (maybe for incorporation into a spreadsheet) at the choice of the user, perhaps from a mini-menu.

Library of different services

If the user is to access a range if services it is essential to be able to call them up with the minimum of effort and preferably just from a name or 'short code' option on the screen. Each entry in the library will include the hardware profile, phone number etc and once set up, the user will not have to bother every time he wants to access a particular service.

Help

Not everything is easy and not everyone is perfect. Many packages provide on-screen help, often as a pull-down menu. This help is often *context-sensitive* meaning that the 'helper knows where you are', so at any point, when you activate the *help* facility, it tells you what you are doing or what you have to do next.

An extension to this is the *help desk* - personal assistance provided by the software supplier (and sometimes by the modem supplier) at the other end of the phone, which you can get if you are in difficulties or if you want information.

(Note that these help facilities are not unique to comms software - most quality packages provide them these days.)

Point-of-sale facilities

Many companies, especially the larger ones, use their comms terminal with an eye to publicity and public relations. With this in mind, comms software suppliers may provide the possibility of adding your company logo to each screen sent, or customise it in other ways.

Another possibility is to collect screens and store them on disk for *carousel* display ie, scrolling through a library of screens and displaying them for general view. A choice of which screens are to be shown, forward or backward scroll and the speed with which they appear, are all possible (see Workmate below).

Forms design

Particularly when dealing with database access and transaction processing it is handy if the comms packages provides some applications support in providing customised forms design. This means that the user can set up screens appropriate to the data to be entered in the applications(s).

Page amendment

Having captured pages from various sources, the organisation may want to edit them, alter their format, add text or data and generally prepare them so that they can then be re-transmitted to members of the company or made available as part of a service to external users. Figure 7.10 shows a trivial example of what can be done!

Figure 7.10 A viewdata page 'suitably amended' (courtesey JCC Ltd)

This kind of facility could form part of the operation of a useful value-added service in which a company might collect data or information from several sources and then offer a 'news cutting' service to its customers.

(An application might be a college setting up a student service. It could collect information about student accomodation, welfare, local entertainment and so on, sort out all that was relevant, shuffle it together and make it available, on-line or in the form of a carousel in the student union office.)

Automation

The more sophisticated user will want to access a multiplicity of services but in addition, may want to set up a connected series of jobs that will run on their own. The following is an example of such a job stream:

- each hour, access database A and capture screen 01
- create an e-mail message containing screen 01 and send it to all the people in mailing list X
- run the data from screen 01 through a spreadsheet program and send the result to user 2 so that he can incorporate it into his spreadsheet
- collect the hourly replies from the message sent to mailing list A
- using a spreadsheet, analyse the day's replies and detect any trends
- store this result on a database
- send the results to the managing director.

To support this kind of multiple operation, the comms software must interact, under user control, with the various packages to be used and will also need to be sensitive to time because certain tasks may need to be delayed, carried out at regular intervals or at certain times of the day.

This facility may also be needed with e-mail where messages or groups of messages may need a delivery time attached to them, either because the sender wants to make use of cheap transmission rates, or perhaps just because of time-zone differences. (For an example of this, see Mass Breakout later.)

Miscellaneous features

Some final practical considerations. The software might need:

- to be able to run under different operating systems such as UNIX, MS-DOS, or different versions of a particular operating system

- have a LAN capability. Increasingly more users have terminals situated as part of a local area network (to be discussed in chapter 9) and it may be important to obtain comms software that can be built into the LAN and accessed from any user terminal
- interface with a range of hardware (eg, different PCs, VDUs, printers)
- provide a set of flexible security-access procedures. Many applications involve sensitive data and the software must allow users to build in passwords and other facilities to ensure only certain services can be accessed and only certain data accessed.

There are two comms packages in particular that will interest you. They have been selected because they are widely used, powerful and can illustrate many of the features that we have touched on. The first is designed to enable you to set up your PC so that it can act as a general communications centre and is called *Mass Breakout*. The other is particularly suited to collecting and setting up viewdata and is called *Workmate*.

Multi-function packages

Mass Breakout

Mass Breakout is the latest in a line of communications software produced by PC Communications Ltd., Elmsdale House, The Green, West Drayton, UB7 7PN.

It is distributed as an all-purpose comms package together with one of several recommended modems.

The package provides fully automated access to outside comms services with the use of function keys and menu selection for a particular service and by setting up what PC Communications call *script files*, which are files of commands, enabling the user to link several jobs together.

The package can support simultaneous access to several services - both COM ports and an internal modem can be used if required. Figure 7.11 is a banner (opening) screen which shows how the software has examined the hardware connections and 'knows' which modems it is connected to. Figure 7.12 shows the current hardware status of the computer in use. You can see the allocation of COM1 and COM2 corresponds to Figure 7.11. (The heading *Classic*, relates to the on-board modem, which in this case happens not to be assigned.)

Figure 7.11 Mass Break-out Banner screen

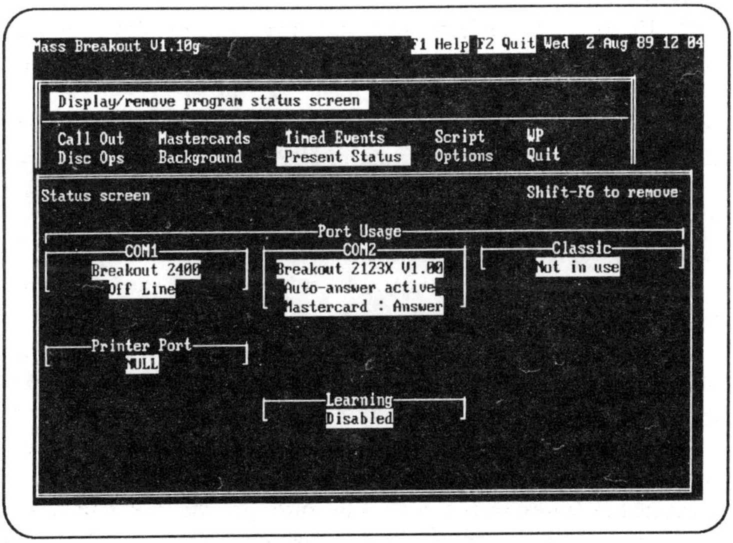

Figure 7.12 Mass Break-out 'present status' screen

The software has been designed to be multi-tasking which allows for simultaneous connection to two or three services, so, you can be sending data at the same time as you are receiving it.

Figure 7.13 show a Prestel page on the left and a BT Gold page on the right of the screen - two independent external connections. Figure 7.14 shows two services actually being dialled out at the same time.

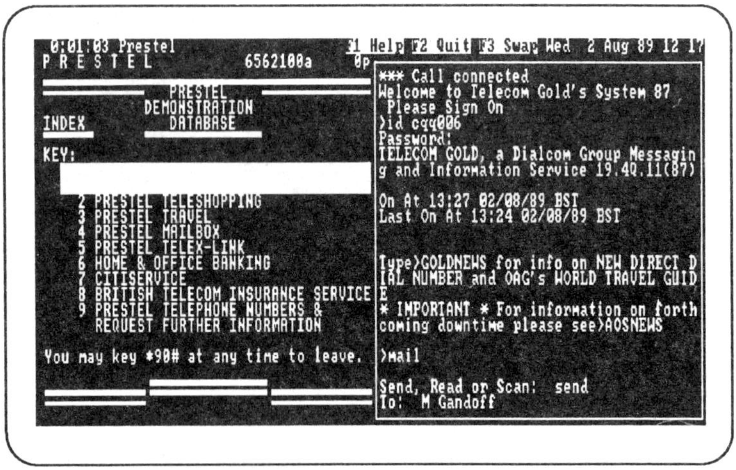

Figure 7.13 Mass Break-out simultaneous service display

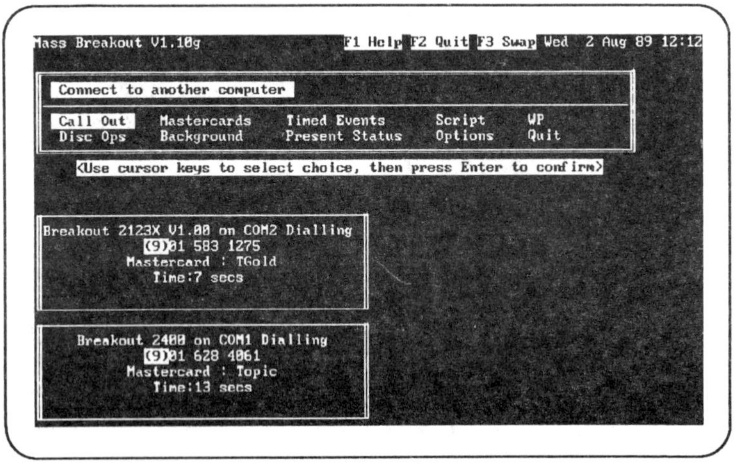

Figure 7.14 Mass-Break-out simultaneous connection

The transmission and connection profile for each service is set up with the aid of a neat 'form' referred to as a *mastercard*. Figure 7.15 shows a mastercard for a Prestel connection.

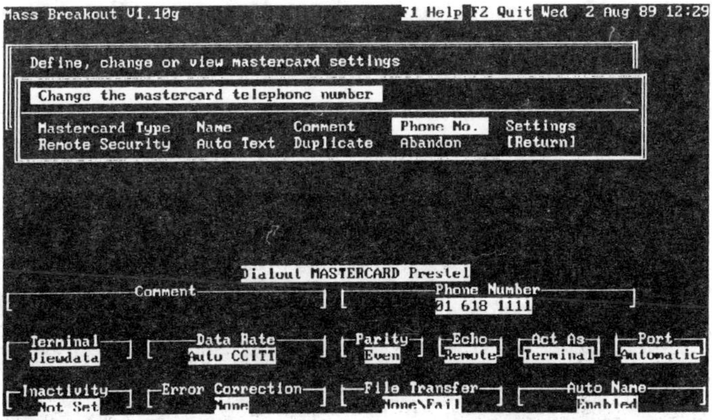

Figure 7.15 A Mass Break-out mastercard for Prestel

Figure 7.16 shows an interesting service we created, called *Lazy*. If you look at the top of this screen or the previous one, you will see that we are examining the mastercard through the *define, change or view mastercard settings* option and in Figure 7.15, we

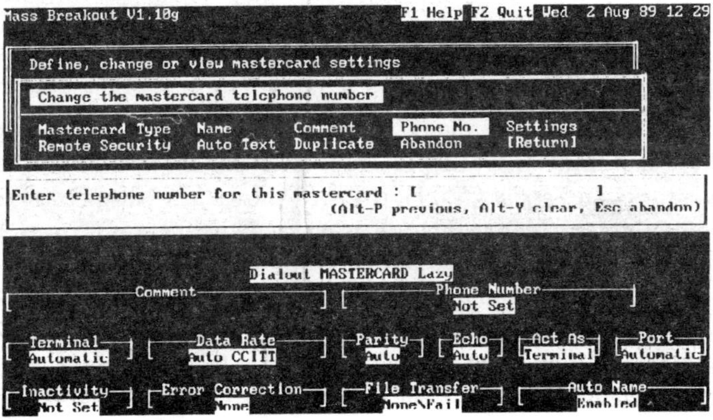

Figure 7.16 A Mass Break-out mastercard for a 'lazy' service

have just set the telephone number entry (the others, such as *terminal type* and *data rate* were done previously). In Figure 7.16, we are also setting the telephone number, **but nothing else**.

You may recall the advanced modem facilities outlined in chapter 5. Here, we are too lazy (hence the name of the service) to fill in the details and these will be left to the modems at each end to negotiate, when we dial in to the service - how lazy can you get?

Figure 7.17 shows the previous screen from which we selected the Lazy mastercard.

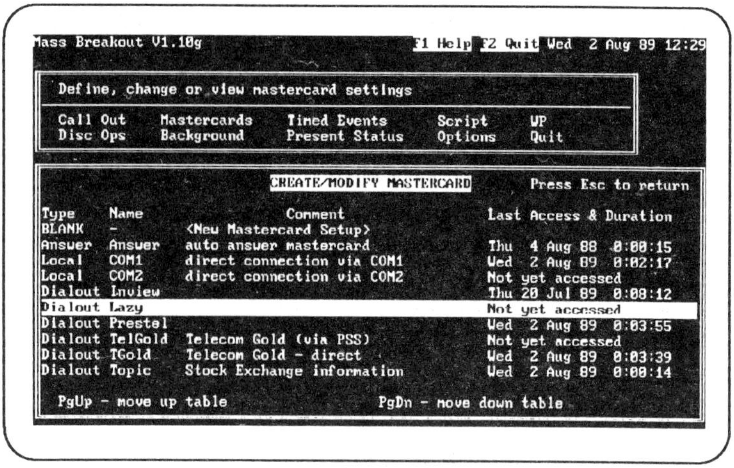

Figure 7.17 A Mass Break-out mastercard selection

The package has many user-friendly aspects. For example, there is a built-in word processor used for the creation of mail messages and *script files*. Figure 7.18 shows a small piece of text, deliberately chosen to include upper and lower case and currency characters. If you hit F3, the screen changes to that of Figure 7.19. - the difference being that the message has automatically been converted into telex format (all upper case, '£' converted to 'POUNDS' etc).

Very complicated log-on dialogues can be prepared (with the aid of the word processor) for automatic connection when needed. Figure 7.20 shows the setting up of a typical piece of dialogue

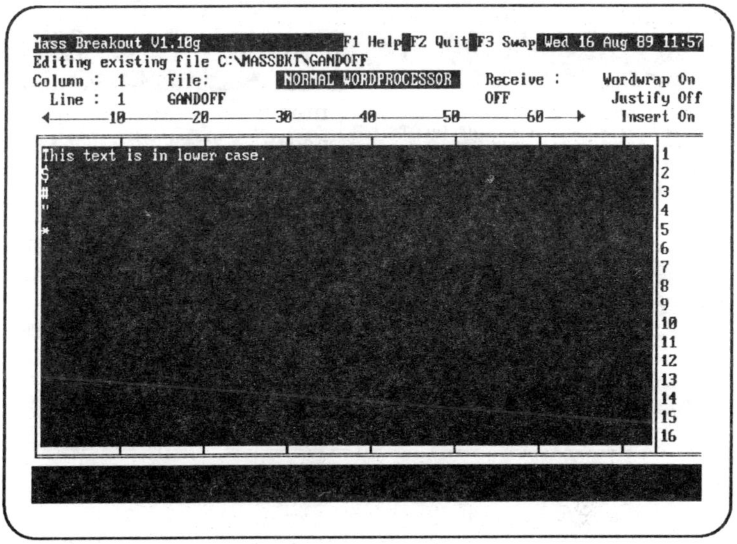

Figure 7.18 The Mass Break-out word processor

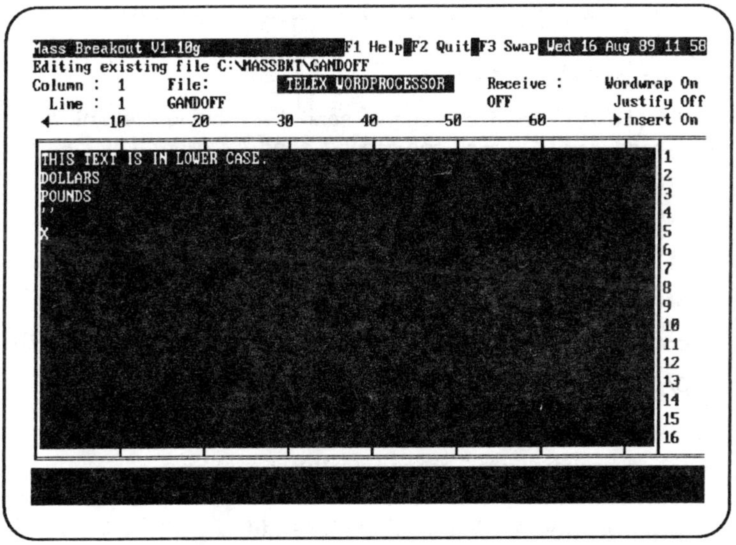

Figure 7.19 The Mass Break-out word processor in 'telex mode'

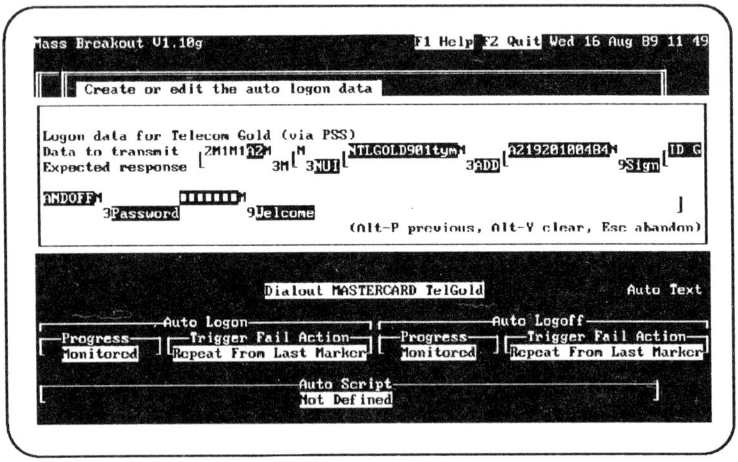

Figure 7.20 A log-in dialogue from Mass Break-out

associated with a connection to BT Gold through the BT PSS. Each line has two levels - the top part is what the terminal sends and the bottom is what it gets back from the remote service.

It wil be of value to go through the wording on the screen which represents the exchange of information one the modems at each end have made contact:

- 2M1M1A2M - wait 2 seconds, send *CR* (carriage return), wait 1 second, send *CR*, wait one second, send *A2* followed by *CR*. (PSS expects *A2* from a PSS user)
- 3M - wait for up to 3 seconds for *CR*
- M - when you get one, send another *CR*
- 3NUI - wait 3 seconds for the prompt *NUI*
- enter the company network user identity (chapter 8) followed by *CR*
- 3ADD - wait up to 3 seconds for the prompt *ADD*
- enter the *NUI* of the company you are trying to contact (and *CR*)
- 9Sign - wait for up to 9 seconds for the prompt *Sign*.

You should now be connected to BT Gold, so:

- enter your BT Gold account number

- 3Password - wait for up to 3 seconds for the prompt *Password*
- enter the password (note that it does not echo on the VDU)
- 9Welcome - wait up to 9 seconds for the Gold 'welcome'.

Now you do whatever you need from the main menu.

We have said several times *wait for up to* so many seconds. If you look at the bottom right of the screen (Figure 7.20) you will see that under *Auto Logon,* we have selected *Trigger Fail Action* as *Repeat From Last Marker.* This means that if the expected reply does not arrive within the specified time, go back a step and try again. If you look carefully, you will see that each marker is denoted by a [symbol. More complex possibilities for fail action could include disconnect, try 3 more times, go back to the beginning and so on.

Finally, in this quick round-up of the package, it is possible to automate the running of jobs by setting up a script file. The package has a language processor (something like BASIC), which enables you to set up a file of commands.

Earlier in the chapter, we looked at sophisticated package facilities; you may recall a reference to automation and this is exactly what Mass Breakout allows you to do. Figure 7.21 shows a small section of the programming needed to set up the log-in

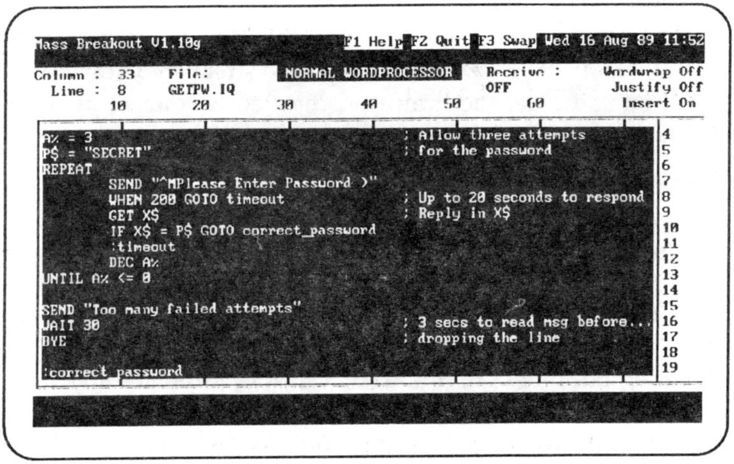

Figure 7.21 A Mass Break-out 'job stream'

dialogue of Figure 7-20. Using the language processor, it is perfectly possible to set up complete 'system runs'.

Finally, as an example of the potential of Mass Breakout, it is interesting to note that one of PC Communications's customers is a supermarket chain which runs a whole operation with the package. The procedure carried out might be something like this:

- during the day, warehouses issue and deliver stocks of goods required by shops in the chain. Details are entered through one or more PCs and stored in a file
- at the end of each day's business the warehouses transmit the daily file to head office. They also send e-mail requests, queries and recommendations
- overnight, the head office PC examines the warehouse daily files, carries out an estimate of what the next day's sales are likely to involve and sends back to each warehouse, details of what they are to order from suppliers
- the e-mail messages are sorted and grouped for delivery the next day to the various recipients so that appropriate action can be taken
- at the end of the week, analyses of goods issued and production bonuses are produced and sent to each warehouse.

This whole cycle is programmed in Mass Breakout for automatic operation.

The package has just one more facility that we must mention-its *learn* mode. If you want to set up a job stream, you can set the mode on and enter the commands needed to connect up to the relevant services. When you have finished, they can be saved as a jobstream for later use.

Workmate

Workmate is a package produced by John Clarke Computing, 5 Saturn House, Calleva Park, Aldermaston, Berks, RG7 4QW.

In many respects, it is quite different from Mass Breakout as a comms package. It is particularly geared to viewdata access and handling but like Mass Breakout, allows for the automation of external service access. The package contains in-built facilities to capture screens from external sources and modify then as required (see Figure 7-10).

It is possible to change background and foreground colours, add in or change features such as reverse and flashing. Special shapes can be built up and double-height or double-width characters produced. New screens can be created and all can be put together to form a carousel for display purposes. The carousel menu allow for the creation of up to 36 different carousel sets, each of which can contain up to 36 pages.

Figure 7.22 shows carousels 0 and X to Z already set up for demonstration and customer training. All the others are available for customer use.

```
No Carousel Name        No Carousel Name
0  STOREKEY.CAR         I  NOT USED
1  NOT USED             J  NOT USED
2  NOT USED             K  NOT USED
3  NOT USED             L  NOT USED
4  NOT USED             M  NOT USED
5  NOT USED             N  NOT USED
6  NOT USED             O  NOT USED
7  NOT USED             P  NOT USED
8  NOT USED             Q  NOT USED
9  NOT USED             R  NOT USED
A  NOT USED             S  NOT USED
B  NOT USED             T  NOT USED
C  NOT USED             U  NOT USED
D  NOT USED             V  NOT USED
E  NOT USED             W  NOT USED
F  NOT USED             X  PICTURES.CAR
G  NOT USED             Y  VIEWDATA.CAR
H  NOT USED             Z  WORKMATE.CAR
 (Press Tab to change file extension)
Select carousel to display
Press F4 for MAIN MENU.   Esc to exit
```

Figure 7.22 A Workmate carousel menu

Once a carousel has been selected, it will run, displaying each page in turn, with an inter-page delay of 0 to 99 seconds. At any time during the display, the cycle can be stopped and you can back- or forward-space through the pages.

This kind of display has obvious advantages for marketing and public relations, for example, many organisations place a viewdata terminal in the front office with a carousel of pages showing the company services and products. Another possibility is to make use of a carousel for training - the user being able to stop the carousel and go back to review an earlier page.

Workmate contains a very powerful facility to create forms for the entry of data to send to a service and to capture data from a service. The details are too involved for this brief overview, but if you look at the mortgage quotation in Figure 10.7, you will see the screen is in a user-friendly form in which the user can enter data that is sent off as the basis for the required mortgage quotation.

Workmate features are accessed from the main menu as shown in Figure 7.23..

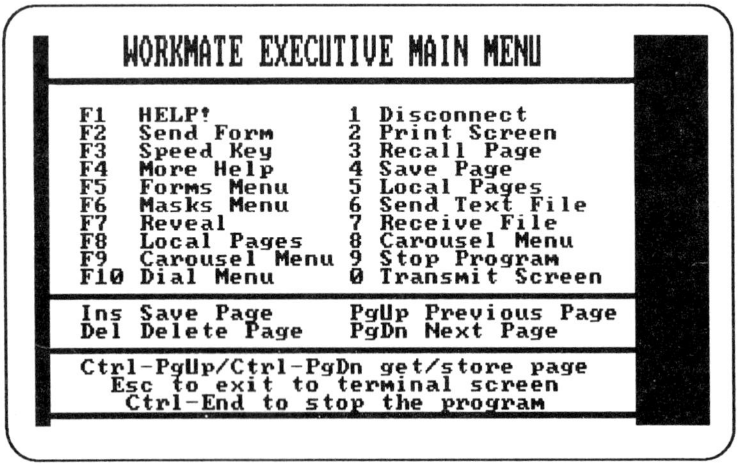

Figure 7.23 Workmate main menu

To make life easier, the package makes extensive use of the function keys and expands their use by the combination of any function key with the *ALT, CTL* or shift keys. This allows for 40 different combinations (which can be set to whatever you want) as shown in Figure 7.24.

Particular commands and sets of command can be initiated by key combinations that JCC call *speed keys.* Figure 7.25 shows a menu of speed keys set up by a particular user. Any combination can be selected to customise the initiation of a particular operation, but note that some combinations are standard in use. The menu shows **90# as the signal to end a PRESTEL session, but if you look at Figure 10.2 for example, you will see that Pestel specifies this combination as end-session anyway.*

The profile for a particular service is set up (see Figure 7.26 for a Prestel example) and then filed.

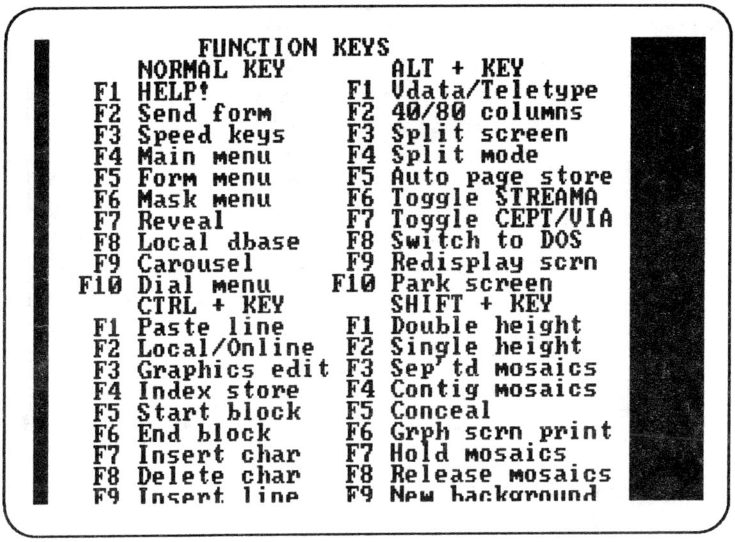

Figure 7.24 Workmate function key possibilities

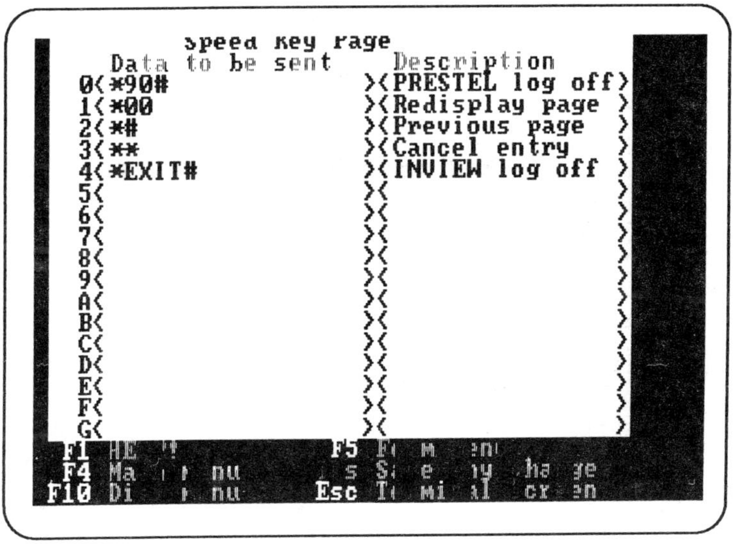

Figure 7.25 Workmate 'speed keys'

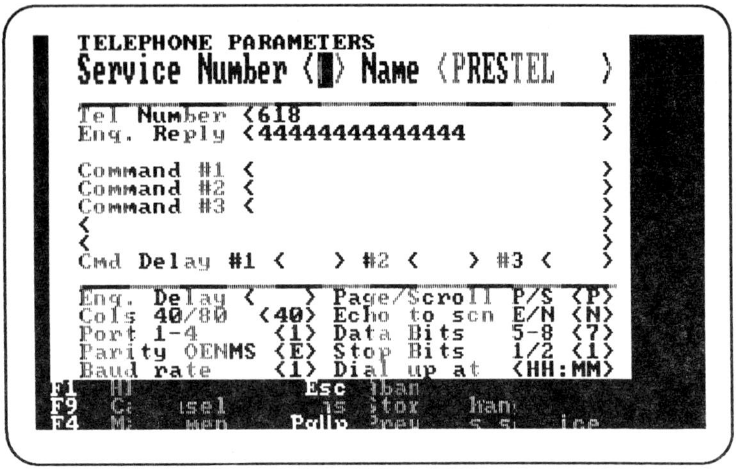

Figure 7.26 A Prestel dial-out profile

At any time, the autodial menu (Figure 7.27) can be accessed and a service profile selected for automatic dial out. Each of the services shown in Figure 7.27 corresponds to an external provider and many of the screens shown throughout this book were initiated from this particular menu.

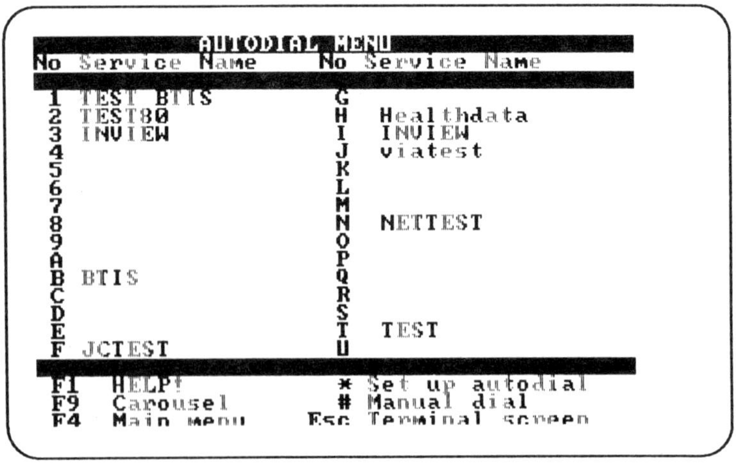

Figure 7.27 The autodial menu

To show you that there is more to the package than just a set of user-friendly screens, let us have a quick look at two screens that indicate some of the more technical aspects.

Figure 7.28 shows the list of pre-determined parameter file configurations that enable Workmate and its facilities to be set up for a particular installation. Figure 7.29 shows one of these - the *line control parameters* specification.

```
VIEWCONF - parameter file configuration   Version 6.10     1st March 1989

                Main menu                    Controls on Next Screens

0 - Quit without saving any changes       Home   - First Field
1 - Line Control Parameters               Left   - Previous Field
2 - Modem Parameters                      Right  - Next Field
3 - Printer Parameters (1)                Enter  - Next Field
4 - Printer Parameters (2)
5 - Screen Handling Parameters
6 - Miscellaneous Parameters              Up     - Previous Option
7 - Message Colours on System Screens     Down   - Next Option
8 - Screen and Mask Parameters
9 - Split Scn/SAA/Local DB parameters     PgUp   - Previous Line
A - Main Menu Key Configuration (1)       PgDn   - Next Line
B - Function  Key Configuration (2)
C - Function  Key Configuration (3)       Insert- Write Modem Or Printer
D - Special   Key Configuration (4)       Esc    - Return to this Menu

S - Save values to disc and terminate     Q - Quit without saving changes

Please enter your choice (0-9, A-D, S or Q) :
```

Figure 7.28 Parameter file configuration

```
1. Line Control Parameters
Character Description                  7 data bits    1 stop bit      Even parity
Receive and Transmit baud rates        Receive: 1200  Transmit: 1200  Full
Split speed indicator                  Same speeds for transmit and receive
Split speed delay factors              004     048     100
Suppress LF after CR when sending      No
Keyboard inactivity timeout (secs)     100 until warning, 015 until disconnect
End of program modem ctrl register     Use the following byte      00
Communications port and driver         Port:COM1       Driver:RS232
Inter-character delay (Ms)             Normal:000      Sending:032
Turnaround delays                      Send/Recv:000   Recv/Send:000
Send give-up time (factor)             Cant Send:016   Bad Chars:Throw away
Delay after sending special chars      Wait 000 ms after 00    , 00      or 00
NETBIOS send/recv timers & address     010 000 1234567890123456 Add adaptor no

NETBIOS Disc        001 FF 00 00 00 00 00 00 00 00 00 00 00 00 00 00 00 00 00 00 00
                        Dly

The character length may be 5,6,7 or 8 bits.
7 bits is normal for VIEWDATA and TELECOM GOLD.
```

Figure 7.29 Line control parameters

Look carefully at some of these settings - they will help you to revise some of your chapter 5 knowledge. In particular:

- the baud rate settings
- the port specification
- the keyboard inactivity setting - a warning that you have been idle for over 3 minutes and connection will be logged off after a further 15 seconds
- the delay between characters on send and receive.

In conclusion, just one screen to remind you of the Hayes AT commands. In Figure 7.30, Workmate has kindly displayed the Hayes dial command as it is executing it.

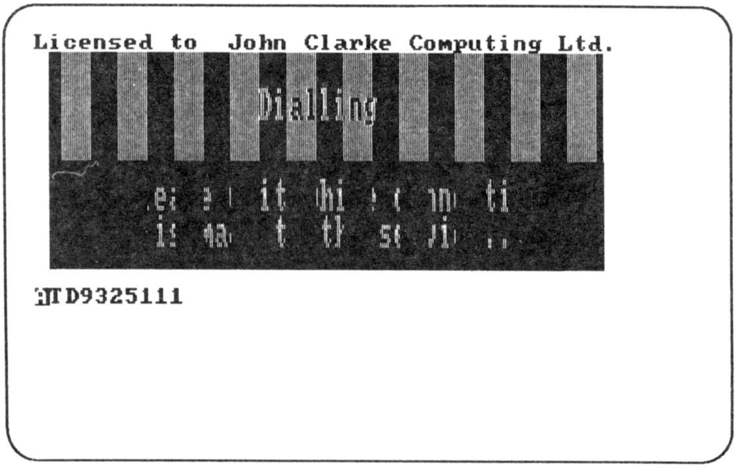

Figure 7.30 A Hayes command in action

Recap

- The chapter shows you why comms software is needed and who makes use of it. Several kinds of service are considered which you will meet again in chapters 9 and 10

- the communications profile is considered together with all the parameters that must be specified so that the user's PC comms software can instruct his modem to talk intelligably to the modem at the other end
- BASIC is discussed together with a introductory description as to how it can be used for special-purpose comms programming (as an opportunity to revise knowledge of the V24/RS232 interface and demonstrating error control and flow control in practice)
- some special considerations that apply when we want to access viewdata- based services are discussed, particularly the extra error-reduction techniques that are not avaialble waith other services
- comms software is considered from the sophisticated user's point of view and a range of possibilities which can help the user to support a DP or business application are introduced
- two PC-based general-purpose comms packages are introduced, both of which demonstrate just how much support a user can get to help in the use and application of comms services and facilities. This also gave an opportunity to show a wide range of VDU screens.

Typical questions

Question 7.1

A PC with a modem attached, has been switched on and is ready to execute a program. Discuss the functions of all the software that would be needed on the PC for a user to be able to send electronic mail to another user

Question 7.2

a. why is terminal emulation software needed?
b. explain briefly what actually happens when a comms port is OPENed
c. what is meant by 'log-on' dialogue? Suggest the dialogue that might apply to a computer conferencing facility and explain the questions and answers at each stage

Question 7.3

The student union of a college has been given the opportunity to make use of a PC for displaying a carousel of information that could be of interest to students in general.

a. make recommendations as to the kind of screens that might be shown
b. where would the data to make up the screens come from?

8: Networks and OSI layer 3

Objectives

After reading this chapter, you should:

- appreciate the significance of the digital data network
- be aware of the main aspects of packet switching
- have an understanding of X25 and other X series recommendations
- be aware of different connection mechanisms applied in data networks
- appreciate connection between dissimilar networks
- understand methods of network routing
- appreciate the need for network management and control
- be aware of some national and international data networks
- appreciate the need for 'value-added' services from a network
- appreciate the significance of ISDN.

Introduction

Chapters 2, 4, 5 and 6 should have given you a good understanding of OSI layers 1 and 2. They have also introduced several concepts relating to networks. Now we must look in more detail at the problems of running and managing a network and some of the protocols involved.

I had originally intended to call this chapter 'OSI layer 3' and spend a fair amount of time dealing with protocols, but after a lot of thought, I now feel that at the level of your present study, it is much more important for you to appreciate what happens in the network rather than how it happens.

We will obviously have to go into some techniques and we must say something about X25 and layer 3 protocols, but you will find that most of this chapter is concerned with network functions, how we try to ensure that the network performs according to our requirements and examples of networks in use.

Objectives of layer 3

What should a network do

As you know, a network is a complex of terminals, switching centres, processing centres and connection media.

Standards, protocols and the whole philosophy of networking are geared to:

- optimising network performance and supplying a guaranteed minimum quality of service
- minimising delay in the handling of network traffic
- maximising throughput
- handling exceptional conditions and peaks
- providing preferential transfer when needed
- selecting the best route (path) for a message
- providing a high degree of standardisation
- providing mechanisms for connecting similar networks
- providing mechanisms for connecting different networks
- providing a full range of mechanisms for monitoring and controlling the performance of a network and adapting network functions to meet current conditions
- collecting network performance information and statistics so that improvements and expansion can be facilitated.

These objectives apply irrespective of the physical structure of the network and its geographical spread. We will be mainly looking at the public data WAN, a data network standardised for public use and conforming to X25. What does the network link?

By definition, this kind of network will be a mesh (Figure 8.1) - a multiply-connected mix of any of the following:

- character terminals individually connected
- packet terminals individually connected

- terminal clusters linked via a controller
- user-owned DP minis and mainframes to which terminals and clusters are attached or linked
- externally-provided minis and mainframes (which supply DP and other services)
- network protocol converters (that can bring non-standard data into X25 format)
- switching/routing nodes (exchanges)
- concentrators for bulking messages for deferred and/or higher speed transmission as required
- network management/control computers
- other networks, especially privately-owned X25 networks
- other private networks that are not X25-conforming.

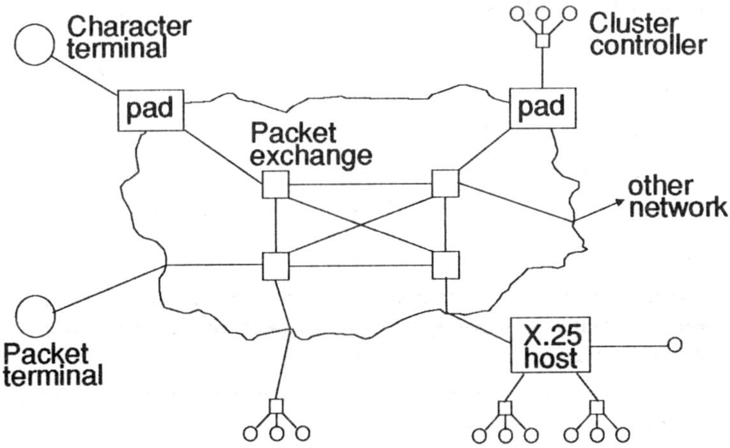

Figure 8.1 A mesh network

The data network

Why not analogue

The PTN is (or at least was) a voice network, designed for analogue transmission via point-to-point and continuous connection. For voice, it provides exactly what is wanted but it has serious disadvantages for the analogue transmission of data:

- a physical link must be maintained throughout the conversation (part wire, part optical fibre, part microwave). During gaps in transmission, the resources providing the link are not used and its transmission capacity is wasted
- the network cannot give priority to urgent messages, which may result in unacceptable delays
- because the data is represented in analogue form, it cannot easily be managed and controlled with digital computers
- modems are needed to enable 1/0s to be transmitted
- because of the low quality of the weakest links within the PTN, a speed currently of about 220 characters per second is the maximum the PTN can handle
- a wide range of level 2 protocols are in use and there is little incentive for standardisation in an analogue network.

In the light of these, it is not surprising that the demand for services based on digital networks is growing. Note however that there are two counter-opposing developments. On the one hand, advances in modem technology mentioned in chapter 5 mean higher transmission rates from the analogue network.

On the other, digital technology is leaping ahead for voice and data partly because of the convenience of its standardisation and partly because of increased transmission rates.

A few questions answered

- a digital network is one that handles digits. So why is it different from an analogue network - surely this handles 0s and 1s too?

Yes, but in analogue form. In a digital network, data and voice are carried as a series of electrical pulses without the need for modulation. As we saw in chapter 5, voice can be digitised by sampling or by other means, so that it is also in the form of pulses.

- are there any advantages apart from the removal of the need for modems?

Yes, in particular the greatly increased security and data transmission speeds that come from using digital transmission and much better quality network hardware.

- how does the network actually handle voice and data in such a way that computers can manage them?

Data is *packetised.* In other words, DP data streams and digitised voice, are grouped and/or broken up into convenient units called *packets* (analogous to blocks or frames in layer 2), transported across the network and then reassembled in order, at an exit point. In fact a digital network is more often referred to as a *packet network.*

The actual size of the packet will vary according to the conditions that apply when the request to carry the message arrives.

If you refer back to chapter 5, to the section dealing with advanced modem facilities, we looked there at how and why a sophisticated modem adapts to network noise and selects the appropriate size for a frame. This balances the advantages of a large frame against the possible disadvantages of having to retransmit a large one if there is a failure. The digital data network does the same thing.

- how does the network resolve the problem of differing level 2 protocol standards?

X25 (coming up next), which all public and many private networks conform to, supports the use of HDLC. Hence it can accept input from asynchronous terminals and those generating data streams in a variety of level 2 protocol formats. All of these can then be packetised, the user is not aware of this and the end-to-end level 2 framing is maintained (refer to chapter 6).

If you look at the literature relating to wide-area networks, you will meet X25 (we have already introduced it in chapter 5) and we must look at it now, partly because it is relevant to networking, in particular packet-switching and partly because it resembles OSI layers 1 to 3.

X25

X25 is the CCITT recommendation for a **DTE-DCE interface in packet mode for operation on a public data network** and it predated OSI by several years.

DTE here means any 'terminal' (which is at **this** end of the link) that can act according to X25. DCE can be taken to mean *Packet-Switching Exchange (PSE),* the exchange that handles connection and routing in a PDN.

X25 has three component levels: *physical, link* and *packet*, corresponding roughly with OSI layers 1 to 3. It is only concerned with these layers - the network is there to deliver messages - anything to do with what the messages are part of, or how the user generates or uses them, are handled in higher layers of OSI.

X25 physical level

This provides the physical link (as discussed in chapter 5 under 'sophisticated interfaces') by utilising X21 for digital users and X21bis for RS232 (analogue) connection.

X25 link level

This makes use of HDLC ABM (see chapter 6) generally known as *LAP-B* (*link access procedure balanced*), or HDLC ARM known as just *LAP*.

The function of this level is to carry out error checking and request retransmissions.

X25 packet level

The protocol makes use of the control and data packets referred to already. We will go into these in slightly more detail:

- Control packet - the major contents of this packet are as follows:

  general format indicator (4 bits)

  logical channel group (4 bits) /logical channel (8 bits)

  These allow for multiple connections from one terminal along the same physical link and are used to specify the required 'logical' channels.

  The group item allows for 16 different groups and the logical channel gives 256 logical channels, so in theory a single X25 connection can handle 4096 logical channels (ie, 4096 separate conversations).

  packet type (8 bits) - such as *call request, call connected,reject, calling address/called address* (see X121 below), *facilities* - variables needed to negotiate and set up the facility during connection (e.g. the maximum packet size that can be sent).

  A packet switched network can act as a *value-added network (VAN)*. We will discuss this later, but in particular, the 'facilities' field allows for functions and activities such as *reverse charging, fast select (minicall)* and *national option markers* - facilities specific to a particular country that are not part of X25 Also, note that there is a command type *expedite,* which introduces another aspect of the network - the possibility of prioritising a user message. X25 allows for data to jump the queue through the network, possibly against the normal flow of packets at the time.

user data - holds data for minicalls (up to 128 bytes long)

- data packet - a 16 bit top end similar to the control packet and a part for data (generally up to 128 bytes long: larger units up to 1024 can be negotiated - see 'facilities' above)

  The third byte contains;

  packet received acknowledgement number (window up to 8)

  more bit which specifies that the data in the packet is part of a larger string.

  packet sending sequence number (window up to 8)

  packet type identifier which is a 0 for data packets.

Associated with X25 there are three other X series recommendations X.3, X.28 and X.29 which are often referred to under the combined name of *Triple-X.*

Other X series recommendations

X.3

This recommendation provides the guidelines for communicating with a PAD and relates to how the PAD should operate. In effect, we are able to 'program' the PAD so that it can communicate with a particular terminal and the parameters passed to the PAD specify what we want. Similarly, the terminal knows what the sending PAD is talking about.

There are 22 possible parameters, some of them being:

- echo (parameter 2) - specifies whether the PAD sends back each character (remember echo-checking) as it transfers it to the receiver
- echo mask (parameter 20) - if parameter has been set 'on', the mask allows you to select which characters will be echoed. For example, you may not want to see carriage return/line feed, ACK or NAK
- data forwarding signal (parameter 3) - allows selection of the signal that informs the PAD you have finished sending a particular block of data and want it forwarded
- line speed (parameter 11) - tells the PAD the bit rate that the terminal can handle
- flow control (parameter 12) - determines whether X-ON/X-OFF will be applied
- character delete (parameter 16) - how to define the 'rubout' control character ie, 'ignore previous character'

- line delete (parameter 17) - the line 'rubout' character.

  (Note that the 'echo mask' - parameter - could be set to avoid either of these rubout characters being echoed.)

To make life easier, the user of a public data network will often be provided with a choice from a list of parameter groups that cover all the likely combinations. In this way, a PAD can be 'reprogrammed' quite easily with a simple two-character code.

Pause for thought

As we have said before, although technically a PAD only provides a linkage between a character terminal and the PDN, some PADs are adapted to accept particular terminals and protocols, such as IBM. Also BT and MCL allow for special input for viewdata, credit transfer and so on (see VPAD, TPAD etc below).

X28

This describes the exchange of control information between character terminal and PAD (note that a PAD can support 8, 16 or 24 asynchronous terminals).

X29

This relates to the exchange of control information between a packet terminal (or a packet host) and a PAD (and between PADs).

Two further X series protocols are worth mention.

X75

This describes the signalling necessary to enable PDNs to inter-communicate.

X121

This is the basis for identifying users in a network or when connecting networks. It defines a 12-digit *network user address (NUA)* which may have two further digits. The first four digits specify the network, being referred to as the *data network identification code (DNIC)*: the first three digits are the network national code and the other digit is for the network supplier. The remainder of the NUA defines the exact location of the receiver. For example, 234 is the UK and 2341 is BTs IPSS,2342 is BTs PSS.

310/311 are the USA; 3106 is Tymnet and 3110 is Telenet. (Figure 8.2 shows the elements of the NUA.)

Digits	*Significance*	
1-3	Country	
4	Network	
5-7	Local area	} DNIC
8-12	Local number	
13-14	Optional sub-address	

Figure 8.2 Network User Address under X.121

You can usefully refer back to Figures. 7.20 and 7.21 which show an external service being contacted via the PSS.

Now let us look at the idea of handling data packets. Bear in mind though, that digital networks are not necessarily packet-switched. LANs for example, usually employ digital transmission but they do not follow the same protocols or packet format used in public data networks.

Packet switching

Why packet switching

The transfer of packets by switching them around through the most 'appropriate' route, is fundamental to most digital networks so, why don't the terminals and host computers connected to the network all generate and transfer packets of the same form and size as those used within the network? Of course they do, if they are specifically designed to be X25-compatible.

However:

- DP applications for host computers (and PC-type terminals) often involve large data blocks - typically based on sections of disk storage, such as one sector or track of disk, or even based on memory (RAM) blocks, such as 64K. This is particularly so when dealing with file transfer or the transfer of large quantities of data (such as sending documents by means of EDI)
- character terminals are usually used for comms because the hardware and software available to drive them is simple, reliable and cheap.

However, they are usually geared to asynchronous character transmission, not the handling of synchronous packets.

X25 is designed to standardise the synchronous transfer of packets of data whether character, binary or anything else. (As you know from chapter 6, protocols and appropriate frames can be applied to overcome some of the problems of character transmission, different applications leading to different protocols, each in themselves standard but often widely differing in content and mechanism.)

What can a packet network do

In general, a packet-switched network will:

- employ open system interconnectivity in its design and construction
- handle digital transmission
- provide pre-defined or pre-agreed levels of service
- be fast and relatively error-free
- be fully compatible with other packet networks, private and national and international
- be able to accept analogue transmission at special input 'ports'
- be very adaptive to unusual conditions
- provide the network supplier and the network users with full reporting of usage and charges to be made to users.

Data is packetised, either at source (packet-terminal or X25 host computer), at an input port (gateway) or perhaps at a gateway exit to another network and each packet must be suitably tagged with source and destination.

Because the network is highly adaptive, it can determine the most useful route for the packets and the most convenient size in which to form them. It will then transfer (convey) the packets from node to node until they reach the node nearest to the 'exit'. There, they will be sorted back into their original sequence and passed out of the network.

Pause for thought

Why do packets get out of sequence?

If you can answer this, you are well on the way to understanding how a packet network operates. An example of some typical processing may help you here:

- a user message consisting of 100 characters is passed to a network node, say node V
- the message might be chopped up into ten 10-byte packets, the first three going into a 50 byte buffer that node V maintains
- they fill the buffer because 2 messages from other users (or even the same user) have already been loaded into it
- the buffer contents are then passed to node W and V starts filling up the buffer again
- shortly afterwards, node V fills up its buffer yet again and sends it on, this time to node X (because node W is busy)
- node X quickly deals with the packets and passes them on down the line
- while this is going on, node W hits trouble and has to request a retransmission from node V
- by the time it has sorted out the problem, packets entered into the network later have reached their destination node, which has to hold them until the 'earlier' ones arrive.

Unless the original packets are given sequence numbers when created, the final node will not be able to put them back into order for delivery to the receiver.

Main packet network functions

The example just discussed was chosen deliberately to introduce many network functions:

- *routing* - as you can see, a node has to decide which is the next node to pass packets onto
- *packet formation/assembly/disassembly* - the receiving node must form up (assemble) packets from characters (which might be received

in a number of frame formats - single characters, viewdata frames, BSC etc). Having sequenced them, it sends them on.

A later node may be operating under very different conditions and it may need to change the size of the packets being handled before it passes them on.

The 'final' node, after sorting out the original sequence, will need to recreate (disassemble) the data into the form in which it was passed in

- *buffering* at a node - as the node is in effect, a computer, it does not seem reasonable for it to handle single packets as far as transfer is concerned and it will need storage space to bulk them up. It also needs buffer space to hold packets waiting for another node to become free
- *packet confirmation/rejection* - just because we are involved with layer 3, layer 2 aspects do not disappear (remember the OSI model only separates the layers for humans to examine - it does not isolate the operations that are carried out).

We still need to:

- ensure that a call can be set up, shut down and continued
- carry out error detection (such as CRC)
- employ a form of RQ.

For all of these, X25 makes use of continuous (and obviously duplex) RQ based on HDLC under LAP or LAPB (see chapter 6).

Network connection services and mechanisms

Two basic techniques, called *services,* are made use of in packet networks for the delivery of messages. They are called *connection-oriented* and *connectionless* services.

Connection-oriented service

For the duration of the connection and the whole ensuing conversation, a logical route through the network is assumed to exist - not necessarily a physical one such as is the case with a LAN.

For a connection-oriented service, this logical route is called a *virtual circuit (VC).* There is no fixed physical route - the network decides on the best way to send the packets. For a conversation to proceed, it selects and sets up the necessary VC and closes it down once the call has finished. (Note that the word 'virtual' in this context means 'of theoretical existence' not as it is used in conversation to mean 'almost'.)

Establishing the VC takes a certain amount of time but once established, data will flow until the conversation is over without the need to keep setting it up. In effect, once the VC has been set up and given a circuit identity, data can be passed into and through the network. You will recall from chapter 2 that HDLC makes use of control and data frames.

A control packet will contain among other items:

- the channel identity
- the packet objective or 'command type' e.g. 'set up call' or 'expedite'
- the sending and receiving addresses
- a 128 byte 'user area'.

A data packet contains among other items:

- the data to be sent
- the channel identity
- a sequence number.

A conversation proceeds as follows:

- start-up - a *call request* command (control) packet is entered and passed to the other end as an *incoming call.* If acceptable, the receiver replies with a *call accepted* control packet, the system establishes the virtual circuit and conversation can start
- data transfer - the sender will transmit a data packet containing the VC identity and the data to be sent
- once finished - either end can initiate a *clear request* packet to end the call which will be answered with a *clear confirmation* packet which results in the close-down of the VC.

In order to be of any use to the user, this service must provide some guaranteed probability of delivery, with data arriving in the same sequence as sent and with a guaranteed minimum level of error.

Note that when the call has been made with a control packet, subsequent data packets **do not need to include the sender or**

receiver address because the group and channel are defined during call set-up.

The virtual circuit is intended for connections where the data volume although larger than might be expected via the PTN, is nevertheless, random in nature. Its proper name is a *switched virtual circuit*. The situation here is very similar to the choice between dial-up and leased line access to the PTN; a *permanent virtual circuit* may be employed when a regular need for connection between ends makes the permanent connection worthwhile.

Connectionless service

This is very different from a connection-oriented service. In effect, a lump of data called a *datagram* is passed into the network for it to deal with as it can.

Pause for thought

A datagram service is more like a postal service than a telephone service - it does not require the use of a virtual circuit so one does not need to be set up or closed down. It is much like sending a letter - the envelope is addressed and the letter is placed in the postbox. The GPO routes the letter by van, train, plane or whatever and eventually delivers it to the addressee.

Compare this with a telephone call - you dial out, make the connection and then talk until you have finished.

This is obviously of use when we are sending short bursts of data such as arrive from an asynchronous terminal - lines of text or business transactions.

How a datagram is sent

X25 allows for datagrams with a special format in which the data to be sent (provided it is short enough - usually not more than 128 bytes), can be included in the control frame that is used for call set-up with a connection- oriented service. In other words, we use the user area item in the control packet (see earlier), rather than having to send a control packet and perhaps one data packet.

Note that this use of the control packet for data is called *fast select* in CCITT terminology and a *minicall* by BT.

The service level provided for a datagram is lower than for a virtual circuit and in times of very heavy traffic, the network may even abandon a particular datagram. There is no guaranteed delivery and if the receiver does not confirm receipt, you just have to send it again.

In addition, there is no guaranteed minimum error level and even worse, the sequence cannot be guaranteed, partly because one chunk may be lost altogether and partly because packets may go along different routes and get 'desequenced'.

Once we start dealing with more continuous transmission, such as with file transfer, or the sending of bulked (concentrated) business transactions, it does not make sense to have to send a set-up frame with data attached each time we have a message to go.

Why use a datagram service

When the whole chunk of data to be sent at any one time is quite small, failure to deliver is not vital but short delivery time is a major concern and there are times when we need to save the set-up time in order to get a very short message across the network quickly. This particularly applies in process control applications - if the system detects a severe problem and sends an urgent message, if it doesn't get there very fast, it might as well not get there at all - the result is still disaster.

When we link into a network, or link one network to another, we must accept that different protocols will apply and compatibility will be a big issue. We must allow for this when we set up a general-purpose network.

Internetworking

The main problem is the many different kinds of network and network user.

For example, we might want to link:

- a character terminal via the PTN through a PAD
- an X25 (packet) terminal via its terminator
- a character terminal to an X25 host

- a group of character terminals via their X25 host computer
- a LAN into a larger LAN
- two similar public WANs
- a private WAN to a public WAN
- two similar LANs
- a LAN to a WAN (very difficult usually).

There will be the need for some kind of interfacing mechanism which can resolve the differences that may arise and in the next section, we look at the various hardware techniques that accomplish this.

Network protocol conversion

A *Network Protocol Conversion Unit (NPU)* is the name given to the 'device' that allows access to a network for users whose terminal does not, or cannot conform to the network protocol. In theory it should be possible to arrange for this conversion for any incompatibility situation. In practice, it may be just too expensive. There are many Ethernet-based and ring-structured LANs (see chapter 9 for further details). The two types of network usually use totally different routing mechanisms, packet formats, electrical interfaces and so on: the cost of software and hardware needed to link such networks would probably be more than that of the network itself.

Often the only satisfactory answer to connect the different LANs via a mainframe which has the necessary hardware and software to provide the compatibility. In other words, set up your own NPU on the mainframe.

There are very many character terminal users who want access to facilities via X25 WANs and it is not surprising that there are lots of PADs around that provide this facility.

Similarly, there are quite a lot of organisations that have many users and applications which demand fast, high-volume linkage, perhaps between their London and Scotland mainframes. For this kind of company, it is worth arranging that the mainframes link directly into the data network. In other words, regardless of whether data to be transferred comes from:

- the user's character or packet terminal connected via the mainframe

- the mainframe itself (busily running applications programs)
- outside users hiring the mainframe as a communications centre, the mainframe (host) **must itself conform to X25.**

If this is the case, the actual linkage from host to network can be via a *packet switch*, an exchange within the network that can handle digital and packetised data. There is no need for a NPU, because **the host and the network conform to the same protocols**. Under a magnifying glass, an X25 host-to-X25 network may look like that in Figure 8.3. Here, an X.21 physical circuit employing the LAPB procedure, multiplexes a whole set of independent X25 virtual calls to a packet switch, and hence into the WAN, and hence....

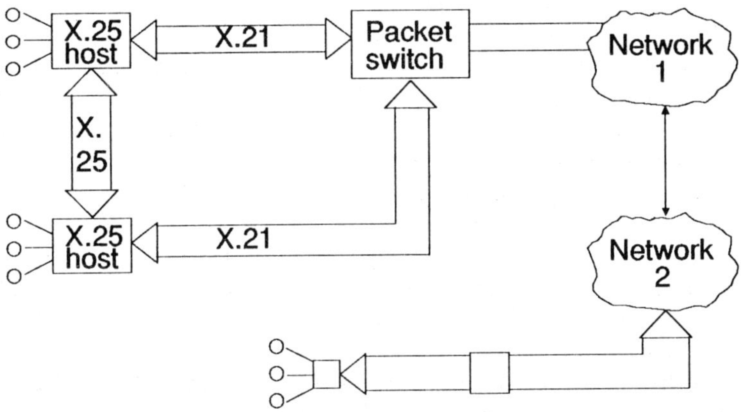

Figure 8.3 X25 Host-to-Host connection

The diagram also indicates the possibility of direct, network-independent host-to-host, X25 communication (what a nice way to enforce standards).

So, we have seen why internetworking is required and we can now examine the range of protocol conversion devices that are in common use.

Packet Assembler/Disassembler

The *packet assembler/disassembler (PAD)* is the most well-known example of an NPU and if you refer back to the X series recommendations, you will recall that the PAD provides the link between an asynchronous character terminal and packet network.

The PAD can either be an integral part of the PSE within the PDN, with individual X28 linkage or a separate unit (remote PAD) at the host (or multi-terminal) site with a full X25 link to the network. (BT offer a range of this latter kind of PAD product called *Datelmux* comms processors. Under software control, they can be configured to act as a multiplexer/PAD for PDN and private network use.

The main difference in practical terms between the two forms of access is in the handling of errors caused by line noise. The character terminal transmits to the PAD in simple character form, while an X25 host or terminal complex employs HDLC which obviously includes the (OSI) layer 2 mechanisms to request retransmission on error.

PAD function summary

- packet formation from asynchronous character strings
- packet deformation - recreation of original character strings for transmission to receiver character terminals including character framing bits and parity bits (stripped off during packet-formation)
- providing mechanisms to send a packet or batch of packets on into the network - when requested by the user, when a buffer is full, when a connection becomes available or after a time-out
- interpreting X3 commands and providing the functions requested (including the editing of data as required).

Bridge

A *bridge* is the LAN term used for a unit that links two networks that are fundamentally the same. Its main aim (assuming that the two networks apply the same mechanisms and protocols) is to enable a user in one network to connect up with one in the other network ie, it handles the problem of 'cross-addressing' between the networks.

Gateway

In theory, a gateway is an NPU, in that it enables linkage to a network from a terminal that does not support the network protocols.

In practice, the term *gateway service* is probably more useful since we are as much interested in the service behind the link and the associated management as with the link itself.

A LAN may have a gateway to an external service, so that all users can link say to external e-mail. The LAN software can provide access to one 'gateway server' terminal through which linkage outside can be made and this service is very similar to others provided by the LAN such as file and printer service (details in chapter 9).

If you pay for access to the BT facility (once called *BT GOLD)* now provided under the name *DIALCOM* (which also includes *PRESTEL),* you can obtain all the facilities of a public e-mail service **including a telex gateway**. This enables a user to send a telex without being a permanent user of the telex network with all the protocol and format conversion this requires.

Router

A *router* is a rather unusual kind of gateway and can be compared with the suggestion above where there is a need to connect two quite dissimilar networks and you need to set something up yourself. The router concept applies particularly when we try to link networks that employ *MAP* and *TOP* (see chapter 3).

Essentially, TOP relates to technical design and MAP relates to production and the two protocols were developed independently. When the 'manufacturing unit' (using MAP) wants to receive the results of the 'design unit' (using TOP), the router sorts out the differences between the packet formats and sizes and also resolves the different kinds of addressing employed.

Now we will deal with some more general aspects of networks. We will first look at general methods for network routing, then talk about the service levels expected from networks, then we can say something about the management of networks.

Network routing

A public data network implies central control with the aid of powerful computers. One of the problems that these computers help to resolve is the selection and provision of transmission paths for data ie, the provision of a route along which to send packets. This 'routing' implies finding the best route through the network, 'best' meaning the quickest and cheapest both for the user being carried and for the owner of the network. In a more limited sense, it applies to a particular node which must decide which node is the best one to pass a packet on to.

In a wide area network, the network supplier is obviously looking to be able to support as much traffic as possible so as to maximise revenue but, at the same time, users will want speed and reasonable cost. In addition, with packet-switching, messages are passed from node (switching centre) to node so the network must be sensitive to breakdown or malfunction as well as peaks and troughs in traffic intensity.

Several routing mechanisms are used that attempt to allow for such problems both on their own and in combination, depending on the complexity of the network and the kind of services it has to provide).

The service provided by the network and the routing to support it are to some extent determined by user request - a positive choice often has to be made between high throughput level and short delay on connection request.

Routing methods include:

- *deterministic routing* where there is a rigid procedure irrespective of the level of traffic and errors/malfunction. Possibilities include *random selection* of the next node to pass the packet on to, *flooding* where the packet is copied and passed on to every node that is able to forward it, making use of a *hop table*, which lists the alternatives at any time and uses mathematical optimisation procedure to select the next node on the lowest number of 'hops' the packet requires to complete its 'journey'
- *adaptive routing* where nodes can adapt to current conditions. One possibility is to pick the adjacent node with the shortest queue
- *isolated adaptive routing*, where each node takes care of itself without regard to conditions at other nodes
- *distributed routing* where each of the nodes has responsibility for deciding on the best routing policy at a particular time based on its own observations, together with information passed across from (and to) neighbouring nodes.

With this method, it may take time for nodes to pass information over to each other and there is the possibility of two nodes overloading each other because they are both trying to do the best for themselves.

The most common method employed arranges that nodes set up tables showing expected time for messages to reach other nodes and eventual destinations

- *centralised routing* where each transmitting node passes information about its own situation (current capacity,queue length for messages waiting to come in and to go out etc) to a central controller, which then reviews the overall network situation (or the sub-section it is responsible for) and passes routing instructions to each node.

  The danger with this is the possibility of overload at the centre (and this is one of the reasons why public data networks need such powerful computers to control them).

Any routing mechanism employed will have advantages and disadvantages and steps must be taken to avoid some problems inherent in the method used.

Here are two examples to point out some of the dangers:

- nodes A and B have passed whole chunks of packets to node C for re- transmission which passes them on to node D. What is to stop D passing them back to A or B (presumably it will have enough sense not to pass them back to C - unless all forward routes from itself are blocked)? This could result in an endless loop and the packets never actually arriving at their destination
- nodes A and B are rapidly becoming busy and both request information from neighbouring nodes C, D and E as to their ability to handle traffic passed to them. Both receive the answers at the same time and both decide to hammer node D at the same time. This could result in D becoming overloaded.

  The routing mechanism(s) must allow for these kinds of occurrence.

There are different kinds of network and whether looking at a LAN, a WAN or a combination, we must have some general classification of the expected performance of the network.

Network service levels

A general classification is needed because:

- we need to be able to discuss and compare similar and dissimilar networks

- at the next OSI layer, the transport mechanism will need to implement procedures to support the required service level.

At layer 3, we can distinguish three types of network where 'error' includes problems such as a lost or duplicated packet as well as simple parity and CRC errors. The principle applied is that the more reliable the network, the less chance of error and the less need to signal that one has occurred:

- type A - the likelihood of errors whatever their cause is not low but no indication is given by the network
- type B - errors are more likely but the user (or the host handling the user) is informed when they occur
- type C - a very reliable network type (such as a quality LAN), where the likelihood of errors is very low and the network generally does not report on errors. It is assumed that either higher level protocols will pick up these errors or the sender will rely on confirmation within a maximum time.

Having set up a network, like any other system, it has objectives to be met and accordingly, a level of performance to be kept up. Network management is concerned with this.

Network management

The overall purpose of a network is to provide communications in support of human applications. You have already met examples of networks and later in this chapter we will look at many public and private networks. You will appreciate that just like any other system, control measures are needed are applied by humans and with sophisticated design, by the network itself.

Network control tasks

- ensuring that basic network functions are carried out efficiently and as expected and taking action where this is not so ie, **adapting** the network to current conditions
- minimising failures and detecting, locating and 'repairing' faults as soon as possible
- ensuring that functions and facilities are available so that users are satisfied as to reliability, repeatability, uniformity, cost, response time and delay

- gathering data on the running and performance of the network so as to spot potential and actual problem areas
- making decisions in the light of performance statistics as to the overall strategy and tactics employed to see if major changes should be considered.

Flow (congestion) control

As with level 2, there are many ways to reduce the problems that occur when one end cannot cope with the incoming flow of data including:

- routing - if a particular node is tied up, it can let its neighbours (or the central controller) know and until it sorts itself out, packets will be diverted from it
- *datagram discard* - dumping datagrams either without warning or if they have not been delivered within a certain time (remember that datagrams do not have guaranteed delivery)
- *global packet permit* - restrict the number of packets that can be passed overall across the network (depending on the buffer space available at the various nodes)
- *throttling (choking)* - the nodes (or the central controller) signal the host computer or user terminal and advise that a particular link is getting busy and that the packet transmission rate must be reduced.

Network performance monitoring

In order to manage the network, the management mechanisms must be aware of what is happening at any time and to ensure that objectives are being achieved, statistics must be gathered. Useful statistics collected during network processing could include:

- total packets received and transmitted by each node
- spare processing and transmission capacity at each node
- total packets destined for a particular node from other nodes
- average queue lengths and delays at each node
- total time and times of day when a node is out of action
- total bad packets received at a node
- total packets retransmitted by a node.

Network management software can make this kind of data available in printed form for problem isolation and long-term analysis but increasingly, use is being made of 'snap-shot' information from VDUs.

From the information collected, the network can adjust itself or request manual intervention to sort out a particular problem.

Test data

One other facility that networks may supply is the provision of testing routines and test traffic patterns so that physical links can be tested and control software debugged and tested for effectiveness. For example, we must be able to set up a strings of packets with a predetermined number deliberately corrupted for different testing reasons. These could include:

- parity/CRC failures
- duplicated packets
- missing packets.

We may want to carry out a test pattern at any time and two possibilities exist:

- generating a random pattern as needed by statistical methods (something like an extension of random number generation)
- using a file of data previously created, either by saving a number of random patterns or by collecting live data and deliberately 'mucking it about' to increase the level and kind of errors needed for testing.

The rest of this long chapter covers three areas.

The first introduces the concept of value-added networks, who supplies them and the services/facilities offered. This leads on to the range of public and private networks, who supplies them and what they can do for VAN providers and the general user. The final section touches on the recent 'Integrated Digital Services Network' concept.

British Telecom packet network facilities

The three major UK network suppliers, BT, MCL and Kingston, all operate packet switched networks - BT was the first.

By the late 1960s, BT (as the then General Post Office) was becoming acutely aware that the use of computers was expanding and that the combination of voice and data transmission requirements were far outstripping what they could provide. In those days (in fact up until 1981), the GPO was the only public network supplier (and incidentally the only modem supplier as well).

The choice offered by switched or leased-line access to the PTN and the telex and telegraph networks was OK for the small application, but was just too expensive for large-scale or fast use. Once X25 was adopted internationally, packet-switching technology started to take off (supported by the major advances in digital technology) and packet networks were implemented, initially in the USA.

PSS

BT obviously used some of these ideas and eventually was able to offer a pilot packet-switched service in 1977 and extend it, in 1980, to a full service called *Packet SwitchStream* (the name was subsequently changed to *PSS - Packet Switchstream Service).*

The network relies on *System X* digital exchanges and computers connecting via 64Kbps data channels, multiplexed up to 2Mbps (32 x 64Kbps) using byte-oriented TDM.

Pause for thought

The term 'System X' is a specification for a type of very large, computer-controlled digital exchange and several companies have supplied such exchanges to BT, MCL and Kingston, in particular Thorn-Ericsson, Plessey, Northern Telecom and GDT. Services provided by BT under the general name *X-Stream* use the Thorn-Ericsson *AXE-10* exchange and BT offers a range of totally digital X-stream services from their network.

They can be divided into two classes:

- those used by organisations with large volume requirements, specifically wanting connection on a **point-to-point** basis (*X-Stream*)
- those for general connection via a digital network (*Switchstream*).

Point-to-Point X-Stream

- *Kilostream* is the name of the service providing full-duplex, synchronous linkage at a range of speeds up to 64Kbps and is handled by a series of local exchanges and two main network control centres

  Terminal linkage is through a 4-wire local line via a *Network Termination Unit (NTU)* something like a digital modem, which provides the X21 (or X21bis) physical interface to the network. Data is carried higher up the network at 2mbps and is split down again to Kilostream by the local exchange before passing on to the receiver

- *Megastream* is something like Kilostream but the basic user linkage can be at 2Mbps or optionally at 8, 32 or even 144Mbps - remember in chapter 5 we discussed opto-electronic devices that can allow transmission at well over 500Mbps.

  Support for the Megastream link can be provided by TDMs which can make use of the basic 2Mbps for a variety of purposes and giving channel combinations of speech (analogue or digital) and data at different speeds.

  Suppliers of digital PBXs use the same signalling and other standards as the network, so it is possible to drive a Megastream link from a PBX

- other services include *Satstream* which provides point-to-point access via dedicated satellite dishes to Europe and the USA at up to 2Mbps, and *International Kilostream/Megastream* which enable Kilostream and Megastream users to link up with users of similar services abroad.

Switchstream

This is the generic name for the BT packet-switched data network service range.

At the higher level, instead of being 'in-band' ie, as an integral part of the data information being sent along a channel, signalling information is collected from all 32 channels of a line and passed down one channel used for *common channel signalling* (we will meet this idea again in ISDN below).

Access to the Switchstream service is either:

- call-out only, via PAD by PTN dial-up/leased line (V21/23)
- call-out/in - X25 user packet terminal via a dedicated link to the PAD called a *dataline*.

(Note that 'minicall' access is only possible with packet terminals).

A dataline is designed to handle the speed required by the terminal - 300/1200bps for character terminals and 2400/9600/48,000bps for packet terminals). The cost of renting a dataline is independent of distance.

It is also possible to link several user datalines into a *Multiline* so that calls can be shared between the users.

Options are available within the service, some similar to those being developed for voice (remember the X25 control packet 'facilities' above). They include:

- *call redirection* - if a terminal is not in use
- *reverse charging*
- *closed user groups* - private linkages of geographically separated users
- *channel direction specification* - incoming-only, out-going-only or both ways
- *dynamic terminal parameter specification* (see X3 above)
- *window size selection* which permits a choice from 1 to 7 (refer to chapter 6 to remind you of HDLC and continuous RQ; packets are sent in blocks allowing selective retransmission up to the window size)
- *banner insertion* - a 64-character message can be attached to the beginning of a call to appear as a 'banner' when the receiver picks it up
- *fully itemised billing.*

Extensions to Switchstream

BT has extensions to Switchstream, one group being *Multistream* including:

- *EPAD* - designed to close the gap that exists where character terminals do not have line error checking/retransmission facilities.

  The software for this can either be in the terminal, the modem or a BT interface between the terminal and modem. It allows for a selection of error-detection techniques including the main CRC methods and a range of horizontal/vertical parity-checking
- *VPAD* - designed to make life easier for viewdata (videotex) users (remember the 'tapping the telephone' demonstration in 'Workmate' at the end of chapter 7)
- *TPAD* - used in credit-card checking and authorisation where a fast connection is needed. It involves a telephone handset with a credit

card reader and supports voice referral after a credit card has been read and sent to the credit agency. This procedure is called *APACS 40* (as recommended by the Association of Payment and Clearing Services.

Other Switchstream extensions include *BPAD, RPAD* and *SPAD* which provide convenient linkage between a character terminal and a range of IBM-supported networks

For user organisations with large-scale Switchstream needs, BT supplies a *Packet Netmux*, an X25 processor that can cope with more than 80 different character and packet terminals.

Interstream

The *Interstream services* are in effect a set of gateways to other networks:

- *Interstream one* provides a link to telex
- *Interstream two* - designed for PSS and PTN access from BT's special *teletex* user terminals. Teletex is an advanced form of electronic mail/messaging that comforms to CCITT X series recommendations, but which does not seem to have taken off very well in the UK
- *Interstream three* - linkage between telex and teletex through the PTN or PSS.

IPSS

BT also provide a gateway service called the *International Packet Switchstream Service (IPSS)*. This allows access to the international X25 network and enables a user to connect with over 50 packet networks in over 35 countries.

The Mercury Packet network

We have already discussed MCL as the main competitor of BT and it is appropriate to say something about its data network facilities. Like BT, MCL has a country-wide physical network based partly on microwave and mainly optical fibre, controlled by massive GPT system X exchanges. Again like BT, a wide range of voice services is offered. Data services cover the same range as BT but are classified and offered on a rather different basis.

MCL do not offer the exact equivalent of PSS as a public switched data network. Instead, the *Mercury 5000* service is supplied to other companies as the basis for their own managed data networks. In practice, this means an organisation wanting to provide a service (such as viewdata or specialised database) can get MCL to supply the physical network in a way that is completely transparent to the user (he thinks that the VAN supplier is also the network supplier). For example, *International Network Services* is a company owned by ICL and GEISCO which offers *TRADINET* and *BROKERNET* based on an MCL packet network (more in chapter 10).

Access can be dial-up or leased to a *network protocol processor* which allows for most protocol conversions to X25 and supports MNP (chapter 6) and APACS 40 (see TPAD above). Access is also possible from terminals in several videotex modes.

Dedicated X25 links are possible into X25 ports on 5000 service exchanges and the network can handle all the IBM protocols for linking MDNS services into one based on OSI.

The 5000 service offers some very powerful network management facilities including:

- alarm mechanisms that automatically inform technical staff of any faults so that swift action can be taken
- Automatic logging of any network 'events' (problems of any kind) so that they can be analysed later on (if a fault occurs regularly it may be a clue to something else)
- short- and long-term capacity planning, carried out to ensure that the network can always cope with demand, all significant elements of the network being constantly monitored
- a telephone help desk - provided for customers and behind the network is a fault reporting system which can help in fast diagnosis of problem causes
- customer can be supplied with detailed usage statistics - daily totals and breakdown to individual user or call.

General packet users

The equivalent of BTs IPSS is *Mercury 5100* providing V21/V22 dial-up access or leased X25 access at 2400, 4800 or 9600bps. This connects to the USA and other countries via massive satellite dishes in London (East Wharf) and Whitehill (Oxfordshire).

Point-to-point packet service

The *Mercury 1000* service is designed for point-to-point linkage at 64Kbps up to 2Mbps (cf Kilostream and Megastream) but instead of separating a 64K service from the 2M, MCL technology offers in effect '64 x n', ie, any number of 64Kbps links up to a total of 2Mbps (using TDM). A particular '64' can be subdivided into voice or data channels or multiplexed up to provide a high-volume link.

This service is operated by *Mercury Data Network Services Ltd* a separate company within the Cable and Wireless group.

Mercury 2100 Premier is an ISDN service (see below).

Kingston Communications (Hull) plc

Kingston has been in operation as a telephone service since 1898 and after the 1984 Act, the Hull City Council decided to operate the service under the above name (from January 1st 1988).

Like its competitors, it offers a wide range of telephone services, linkage to MCL being via centres at York and Leeds and to BT through its digital main switching units at York and Sheffield.

Late in 1984, the company installed GEC/Plessey System X exchanges and now, over 80% of telephone subscribers are linked via optical fibre. Over 95% of incoming traffic from BT and MCL networks is via fully digital links.

Network testing/monitoring is based on the Hewlett-Packard *remote access and test system (RATES).*

Kingston introduced a packet network in 1987 which exploits the optical fibre circuits and offers dial-up/leased access or dedicated links (like Kilostream/Megastream and MCL 5000/1000).

Now let us look at just one private UK packet network. Then we will examine packet networks abroad.

JANET

The *joint academic network (JANET)* links over 100 UK universities, polytechnics and government centres. It allows the linkage of users with hosts and other users for general data and information access, software (via large computing facilities in Manchester and London Universities), e-mail and computer conferencing. (A recent estimate came up with a figure of 1,000Mb per day as the amount of data that is transferred within JANET.)

It currently makes used mainly of leased line/PAD access at 9.6Kbps, but some users have recently-upgraded dedicated BT and MCL facilities to connect up along high-speed leased analogue lines (48Kbps), or directly via BT's enhanced PSS services (Kilostream or Megastream). It also provides gateways to PSS and *Internet* (the USA research network) as well as European networks.

JANET attempts to be OSI-conforming as far as possible, and although it was developed before OSI was properly specified, it makes use of many features that try to achieve something like OSI. One of its interesting features is that it allows an interface to an end-user LAN.

X25 networks abroad

ARPANET

The first wide-area packet-switched network was *ARPANET*, developed in about 1968 by the US Department of Defence - *advanced research projects agency (ARPA)*. Its aim was to provide an efficient data transfer service for universities and research centres (something like JANET now offers).

It is a datagram-oriented service and links over 100 of these across the whole of the USA (including a satellite link to Hawaii) and in Europe. Users need digital linkage, which can be at up to 56Kbps.

Most other UK and overseas packet networks rely on ideas that are used in ARPANET.

TYMNET

Shortly after ARPANET, the information systems group of the USA aircraft manufacturer *McDonnell Douglas* set up *TYMNET*, a commercially oriented network which currently supports over 5000 simultaneous users in the USA and can service foreign users too. Its particular advantage is its ability to handle a wide range of protocol conversion, in particular to support IBM 3270 devices. TYMNET users have PTN access at 9.6 and 56 Kbps through over 1300 network nodes. It also provides electronic mail and a few other user-oriented services. Estimates state that the network copes with over 7 million connection sessions per month.

TELENET

TELENET is a product developed in 1975 by a subsidiary of the USA company *General Telephone and Electronics (GTE)* to support users of Tymeshare computers and operates in the USA and many other countries.

TRANSPAC

TRANSPAC is the French equivalent of the UK PDNs and has been in operation since 1978. It offers a range of connection services including leased line and switched at rates from 48Kbps up to 2Mbps, but with more choice than is available from the UK network.

EURONET

This is the 'European common market network' and has been operational for about 10 years. It was originally intended to supply scientific and technical information but has been extended as a PDN for business use. Its main packet exchanges are in London, Paris, Rome and Frankfurt with subsidiary access points in Amsterdam, Brussels, Copenhagen, Dublin and Luxembourg.

Some networks provide communication facilities, ie, enable linkage of users, computers etc. Others, based on these networks provide additional services.

VAN/VADS

Now, we can introduce the concept of a *value-added network (VAN)*.

Added value

To qualify as a VAN, a network must add some extra facilities to a basic telecomms network. These were introduced earlier and to remind you, include services such as:

- fast connection/routing to other users and to other networks
- network usage monitoring/analysis
- detailed accounting/billing
- message storage for retransmission
- broadcasting a stored message
- encryption.

The government has introduced the more modern term *value-added data Service (VADS)* to replace 'VAN'.

A VAN/VADS may provide all of these services and all the user applications needed as well as an overall managed network allowing for the supply of fully managed network services. In this case, it is called a *Managed Data Network Service (MDNS).*

In order to operate a VAN or VADS a government licence is required, the intention being to provide some protection for the major licensed PTOs and prevent a free-for-all rat-race which might not be in the general interest. (In fact, the rat-race has already started because companies are finding many ways to bend the rules.)

VAN/VADS services are provided by the PTOs and by organisations which have their own private networks that interface with the public network. In many cases, access must be via the X25 public data network.

VAN/VADS applications

Applications supported include:

- electronic mail and mailboxes (often backed up with word processing and text editing and translation services). E-mail can be for general use, or for specialised users linked to information access such as for reporters and journalists or legal or business advice
- videotex-format data/information access
- text-oriented data/information access
- voice management facilities such as radiopaging, telephone answering and messaging and the provision of voice conferencing
- message-handling service - a sophisticated facility where messages can be sent and received in a variety of formats to and from a range of different terminal types (in some cases, conforming to X400 - see chapter 3). (Note that some conversion and editing may be needed. For example, remember from chapter 2 that telex uses a limited character set. Similarly, if a fax image is sent to an e-mail terminal, some of the 'shapes' may need to be simulated with characters
- financial services - this includes financial database access, EFT, EDI, credit checking and many specialised services for particular kinds of business and industry such as insurance, airlines, holidays and stockbrokers.

Note that we have already touched on some of these services in chapter 7. We will also have much more to say in chapter 10.

In summary, the VAN/VADS supplier can provide a network based on his own and/or part of one supplied by a PTO, but must not just provide connection and routing. Some extra facility must be made available as value added to the basic service.

The cost advantages associated with VAN/VADS usage are that charges are based on connect time and/or the number of characters or packets transmitted, rather than distance travelled within the PDN; connection charges are to the nearest access point (PAD or interface processor) which are affected by the distance and time of day like ordinary voice calls.

ISDN

As we have seen, from the user's point of view the wide range of services and applications 'at the other end' of a digital or analogue network involve a bewildering range of connections - dial-up, dataline, two-wire, four-wire, Kilostream etc etc. This is due to the development of digital transmission, packet networks and the many advances in technology and techniques, particularly in the last 10 years.

It has been recognised, in Europe (CCITT) and internationally (ISO) that there is an increasing need for an internationally-agreed set of standards that can be applied in the development of universal linkage to an all-purpose network. This general concept is not fully implemented yet, but it is expected that by the end of this century, we should have available an *integrated services digital network (ISDN)*. ISDN is really beyond the scope of your studies, but since it is already available in a pilot form, you should know a little about it. There are several quite difficult concepts involved and you can ignore it altogether if you want to.

The telephone network is almost completely digital for practical purposes and can be referred to as an *Integrated Digital Network (IDN)*. The logical extension is in the supply of a network that can handle voice, viewdata, data, telex, video, fax and everything else ie, an *integrated services digital network*.

This will make use of the same switching exchanges and connection paths for the total mix of analogue and digital services.

Its main feature is **a fully digital link from one end of a conversation to the other**. With most networks, we are involved with some mix of analogue and digital - ISDN provides **end-to-end digital connection.**

CCITT 'I' series recommendations

CCITT recommendations in the 'I' series, relate to ISDN (you will recall from chapter 5 that the V series are for analogue and the X series for digital networks). These recommendations (provisional at present) include service definitions, the basic configurations of multiple channel links and a whole set of others relating to interfaces of various kinds.

The general set of recommendations are included in recommendation *I110*. They include an ISDN 'functional architectural model' which shows the connection- related functions that should be provided by a local ISDN exchange and how these relate to the end-to-end terminal connections. Recommendations also relate to 'reference configurations' which define functional groupings such as:

- *NT1* (network termination 1) - a connection point that can handle the physical interface only
- *NT2* - a more complex end-connnection with OSI layer 2/3 capabilities as well as layer 1 (eg, a digital PBX or a sophisticated LAN)
- *TE1* (terminal equipment 1) - a terminal, such as a fully digital telephone that can interface directly with the ISDN
- *TE2* - with a V24/V28-like or X21-like interface and which needs a further interface (*terminal adapter*) in order to link into the ISDN.

Connection paths

There are two types of channel that are fundamental to ISDN:

- *B channel* - 64Kbps for voice and/or data
- *D channel* - 16Kbps for control and signalling

  These are used in combination and typically:

- 2B+D is two 64K B channels and one 16K D channel making 144Kbps in total
- 30B+D - actually carried out using TDM and hence called *time slots* rather than channels. The 32 slots are usually numbered from 0-31 and the recommendation is that slot 0 is used for timing and

synchronisation, slot 16 is the D (signalling) and the other 30 are the Bs. (MCL makes use of slot 0 for network monitoring and control as well)

Let us now look at how they are applied in ISDN.

IDA

IDA (Integrated Digital Access) is the service whereby a user can get at the ISDN facilities and there are two fundamental mechanisms for this:

- *basic access interface service* (covered by CCITT recommendation I430) - for the small user (e.g. PC or featurephone) based on 2B+D
- *primary rate access* (CCITT I431). This is based on a 2Mbps digital link with 30B+D and is designed particularly to link an *ISPBX (integrated services PBX)* to an ISDN System X exchange. (Note that *23B+D* is the standard in the USA). BT has a pilot scheme for its **basic** access in operation referred to as *single line IDA*. BT's **primary rate** is known as *Multiline*. MCL,s 2100 Premier service mentioned above is equivalent to BT's multiline IDA and been in operation since 1989.

The ISPBX mentioned just now, uses all of the ISDN features to transfer data and voice along the B channels, so that how the ISDN conveys these and how the D channel is used, are completely transparent to the users.

There is no logical intermediate in the UK between the 2B+D and the 30B+D - an obvious problem for the medium-sized user of ISDN. In other countries, a wider range is often available, in particular, France has a service that gives a transmission capacity of up to 1Mbps.

So far, we have ignored standards relating to signalling mechanisms in analogue and digital networks, since they are really within the realm of telecommunications. For those who are really interested, international ISDN signalling standards are yet to be fully agreed, but pending a full take-up of recommendations such as CCITT Q931, both BT and MCL make use of what is called *digital access signalling system version 2 (DASS-2)*.

Now we can just touch on what people are expecting from ISDN.

Where ISDN might go

Expected developments include:

- completed specification and adoption of standards
- further development of terminals and terminal access devices
- direct connection from private networks
- *shared tenant service* - several companies on the same site/building making use of the same linkage
- simplified licences so that simple ISDN service resale can be permitted
- agreement on charging arrangements.

At present over 70% of all large switches in use are fully digital and most large organisations employ integrated digital exchanges (ie, that are ISDN- compatible) and it has been projected that by 1990 ISDN primary rate coverage will be available to over 90% of all possible large users.

In summary, an ISPBX can link many users via a multiline link to an ISDN exchange. A terminating unit can link one or two terminals/telephones via a single line link to a similar exchange. From here, the user has gateway access to all the other services (including the packet networks) that he wants to access.

Recap

- it then gave a simplified view of the main methods for connecting users, in particular the virtual circuit and the datagram
- the problems of internetworking and protocol conversion, introducing the terms gateway, bridge and so on were considered
- the next subject for consideration was how networks determine how to route packets, and several mechanisms were introduced
- we looked at some of the practical problems of monitoring network performance and managing a network to achieve a satisfactory performance level
- the next section tried to simplify the data network services provided by the main PTOs and for comparison introduced JANET, a private

network. Also for comparison, it listed some international data networks

- the penultimate section gave a short introduction to value-added networks in preparation for more detail in chapter 10
- the final section provided an overview of the integrated services digital network and put it into perspective within other digital networks.

Typical questions

Question 8.1

Give an explanation **in not more than 20 words** each of the following terms:

a. network routing
b. X25 physical level
c. virtual circuit
d. 2B+D
e network user address
f packet terminal

Question 8.2

You are investigating the service provided by a WAN and are concerned with performance of a particular switching node. Based on what we have said about network monitoring test patterns:

a. how can such test patterns help in determining node and network performance?
b. give a broad outline for a basic set of tests that might be carried out in order to gather information about the performance of the node.

Question 8.3

As a typical Computing or Business Studies student, why might you want to make use of the JANET network?

Question 8.4

A PAD is a particular kind of network node that will communicate with other nodes and with user terminals. Explain briefly:

a. why this communication is necessary
b. the main framework recommended for this communication

9: Local area networks

Objectives

After reading this chapter, you should:

- have a general idea of how to define what is wanted from a LAN
- appreciate the main reasons and justification for using LANs
- understand some of the hardware considerations associated with LAN set-up and operation
- appreciate the problems of estimating LAN requirements and performance
- understand the problems of managing a LAN
- have a working knowledge of a commercially available LAN.

Chapters 1 to 7 were not really interested in the actual size of the network being used for carrying conversations. Well this one is. In particular, we cover what are called **local area** networks. We will try to define the term and explain why and how users are linked in this way.

The chapter will give a general view of LANs and will not try to review the very wide range of LAN hardware and software that is available. (We will however, spend a little time looking at one package in particular.)

Network topologies

By now, you should have a pretty good idea of what a network is and and we can look at the special problems of a LAN in particular, the need for very high-speed transmission and the various mechanisms that try to ensure an acceptable level of service to all users.

Network nodes

First, we must introduce the term *node*. This is used for any 'element' connected to the network that has some part in its running. A node could be a main processor, a server (see later) or any piece of hardware that assists the network. In some networks, a user workstation (terminal) can also act as a network node.

Now we can examine the four main alternatives for a *network topology* (or structure). We will ignore for the time being the intelligence behind the network, ie, the 'mechanism' that manages the network and connects the various users (you should know quite a lot about this from chapter 8 anyway).

Star

With a *star* network, we are usually dealing with a central computer with dumb or semi-dumb terminals connected only to it, apparently radiating out like a star (Figure 9.1). Connection between any two users is through the centre. A typical example of a star network is the public telephone system, where the PTOs have provided a network in which any person can talk to any other, but only via the exchanges that make it up. The star is not a very common LAN topology.

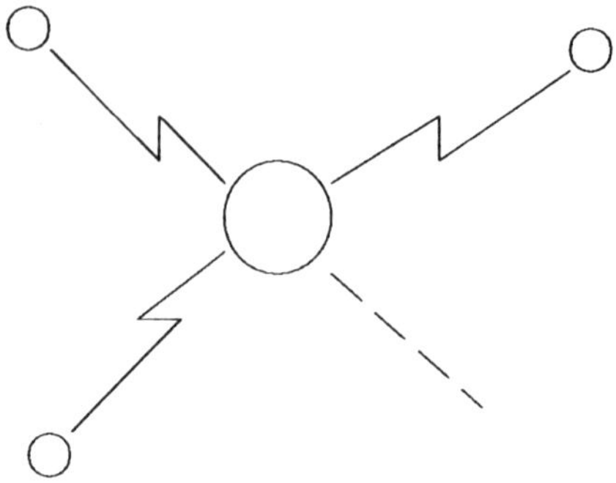

Figure 9.1 A basic 'star' network

Ring

A *ring* network has all users connected to the one on either side in a physical ring (Figure 9.2). Any conversation from A to B must pass through all the users that lie on the route. The network must have some central control in order to manage connections and the functions of the network, but it is not at the physical centre as in in a star network.

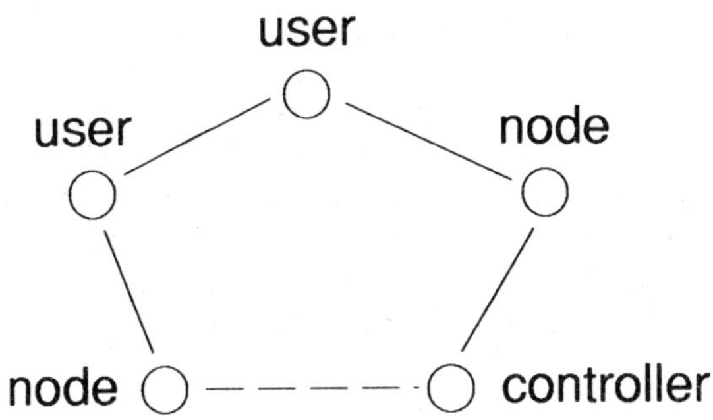

Figure 9.2 A basic 'ring' structure

Tree

A *tree* or *bus* network is structured so that users and nodes are attached to a main trunk (or *backbone*) and form branches like on a tree (Figure 9.3). With this structure, everyone can talk to everyone else. The central intelligence is accessed along the branches, usually using a broadcast technology. An advantage of the tree network is that a message may have a much shorter path than with ring networks where **all** messages may have to pass **through** all users, although messages must still be via the central intelligence.

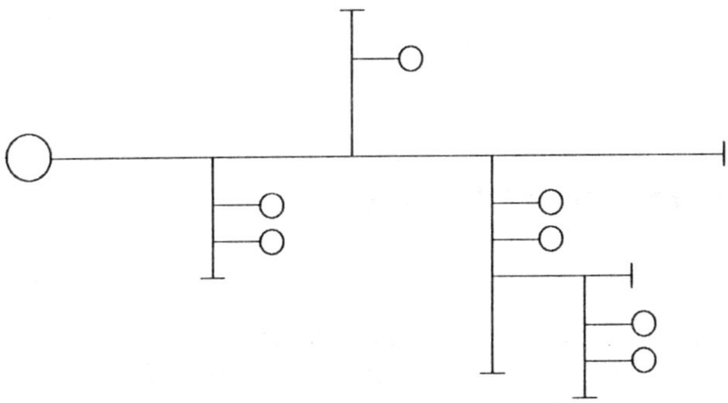

Figure 9.3 A tree or bus structure

Note that the way that the terminals come off the network can be referred to as *multi-drop* (compare point-to-point and multi-point in chapter 2).

Mesh

This is very common in public and private wide-area networks but is not easy to implement in a LAN. The idea is for users to be partly or wholly inter-connected as shown in Figures 9.4 and 9.5. The degree of meshing will be determined by the complexity of the application and the trade-off between centralised and de-centralised connection. If there is a central facility, everyone can talk to everyone else, but in practice, conversations are likely to be only between certain users or groups of users.

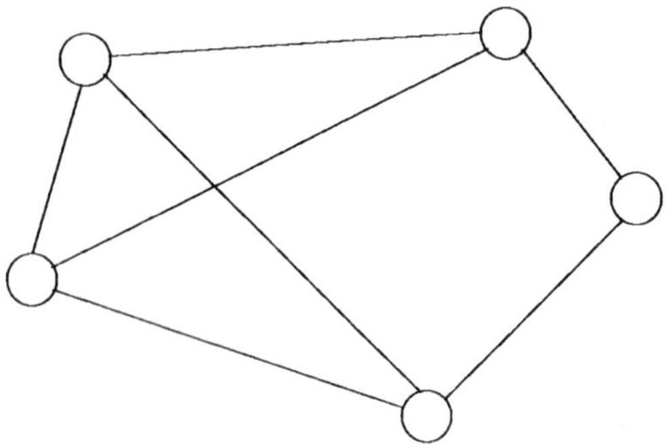

Figure 9.4 A simple mesh network

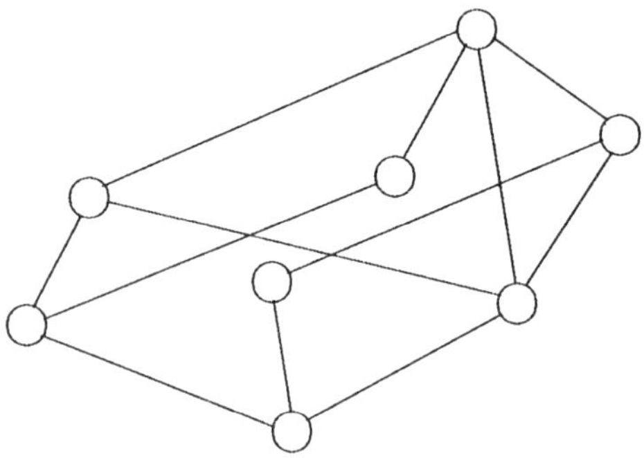

Figure 9.5 A more complex mesh

Now let us say a little about why a LAN is needed, then we can try to provide an explanation of what factors make us regard a particular network as a LAN.

The need for a local area network

Many organisations will have a number of computer users with differing requirements in a limited physical area. When linked with the technology generally referred to as a local area network, they can share hardware, software and other resources in avery efficient manner. Being linked together, whether in the office or the factory, users can take advantage of the common resources and facilities to share work and efforts and utilise the wide inter-communication possible. Resources and facilities include programs, disk space, printers and external communication links (such as for telex, e-mail and viewdata).

A typical example might be the workstations used by a team of word-processing or desk-top publishing clerks. Standard letters, paragraphs, mailing lists etc, used by any or all clerks can be stored on a shared hard disk and copied therefrom as required.

Individual letters, notes, names and addresses and so on, unique to a particular clerk, can be held on a workstation floppy or hard disk.

Network and applications software can be updated transparently to the user and different users can have different versions of software. Using electronic mail, messages and text can be passed around to all users. They can also taken advantage of developments such as computer conferencing to make life easier. Further facilities such as gateways to external services or company mainframe can be implemented once and then shared, thereby saving on costs.

Printer usage by an individual clerk may be intermittent and too low in volume to justify a dedicated printer (solely for his use). The LAN could support a *draft quality* printer for rough copies, that all clerks can use, together with a high-speed, high-quality laser printer for final, top-quality letters or perhaps for processing the output from computer-assisted drawing software (such as for engineering or construction) or electronic publishing packages.

As we have said, the LAN is structured to provide shared resources. In its simplest form, it can be considered as in Figure

9.6. A number of users will carry out a number of applications making use of certain resources. As it is a network, they will share resources and communicate with each other (known as *inter-working*). Facilities must be provided to allow for connection between users, resources, the transmission medium and so on.

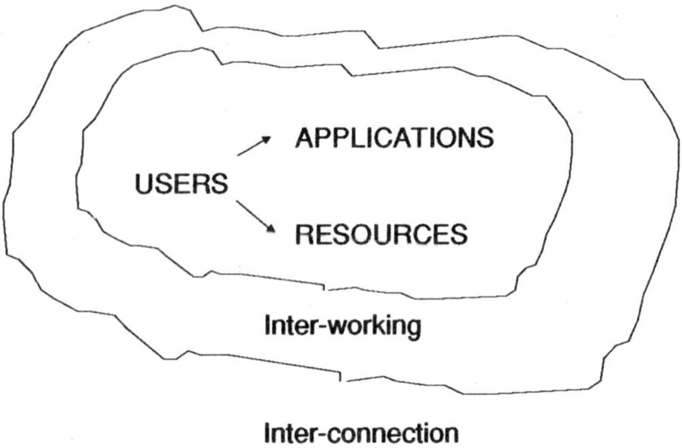

Figure 9.6 A simplistic LAN

LAN technology is usually based on the transmission of packets. Because of short distances, very high quality equipment and the general 'high-tech' involved, LANs have high speeds (of the order of megabits/sec) and low error rates. The electronics and media associated with LANs make this possible in a way that cannot be achieved in WANs except at their very highest level.

The other reason for low error rates is that basic LAN technology does not usually require switching devices - 'everyone is connected to everyone else', so a message addressed to a particular receiver will eventually get to him.

What is a local area network

It is very difficult to define a LAN and to be able to say if we are dealing with a LAN, we need to look at the overall profile of the network. Some of the factors that will help us to decide are:

- the physical separation of users, servers and services - typical descriptions of a LAN refer to one room, one floor, one building etc. Actually, some LANs can span 1000s of metres
- the topology of the network - most LANs are based on a ring or bus structure although variations do exist. A pure star is not very common
- the speed at which data can be transferred - as we have said, LAN technology allows for rates of *at least* 500Kbps - anything less is probably not a LAN
- the processing power, services offered and number of users that the network can support - LAN processing power is usually based on microprocessors (such as are used in PCs) and although these are becoming very powerful if the network makes use of non-PC processors and relies on disks, larger and faster than would normally be available with a PC, it is probably a mini or mainframe-based network. It is debateable whether this would be called a LAN (or just a small network). On the other hand, although there are PC-based LANs that can support dozens of users, anything over say 100 users is very fancy LAN indeed
- the distribution of processing power - one of the main advantages of a LAN is that all users can share hardware resources. It is also very convenient if the workstations are to an extent intelligent - ie, have some applications processing power of their own. The more work that a terminal can carry out, the more power the controlling computers have available for running and managing the network itself. In fact almost all LAN terminals are by definition, intelligent - the LAN is really a way of sharing out this intelligence (ie, processing power) to the best advantage. In this way, application and network processing are shared out instead of all being in the hands of a central processor (compare this with a mainframe and star-linked terminals)
- the basic technology for management, connection, routing and control - the LAN might vary from a couple of PCs linked together, sharing a printer with a T-switch to massive ones where routing and connection is based on the same digital PBX used to handle the telephone calls in and out of the organisation. Obviously the management and control of LANs vary from the simple to the extremely complex
- the shared facilities available - these include file service, printer service, library service, gateway service, messaging (electronic mail) and assistance with management and control. A LAN should as a minimum support one file server and one printer server.

- what you think it is - I think my college mainframe with a star arrangement of over 100 user terminals is not a LAN even though it covers a fairly small physical area. Apart from some simple file-handling functions, the terminals are dumb, while the main peripherals are large and are sited in or near the computer centre, rather than being under the control of the network users. Furthermore, the central mainframe is extremely powerful in terms of its support for servicing users and their requirements for filing and printing - far more than you would expect from a LAN. The college is phasing in a Digital Equipment Corp, *VAX*-based network based on the *DECnet* version of *Ethernet* (which we will deal with shortly). Although it will support roughly the same number of terminals as the original mainframe, it can have peripherals attached at almost any point and in particular, the terminals can be as intelligent as we like (such as Apple Mac and IBM PS/2). This is a LAN.

(It is interesting to note that whatever you or I think a LAN is, there are well over 10,000 LAN installations in the UK.)

Now we must look at the various entities that make up a typical LAN.

The main 'components' of a LAN

The actual structure of a LAN will depend on the number of users to be supported, data volumes, the range of applications, the distances involved and so on. In general, there has to be intelligence to handle file usage, printing, external access and general management of the network - assigning priorities and handling errors and breakdowns.

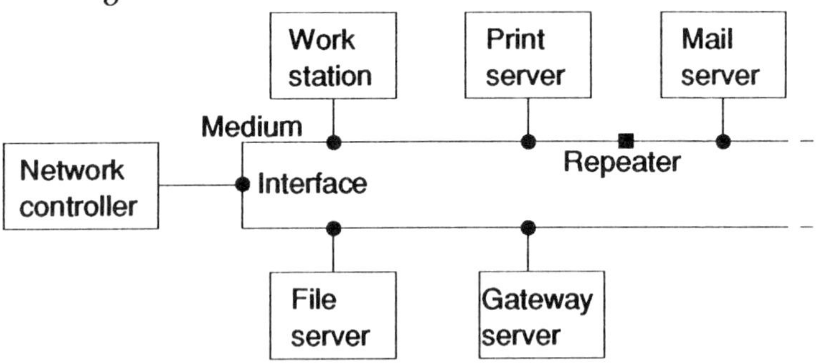

Figure 9.7 Conceptual LAN components

The typical LAN as shown in Figure 9.7, regardless of its topology, will involve some or all of the following:

- *network controller* - there must be some computer intelligence that allows users to talk to each other, recover from faults, share out resources and so on. The network controller is an interface card often as an expansion card added into a PC (sometimes built into its motherboard). It acts as a link between the terminal and network cable providing multi-user facilities and overall network control. It may even act as a medium interface in sophisticated LAN set-ups where several sub-networks based on different media are linked together
- *file servers* (one or more) - each file server is a program responsible for a disk and the directories and files stored on it. It ensures that users have access to the files and records they are entitled to while, at the same time, preventing multiple access. This may be accomplished by *file locking* where only one user has access to a a particular file at any one time, or *record locking* where several users can access a file but only one user can access a particular record at any one time
- *printer server* (one or more) - part of the network will involve a program that controls the use of a printer, queuing up print requests and storing them on disk until the printer has finished the previous ones
- *library server* - the term 'library' is used for a file containing software in a form that can be executed (run) by the network controller, other servers and the users. It may be operationally convenient to arrange that different users have access to different sofware libraries. There are several reasons for this, in particular, the possibility that different versions of software may be needed and we may want to separate them so that different users use different versions, perhapsone set for home customers and one for export.

  Another common reason could be that proprietary software (spreadsheets, word processors, data base packages) have been purchased on a *multi-site licence* basis. For example, the licence may allow up to four users to run the software. If you have eight users on the system, if the software is freely available, the licence agreement will be breached.

  It is not just a question of limiting the number of workstations. With many LAN installations, many users can make use of the system at different times. (At Thames Valley College the 100+ workstations are used by over 2000 students and staff.) It will be up to the network controller to ensure that a particular library is accessed by particular users. The system will know who has privilege from user number/password entered at log-on

- *communications server (gateway server)* - this will allow users to access gateways to external services including viewdata, telex, mainframe database access and linkage to other LANs
- *workstations* (user terminals) - except for a pure star arrangement, user terminals cannot be **completely** dumb, because they usually participate in the network itself even if only to create their messages in the right form for passing on to other users or nodes. In addition, for many users, the workstation is taking the place of the dedicated PC they used to make use of and they still need access to local disk storage. No dumb terminal can do this although it can request access to resources through one of the network nodes. Note that many LAN setups allow a server to operate at the same time as it is being used as a workstation. It is up to the network control software to handle this as needed. (When we look at Tapestry, at the end of this chapter, you will see that a terminal can act as a user workstation, a printer server, file server and library server at the same time - **provided it has the processing power to be able to cope**)
- *node* - this is the general term for any LAN element that contributes to the running of the network - PABX, controller, switch, server and so on, rather than the user workstation (intelligent or semi-intelligent)
- *transceiver* - this sends and receives messages to/from network. (Note that network controller and transceiver are both network nodes)
- *repeater* - where we want to site a terminal a long way from other parts of the network, it may be necessary to use a repeater to boost the transmitted signals (see chapter 5)
- *transmission medium* - common transmission media used in LANs are twisted pair and coax, although some more recent developments have included optical fibre. It is uncommon for a radio link to be involved. However, chapter 5 referred to the possibility of microwave, laser (or even infra-red) links over short hops and these can be used. The problems of interfacing the LAN to the transmitter would probably be prohibitive unless it was shared out in a very large LAN - in which case, presumably, some use of a private or public digital network would be required.

  The IEEE has recently started work on a LAN standard that includes optical fibre specifications for Ethernet transceiver and repeater (coming up soon).

Now let us look at some of the human aspects of operating a LAN.

LAN manager status

In theory, all server functions could be carried out entirely by the network software, but in practical situations, human intervention is usually required. The most important person is the *network manager* who will be responsible for setting up andmaintaining the general configuration of the network. There should only be one network manager but if he is also a user, he may have other kinds of manager status. He decides which users will be recognised, which nodes will act as servers, how software libraries will be organised and who will be allowed to act as a *server manager*. A sophisticated LAN will allow the network manager to assign server manager status to privileged users, so they can look after a particular server. This may be specific so that *own server* applies to just one resource (such as a particular printer) or *all servers* (such as all printers or even all resources). Typical LAN privileges could include:

- *printer server manager* - each printer needs someone who can look at the print queue and remove a long print-out that was put there by mistake, handle paper changes and paper wrecks. He may also rearrange the print queue and flush out jobs if necessary
- *file server manager* - this privilege allows for attachig and changing passwords to disks or files and adding or changing the list of users who have access to particular storage elements
- *gateway server manager* - he may add new external service links or change existing ones
- *mail server manager* - someone has to remove old messages and monitor the use of the various mail facilities.

Pause for thought

Before looking at techniques, let us stop and overview some of the advantages of LANs, both to the organisation putting in and managing it and the user who will operate from the workstations:

- *centralised control* - management can monitor usage of the LAN and control its facilities and resources centrally in a similar way to the more conventional computer network with dumb terminals
- *resource sharing* - leading on from this, the optimum usage of hardware, software and time resources can be achieved

- *applications management* - similarly, with central control, users can be provided with a range of applications software with differing versions if necessary
- *modular build-up* - if properly planned from the start, the structure of a LAN and the way it operates allows an organisation to expand the network in regular steps as the demand for services increases
- *location flexibility/movability* - it is often fairly easy to change the location of a workstation or other node and add extra ones without a major modification to the LAN
- *application integration* - the siting of workstations at the place of work and the wide range of applications software available, means that users are as involved with office technology as they are with data processing applications and in many cases, these are easy to integrate and equally easy to access
- *interconnectivity* - LAN techniques and hardware arrangements allow any user to communicate with any other either on a one-to-one basis or by broadcasting (one-to-many). This makes it ideal for electronic mail and its derivatives (see chapter 10).

Just one more point; to remind you, the network **controller** is a piece of hardware, the network **manager** is a person.

Now we have some idea of the hardware and functions of a LAN, we can examine some techniques used in LAN technology.

Connection/access to network services

There must be some mechanism that allows the network controller to arrange which node or user gets processing service from the network and there are several basic techniques used. The first two are very common in LANs, the others apply more to WANs, although are of importance with modern PBX-routed LANs.

Broadcast

LAN broadcast techniques were largely developed from early experiments at the University of Hawaii in connecting terminals to a mainframe, using radio transmission. Signals are generated on a shared radio channel and everyone listens to everyone else (ie, monitors all signals).

Polling
The controller calls all terminals in some sequence and either sends or receives messages. This is most common in star arrangements where a mainframe or minicomputer services many user terminals.

Point-to-point
As we saw much earlier in the book, this usually means a conversation between just two users, but if we allow for *non-store-and-forward*, we then have a technique that could lend itself to a ring (and usually is). For example, B has just received a message from A. If it is for him, his terminal grabs it. If not, it passes the message on to C's terminal, which makes the same decision, and so on. In other words, a kind of multiple point-to-point.

Select
The controller decides who it wants to send to/receive from. Obviously this allows for a high degree of prioritisation and for LANs, although not a complete technique, is often superimposed on one of the others.

So, we can see many users sharing many resources within the LAN, but whether star, ring or bus, we must now consider the problem of how to ensure that access to resources is fair and network resources not wasted.

Contention resolution methods

There are three main methods of accessing resources in common use.

Carrier sense multiple access
This applies mainly to bus networks where broadcasting is used. It was developed from the University of Hawaii *Aloha* technique used in radio data broadcasting where a sender, detecting that the transmission channel was busy, would wait and try again later.

In a LAN, if two transceivers try to transmit at the same time and clash (collide), both must stop otherwise data packets will be damaged. The technique tries to avoid these so-called *collisions*. But at the same time, it must reduce idle time - where the transmission channel is not being used at all (particularly the situation where everybody knows it is busy and everybody waits for the channel to become free). The way this is done in broadcast systems is called *carrier sense multiple access (CSMA).*

The basic idea is that the transceiver listens for the carrier signal on the channel to see if it is busy and only if it is not, will it try to transmit. If it senses that the channel is busy, it must retry at a later time.

If it re-tries immediately, we refer to *1-persistent CSMA* (the probability of retransmission after sensing busy, is 1). We can implement the technique with different values for *persistance* - the lower the persistence, the lower the probability of an immediate retransmission, so the less chance of a further busy. Conversely, the more time is wasted while re-transmission is held up.

If the sender does re-transmit immediately, it may be some time before some of the other stations notice that the channel is busy because of transmission delay, so they may transmit at the same time. The problem arises because a particular station may have transmitted a packet which has not yet reached another (the LAN cables may very long and data rates high - typically 2 nanoseconds per metre) and most of the packet could be transmitted before the collision is detected. When two or more senders transmit simultaneously, the messages corrupt each other, the receivers will not acknowledge acceptance and all messages will have to be re-transmitted.

One solution adopted is for a 'loud noise' to be transmitted by the sender that first detects the collision. While the others are waiting for this to arrive, the originator holds off until the channel is quiet again.

In simple CSMA systems the transmission time for the whole of a message is lost to the sender. A considerable increase in performance can be gained if collision is detected as soon as possible so that senders can abandon the rest of the message theyare trying to transmit.

To this end, extensions to basic CSMA exist, in particular *CSMA/CD* which is based on *collision detection (CD).* If the sender detects a collision at the start of transmission, no data has been sent so no data is lost. However, if the collision occurs during the transmission of a packet, the method requires it to wait for a short time and try again. If there is a further collision on re-try, it must wait again and keep trying until it can seize the channel.

The method used to determine how long to wait before re-try often incorporates a *back-off algorithm*. In effect, a random number is generated which is the basis for a time period during which the sender 'backs off' for a while. The calculation must allow for retries so that it is sensitive to the fact that a collision may have occurred several times.

The next two techniques are used in ring networks.

Time slotting

Making use of reserved time intervals (time slots) is called *time slotting* and is a form of time-division multiplexing. If each user is only allowed to transmit in a particular time slot (say user 1 in the first 1/10 second, user 2 in the second and so on), collisions can be eliminated altogether. This is not very efficient because an unused slot is a waste of **time** - a scarce network resource. In some LANs a mixture of rigid slotting is employed for some of the time with free-for-all CSMA/CD for the rest.

Token passing

A totally different approach, often used in rings networks, is *token passing*. Here, 'empty' packets, called *tokens* pass round a network until required by a sender terminal which attaches its network address, data and the intended receiver terminal's network address to the token. This then passes round the network, through all the various nodes (users, servers and other hardware units, such as repeaters) until it is received. The receiver's terminal then extracts his data, frees the token and it passes on. Note that the control intelligence (the network controller) must handle priorities to prevent one user from hogging the system or a particular facility. A dedicated monitor node is usually responsible for token generation and management.

In modern ring structures, the token is expanded into a packet with data and a CRC block. When the recipient collects the data, an error check is performed and a flag set to show the error status. The packet is then returned to the sender, either to be freed for someone else, or so that a re-transmission can be effected if necessary.

Communication techniques

Baseband techniques are most commonly employed in smaller LANs. Signals are not modulated but are sent as pulses, all nodes (users and servers) sending and receiving at one frequency. The digital DC pulses generated at the workstation (or transceiver) are passed in this square wave form through the medium and because of the high quality circuitry and absence of physical switching, they are not degraded, except over long distances (more than 100s of metres).

It is possible to handle more than one channel in a baseband network but only by employing time-division multiplexing. Broadband LANs on the other hand, rely on frequency division muliplexing so nodes can be operate simultaneously. In complex LANs, other channels may be used for facilities such as closed-circuit TV.

Broadband is much more complicated than baseband because it is intended for multi-channelling - different users, or groups of users are are carried at different frequencies. Signals are analogue in form and although data transfer is much faster, modem-like devices (which generate the carriers needed) are required to connect users onto the medium. Multiplexers can be used also, thus improving bandwidth usage.

LANs of many different types are used but most have as their basis one of three technologies, two of which are ring-based, the third being bus-structured. We will now introduce them.

Important networks technologies

Cambridge ring

The original *Cambridge ring* is now obsolete but its developments in the form of *slotted rings*, are important in many LANs. The basic packet circulates around the ring in one direction and contains:

- source address
- destination address
- 16 bits for data
- status bits (packet accepted/rejected, not received etc).

Recent developments have made use of larger packets, whose size can vary.

The ring is based on twisted pair for transmission and has a repeater for each station. All repeaters are powered from a further pair of wires, from the ring itself, rather than from the station, so if a station goes out of action, the ring is not disturbed. Figure 9.8 shows the basis of a ring workstation.

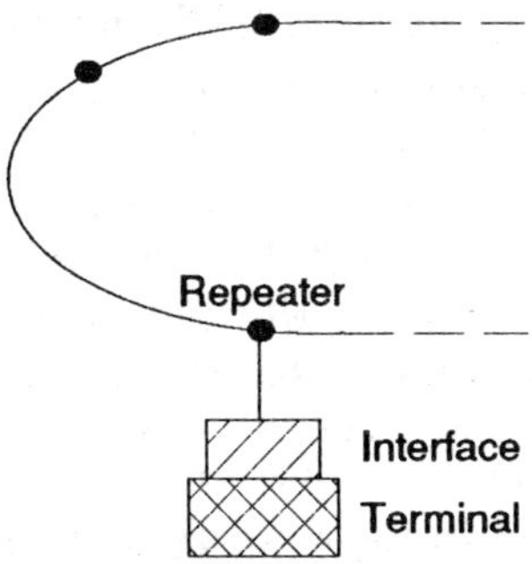

Figure 9.8 A ring workstation

Packets circulate round the ring unless removed. A special node called a *monitor* looks at each packet's status and will remove an abandonned packet or one not received. Each repeater will either pass on an incoming packet if not for its workstation, or accept a new packet from the workstation if no other one is passing.

IBM token ring

A relatively recent devlopment in LANs, the *IBM token ring* uses baseband transmission along twisted pair at up to 4Mbps and can handle 72 nodes in its basic form. (A very recent extension uses specially sheilded twisted wire and is said to handle up to 260 nodes at up to 16Mpbs over short distances).

The technique is based on token-passing. A 24-bit token is seized, data is attached and the token is sent. The receiver extracts the data, sets on the *address-recognised* bit (to show he was the proper receiver), the *frame-copied* bit (to show the frame was correctly received) and sends the token back. Once the frame has been returned to sender and checked out, it can be freed.

Since the frame has a distinct header and trailer, as soon as the packet has been acknowledged, the token can be freed **while data**

is still being copied from the packet. In other words, there is the effect of more than one token (or packet) at a time.

Ethernet

This is one of the most well-known and well-used LAN technologies. It was introduced as *Ethernet-1* in 1973 by the Xerox Corporation and in 1980, Xerox, Digital Equipment Corp and the Intel Corp collaborated in the development and definition of *Ethernet-2*, the standard on which most current Ethernet implementations are based.

Ethernet finds its major application in office environments where there are fairly short transmission paths between the various nodes. Several organisations produce their own version of Ethernet LANs, including Wang *(Wangnet)*, DEC *(DECnet)* and Torus (*Tapestry* and *Icon*). We will restrict ourselves here to the basics of an Ethernet system and not look at the variations.

The technology is based on a bus structure, the medium being coaxial cable, the maximum data transfer rate being 10Mbps and the maximum number of workstations 1024. Baseband techniques are used - signals are placed directly onto the medium and messages are broadcast to all users. CSMA/CD is the contention resolution mechanism used and data is passed round as an *Ethernet packet*, which has the format shown in Figure 9.9 where the items within the packet are shown with corresponding lengths (in octets):

Syncro nisation	To address	From address	Data length	Data content	CRC
8	6	6	2	46-1500	4

Figure 9.9 Ethernet packet format

- *synchronisation* is used as in BSC and HDLC frames (see chapter 6)
- *to address* is of the form block/station and allows for a block of stations to be contacted and a specific one within the block (*block* refers to an allocated group of stations). If the first bit is not set to 0,the system will know that it isdealing with a *multicast* packet (for several receivers).

Then, if all the bits are set to 1, it is a 'tell everybody' multicast packet, otherwise it is for a specific block

- *from address* has a similar format to *to address*
- *date length* specifies the number of data octels in the next part of the product
- *data content* holds the transmitted data and can vary from a minimum of 46 to a maximum of 1500 octets
- *CRC* is a 4-octet cyclic redundancy check field.

The Ethernet-2 specification allows a total distance of about 150 metres with thin coax cable, whereas use of 'thick' coax cable (ie, low-loss) allows networks with a total distance of up to 500 metres. It is usual to lay a length of thick coax (called the *backbone*) throughout the building in which users will be connected. This could be say, up a lift shaft or under floors. When users or groups of users are to be added, thin coax can be tapped off from the backbone.

Each station is connected to the network medium by a *tap-off point* through a *transceiver* which is responsible for packet formation/deformation, the CSMA/CD and the sending and receiving of packets. In this way, each node takes some part in the operation of the network. (Note that suppliers can provide the CSMA/CD logic on a single chip eg, the Intel 82586).

The maximum length of cable from a tap-off point is 50 metres, the minimum distance between workstations is 2.5 metres and the maximum distance between tap-offs is about 100 metres. If extra length is needed, *repeaters* can be added into the network. At the physical end of each run of cable, there must be an electrical impedance called a *terminator*. The basic structure of an Ethernet LAN is illustrated in Figure 9.10.

Care must be taken in estimating the overall maximum length of cable as workstation, transceiver and repeater are all equivalent to specific cable lengths and these must be included in calculations.

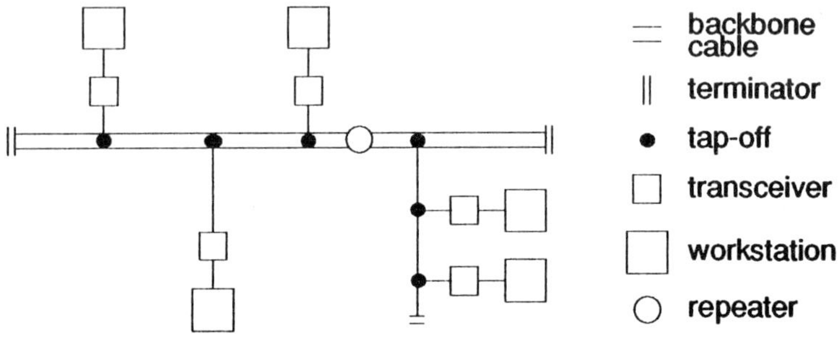

Figure 9.10 Ethernet basic structure

Pause for thought

So far, we have looked at why a LAN might be needed and the main advantages to be gained from its use. We have also considered some of the technology and techniques employed. Now we need to look at the overall running of a LAN and this is in many ways, the most difficult aspect of LANs to deal with. We really need:

- detailed knowledge of the hardware and software used
- a very good idea of what we want to use it for: how many current users, how many future users and how much use they will make of facilities
- a very good idea of purchase and running costs.

These will be specific to a particular network and without them, we can only make generalisations. For our purposes, we can overview some of the thinking that is needed and some of the problems that have to be faced.

LAN management

Selection - how do we decide on the LAN and its organisation?

The first question to be asked is *do we actually need a LAN at all?*. If we are just linking two or three users so that they can share printers, it is probably much simpler to employ a *T-switch*. This is basically a box that connects all the PCs to the printer, so that any one can be connected when necessary. The simpler and older ones have a manual switch while more recent examples can be switched under software control.

As soon as we get more complex than say, just two or three users, we need some management software. If we are going to share files, then unless we pass floppy disks around the office, we will need some file management. A rough guide to indicate that a LAN is needed might be something like:

- 3+ users, each needing action for more than 3-4 hours per day
- 2+ needing access to an expensive printer
- the need for access to other printers
- the need for a range of applications software
- files common to several users
- the necessity for files and software protected from abuse
- users needing to pass data to each other
- a real need for electronic messaging
- the need for more than occasional gateway access to external services
- the need for some central control so that usage statistics can be kept, priorities and privileges can be set up and altered.

If we are dealing with two or three users who only need occasional contact, or are too far apart to consider LAN linkage, we could arrange for modem/PTN linkage with some basic comms software. Within a building, we could even use just null modems to form these links. Remember however, that most PCs at present only support two asynchronous ports (so one user can be connected to only two others) and basic comms software will not support the protocols necessary to enable one user to have a simultaneous conversation with two others.

Estimating

Having decided that a LAN is essential, we must look at what it will be used for and for how much of the working day. We must make some estimate of typical user activity in order to have some idea of the weight that will be placed on the main processor and the transmission medium. This must be application-oriented and we can either look at the applications and see who uses them, or look at these users and see what they need.

A table is of great value here as a working tool and Figure 9.11 shows an example:

Application	*Type of user*	*No. of users*	*Bytes per hour each each user*	*Disk storage needed each user*	*Pages per hour each user*
e-mail	casual	8	500	10,000	5
accounts	experienced	2	130,000	50,000	20
order entry	experienced	2	80,000	100,000	50
spreadsheet	casual	4	200,000	500,000	30
viewdata	casual	2	10,000	30,000	10
word processing	experienced	4	600,000	2,000,000	80
software/system				8,000,000	8

Figure 9.11 LAN user/usage table

From this, we can try to estimate the required number of print and file servers and work out roughly the average data transfer rate. It can only be a guide at this point however, as we never know exactly at any instant how many files are being transferred, how many users are sending print lines and so on, but at least we can say whether we are looking at 0.5 or 5 Mbps.

Files are also a problem: some will be for general use and some for specific users, but we may find it difficult to calculate how many users will want to access a particular file, or take copies of part of it at any one time.

Physical factors

The next thing is the LAN processing capabilities. The management software/hardware itself will need a basic overhead quite apart from the applications and we do not want to arrive at a condition know as *processor flooding*, where the system just cannot handle the work it has to do. Fortunately, this is becoming less of a problem as chip technology advances and there are new processors coming out (*Motorola 68040, Intel 80486* etc) which are very powerful. At the same time, LAN interface cards are getting faster.

Type of medium, network configuration and the contention resolution mechanism are not independent variables that the potential user selects from the list available. They are very much bound up with a particular LAN supplied and all you can really do (unless you are designing your own from scratch) is to look at what is available and be guided by your supplier and perhaps other companies that have installed LANs. Using an estimate table, perhaps like that of Figure 9.11, you should be able to determine a broad specification for your LAN.

Actual topology will be determined by the required user locations and the transmission length involved. Bear in mind that there are operational considerations as well, such as whether existing internal telephone wiring can be re-used, or the possibilities for expansion and change. It is unlikely that the number of users will remain static and we must make allowances for adding new users. Also, people move around within an office or building and it is not a good idea to set up a LAN that cannot easily cope with this kind of change.

Applications

Software suppliers are usually very aware of the LAN environment in which their packages will run, but the MS-DOS (or PC-DOS) operating system used with most PCs these days, does not support true multi-user processing (particularly important with regard to multiple file access). As this is essential in a LAN, the LAN software must handle this itself and you must be sure that a particular package can run under the LAN multi-user environment. Conversely, if the package has been built for multi-user use, is it compatible with the LAN you are going to run it on?

Applications can be classified into those that are supplied with the LAN and those DP and electronic office applications programs you want to run. Built-in facilities usually include some kind of e-mail or messaging, backed up with a simple word processor. Some LANs provide the minimum, while others are quite sophisticated (see the review of Torus *Tapestry* at the end of this chapter).

If the number of applications required is fairly small, the user can be presented with a simple menu, but with sophisticated and complex LANs, much care must be given to the kind of dialogue that the user is presented with. However simple we try to make it for the user, the fact is that a LAN provides decentralised facilities and with these come some measure of decentralised **responsibility**; everyone must play his part and follow the rules - failure to do so leads to chaos.

To make life as easy as possible, while at the same time trying to reduce situations where a user can break the rules means we need to employ some very clever VDU screen design.

The dedicated user (who uses the workstation regularly as an essential part of their job) is no real problem once trained to handle their job on the LAN.

It is the casual 'hot-shot', who thinks he knows a thing or two, that can cause most trouble. In any organisation, there is always someone who has played with computers, has managed to 'rip off' a few clever applications packages and tries to install them on the system. Quite apart from the possibility of infecting the system with viruses, storing unsupported software in live libraries and running unscheduled programs makes life very difficult for the LAN manager and will only confuse the bread-and-butter users.

Another consideration is the possibility of linking applications between different systems. Gatewaying out is not usually a problem (one workstation can act as a gateway server and provide an exit for users), but it becomes more difficult if we want to bridge several LANs or gateway to a mainframe. Then we have to consider the network protocols involved and the difficulty for example, of linking an Ethernet complex to an X25-compatible mainframe.

Number of users and siting

Some questions that may need answers:

- will everyone have a terminal or can some be shared out?
- will a particular terminal provide enough extra information or reduced work-load to justify its existence and the extra load on network facilities?

- does a particular manager really need his PC in the network for the few spreadsheet calculations he wants, just so that he can occasionally make use of the laser printer?
- are there users within the organisation that need to communicate either text or data, who are currently not connected at all?
- do the applications dictate the siting of terminals? Presumably a group of work-processing or desk-top publishing operatives would expect to sit close to each other, but do we want the sales clerks to be near the accounts clerks?

Installation

Setting up a LAN is not cheap and it is important to think of installation and of future use. Some questions that may help include:

- are there enough PCs already in use and are they compatible with each other and the LAN software/hardware?
- do we need to buy more printers and if so, what kind?
- can we make use of existing cabling and trunking?
- will we need to drill through walls, take up floors, lay down a backbone etc? (Not only do these involve expenditure but they are a source of disturbance within a busy organisation)
- Is there any way we can plan for future expansion?

Finally, having determined (or estimated) the number of users, file servers and printers, we should allow at least 50% slack for all the extra users who will want to jump on, once things are going well and the extra input that will appear once users start to find new applications - particularly for word processing, DTP and electronic mail.

LAN management and control

User considerations

A clear definition of user responsibilities for system usage and activities must be laid down and supported by a set of privileges at different levels. It must be possible for overall control to be maintained by one network manager, who will need regular usage statistics and a good LAN should provide these. Typical useful averages and totals obtained could include:

- user response times
- print queue lengths (how many jobs waiting for results to be printed)
- log-on times (who logs on, when and for how long)
- number of accesses to a disk/directory/file
- the number of packets needing retransmission
- node breakdowns.

LAN operational problems

When we make use of a wide-area network, the responsibility for ensuring that the hardware delivers a minimum service level is the responsibility of the network provider. With a LAN, **we** are the network provider and if operation of the network is to be a success, there are a number of problems that must be allowed for. Many occuring in the day-to-day running of a LAN result from some kind of hardware failure and include *outrages* (severe problems that really upset the network) such as:

- a break in the transmission medium
- a workstation breakdown
- an Ethernet transceiver *jabbering* (stuck in transmit mode)
- a monitor or other node failure
- sabotage.

Some of these problems can be removed fairly simply. For example, one possibility allows for a complete breakdown of the workstation, by connecting it in parallel with a relay (power-operated switch). While the PC is on, the relay takes power from it and stays off. When the PC loses power, the relay comes in (see Figure 9.12).

A jabbering transmitter can be detected by building in time checks - if a transmitter has hogged the system for more than a defined maximum period, the network can spot it.

To allow for monitor failure, it is possible to put in a *shadow* (a back-up device that comes in if another fails).

Techniques are available (such as *time domain reflectometry*) using the electrical properties of the medium, to spot where a break has occurred due to a cut or damaged cable. Some LAN

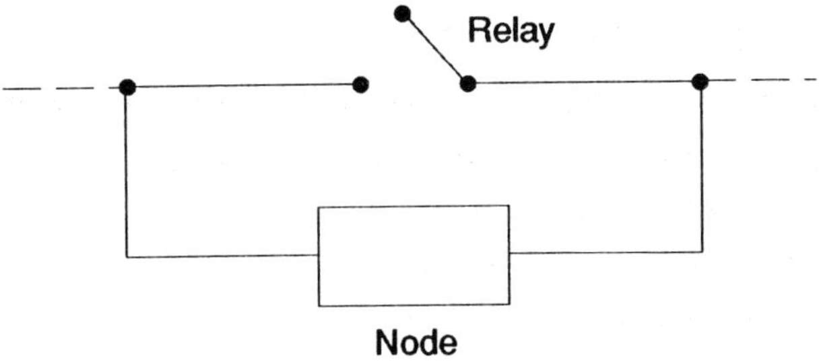

Figure 9.12 Node failure allowance

implementations employ a double medium as a *folded ring* so that although any individual node can fail, the 'integrity' of the ring is maintained. Figure 9.13 shows how the Racal *Planet (private local area network)* uses this neat, folded ring technique to overcome the problem of a broken cable.

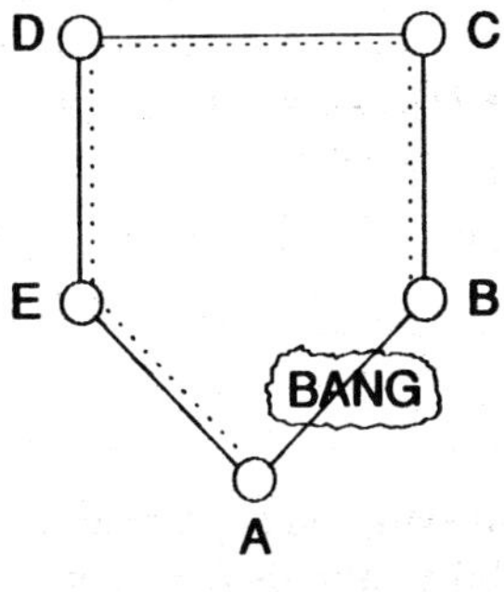

Figure 9.13 Racal PLANET medium outrage handling

While everything is OK, transmission makes use of one of the cables, (say the outer in the diagram) and tokens pass A-B-C-D-E-A. If a node goes down, it is immediately sensed by the controller which reconfigures the ring so that the other cable is used. The diagram shows a break between A and B and after re-configuration, tokens between A and B pass along the outer cable in the path A-E-D-C-B, then back along the inner cable in the path B-C-D-E-A. If A is completely disconnected, the ring can be adjusted to include just E-D-C-B or B-C-D-E.

In the last 2-3 years, as with standards in many other areas, LANs have been the subject of an enormous amount of work. There is no way in a book of this level, that we can hope to give you the full current situation, but at least we must state the titles of the most important references.

ISO standards for LANs

As part of the overall OSI specification, there exist standards relating to LANs, which overlap in layers 1/2. They are based on similar IEEE standards and the most important include the list shown in Figure 9.14.

Reference	*Subject*	*IEEE Equivalent*
8802/3	CSMA/CD (based on Ethernet)	802.3
8802/4	token-passing bus access	802.4
8802/5	token-passing ring access	802.5
8802/7	slotted ring access (based on Cambridge Ring - BS6531/6532)	802.7
8802/2	logical link control protocol	802.2

Figure 9.14 ISO standards for LANs

Each of the first four standards provides a common service referred to as *medium access control*. Above this is the LAN logical link control protocol (the last standard in the list), which is similar to OSI layer 2. This can provide addressing and error detection (LLC1) or be closer to LAPB (see chapter 6). If designers, suppliers and implementers of LANs conform to these standards, life is made much easier particularly when linking a LAN to an X25 WAN. Note that recent modifications to the Ethernet specification mean that it almost exactly satisfies 8802/3.

As we have said, there are many LANs on the market generally based on a ring or a bus and given that a particular kind of LAN structure is wanted, there are often many alternative suppliers, whose software can support the structure and usage needed. We will now have a quick overview of *Tapestry*, a LAN marketed by *Torus Systems Ltd* of Cambridge.

Torus Tapestry

This is just one of many commercially available LAN software/hardware packages, but I am fairly familiar with it, having used it in teaching for several years and I think it is well worth introducing. It is an Ethernet structure based on IBM PCs (XTs in my college), using coaxial cable as the medium. Each PC has a network controller card fitted and the coaxial cable fits in to the back of the PC via a coaxial socket.

CSMA/CD is employed with an interesting extension. Although the LAN basically uses baseband transmission, all messages are passed to a transceiver, which relays them at a different frequency. In other words, 'send' is at one frequency and 'receive' is at another - in this way the number of collisions is in theory halved.

Each file server is a PC responsible for a hard disk, called a *cabinet*. Cabinets have the *drawer* as a sub-division, each of these actually being an MS-DOS directory. The logical structure of a Tapestry disk is shown in Figure 9.15. A cabinet can be password protected; drawers within a cabinet can be restricted to a particular user and files within a drawer can have various levels of security.

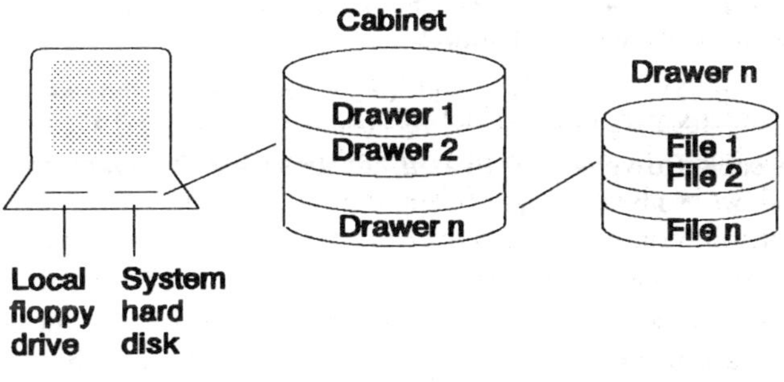

Figure 9.15 Tapestry disk structure

Each user of the system is given a user name and password, both of which are needed before the system will let you in. Users have access to local files on the PC hard and floppy drives and you can import or export data between local and system areas as you want.

Each user has access to electronic mail and can prepare messages with the text editor, send/receive messages, set up a mailing list for message broadcasting and examine a diary to see what messages have been sent and to whom.

PCs can be assigned as gateways, one for each type of service. Thus gateways providing modem access to viewdata, a direct link to a mainframe or perhaps a special link (bridge) to another LAN, are all possible. Once a gateway has been set up and the services it can access defined, any user can go through it.

Priviledge and security is not easy to maintain without someone having a lot of authority, but is fairly easy to set up. Only one person should have 'network manager' status and it will be his job to configure the network and the users. This will include decisions on:

- which PCs will act as file, printer and gateway servers
- how to organise the software libraries
- the actual siting of the PCs, printers and users
- who will act as server managers for each server
- what will be the passwords, who will be given acces to them and how often should they be changed
- any operational rules or conditions such as reminding users that all mail messages to be left on the system for more than 3 days, should be copied to a private save area, because the mail server manager will remove them regularly.

Dialogue associated with Tapestry is entirely menu-based, choices being based on a series of icon screens, using a mouse, the cursor control keys to line up on the icon or by entering the first character of the selection. (Note that for some screens, the function keys are used for selecting further options - where this is the case, we will refer to say, F3 for function key 3.)

At any time, some 'help' can be provided with F1, in the form of a *pop-up list* - a menu that come up from the bottom of the screen (compare this with a *pull-down* menu that comes down from the top).

Other functions appear in a banner at the foot of the screen and like help, are obtained with the function keys. The system has a rather nice protection mechanism. If a user does not have a particular privilege, the main icon or banner function just does not appear. For example, the home screen in Figure 9.16 shows network manager from F6. This only appears on the screen if the log-in is by the network manager.

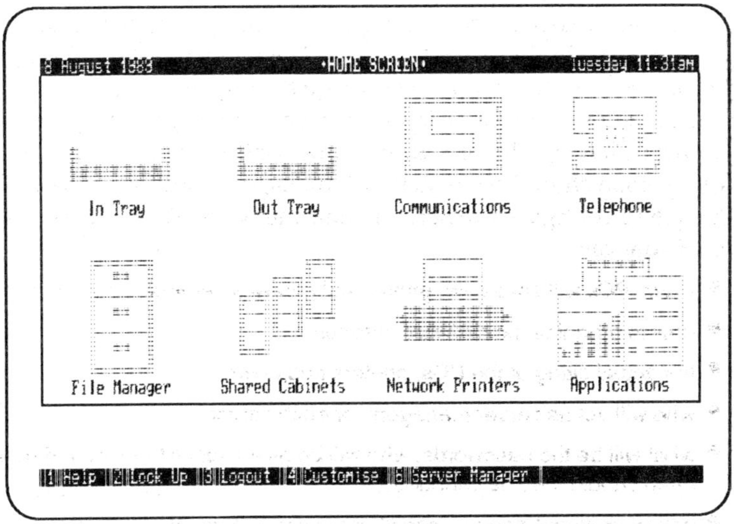

Figure 9.16 The Home screen

In this short overview, it is impossible to detail every aspect of the package. However, the various screens illustrated will give you some idea of the scope of the package.

Home screen facilities

The *home screen* appears as soon as you have logged on with a valid user number and password. As you can see from Figure 9.16, there are eight options available. On selection, option screens are displayed. From these you can always return to the home screen by selecting the *home* icon. Options include:

- *in-tray* - allows you to look at any messages sent to you

- *applications* - allows you to access any applications software that has been set up for you. For example, a spreadsheet, such as Lotus, a data manager such as Smart, or an expert system shell, such as Xi-Plus
- *network printers* - the screen relating to the three printers set up for practical work at Thames Valley College is shown in Figure 9.17

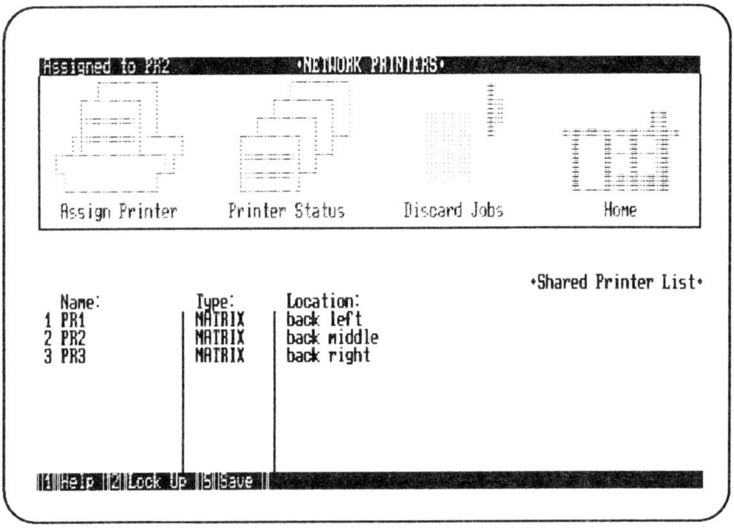

Figure 9.17 The Network Printers screen

- *shared cabinets* - whose screen is shown in Figure 9.18. (Appendixes 2/3 will refer to this tapestry configuration. As you can see from the diagram, there are three cabinets, corresponding to the system manager, the sales office and the warehouse)
- *file manager* - allows access to the user's local files. See figure 9.19 in which we have previously selected the **TOP** drawer of the disk with the *open drawer* option. If you look carefully at the files shown in this top drawer, you will spot one called MESS1.MG, which is the message being displayed in Figure 9.21. The other, called OTHERS is also referred to in this screen. As you can see, the screen contains many options to allow you to 'do things' with the files. For example, *set drive* enables you to change the drive specification from 'C' to 'A', so that you can operate on the local floppy drive

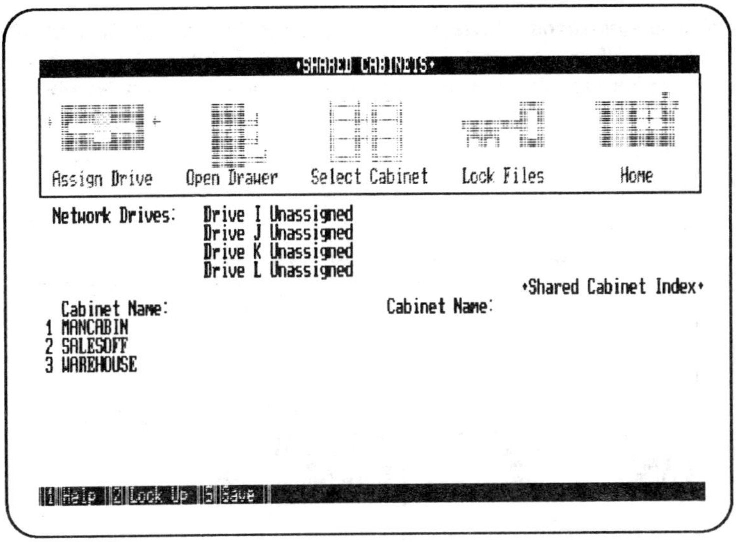

Figure 9.18 The Shared Cabinets screen

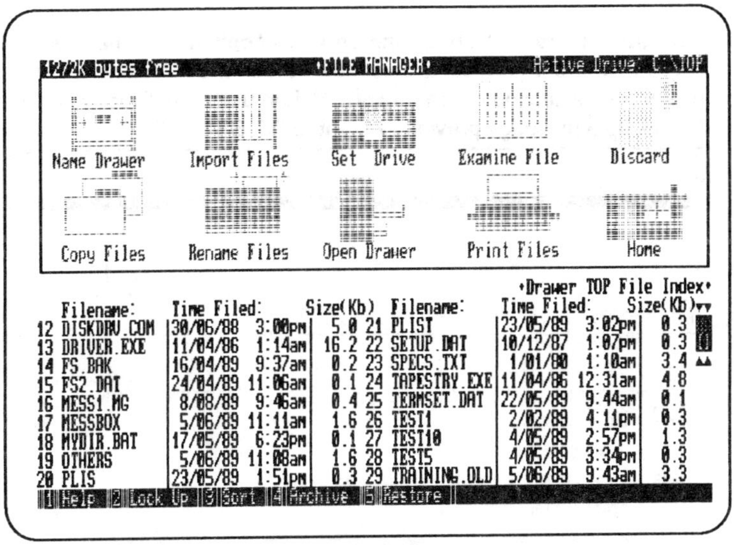

Figure 9.19 The File Manager screen

- *communications* - allows access to the three services shown in Figure 9.20. BVS is the Berkshire County Council viewdata service that provides local trade and general information service. HARRIS is a direct link to the college Harris mainframe. LIBRARY is the local Slough Public Library service that gives information about library services and books in the library

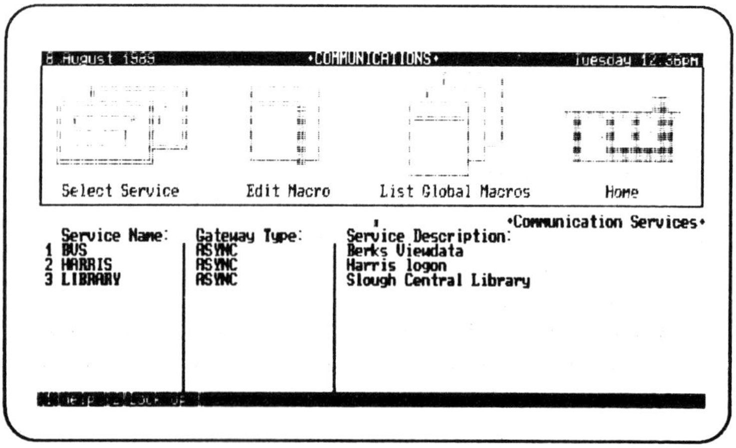

Figure 9.20 The 'Communications' screen

- *out-tray* - Figure 9.21 shows the *send mail* option from the *Out-tray* screen, where I created a message (under a particularly relevant subject) by selecting *prepare mail* and then used the Tapestry editor to pick up a message previously created (MESS1.MG).

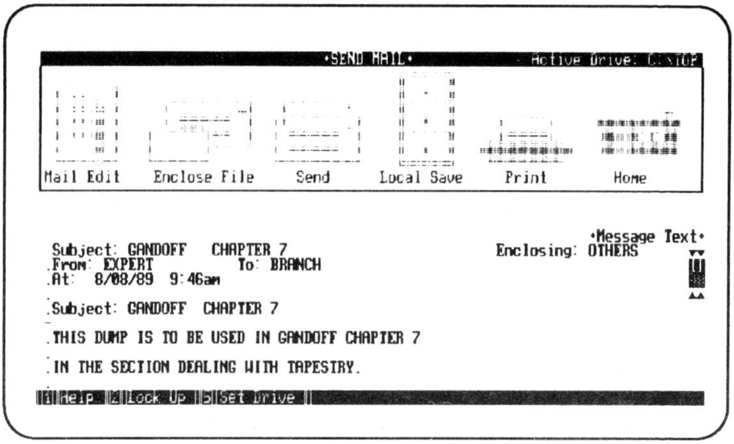

Figure 9.21 An 'Out-tray' screen with a message/enclosure

The *enclose file* option allows a user to attach the name of a relevant file to a message - I have sent a message about chapter 7 and told the receiver he will find more in a file called OTHERS. To keep the message, you select *local save* and when you send the message (select *send mail* and specify which users you want it to go to), the system saves it for you. If you want to send messages regularly to a group of people, you select *create mail list* from the out-tray screen and produce a group mailing list

- *server manager* - allows a server manager to observe his responsibilities. From the home screen, F6 brings up the screen in Figure 9.22 (this particular user has manager status to everything) *Applications* allows the server manager to set up and change the applications software that users have access to. *Printer server* allows for operations on the printer, such as installing new network printers, restarting and rearranging the order of jobs in the queue.

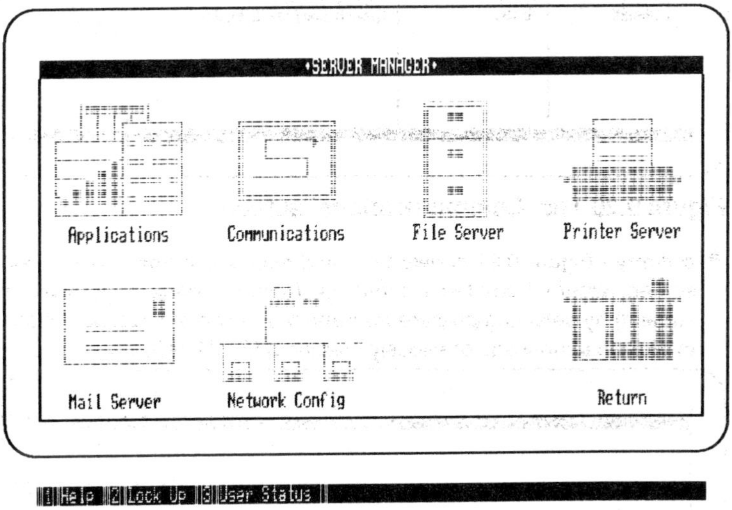

Figure 9.22 The Network Server Manager main screen

The *communications* option of the server manager screen is shown in Figure 9.23. As you can see, there are four external services that can be accessed, the three you have already seen in Figure 9.20 and a new one that I have just added called GANDOFFSHOUT (it is not a serious service!). Note that the screen allows for *instal,* the creation, *alter* the changing and *discard* the removal of a service. *Edit macro* allows for the set-up of a log-on dialogue (see chapter 7)

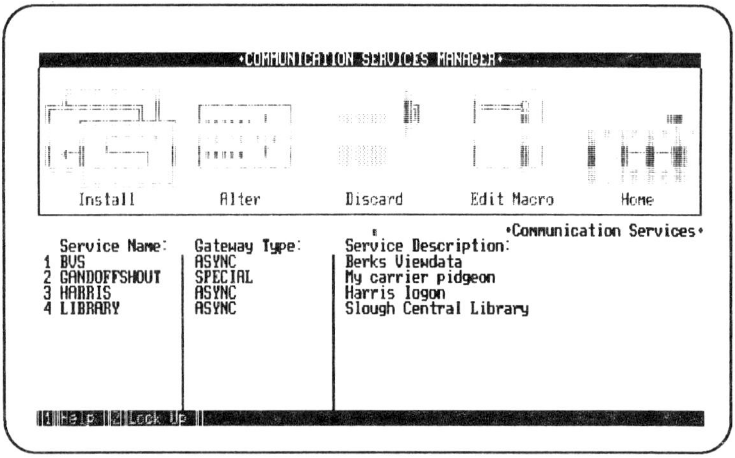

Figure 9.23 A Communications Server Manager screen

- *mail server* - allows the mail server manager to monitor and maintain the e-mail system. The mail server screen (shown in Figure 9.24) allows the manager to sort mail into order by name, date etc. He can also discard (remove) mail. (As you can see, while I was messing about with Figures 9.21 and 9.24, I sent three messages on the same subject and with almost the same content. All of these are rubbish now and should be removed, otherwise the disk space allocated to messages

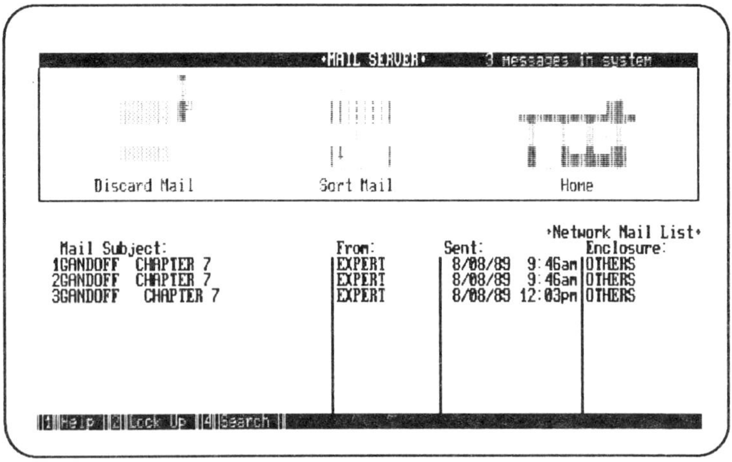

Figure 9.24 The Mail Server screen

will fill up and no more will be accepted. It will be the mail server manager's job to do this.)

Network configuration

From the network server manager screen (Figure 9.22), the option *network configuration* produces the screen in Figure 9.25 - a list of the user names that have access. (The package has been configured for a case study and the names correspond to the sales office, the warehouse etc.)

This network configuration option is the most dangerous option in the system. Once a user has access to it, it is possible to delete users, change passwords and generally do some dreadful damage. At the college, only user **EXPERT** has the privilege of this option and then only if he logs on with the password **METSYS.** (Both of these will be changed long before the book is published).

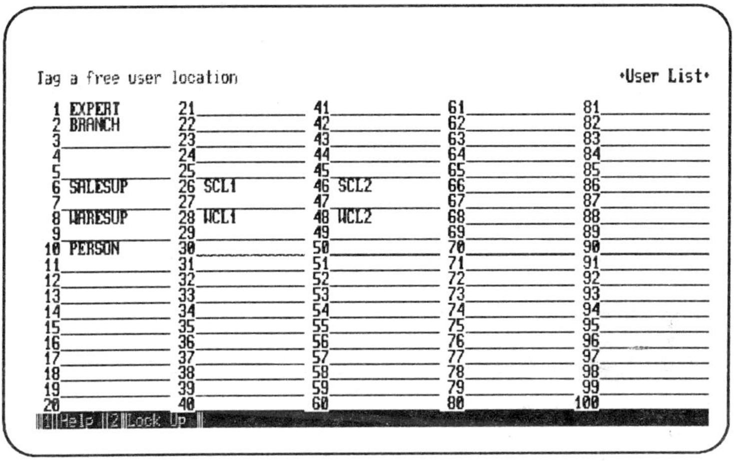

Figure 9.25 A list of users

F5 enables a new user to be added and Figure 9.25 show the screen where I am just about to pick a location in which to add a new user **ADDED-HACKER**. F3 changes the screen to show the node list, the list of PCs that make up all the workstations. Figure 9.26 shows this screen where location 3 has been selected to allow for the addition of a new node called **HACK-IN**. Figure 9.27 show a new user, Mr. **ADDED-HACKER** being added to the list. He

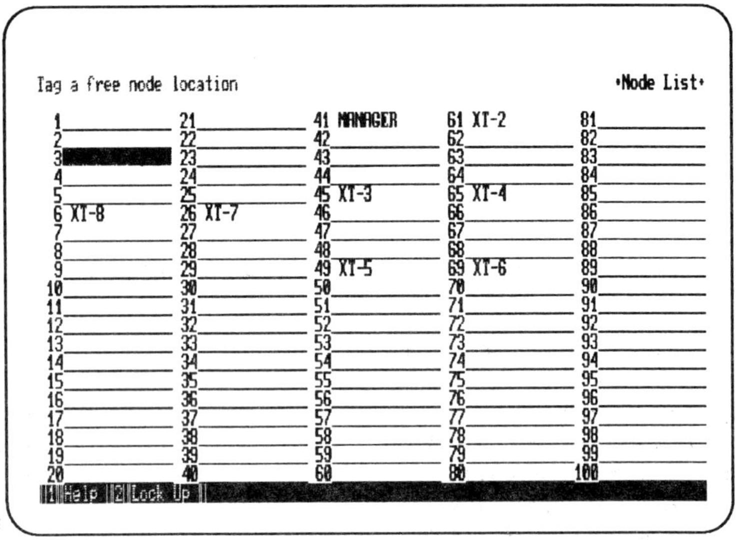

Figure 9.26 A node list waiting for an edit

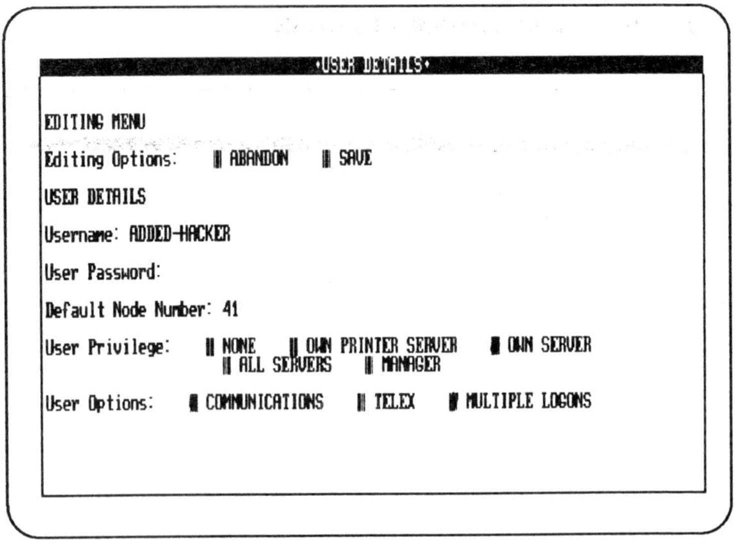

Figure 9.27 Adding a user - ADDED-HACKER

has been given *own server* status, can carry out communications and is allowed to log on simultaneously at several nodes.

Finally, having selected the name **HACK-IN** for location 3 on the screen in Figure 9.26, Figures 9.28 and 9.29 show the addition of this new node. As you can see, it will act as a printer server and software library server. As a gateway server, it provides an

```
                              •NODE DETAILS•

EDITING MENU
Editing Options:    ABANDON    SAVE
NODE DETAILS
Node Name: HACK-IN
Software Library Node Number: 0
Network Address: 00 00 00 00
File Server:    NO    YES
Printer Server:    NO    YES
Gateway Server:    NO    YES
Software Library Server:    NO    YES
                                                        Continued ...
```

Figure 9.28 Adding a node - HACK-IN

```
                              •NODE DETAILS•

Software Library Server:    NO    YES
GATEWAY SERVER DETAILS
Gateway Name:
Gateway Type:    ASYNC    TELEX    REMOTE    3270 BSC
                   SPECIAL
Service Code: 0
Modem Port Number: 0
Modem Parameters: prayers
Modem Type:    SMARTMODEM    DACOM GT    DACOM AD    XTEC    DIRECT
                 QUATTRO
Dialling Method:    TONE    PULSE
```

Figure 9.29 Adding a node - HACK-IN - continued

asynchronous link via a Quattro modem, dialling out being by DTMF (not pulse-code).

If you examine these screens very carefully, you will find that you have been able to revise and consolidate a lot of your knowledge about LANs. It can only give you a taste of what is possible, but I hope that it is enough to whet your appetite for work in the future.

I am grateful to Torus Systems for permission to discuss Tapestry and show the screens and also to Thames Valley College for allowing me to use our implementation of the system.

Recap

- we first looked at the basic network structures and showed that ring and bus are the most common in LANs
- we then tried to explain what a LAN is and why it is needed as a means of achieving efficient DP within an organisation
- what a LAN is, can only be answered by looking at what it is used for, who is using it and how much
- why it is used is mainly because resources are needed by all users but not always all the time; the technology behind a LAN enables these resources to be shared out in an economical and fairly efficient manner
- hardware components that can be employed in different LANs, in particular the network controller, transceivers and the various servers are considered
- personal responsibility, in particular the status of the LAN manager is discussed
- some of the technology and techniques associated with LANs that ensure a fair distribution of resources are covered and an overview of the main ring- and bus-based LANs is put forward
- practical problems of estimating for, selecting and running a LAN including measures to cope with hardware failure are discussed
- the LAN Tapestry is looked at, demonstrating many features of a popular LAN.

Typical questions

Question 9.1

A manufacturing organisation occcupies several sites and has three minicomputers servicing about 75 users. The factory and main offices cover the area of a circle about 100 metres in diameter. Research and development and quality control are about 10 kilometres away on a site about half the size of the works.

a. give your views on whether the whole complex constitutes a LAN
b. if you feel that it is not, suggest how the overall network might be structured into a number of connected LANs.

Question 9.2

Bodyshop Ltd is a personnel recruitment/selection agency for permanent and temporary staff who are seeking office and secretarial appointments. It employs an office manager, a staff interviewer, an accounts clerk and two typists, all of whom make some use of PCs and the company has decided to install a LAN to cover all its DP requirements.

a. make list of 10 application areas that the company could have supported by the appropriate software
b. discuss the factors you would need to know about in order to make some recommendations on the LAN.
c. what do you feel should be the responsibilities of whoever is placed in charge of the LAN once installed?
d. what steps can be taken to reduce the problems that will arise if LAN hardware fails?

10: Applications and future trends

Objectives

After reading this chapter, you should:

- appreciate the role of data communications within data processing
- appreciate how integrated data processing and data communications are applied in commercial organisations
- appreciate how data communications technology has changed the function of systems design
- appreciate how an organisation selects comms services and facilities
- be aware of and be able to classify the various 'value-added' services
- understand the significance and framework of videotex and other methods of data/information access
- understand the significance and framework of methods of text and data interchange including e-mail, fax, EFT and EDI
- appreciate what is available from the user's home
- have some idea of future trends in electronic data transfer.

Introduction

The purpose of this chapter is to help you to put into perspective, what you have learnt from all the other chapters. We will look at the internal and external services and facilities available and see how they can be incorporated into computerised systems. We will look too at comms in practice and give a summarised view of DP comms and telecommunications and how they fit together.

By the time you have finished this chapter, you should be in a position to say why comms is so important and have a clear picture of many of its ramifications to business, industry and the private individual.

We will start by examining the stages in planning the introduction to comms into a company. We will then look at a 'typical' company and summarise its DP activities in the light of possible comms applications. Then we will look in more detail at these comms applications, who provides them and how they can be used.

We will finish with some ideas about comms and the individual and make just a few some predictions.

System design and comms

In order for a company to implement comms applications, it is essential to look at all of its DP applications, all of its voice communication needs and all the external services available that might be integrated into its systems or be used to support them. Then it can try to organise its DP in the best possible way. (Before continuing here, you should re-read chapter 1 to remind you of the relation between DP and comms.)

Now, let us start with a plan of campaign to examine what is currently done and what might be wanted:

Define the company DP requirements

Obviously the company must know what it wants to do with its computers - what business applications it needs to support with the aid of computerised systems. Although not every application will always be fully computerised, most of the following departments or functional units will have some computer involvement;

- marketing, public relations/publicity - ensuring that potential customers know about the company's products and services and that the company appears in the best way to the public and to industry at large
- sales, customer service and order processing - attracting and dealing with particular customers, taking their orders for goods and making sure that they are happy with the service they get; passing records to marketing, of the progress of salesman and sales campaigns as well as general information, so that advertising and publicity campaigns can be run
- production/machine scheduling/control - organising the factory production processes so that raw materials/components, machines

and staff are all available and used in the most efficient way, so that orders can be met quickly and cost-effectively; ensuring that production machines, computers and so on are used properly, regularly serviced and replaced when they become uneconomical to continue running

- purchasing - making sure that raw materials, components, packaging material, and office and other 'consumables' (such as stationery) are ordered from suppliers and delivered when they are needed, at the best possible prices and the shortest delivery times
- stock receipts, stock issues - checking, entering and recording deliveries of goods ordered from suppliers, checking out finished goods for packaging and delivery to customers
- stock handling, packaging and stock control - ensuring that goods are kept in the best way so that they can be kept in the best condition and retrieved when needed for orders; packing the goods for safe delivery; trying to ensure that there are always enough finished goods and raw materials/components and without there being too many (so that money is not unnecessarily tied up)
- loading/delivery scheduling and vehicle control - ensuring that delivery vehicles are routed in the most efficient way and that goods are loaded on to the vehicles to support this; ensuring that vehicles are regularly serviced and generally 'legal on the road'
- payroll, personnel and manpower planning/recruitment - making sure that staff are paid according to work done, (wages, bonuses commissions ans so on); trying to ensure that staff are contented and work in the most efficient and effective manner; trying to anticipate when extra or replacement staff will be needed and ensuring that they can be found
- accounts - ensuring that company bills are paid, trade debtors are chased up for payment, there is always enough cash for day-to-day running and to fund long term investments such as machine and vehicle purchase; making available an up-to-date view of the profitability of the organisation and ensuring that any surplus funds are invested wisely.

Define the staff 'location' requirements

It is unlikely that all the potential users of the computer will be within sitting distance of it. We must decide on the method of connection between the user workstation and the main processor that will service it - either for data entry or information access. Several questions should be asked, including:

- are users directly connectable as on-line terminals to the mainframe services?
- are they within the connectable maximum for LAN workstations?
- are there users with similar requirements that can be 'clustered' into a subsidiary network?
- are any external (modem) links needed to services such as database access or fax?
- are any external modem links needed, such as to the company processor services from employees or customers outside the main site?

This latter could include the possibility of:

- customers dialling in to access stock data (perhaps via videotex screens)
- sales staff entering orders or enquiries through mobile terminals via the cellular network
- employees 'teleworking' from home (perhaps it is convenient for some staff to do all their work from home using a terminal/modem link).

Consider the effect of staff 'location' on DP

Now that computing facilities are available all over the site (and possibly outside it) to anyone with access to a terminal, we will be dealing with a much wider range of users and user skills. Further questions to be posed include:

- what form will screen dialogue need to take to enable users to select from the services and facilities available?
- who will want to make use of which facilities and who will be allowed access?
- what extra security measures are needed to prevent unauthorised access to services and data within and outside the company?
- will identification/data entry hardware be needed? (eg, magnetic card readers for on-line employee identification access to restricted areas, bar-code readers in the warehouse being used for stock entry etc)

Define the voice communications requirements

These must be defined because their provision may rely on the same hardware and software as that needed for data comms. Yet more questions include:

- can the digital PBX be used to control the LANs linked to the mainframe?
- will telephone users want computerised assistance (such as directory dialling) and are these also users of other services, ie, telephone services available from their data terminal? (Directory dialling is an example of what is called *computer-integrated telephony (CIT)* and is covered later on)
- is the level of voice communication sufficiently high to require digital linkage and can data be carried at the same time?

Examine and select from the range of possible 'external services'

Although later in this chapter, we will go into more detail, the following is a summary of external services:

- *EFT* - confirmation of creditability and transfer of credit from customer to supplier without cash being involved. It automates retail transactions at the point of service (shop, supermarket or in the home) and allow for banking and shopping. It is based on a universally acceptable identity card authorising credit transfers from the customer's bank to that of the supplier
- *EDI* - the transfer of documentary information such as invoices and payments, between computers, without the need to send the actual paper
- *Videotex* - user-friendly access to the data, information and services provided by a wide range of companies
- *Telex* - an international standard means of communication using limited-format text
- *E-mail* - communicating via mailboxes with other people and services provided by a wide range of companies. (Note that e-mail organisations often provide videotex data and information access and videotex companies often provide e-mail!)
- *Fax* - the transfer of images via a modem-telephone line. Usually by placing the document to be sent into a special-purpose fax machine, but more recently directly between PCs which are fitted with a *fax card* - a special circuit board that has a modem and fax software on-board
- *'Voice' services* - radiopaging and telephone messaging (often linked to other services). Possibilities include receiving a voice message telling you that there is a telex or fax waiting for you.

How will they be incorporated into the new system?
We may have to modify parts of the system to include the services we decide to make use of. This often means ensuring that existing manual and computerised procedures can interface with them, especially if:

- the user needs to pass data to them, perhaps transferring documents from an existing application to a remote EDI service, or authorising payroll credit transfers to *BACS,* a central clearing organisation that will transfer the funds to each employee's bank account
- the user wants to capture data and use it in a particular application, such as obtaining an insurance quotation and incorporating it into a letter to a client, or obtaining government or industry trade figures to bring them into a spreadsheet and then compare them with those for the organisation.
- the user application involves capturing data and then editing and modifying it to make available to other users (see 'videotex' later in this chapter)
- data needs to be gathered from a number of users within the organisation before being passed to the external service.

How will we connect locations to the central and external services?
Once we have decided on the services needed and who will access them, we must sort out the mix of LAN, sub-LAN, private network, analogue/digital network for all the various applications. (If you refer back to chapter 2, **having defined 'network A',we must now define 'network B'.)**

- *Network A* - all the DP applications (as specified above in 'DP requirements'); all the internal comms applications (e-mail, videotex, etc) that we have decided to implement; all the external services needed
- *Network B* - direct terminal-mainframe links and LAN links (within the LAN and LAN- mainframe); analogue links; digital links
- *Extra hardware* - transmission media (optical fibre, co-ax, microwave dishes etc), modems, line drivers, multiplexers, terminal cluster controllers, digital terminators.

Having decided on the plan, we can now look at a 'typical' business organisation and review the DP it is likely to carry out. Then we can carry out a broad examination of how its DP requirements can be serviced more efficiently and more cheaply by the extensive involvement of comms.

A 'Typical' company

What DP does the company carry out now

It is impossible to define this 'typical' organisation so let's do it - and accept that although not entirely satisfactory, we need some kind of framework on which to build our ideas.

Let us take a company that sells products. We need not specify what it sells, but the product range is based partly on finished goods bought in and repackaged and partly on goods produced in the factory from raw materials. Customers are mainly other companies, to whom goods are delivered but some orders are dispatched by post or rail.

Its main functional areas (for simplicity, assumed to be located on one site) are as follows:

- *computing* - the company mainframe computer on the site supports an Ethernet-based network of terminals, some in subsidiary Ethernet LAN configurations and some as stand-alone. The mainframe has three modem dial-up links and the organisation has a packet-switching identity (chapter 8) for access to X25 networks. All company files/databases are held on the mainframe disks
- *sales* - the sales office will action orders placed in writing or by telephone. They will also need to reply to telephone enquiries about products, order progress and delivery times. The mobile sales force will want to know which customers to see and record results of visits. Any orders generated will need to be passed to the sales office for action. The office has six terminals in a LAN: three for enquiry/order entry, one to assist the salesmen, three for order confirmation and general company correspondance (acting as the general company typing pool)
- *payroll* - all staff are monthly paid by credit transfer. The salesmen are reimbursed monthly for travelling and other expenses in cash. They receive a commission, one month in arrears, on sales generated. Some production staff receive a bonus related to work carried out. This is paid in the current month. The office has three 3 terminals in a LAN

- *factory production/stock* - goods for production are held in the factory store. From order information, the factory produces or makes up deliveries for dispatch. Purchasing is informed of shortages of raw materials. The factory has six terminals in a LAN: three for production support, one for general planning, two for production scheduling and two individual terminals for stock issue/entry recording
- *purchasing* has two terminals in a LAN; one for purchase order generation and one for records and order progress
- *despatch* - deliveries from the factory are suitably packaged. Small or non-urgent deliveries may be posted, but the majority are handled by delivery vehicles. Purchasing are informed of shortages of packaging materials. A daily loading and delivery schedule must be produced for the vehicles. There are three terminals in a LAN: one for delivery scheduling, one for dispatch recording and one for vehicle control
- *accounts and finance* have four terminals in a LAN: two for orders and invoicing, two for management and control and two for external enquiry.

Pause for thought

Although a very broad specification of company activities carried out, this should be enough for you to think about what could be changed and added to take advantage of comms facilities. So, spend some time thinking about the questions:

- what comms facilities could be employed?
- where could they be used - internal/external?
- what would be the advantages?

Orient your thinking towards:

- the reduction in the amount of paper required
- more efficient communication within the organisation and outside
- more effective management information
- more effective information for sales, production and accounts
- more efficient use of vehicles.

The problem that has been set here is very complex as it requires DP as well as comms knowledge. You are not expected to provide anything like a complete answer, but it will help you considerably to summarise what you have learned and it will give us a focus for the rest of the chapter.

In order to answer the question just posed, you need to have an overall view of all the external services that are available to the company. Then you can decide how to integrate them with the DP requirements. Some suggestions for an answer to the problem will be found in the penultimate section of this chapter.

We will now examine the many external services available. I found great difficulty in deciding whether to deal with VANs or viewdata first in this chapter. The problem is that many external service suppliers provice access via viewdata screens so should we complete what we have already said in chapters 2, 5 and 7, about viewdata, or should we look at the services in general and then say something about the technology behind viewdata?

As you are already fairly familiar with viewdata, particularly from chapter 7, I think you know enough about it to be able to appreciate why it features so often in external (and internal) services, so we will look at VANs next.

Value-added data network services

Some four or five years ago, the concept of a value-added network was introduced and as we said in chapter 8, this implies that over and above the provision of a data highway, the network supplier could support user services to add some value to a basic telecomms network. The current name for such a network is *value-added data network (VAD).*

To obtain an operating licence from the Department of Trade and Industry for a VAN/VAD there are various conditions to be met. They can be summarised as:

- no simple resale of services, ie, you cannot rent network facilities from a PTO and then 'sublet' surplus capacity to other users
- if speech is included, it cannot be charged at a lower rate than the PTOs charge
- where OSI recommendations apply, they must be followed
- where implemented, the network must not be cross-subsidised from other parts of the business (very difficult to enforce!).

The following are not allowed:

- a speech-only connection/routing service
- a Telex-only service
- mobile radio over land
- a basic packet-switched service (ie, in direct competition with BT and MCL).

So, the granting of a VADS licence requires the VADS supplier to offer more than just a basic network. The actual 'value added' in a VAN/VADS includes any of the following:

- sending a message to two or more addresses (broadcast)
- storing messages and data on behalf of the customer
- speed conversion - allowing slow terminals to talk to faster ones
- deferred transmission (holding message for later transmission - either to save on costs or because of time-zone differences)
- conversion of codes and formats and protocol conversion perhaps to enable a terminal to link into an otherwise incompatible mainframe or other terminal
- connection and routing
- protocol conversion and gatewaying to other service-providers and services.

Fairly recently, there has been increasing emphasis on the last three of these and many organisations now provide a connection and routing service that makes it very easy for a user to gain access to facilities offered by other organisations.

The situation is very confusing but is illustrated in Figure 10.1 and can be summarised thus:

- the PTOs provide the basic transmission network
- the *private network supplier (PNS)* makes use of a combination of PTO networks and their own to provice a 'private network'
- the *service provider (SP)* offers various services (e-mail, EDI etc) via the private network supplier
- the *information provider (IP)* makes data, information and software available to support the service, the service provider supplying the gateway to the IPs mainframe computer

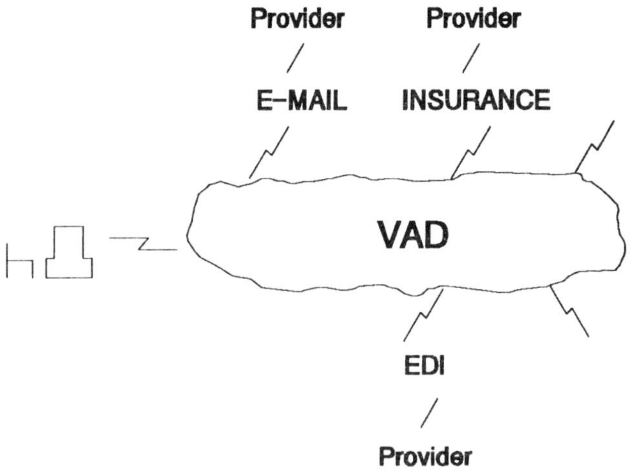

Figure 10.1 User access to VAD services

What makes the overall situation complicated is that some PNSs act as SPs, some IPs are also SPs and some services are available via more than one SP. For example, BT make use of part of their

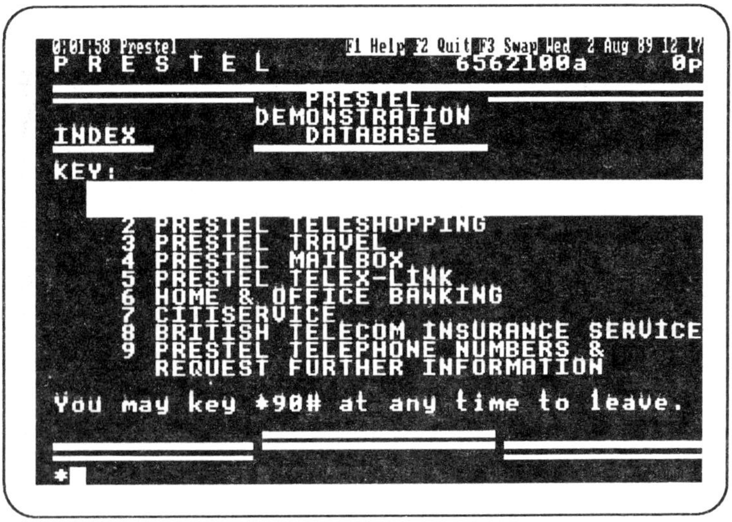

Figure 10.2 PRESTEL demonstration screen

overall network as the equivalent of a series of VADS in particular Prestel as its 'private network' (see Figure 10.2). Through this, you can access a number of services (as we will see later on), but you

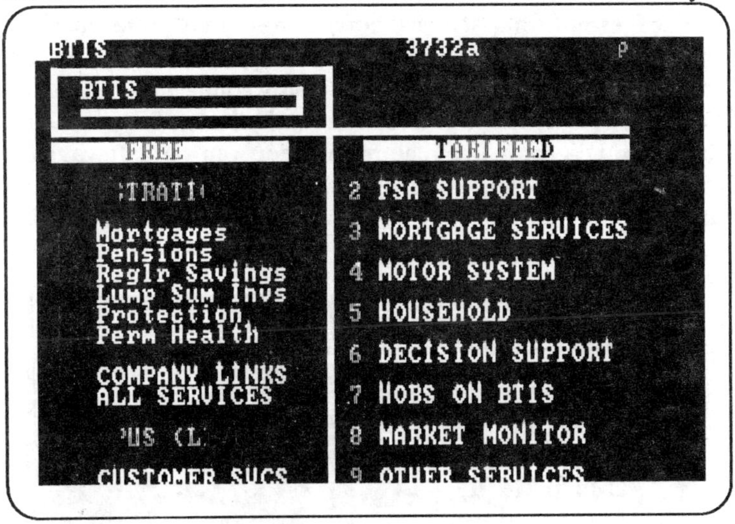

Figure 10.3 BITS insurance and investment

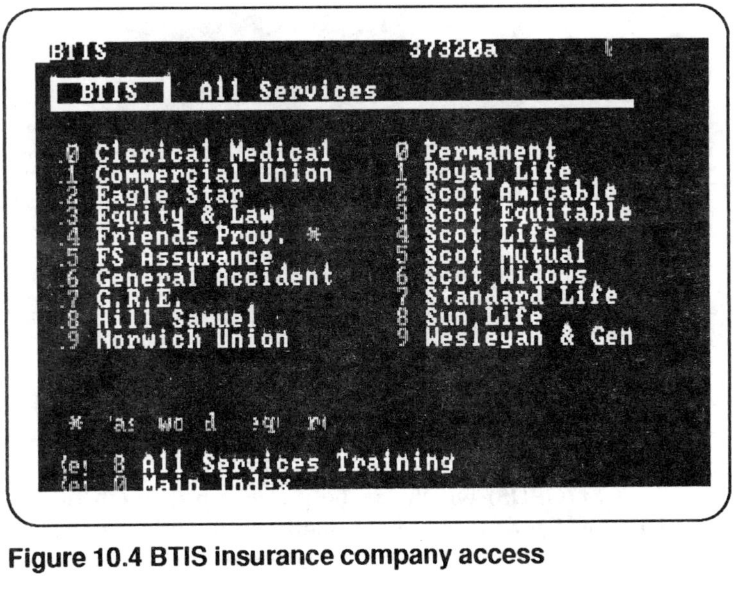

Figure 10.4 BTIS insurance company access

can also get through to *BT Information Service (BTIS)*, which is one source of a range of financial services with BT as the SP as well as the PNS.

The Prestel-format screens shown here, demonstrate what BTIS can provide. Figure 10.3 (page 3732a) is a general view of available services, those on the left being free (only connection charges are paid, the data accessed is free). Figure 10.4 (page 37320a) shows the insurance company mainframes you can be gatewayed to from the main menu, while Figure 10.5 (page 37324a) shows the user training that can be provided in order to use the services.

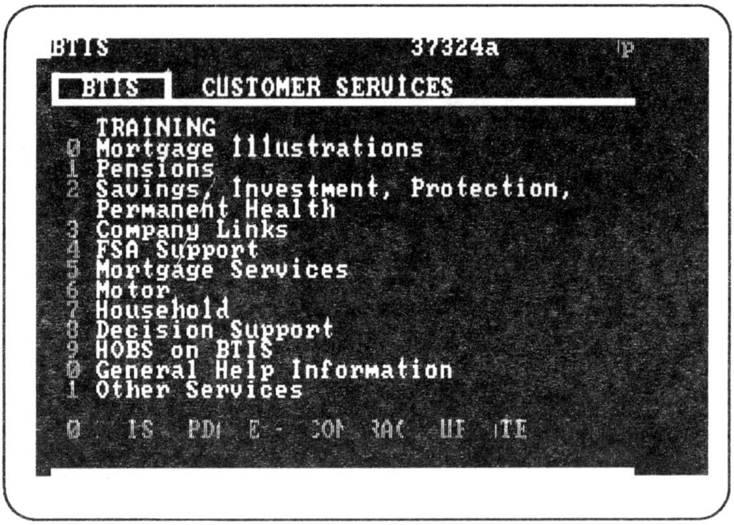

Figure 10.5 BTIS services training back-up

Another VAD organisation is *Istel*. This large private network is owned by National Westminster Bank and the Canadian Bell company.

Microlink, the viewdata service for microcomputer users is available from Istel which also provides a service called *Inview*. The screens show the main menu (Figure 10.6) and a mortgage quotation (Figure 10.7) provided by (*On-line Proposal for Underwriters (OPUS)* which can be picked up through Inview. (Note that we have taken a slight liberty with the screen to show how JCCs *Workmate* can be used to tailor videotex screens.)

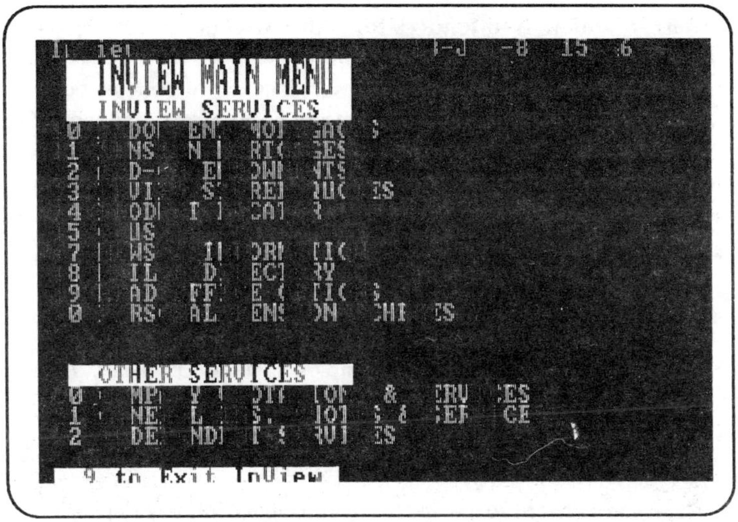

Figure 10.6 Inview services

Yet another network supplier is *International Network Services (INS)*, owned by ICL and GEISCO. Two services they provide are

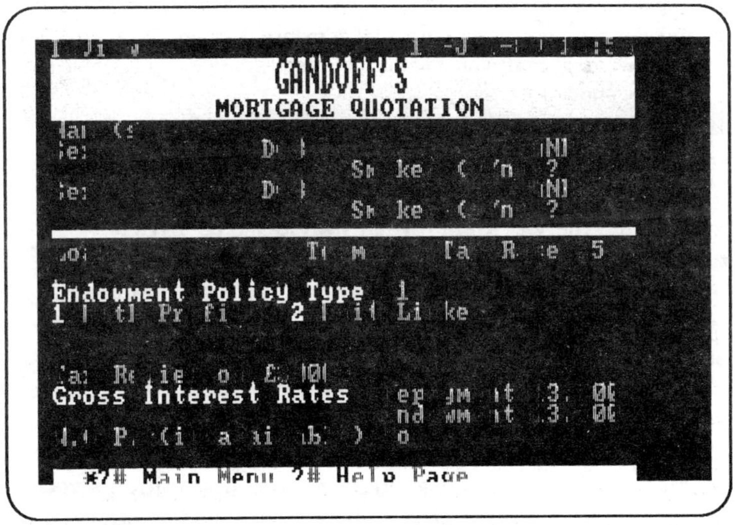

Figure 10.7 A mortgage quotation

Brokernet which is intended for stock exchange dealings and *Tradinet* which provides EDI (see later).

The user accessing the various services is not concerned with how the connection is made to other company databases. The VAN supplier takes care of this - as far as the user is concerned, the required service is just an option to be selected on the screen.

The major facilities provided by the service providers are:

- videotex format data/information access (such as Prestel and Inview)
- text-format data/information access (e.g. *Dialogue* and *Blaise* - a bibliographic service provided by the British Library)
- electronic mail/messaging (examples include *BT Gold, Prestel messaging* and MCL's *7500* service)
- financial services such as credit card verification, insurance quotations, market news, banking and so on
- access to software so that users can run other company's applications software on their own data (from their terminals).

Videotex

In its widest sense, videotex just means 'text on the VDU screen' but we can identify a special form which is called *viewdata* and which has two meanings;

- any computerised service internal or external, where the access is via screens in a format similar to that of Prestel screens (such as the many already shown)
- the provision of such a service, or even the actual provider of the service.

Essentially, the viewdata format provides a user-friendly access to data or information in a page format that is recognised internationally (although numerous different standards are followed). It is usually based on a hierarchical (layered) menu access with what can be called 'dive-ins' where entering a particular page number can give immediate access to the page.

It can be used to provide a front-end operating environment to all kinds of services. For example, there is no reason why an organisation could not use videotex to all application screens - sales, payroll etc. (You have already seen in chapter 7, how packages such as JCC's Work-mate can be used to format data into viewdata screens.)

Pause for thought

Many companies employ this kind of format. To observe it in practice, the next time you go shopping in a town centre, look for a travel agent (such as Thomas Cooke or Thomsons) and either look through the window or go inside and examine the screens in use on the agent's viewdata terminal. You will find that they are very similar to the viewdata screens you have seen earlier.

In fact, Thomas Cooke are owned by Midland Bank who provide a network for customers of the travel business. This allows access to airline, road, rail and sea ferry schedules, foreign exchange rates and much other information that helps holidays to be booked. Other travel agents provide similar services to their staff and customers.

Viewdata is similar in format to Teletext (*Ceefax* and *Oracle* in the UK). Teletext is essentially a series of viewdata screens that are broadcast by the BBC and ITV as a set of frames in a regular 'carousel'. The user selects the page to be viewed and when it arrives in its place in the carousel, the specially adapted TV set captures it and shows it to the user.

Viewdata is similar but is interactive - you select what you want, see it and reply if the application suits. Viewdata and teletext also have the similarity that they both involve the computer control of data available.

(Note that you must distinguish between videotex and other data and information services which are **text-based** and not pictorial.)

To access viewdata, you need a terminal and modem (V23 usually). The terminal can either be a specially adapted TV set, a special-purpose, dedicated viewdata terminal or a PC with the relevant comms software (chapter 7).

Public Viewdata is provided in the UK by Prestel, Istel etc. Viewdata in other countries includes for example:

- *Captain* (Japan)
- *Teletel* (France) - the special Teletel terminal is given free to users of the service
- *Telidon* (Canada)

Information providers include:

- commercial organisations - banks, building societies, insurance companies stores, airlines
- financial/equity intelligence companies - Extel, Dun & Bradstreet, the Financial Times, Dow-Jones
- publishers - Readers Digest, New York Times
- special services - farming, carpet sales, betting shops, legal, education, engineering, parliamentary, journalists.

Free services are often provided by local government, e.g. borough councils offer public-service viewdata as do county libraries (remember the Tapestry gateway to BVS and Slough library referred to at the end of chapter 9).

Many service providers offer commercial (Figure 10.8) and personal services (Figure 10.9) and are designed to attract users in the home as well as in the office.

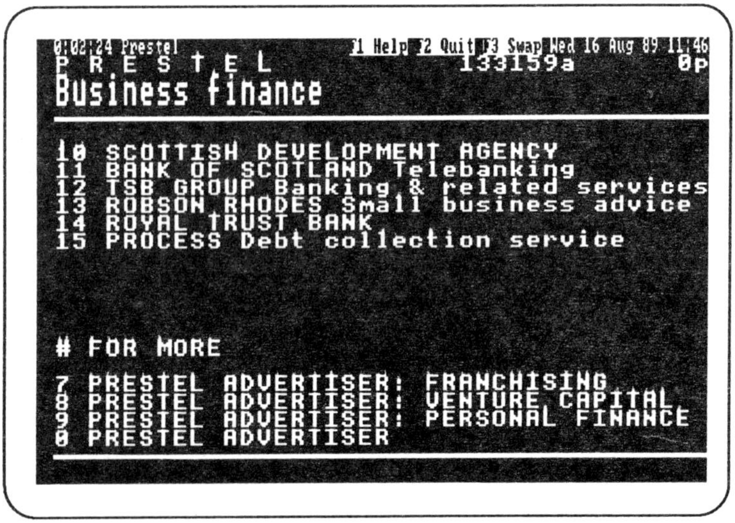

Figure 10.8 PRESTEL commercial services

Viewdata format

Most viewdata is in a standard 40-column format looking like Prestel. The page has basic text (possibly prettied up with simple diagrams), a page number and where further access is needed, a

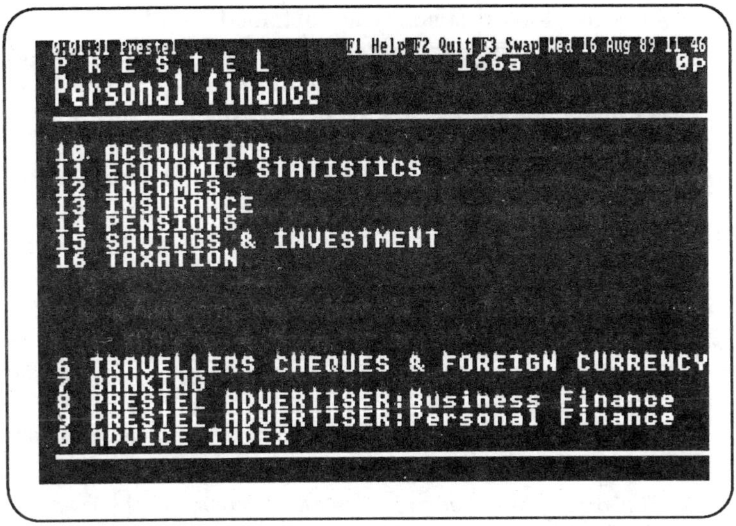

Figure 10.9 PRESTEL personal services

hierarchical menu structure. Figure 10.10 shows Prestel page 656227b - the menu instructions are quite clear!

Figure 10.10 PRESTEL messaging

Special functions are usually not obtained with function keys (because these vary from terminal to terminal) but by combinations of other keys (see the bottom line of Figure. 10.2).

Other viewdata formats are available, usually giving a better definition than basic 40-column viewdata. Some financial services are based on a rather less common 80-column viewdata. Other services can provide information on screens that can make use of curves.

There are not very many universal standards relating to viewdata, but we can identify two de facto standards:

- *NAPLPS (North American Presentation Level Protocol),* which applies in the USA and Canada. It is based on recommendations of ANSI and the Canadian Standards Association. It was developed from specifications produced by the Bell Telephone Company, AT&T and Telidon (the French teletext service)
- *CEPT (Conference of European Posts & Telecomms)* which is applied by Prestel and Telitel (France).

The basic standards relate to:

- the characters that can be used - alphanumeric, special (such as diphthongs, musical notes, playing card suits)
- basic screen format - character sizes, use of colour, intensity (brightness), reverse video, flashing
- more advanced facilities (many still to be agreed) - windows, image movement
- the actual method of producing shapes - *Mosaic* (dots): Prestel screens are produced this way (you can see how jagged the shapes are), *Alphageometric*: much less common at present and based on 'display units' rather than dots giving much smoother pictures, *geometric primatives*: (building blocks for complex drawings)
- the control functions needed.

To access public viewdata services, the user connects to a service provider, via a network provider (as shown in Figure 10.11). The service provider may gateway to other services including private mainframes and other private viewdata networks.

There are many kinds of screen format that are widely different from viewdata. For example, many PC users make use of Microsoft *Windows* or Digital Research *GEM*, while mini and mainframe users are presented with a variety of screens

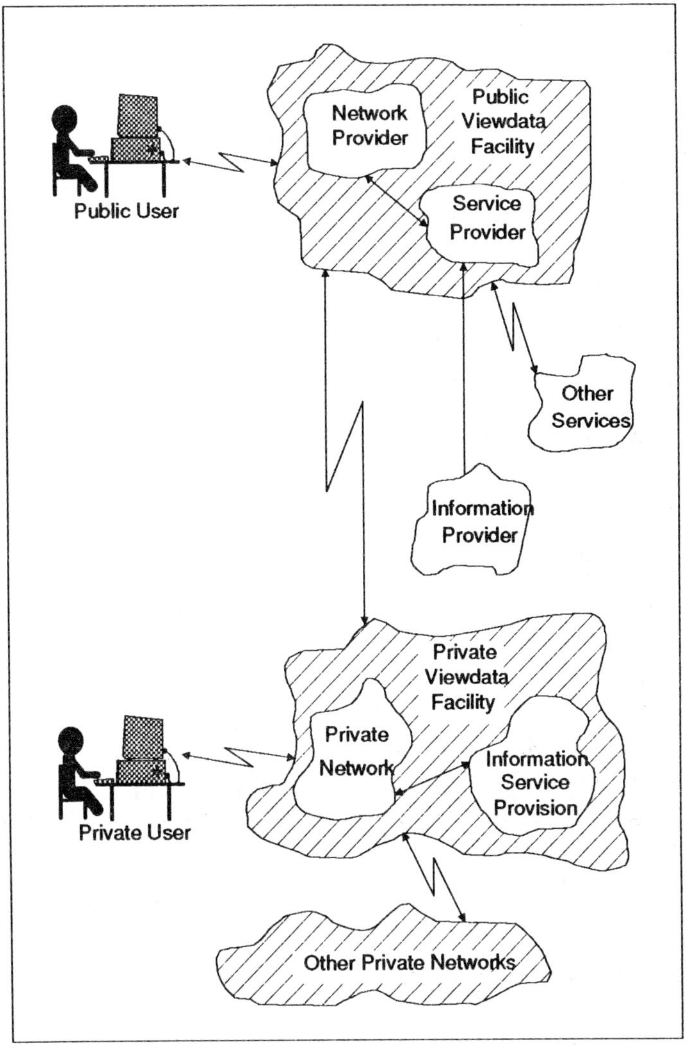

Figure 10.11 The basic structure of viewdata services

depending on the general format that the manufacturer has decided to use.

A number of packages even allow you to build up your own special-purpose screens, for example, *SMARTware* by Informix allows you to define data entry screens that can be used to enter data which can then be passed into a spreadsheet for calculation. It remains to be seen just how long 40-column viewdata will last as a major front-end - because of its ease of use and because people are familiar with it from its widespread use and from teletext, I believe that it will be around for quite a few years.

Electronic commercial data and credit transfer

EFT

Electronic Funds Transfer (EFT) is the electronic transfer of credit between users, sites, banks, companies and so on geared to a 'universal' identity card that can authorise credit.

Identification is based on an account number recorded magnetically on a plastic card and it enables a customer to obtain goods or services without cash (such as the purchase of petrol or clothes etc at a department store). It can also be used for 'remote shopping' such as the booking of theatre and airline tickets, just by quoting the users' identification. Later, the company will send a documentary confirmation of the transaction. It is usually necessary to check on the credit of the customer (often by accessing a remote credit-checking service) and to see if the card is on a stolen list.

Once everything has been shown to be in order, the credit transfer initiated by the customer card transaction produces an automatic debit of the customers account and a credit of that of the store.

To assist this kind of business BT supplies *Cardway*, a facility for converting the serial data from credit cards into packets for digital network transfer.

Barclays Bank have *PDQ* with hundreds of terminals that accept *Diners Club, Access, Visa* and other credit cards. Lloyds Bank have *Cardpoint* while Natwest have *Streamline* which can be used at Texaco petrol stations, Waitrose etc.

Switch is the facility provided by Midland Bank in conjunction with Natwest and the Royal Bank of Scotland in which a charge card or *debit card* can be used for credit purchases in many places, with immediate debit of the customer's bank account balance.

Data resulting from the transactions is collected by a special terminal which can be called up and the end of the day by the bank mainframe, or the company can pass a magnetic tape from their mainframe to the bank, or the company could use EDI (coming up soon).

The ATM

Although not quite the same as other forms of EFT, the major banks in the USA and then in Europe introduced the *automatic telling machine (ATM)* - the 'hole-in-the-wall' banking service. (Remember that we used this as the setting for a layer 2 protocol example in chapter 6.)

For this service, the user puts his card into a magnetic-card reader and the ATM asks for a *personal identification number (PIN)* to be entered through the keyboard. Once this has been OKd, the user can draw out cash, order a statement or even transfer funds between accounts.

Before transmission, the electronic data is encrypted to reduce the possibility of hacking between the ATM and the bank central computer, otherwise it might be possible to pick up stray radio transmission and capture PINs for fraudulent use. (Another fraud possibility that has been tried is to turn off the money-dispensor in the ATM. We assume that banks take every step to ensure that such thieving is not successful.)

The facility is offered by a number of building societies as well as the major banks and several ATMs accept the cards of other companies. (Midland, Natwest and TSB cards are all interchangeable.)

Link is a facility involving over 700 ATMs provided by an association of Abbey National and Nationwide Building Societies, Girobank, the Co-op bank and *FTS* a group of financial institutions including banks, building societies, American Express and Diners Club. It is based on BTs Kilostream.

Matrix is provided by 7 of the large UK building societies and can be accessed from over 400 ATMs.

In the USA and Canada, there is a service called *Plus* which is based on 11,000 ATMs and which was planned to tie in with Link this year.

With an appropriate terminal and a card reader, EFT can also be made available from the home (see later in the chapter).

Note that the term *EFTPOS* meaning *EFT* at the *point of service*, implies making use of credit card transactions at the point **where the computing service is needed**, ie, where the transaction originates (at the store till, supermarket check-out etc) and where an immediate debit of the customer's account takes place.

The Smart card

The *Smart card* was invented and first used in France. It is basically a conventional plastic credit card with a magnetic strip, **to which has been added a ram chip**, ie, a piece of integrated circuit memory. In Europe, this typically has a capacity of 256,000 characters, but Japanese cards are available that hold 1 million characters. In the USA, a different technology has arisen, where the memory is stored optically and accessed by laser. These cards have a capacity of up to 2 million characters.

Over 30 million smart cards are already in use just in Europe, and once some degree of standardisation of use has been agreed, it is expected that world-wide usage will grow at the rate of many millions per year.

The possibilities for use of the card are enormous since it can hold complete sets of records. For example, in credit purchase, there will be no need for a credit check, since the full details of the user's account with the store can be held on the card.

The same applies in banking - the ATM can read all the account details from the card and issue cash etc, without having to check with the head office mainframe. This saves on-line transmission costs, providing a major reason for their adoption.

An obvious use is in situations like cashless telephoning. BT already provide a phonecard for this purpose (although it is not actually a smart card). It could be used similarly in any other situation where payment is made now by tokens, such as car parking.

It can also be used for access identification to secure areas and deposit boxes.

An even more interesting possibility is to use the card as a kind of portable electronic file and there are already plans to do this with medical records. A complete history of medical and surgical treatment for a patient could be kept on the card and once much higher capacity cards are available, it will not be very long before X-ray images could be held as well.

Security applications exist too. Perhaps a digital map of the user s fingerprints could be stored on the card, which can then be compared with the real fingerprints read by the terminal. For total secrecy, it is possible for the card to be formatted so that the user can put his own PIN and password on it so that not even the bank or store knows his identity.

Variations on the card include the addition of a processor along with the memory and the integration of the card into a unit that also contains the reader and can interface with other terminals.

EDI

EDI (Electronic Data Interchange) is one of the biggest things in data processing these days. It has been called 'paperless business trading' and is a standardised form of computer-to-computer inter-transfer of business information that would be employed in documentary form if computers were not used.

In the UK, Istel and INS are the main suppliers of VADs for EDI and typically, they offer a switched network service that enables users to send documents such as orders and payments, without having to worry about addressing and routing. Various standard formats need to be applied and the network software handles the necessary conversions between formats.

The supplier usually supports a kind of store-and-forward EDI, where 'documents' are sent to the network and forwarded as required (just like mail from an e-mail mail-box), but is also possible to have a form of conversational EDI, whereby documents are sent immediately to the receiver who can acknowledge them immediately.

Examples include:

- transferring employee payroll from company to bank and hence to employee bank account
- sending bulked credit card transaction records from department store to finance company
- sending a batch of invoices from a manufacturer to all its customers
- sending a batch of orders from a supermarket to its suppliers.

Tradinet, the INS service is claimed to have over 1000 customers at present. The service provided by Istel is called *EDICT.*

One of the major problems of EDI at present is the fact that different industries and groups of companies have different document standards - imagine trying to design a standard invoice that could be used for your car service, by a supermarket delivering goods to a local restaurant or by a solicitor after selling a house for a client. The goods and services provided are very different and it would be almost impossible to standardise 100%.

EDI Standards

The UK *(Article Numbering Association (ANA)* took a major lead in the development of EDI and its standards by introducing *Trading Data Communications (TRADACOMS)* standards. These suggest a basic syntax for EDI:

- document format and exchange must be independent of the computer hardware involved
- it must be independent of the comms network protocols applied
- it must not affect the existing user DP structure
- it must be flexible - able to handle variable length data and other fields (such as format control characters).

The syntax supports 18 different types of transaction including order, invoice, credit note, statement and delivery note. The particular standard is called *United Nations Trade Data Interchange (UNTDI).*

Pause for thought

Does this need for document standards remind you of anything in particular? We have a situation where many users want to send documents in a variety of environments for a variety of purposes. Surely this is extremely similar to the need for X400? Look back to chapter 3.

International EDI standards, something like X400 are in preparation. They identify the following entities:

- *file* - a group of documents
- *message* - a logical portion of a document (e.g. header, body, trailer)
- *segment* - a sub-section of a message
- *special 'data elements'* - the format of specific items of data such as addresses, dates, part numbers and so on.

Rules are being developed which allow for the combining of segments and messages to form documents, non-standard character usage and start and end transmission control records.

There is a possibility in the future for an international syntax and a scheme called *EDI for admin commerce and transport (EDIFACT)* is designed to look at ways to resolve the differences between UNTDI-based and 'specialised' syntaxes (that apply in particular industries and trades).

The demand for EDI is such that national and international standards will have to be agreed and adopted fairly soon - there is much talk of international EDI at present.

Advantages of EDI

There are many advantages to be gained from EDI, some of which result from savings and others from increased sales because dealing with EDI-oriented companies is easier and cheaper for others. They include:

- high-speed communication of orders, payments and so on, means that goods can be ordered later than would normally be the case, so less goods need to be stocked (less storage space, less money tied up in unsold stock)
- reduced clerical, handling, mailing and delivery confirmation costs
- automatic receipt acknowledgement
- security - less time and effort is involved in chasing up lost or late documents (they are much less likely to occur)
- trading advantage - if an organisation already makes use of EDI, it is bound to give preference to suppliers that do so as well
- improved cash flow - you can pay later and you receive payments quicker
- for the future, if EDI standards are agreed, it should be possible to agree on a standard for electronic legal documents within an EDI framework. At present, business deals may be confirmed by telex, letter, telephone etc and different legal significances are placed on these in different countries and different industries.

Let us now survey and summarise possible means whereby one party can send information to another.

Miscellaneous applications

1-to-1 methods

- *Fax* - originally intended for non-text material such as fashion drawings, cartoons or engineering designs, fax is increasingly being used for sending text and taking copies. If I have just produced some figures on my spreadsheet and want you to have a copy, I can make use of the fax card in my PC (or link my PC to the office fax machine) and send you an image of the screen and at the same time store a copy of it on my disk. Neither of us needs to keep an actual paper copy (unless we want to)
- *PC-to-PC* - as we saw in chapter 7, there is plenty of software around for handling file transfer. All you need to do is set up the document as a file and then transmit to the other end
- *telex* - still very popular in the business world, partly because it has international support and partly because many financial institutions will accept orders, contract confirmations and funds transfer requests in telex form, but not by e-mail or fax.

1-to-many methods

- *E-mail* - originally intended for 1-to-1 use - I send a message to your mailbox and you reply when necessary. Increasingly being used for *broadcasting* where a company can automatically send publicity material, notifications of price changes andso on, to all the customers on its mailing list. (Note that fax is now being used in a similar way.)

  The e-mail delivery and management can either be part of the user's software (on his PC or the company computer) or provided by an external supplier
- *Viewdata* - we can think of one information provider making his profits by being able to send his information to the many users that want access to it. As with e-mail, this could be company-based or externally provided

Many-to-many methods

- *Teleconferencing* - a derivative of e-mail whereby a set of general mailboxes are provided and people can have remote conversations - perhaps considering a particular problem and possible solutions or the results of carrying out recommendations. It has been suggested that this is likely to become one of the largest of all computer/comms application areas within the next couple of years. (Note that this facility is used by amateurs and hobbyists in *bulletin boards* - coming up soon.)

Voice response

An interesting application mentioned earlier, is to make use of **the telephone itself** as a data terminal. In the USA this has been very popular in the automobile industry and it has been taken up in Europe for the same purpose. A number of banks have started to provide a similar facility as an alternative to using viewdata or the ATM for statement details.

The supplier of the service maintains a computerised library of words and statements that can be used for replies to questions.

The user connects to the central computer by dialling its telephone number and then uses the DTMF tones generated by the telephone as codes for the digits pressed. At all stages, the computer confirms by 'voice'.

For example, having connected to your bank's computer, the voice response system might say:

Good morning. Please enter your account number.

You press the telephone keys corresponding to your account number. The computer then says:

Good Morning Mr. Smith. Please enter your request.

To use the service you will need to know the menu selection codes, which might be:

Code	*Significance*
1	current balance
2	send statement
3	send chequebook
4	make payment
-	
-	
9	log off

If option 1 is selected, the voice tells you how much you have in your account. If you select option 4, the computer asks you to enter the number of the account you want to transfer funds to. This could be set up to be the electricity company, a department store or whatever.

To use the facility, you really need a phone that generates DTMF tones, not pulses. If you don't have one, the service provider will supply a small, hand-held keypad with a loudspeaker built in called a *codec (coder-decoder).*

You place the unit over the mouthpiece of the non-pulse telephone and when the keys are pressed, DTMF tones are generated and sent down the line.

This means that you can access the service from any telephone in the world, provided you have the codec and can actually make a telephone connection to the computer.

Bulletin boards

These are text-based mailbox systems, usually operated by amateurs for specialist groups - mainly computer enthusiasts. They provide facilities for exchanging notes and news, the possibility for conferencing - swapping ideas and suggestions on problems, exchange and mart - for buying and selling equipment and for 'downloading' software - transmitting copies of useful software.

Some bulletin boards are free, while others make a charge. Examples include:

- *The Crow's Nest* - 0793 467863
- *The Crystal Tower* - 01-886-2813
- *London Connection* - 01-657 3240.

Computer-Integrated Telephony (CIT)

This is a very exciting application that beings together DP and telephony.

Earlier, we discussed the possibility of storing a telephone directory on a PC - a list of numbers can be made to appear on the VDU screen, you select the one you want (by mouse or function keys) and an autodialler will call the number you want.

Derivatives of this basic technique are becoming quite common and software can often enable you to do much more sophisticated things, such as:

- produce a list of any customer who has not be phoned for 14 days
- provide the phone numbers of all pharmacists in London NW3, who have placed an order for aspirin this week
- telephone any supplier of metal brackets whose price is more than 5% down on last month.

Even more complex procedures are possible, perhaps the most interesting being for the support of telephone sales or debt collection. The software can select the person you want to talk to and produce a form on the VDU giving details such as when last called and amount owing. The clerk using the phone can refresh his memory from the form and then hit the return key to make the machine dial out. During the conversation, the clerk can take notes or enter order details through the keyboard and when finished, the machine will update its files for the next call.

The software needs to be quite clever if we decide to allow for numbers being engaged. Suppose we want to contact all the NW3 aspirin purchasers, to tell them that their stock delivery must be returned (perhaps because the bottles are incorrectly labelled). The program could bring up each pharmacist in turn and then dial out for you. It will need to know what to do if one or more numbers is engaged. Should it:

- retry every five minutes, as soon as there is a pause
- try three times and then tell you it was unsuccessful
- keep trying but put it lower down the list the more times it tries.

Good software will allow a user to select the basis on which it will handle calls or even make use of adaptive reasoning (refer to chapter 5 and compare this with the way that modems can adaptively deal with error conditions).

As the PTOs are starting to provide cheaper and more powerful telephone services, it seems likely that CIT will be employed by a very large number of users.

Electronic diary

Something like CIT, but even more work is done for the user by the system. The basic idea is for a user to enter details of future arrangements - meetings, dental appointments and so on and have the computer produce a list each day or give a warning that an attendance has not been confirmed.

A very powerful extension to this, is to **link the diaries of several people**. If everyone involved makes sure that their own diary is up to date, it should be possible to ask the computer to do things such as:

- tell me when Fred is next available for a half-hour chat

- book me a meeting with all level 2 managers on the next available Tuesday afternoon
- tell me who attended the monthly progress meeting last week
- send a note to every salesman teminal, telling them that I want their expense forms in, fast!

In other words, as well as a set of diaries, the whole complex could be used for manpower scheduling. It could also be extended to include vehicles, machines, training courses and so on.

A fully computerised diary is a likely candidate for internal comms but, as we will see later on, many members of staff could be off-site, perhaps working from home, their car or on a customer s premises. In this case, the 'diary' becomes even more useful.

Now for some applications that are often accessed from the user's own home.

On-line computing in the home

Home banking/shopping

Many organisations provide viewdata access to their catalogues and price lists through which it is possible to order goods as well.

Most organisations accept orders from terminals and send you an invoice in the normal way, but a more interesting method is to make use of EFT. Here, the customer is provided with a magnetic card reader ('wiper') and after selecting goods, the card details are read in and the account is debited with the sales amount immediately.

Home-banking is equally interesting. The Royal Bank of Scotland provides a service called *Home and Office Banking Service (HOBS)*, which is viewdata- based. (See Figure 10.2, option 6, for access to HOBS from Prestel and Figure 10.3, option 7 for HOBS from BTIS.)

The screens show that it is possible to do almost everything from the service that you can get from an ATM (except of course, cash withdrawal).

Figure 10.12 is a log-in screen and is self-explanatory. Security is preserved with an account number and password (see the screen note about changing your password whenever you like). A statement can be obtained any time (Figure 10.13).

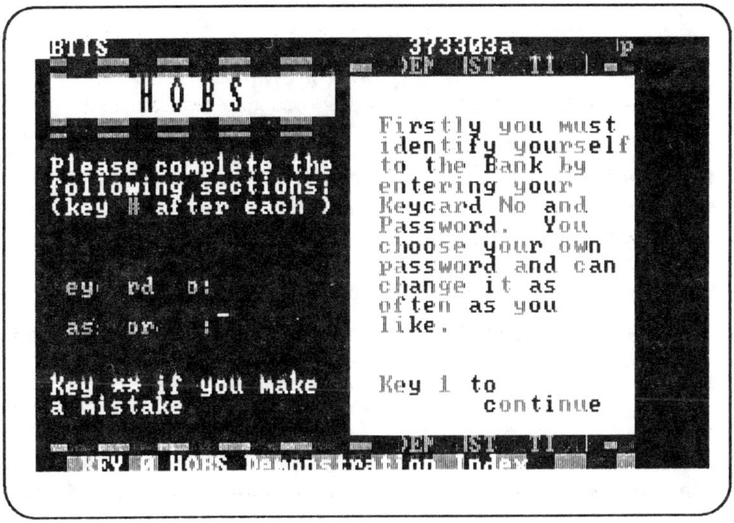

Figure 10.12 HOBBS log-in screen

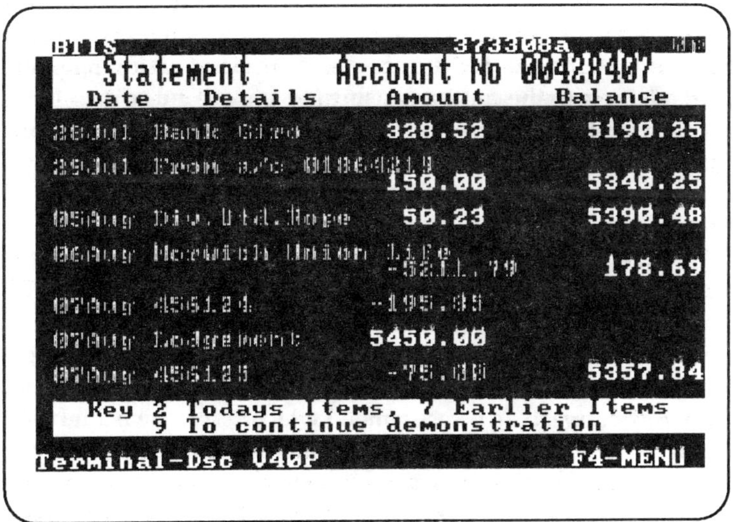

Figure 10.13 A statement from HOBBS

Teleworking

This is a very new idea and literally means working from home with the aid of a terminal, employing some or all of the communication methods already discussed

There are many jobs that do not need to be done entirely in the office, such as market research, programming and designing. The reasons why they are generally done in a office environment are:

- access to equipment and facilities - photocopiers, keyboards etc
- the need for constant communication with fellow-workers
- the need for management to monitor and control workers and work done.

With teleworking, a company has to strike a balance between the costs of putting terminals in employees' homes, the associated data transmission costs and the other hardware and software overheads on the one hand, and the reduction in office overheads and expenses and employee travelling costs and the more relaxed atmosphere in which employees can work.

The employee can receive work specifications and instructions on-line, carry out the necessary work and send the results back on-line. With access to comms software and external services, an employee could import data from the company database or from external providers, could converse with other employees using e-mail and could send reports, diagrams, drawings and spreadsheets to the company using fax, e-mail and so on.

An extension could be a kind of 'distributed' teleworking where a group of employees is controlled by a local supervisor who himself teleworks with head office.

How will our typical company use comms

As we do not have any information on data volumes, numbers of transactions etc, it is impossible to make any recommendations as to extra hardware resources needed and how the network might be re-designed to be more efficient. With the information given, all we can hope to do is recommend which services we think they should consider and why. First the internal comms system.

The scope for internal comms

- *E-mail* - I don't know how any company of more than just a few members of staff can exist without e-mail. For this organisation, there are several possibilities, such as conferencing:

  Have we had any problems with these customers ?
  Anyone got any ideas on the best way to handle them?
  This design problem has me stumped. Anyone met it before?

  Communication could be supported between eg, sales and production:
  How long will this customer order take?
  Can we re-schedule next week to allow for a major priority order?

- CIT - an obvious choice - the company has many customers and suppliers and the automation of outgoing telephone calls is bound to improve efficiency. It could also allow the company to monitor what calls are made by which people, by examining records kept by the terminals used for CIT.

- Diary - should be considered (see the general review earlier).

- Viewdata - although the majority of staff will not have had much exposure to viewdata in their work, most people have seen TV screens showing Prestel or Ceefax/Oracle and at least know what they look like.

  Many DP applications involve user/machine dialogue, including order entry, stock enquiries, job progress and personnel records. All of these could be considered as possibilities for viewdata 'front-ending' - using viewdata formats for all VDU screens.

  As well as introducing a high degree of standardisation, it makes life easier if external viewdata is accessed in the company as well (see later).

External comms possibilities

- *E-mail* - actual business documents (eg, orders, payments) come under EDI, but there are many possibilities where a company might provide e-mail access to its employees or other companies, perhaps to service customer enquiries on stock prices, discounts, availability etc. Similarly, customer orders could be sent this way. Many organisations quote their external e-mail supplier number on a letterhead. Others specify a *DX* number, usually the telehone number that gets an external user into the main menu of the company mainframe for direct document entry.

- *External diary* - might be worth considering (see the earlier review).

- *Mobile terminals* - we don't know how many potential customers for this company, nor what products it sells, but it is not unreasonable to assume that there is scope for mobile terminal usage for in at least two application areas, salesman and deliverymen.

  A sales rep can enter enquiries, request estimates and place orders on-line. It is very impressive for a customer to see this in practice. A lot of time is saved that would otherwise be need for the salesman to fill in order forms and either post them in or telephone the details through to head office. It could also be arranged for the computer to send a daily customer calling schedule to each rep and even be used to record his car mileage and expenses

  For deliverymen - many organisations find it is cost-effective to keep some delivery vehicles with a wide range of stock on board. The computer knows what each vehicle is carrying and as stock is delivered, the driver can enter the details, the stock file being updated immediately. This is particularly convenient for vehicles involved with servicing - the engineer can log in at any time and find out which customer to go to next

  In both of these cases, the immediate connection to a car-based terminal means that major rescheduling can be done at any time - the computer knows what stock is on board and where the vehicle was on its last call

- EDI - another obvious choice! Large customers could place many orders in any particular week/month; the orders and corresponding invoices/goods advice notes etc could be exchanged by EDI

- Viewdata - two possibilities seem obvious: the use of viewdata format for external access to the company computer by customers, such as for the external e-mail referred to above (for enquiries and orders); accessing external VAN/VADs for financial and/or technical information.

If the company has decided to make extensive use of viewdata from external suppliers, there will already be skills available within the organisation staff and it should be relatively easy to persuade other staff to adopt the new dialogue and to train them as well.

It is left to you as an important exercise, to fill in more details than you have been given. To gain the maximum benefit, think about what the company sells and put in some 'test data' for number of customers, total items in the catalogue, total monthly items sold of each product or product range and so on.

This will obviously be a major piece of work and you could do this as a project involving a team of two or three people. Good luck.

Where are we going

There are just too many areas in comms and DP to make predictions as to what is going to happen over the next 5-10 years, but we can at least review some topics where expansion and major developments might be expected:

Hardware

Each generation of processors is faster than the last. PCs are now coming on the market with instruction cycles 5-10 times faster than were available only two years ago. There is likely to be an increased use of the new high-speed *reduced instruction set computer (RISC)* processors which dramatically increase computing speeds. At the same time, the costs of memory and disk drives are falling.

This will surely lead to extremely powerful workstations that can tackle processing jobs that would previously only have been possible on minis and mainframes.

Similarly, as techniques such as teleworking and EFT take off and e-mail and fax become more popular, the number of terminals needed will grow. As their use become widespread, there will be an increasing need for the comms hardware and networks to link to mainframes and other users.

As more advanced techniques are employed in modem design and as the PTN generally becomes more reliable (and hopefully cheaper) so increasing use will be made of analogue transmission to support this increase in the number of low-speed terminals.

We have already discussed the dramatic increase in the availability of digital network services. Further use of packet networks and ISDN should lead to an increased number of high-volume transmission requirements.

Standards

We have reviewed the need for standards and their application throughout the whole of this book. It has taken about 25 years for the comms industry to reach its present level of standardisation but there is still a long way to go.

User applications are beginning to demand standards in hardware, software and applications. If the user cannot obtain software or services to interface with those already in use and following the same protocols and standards, he will go to another supplier. It is in the supplier's own interests to follow standards - if a network supplier does not conform to international standards, no-one will make use of his network.

Users in quite different industries have similar problems and if they all push for standardisation, it must happen eventually. In particular, it is going to be very interesting to see whether there will eventually be some kind of integration of standards such as X.400, UNTDI and the various protocols relating to office and manufacturing documents

Applications

No matter how many we list now, by next week or next month, there will be more. All we can do is mention the areas where it is generally agreed that major expansions will occur:

- teleworking - it is becoming more expensive to live and work in major cities and there would seem to be plenty of scope for this
- teleconferencing - as user rely more and more on their terminals for DP applications and e-mail, it will become quite natural to have discussions and conversations between users at terminals. (One large manufacturer has suggested that over 30% of all keyboards in the world will be used mainly for this)
- computer-aided telephony - telephone calls will become cheaper, mainly because of competition existing between the PTOs. As more people make use of the telephone in business applications, more automation will be needed.
  The more that the software can do to help the user in deciding who to phone and then actually make the connection, the easier it will be to use the phone and hopefully the more efficient. Users already have access to directory dialling, deferred dialling, broadcasting etc with fax and e-mail and it cannot be long before even more users demand it for voice calls
- EFT/EDI - it has been projected that by 1990, well over 10% of all trading transactions will be carried out with a plastic card. Many companies use EDI for all transactions and there are plans in almost all the major countries to develop integrated banking systems based on EDI.

Finally

Hopefully, this book has shown you some of the applications and problems of on-line DP and computing.

The subject is changing, probably faster than any other at any time in history. I hope you can see why I am so excited by it and why I feel that your future career is bound to be helped by the knowledge you have gained.

Recap

- this final chapter takes a detailed look at some of the information needed about an organisation and its computing requirements. The intention is as preparation for a discussion on the introduction of further comms facilities and services to a particular company
- the activities of the company in terms of the DP it carries out are summarised, a range of the facilities and services available to organisations are discussed, suppliers of value-added networks and the services available from these networks arecovered
- viewdata and its providers are discussed
- the increasing trend towards 'paperless business', in particular electronic data interchange and electronic funds transfer, is illustrated
- a number of other comms applications including services available from the home are shown
- the possibilities for further comms facilities that might be available to the 'typical' company are summarised
- some views on the future of comms and comms applications are offered.

Typical questions

Question 10.1

You and I are computer studies students living in different cities. We both have PCs and want to be able to send study material to each other.

Write a sentence on each of six different ways this could be accomplished, stating the advantages and disadvantages of each

Question 10.2

Draw a diagram showing all the processing and communication stages involved when a bank account holder wishes to obtain an on-line statement of account from a videotex terminal

Question 10.3

Make four points on the following:

Why should a DP manager need to be aware of and involve himself in the requirements of his company for voice communication?

Question 10.4

A company employs a team of programmers working from their homes.

A particular programmer will want to discuss problems with others and with his supervisor. He will need to receive copies of programs for amendment and documentary specifications. He will want to send programs after they are written and tested and he will need to send progress reports and details of tasks carried out and hours spent.

Make a list of the services that will be needed to support this teleworking.

APPENDIX 1: BASIC for data comms assignments

This appendix provides the minimum knowledge of BASIC needed to understand the section in chapter 7 and to work on examples suggested in appendixes 2 and 3. It leaves out many aspects of BASIC (which you can pick up from a manual or textbook if you need to). Where possible, we will show a model statement for many BASIC features, in which anything surrounded by { and } is optional.

Main elements of BASIC

Most versions of BASIC require each line to be given a line number for reference - there are no statement labels and you can if you wish, put more than one statement on a line (each statement being separated by *:* a colon symbol):

```
100 A=1: B$ = "YES": C%=20: PRINT A;B$,C%
200 INPUT X
```

Variables

BASIC variables can have their type defined explicitly in the program, or you can leave the language to assign a default value from the name assigned.

Variables must start with a letter from *A* to *Z* and can then contain further alphanumeric characters (usually up to a maximum length of 30). The final character determines the type of variable:

final character	*variable type*
$	non-numeric - character
%	binary - usually 16 bits, complement negative
!	short float - usually 4 bytes, up to 6 significant digits
#	long float - usually 8 bytes, up to 16 significant digits

To define variables explicitly use the DEF statement. It takes the form:

DEFtype Variable1{,Variable2....}

where *type* is:

STR	string
INT	binary
SNG	short float
DBL	long float

and *letter* means that any variable beginning with the specified letter(s) will have the type selected eg:

```
10  DEFSTR A,B,S-Z
20  DEFDBL L
30  DEFINT N,P,R
```

Assignment
A *constant* or *literal* is an actual value that can be assigned to a variable, assignment being with the aid of the = sign, so:

```
10  A=1
```

puts the short float value *1* in a variable *A*, while

```
20  B% = -5
```

puts the complement of the 16-bit binary equivalent of *5* in *B%*, and

```
30  C$ = "ABC"
```

puts the character string *ABC* in the variable *C$*.

Other assignments can be made:

Variable = Variable/Expression/Function

All of these are examples of assignments:

```
100  A=B
110  A=B + C - 35
120  A=B + LOG(C)
130  A=B*(E + LOG(D)) +1
```

An expression can contain the arithmetic operators:

+ add
- subtract
* multiply
/ divide
** raise to the power of

Note that (and) in pairs can be added almost anywhere to improve readability. Note also, that + can also be used as a string variable operator, so:

```
100  A$ = "ABC"
200  B$ = "XYZ"
300  THING$ = A$+B$
400  PRINT THING$
```

produces *ABCXYZ.*

Numeric functions

These consist of the usual functions such as:

LOG meaning *find the natural log of*

INT meaning *find the whole number value of*

RND meaning *produce a random number.*

String (non-numeric) functions
BASIC is not particularly clever in the way it handles data but there are many functions available for manipulating character strings. A selection is given here, of those you may find useful in comms programming. The first three are used to extract substrings from character strings and are similar in how they are used.

**MID$**(X$,n,m)

This extracts *m* characters from *X$* starting at the *n*th, so:

```
100 X$ = "ABCDEFG"
120 PRINT MID$(X$,2,3)
```

produces *BCD*, while:

**LEFT$**(X$,n)

extracts *n* characters from *X$* starting at the left, and

**RIGHT$**(X$,n)

extracts *n* characters from *X$* starting at the right.

Other useful string functions include:

CHR$(n)

used to generate a single ASCII combination, whose binary equivalent has the decimal value *n*. For example we may want to generate a *NAK* in reply to a garbled message. *NAK* is 0110101, for which *n* is 53.

LEN

returns the length in bytes of a string variable, so:

```
100  A$ = "AB"
110  A$ = A$ + "XYZ" + A$
120  PRINT LEN(A$)
```

outputs the value 7.

Input and Output
The keyword *INPUT* is used to enter data from keyboard and takes the form:

INPUT {"literal string";}Variable1{,Variable2...}

Examples include:

```
100  INPUT A,B
120  INPUT "Enter your name ";N$
```

PRINT is used to display data on the VDU screen (or printer) and is rather more complex than *INPUT*. Its general form is:

{L}PRINT Variable1{[,/;]Variable2...}

Examples include:

```
200  PRINT A,B
```

which displays the current values of A and B on the VDU screen;

```
300  LPRINT "TODAY'S DATE IS ";D$
```

prints the literal shown, followed by the current value of *D$* on the printer.

If the separator is a semicolon, BASIC puts one space between the variables that appear. The comma causes it to arrange variable values so that they are well-spaced out:

```
100  A=21: B=-1.503: C=0.032
200  PRINT A,B,C
210  PRINT A;B;C
```

gives as output from line 200:

```
1              16            32
|              |             |
21             -1.503        0.032
```

while line 210 gives as output:

```
1         11
|         |
21 -1.503 0.032
```

Notice that in these and similar following examples, the upper numbers indicate the columns in which the lower, actual results line up: on a real print-out or display, the upper numbers do not appear of course.

Other options are associated with PRINT.

{L}PRINT with no variables

which causes a blank line to be displayed, and:

{L}PRINT TAB(n)

which causes display to start on the line at position n.

Formatted printing

The PRINT statement is very limited in its scope for formatting print lines.

Suppose we have executed statement 100 earlier and want to produce two lines with the format:

```
1        10        20        30        40
|        |         |         |         |
 YEARS   REDUCTION           COEFFICIENT
21       -1.503              0.032
```

As you can see, the horizontal spacing that would be produced by lines similar to 200 and 210 above is quite wrong. There is a derivative of *PRINT* that must be used if this kind of format is wanted.

It takes the form:

{L}PRINT USING "format list"; Variable1{,Variable2,..}

The following example shows its use here *(the lower case b is used to emphasise where blank characters must be inserted)*:

```
200  PRINT"YEARSbbbbREDUCTIONbbbCOEFFICIENT"
250  PRINT
300  PRINTUSING"b###bbbbbb##.###bbbbbbbb###";A,B,C
```

The following is another example of formatted printing:

```
10   A=12.348: B=-9876
20   PRINT USING "Ab=###.##bbBb=b######";A,B
30   PRINT USING "#####.##bbbbbb#####";A,B
```

This piece of logic produces as output:

```
1          10         20
|           |          |
|A = 12.35| B =     -9876
|           |          |
|     12.35 |      -9876
```

Note that line 20 specifies one decimal place too few for A, so BASIC rounds it to 2 decimal places.

The hash symbol # indicates the location of a digit, an extra one being included for the sign (which might happen to be negative). The point symbol . shows the location of the decimal point. Anything else is printed 'as is' ie, exactly as it appears in the format list.

Files

To define a sequential disk file, we use the *OPEN* statement. This has two general formats, the simpler being:

OPEN "M",#m,"name"

where *M* stands for mode, selected from the following:

mode	*significance*
I	*input (ie, records are to be read from the file)*
O	*output (ie, records are to be written to the file)*
A	*append (ie, the file already exists and we are to add records to the end)*

m is the file number that BASIC needs, to know which file you are OPENing and *name* is the identity of the file in the directory. Examples include:

```
100  OPEN "O",#1,"NEWFILE" create a file
110  OPEN "O",#2,"ANOTHER" create another file
120  OPEN "I",#5,"EXISTS" this one already exists
```

Once open, there are several keywords used to send data to/from the disk file. To simplify, we will include the two most often used. These take the forms:

INPUT #m,variable list
PRINT #m,variable list

Examples include:

```
200  INPUT #5,A,B,C$   a
210  C=A+B             b
220  INPUT D$          c
230  PRINT #2,D$,C     d
```

As part of a program including lines 100-120 earlier, this piece of nonsense does the following:

a pick up values for *A,B* and C$ from file *EXISTS*
b carry out a 'calculation'
c pick up a new value for a string variable
d write a new record to file *ANOTHER*

As another example, this logic:

```
100  A=12: B= -6.33: C=12.34
110   PRINT USING #2 "### ##.## ###.##";A,B,C
```

outputs to file 2:

```
b12b-6.33b012.34
```

I trust that this appendix has given you enough BASIC to act as a springboard for the rest of the book.

APPENDIX 2: Suggested comms assignments

I have been teaching this subject for several years and I never find it easy to set assignments. My approach to the subject has been to avoid as much 'heavy theory' as possible and concentrate on applications and the extensions to systems analysis and design that require a knowledge of comms. However:

- students only have about 90 hours for lectures and practical
- there is always a limit on student access to hardware, particularly when used as part of group assignments.

At Thames Valley College, we try to enforce a fairly rigid adherence to general BTEC guidelines - that courses should be heavily oriented to student participation. In subjects for all HND courses, final assessments are usually made on the basis of 50% for examinations and 50% for coursework.

In *Data Communications*, one of our final year options, I usually set three assignments, the first being written and the others requiring an investigation and often, the implementation of a system, perhaps including the design of programs.

Practical assignments are usually designed for group working and students have worked on projects involving from two students up to a whole class of 12 (difficult to control unless one student is prepared to do a lot of work).

I hope that the examples I am going to show, will give you an idea of the kind of practical work that can be carried out.

Assignment specification

I have tried to keep to a standard format for assignment specifications - it helps me to assess, it helps students to appreciate why they are carrying out an assignment and gives them an idea of how to do it.

- *Objectives* - these are the objectives of the assignment in terms of what it will help a student to learn and the skills that will be acquired if sufficient work is done.

In many projects, some of the skills to be acquired are common core skills, such as 'working in groups', 'self-management', 'oral communication' while others are subject-oriented, such as developing a relevant protocol or flowcharting a particular application.

Assignment specifications are never detailed - I expect students to come and discuss what they are to do, it gives me a chance to see how they think and it gives them some scope for enlarging or modifying the assignment to suit their interests or previous experience

- *Scenario* - a statement of the problem area. Students are usually free to modify or extend this to suit the hardware available, the amount of extra time they want to put in and the number of people that will work on the assignment.

This is not the way things occur in real life, but I believe that the more flexibility I can give students, the more chance they have of thinking up ideas and the easier it is for them to coordinate their efforts

- *What you have to do* - this gives some direction on what the project should achieve as much as how I think it should be approached. Past requirements have included:
  specify a system down to program specification level
  investigate software and produce a report
  develop programs to demonstrate layer 2 protocols
  write magazine articles
  produce training material for non-technical staff
  justifying hardware and software to management.
- *Deadline and late penalty* - students always complain that they have too much coursework - but at the end of the course they always say how valuable it was. A deadline for an assignment hand-in is for the student's benefit not for the staff and students must learn to schedule efforts so that assignments are handed in on time.

At my college, we usually knock off 10% of the possible mark for up to one week late and 20% for up to two weeks (100% if any later).

(This section has been left out of the assignment specifications: you can suppy your own.)

- *Additional notes* - this will include assumptions that can be made and recommendations on what to do and what not to do eg:

a. ensure that the material in the report is not too technical - it is designed for users
b. provided protocols are specified in detail, programs need not be written
c. develop the system for one branch only and assume that the others will be taken on later
d. you can assume that all head office files already exist and programs need not be written to transfer any records needed to the warehouse.

- *Assessment* - a very important part of the assignment. It is not enough to say that the assignment counts for say, 40% of the total coursework. The student is entitled to know in detail, how marks or grades can be obtained.

I use a percentage marking scheme for assignments and examinations (appendix 3), but dont be surprised if your college makes use of letter grades or *pass, merit* or *distinction*. It seems likely that all HND assessments will go this way eventually.

- *Workload estimate* - just a broad suggestion. In a college, student effort may have to be entirely during timetabled hours, or there may be scope for open-house computing. Students should feel free to put in more hours than the estimate.
- *Comments* - this will be of further help and usually gives an idea of how the assignment was handled by my students.

Resources and facilities

Current hardware at Thames Valley includes:

- a Harris mainframe with 60+ terminals
- a MicroVAX minicomputer with 50+ terminals in an Ethernet LAN
- 9+ groups of IBM and other PCs in LAN configurations
- many stand-alone PCs.

It is possible to specify assignments linking the Vax to a PC LAN, the simulation of errors and their handling on the Harris etc, but in a busy college, this would be just too disruptive on other students.

Most of the assignments carried out have made use of some or all of the following:

- 8 PCs in Tapestry configuration (see chapter 9)
- pairs of PCs (null modem links)
- RS232 link between the Harris and the Tapestry network.

The Harris has usually acted as 'head office' and the PCs as branches or perhaps individual users. Pairs of PCs are used to develop programs demonstrating layer 2 protocols, such as the ATM problem discussed in chapter 6 or for electronic mail (see appendix 3, question Q6).

Student pre-knowledge

Students are very familiar with MS-DOS, Pascal, COBOL, Symphony and other packages and a good number have exerience of C.

Very few have more than a nodding acquaintance with BASIC - it is our rigid practice to force students to follow the *Jackson structured programming* methodology and it is felt that BASIC is just not suitable for this. Nevertheless, either students have learnt BASIC at school, or they pick up enough from me to be able to develop comms programs without much trouble!

More technical students have developed programs in C, particularly those who gained experience on their placement (at TVC, we run a 4:3:2 term course, the middle 3 terms being for student placement with local companies).

As to what students hand in, some part of the assessment allocation is usually for presentation.

In the suggested assignments that follow, I have given some indication of the total man-hours required, assuming that one student works on the project. Assignment 6 is a big one and has alrady been referred to in chapter 9. It is definitely intended for group working. Assignment 7 could be a series of small assignments or group projects.

List of assignments

1. Magazine articles
2. Report to the college Director of Services
3. Vehicle reservation program
4. Car spares company
5. Electronic mail program
6. Order processing network
7. Port & Folio business market service

Assignment 1

Objectives

- to require students to read around particular subjects and collect and present further material in an organised way
- to demonstrate a working knowledge of particular aspects of the unit content at an interview and collect further information during interview
- to integrate different aspects of the unit content
- to plan work geared to unfamiliar requirements.

Scenario

A group of communications gurus has been commissioned by 'International Systems', a monthly magazine for programmers, analysts and software users, to write a series of **three** connected articles on subjects of interest to readers. The editor will then select the best group of three for publication.

Readers of the magazine generally have a heavy experience of DP and a nodding acquaintance with comms.

Articles are to be selected from the following list:

- the significance of digital exchanges
- BASIC as a comms language
- ARQ mechanisms
- electronic mail and its extensions
- smart modems
- how to select a local area network
- mobile services
- the fully integrated workstation
- security/secrecy measures for transmitted data

- C as a comms language
- teleworking
- efficient multiplexing
- remote financial information
- communications software
- the legal framework of data comms.

What you have to do

1. Interview the editor as to the scope/content/volume of the articles required
2. Draw up a plan of your work showing break-points where necessary
3. Discuss your work with the editor at the first break point
4. Present your three draft articles, with any diagrams, tables etc and some indication of the styling/layout wanted.

Additional notes

Students will be required to interview the editor (G. Mandoff who has more than a nodding acquaintance of comms), for direction on subjects selected and the approach to be adopted. Articles selected must not contain any material used as the subject of other unit assignments, but they may make reference to their own or other student's assignments as research work

No two students may select the same **three** article subjects.

Assessment

- interview 10%
- presentation/documentation 15%
- originality/research 15%
- knowledge of applications 20%
- knowledge of hardware 20%
- knowledge of techniques 20%.

Workload estimate

- research/discussion/planning 2 hours
- interview/discussion 2 hour

- article drafts 12 hours
- corrections 2 hours
- final articles 2 hours

  Total 20 hours

Comments

Students found this assignment difficult - their big problem was selecting three linked subjects. Once they had sorted this out, they generally did very well and most students presented a full desk-top published report including nice diagrams.

Typical groupings included:

- BASIC, C, comms software
- smart modems, teleworking, mobile terminals
- remote financial information, the ingetrated workstation, security measures
- e-mail, teleworking, comms software.

Assignment 2

Objectives

- to revise, expand on and consolidate knowledge gained so far
- to appreciate that this knowledge is to be applied from the DP viewpoint, not from that of the hardware specialist
- to see how this knowledge provides a basis for the remainder of the course.

Scenario

Tems Vallee College (TVC) carries out a wide range of DP activities, some as stand-alone workstations using IBM XTs and a few Apples, the bulk of the work being based on semi-intelligent terminals, linked to two different mainframe computers. Current systems include:-

- student registration/fees
- course/division/school costing and budgeting
- staff, room and resources allocation (eg, computer time)
- other financial systems

- other administration systems.

Many users within the college have some experience of PC and terminal-based systems, but in general, most of the academic and administration staff are very hazy about comms network concepts and facilities.

TVC is carrying out a major re-think of the computing services and facilities it will offer. It expects to set up a main network of mainframes, PCs and assorted terminals as a set of subsidiary, fully bridged networks, with a limited number of gateways to external services.

The *Director of Services* has asked for a brochure to help him decide what the new system should provide and act as a guide for users of the new network to its broader aspects.

What you have to do

To assist in the production of the brochure, you are asked to provide a four-part set of explanatory notes that give some background knowledge.

The director wants the following subjects to be covered:

- an overview of the applications supported by the system
- internal and external facilities from the network
- a basic introduction to the hardware units that might be employed in the network
- how to ensure that errors, not introduced by users, are detected and corrected.

Additional notes

Remember, you are preparing the material for non-computer professionals. Be as clever as you like with suggestions for applications, but **simplify the technical side as much as possible.**

Dont be frightened to include diagrams or screen dumps, especially in the first part (flowcharts are also appropriate)

Assessment

- relevance of ideas for the brochure 25%
- inventiveness/ingenuity of ideas 25%
- presentation skills/clarity 20% of material offered

- level of technical knowledge shown 30%

Workload estimate

- planning/research 4 hours
- notes 10 hours
- discussion/revision 2 hours
- corrections/final 4 hours
  Total 20 hours

Comments

This assignment would be set after about a third of the lectures have been given. Students can provide 75% of the material from lecture notes/handouts, the remainder coming from discussion and some further reading.

The first part of the assignment is to remind students that the subject is strongly DP-oriented (see the second objective).

Students attempting this assignment have generally been far too technical - to put the problem into perspective, I act as a non-technical intended user of the system and ask the following kind of question:

- why are some of the wires black and some yellow?
- what is that box on the floor that connects our two PCs to the wire going to the main computer?
- why are some workstation screens much bigger than mine?
- will electrical interference affect my computer?

Assignment 3

Objectives

- to demonstrate an appreciation of the practical problems of PC-to-PC communication
- to apply OSI layer 2 thinking and specify a suitable protocol
- to develop and test programs to implement the protocol designed.

Scenario

An organisation has many employees that may need access to a company vehicle for immediate use or some future occasion. It

has a transport department that must keep up-to-date information on the availability of cars, vans and motor- cycles.

It has been decided to implement an electronic mail vehicle booking system that will operate like a electronic diary. An employee will be able to request:

- self-drive or driver/chauffeur
- a vehicle type (eg, estate car, 1-ton van)
- a particular model (Sierra 2.3GL, Datsun Omnivan).

Bookings can be made:

- for 'now' or 'as soon as possible'
- for a future date (eg, tomorrow, 2.00 pm).

What you have to do

1. Design a layer 2 protocol with relevant data frames to handle any enquiry from a user terminal to the mainframe that holds the diary
2. Produce a detailed specification for a program to service a user terminal (assumed to be an IBM PC)
3. Make up a suitable set of test data and get the program working in a sutible programming language
4. State very clearly all assumptions made.

Additional notes

- you can assume that a physical connection has been made from the terminal and that the user has signed on with a password before your program comes into operation
- data frames must include enquiries from the terminal and the replies from the mainframe
- note that user dialogue must be designed
- your protocol should allow for some of the following:

a. all the 'questions' that a user will want to ask
b. 'satisfactory' replies from the mainframe (*Please collect ELLW 234 from the car pool, Take any Bedford van after 4.00 today)*
c. unsatisfactory replies (*Sorry! type not available, will another do?, Sorry! no vans free until Tuesday*)
d. garbled messages to/from the mainframe

e. unforseen disconnection.

- if the assignment is to be individual, you need not concern yourself with the mainframe files, nor the mainframe programs that will support the system
- the assignment can be considerably simplified if necessary by assuming just one kind of vehicle, only same-day bookings etc.

Assessment

- understanding of the application 30%
- development of suitable rules and data frames 30%
- clear statement of program logic 20%
- satisfactory program performance 10%
- program documentation 10%

Workload estimate

- investigation of problem 2 hours
- protocol development 3 hours
- program specification and dialogue design 6 hours
- program writing 6 hours
- program testing 5 hours
- write-up/discussion 5 hours
  Total 27 hours

Comments

Some of the questions in appendix 3 ask you to develop similar protocols for similar environments. Also, refer to the ATM problem in chapter 6.

Assignment 4

Objectives

- to consolidate and extend systems analysis and design experience gained in other parts of the course
- to broaden these ideas to allow for a remote, on-line system that interfaces with the one you are designing

- to consider the distribution of data that must accompany distributed processing
- to consider the requirements of a LAN for a particular application area.

Scenario

CMR is a company situated on the Slough Trading Estate supplying car spare parts to the public and to garages/service engineers. Orders whether written, by telephone, or personal, are placed through the sales office.

The company has a large warehouse with goods coming in all day from suppliers and being checked out for issue or delivery to customers.

The overall CMR site is such that all offices are within an 80 yard radius circle.

Two directors are also associated with *Carhire Ltd* in Maidenhead (about eight miles from Slough) and some nice office accommodation is available (with LAN/telephone/power wiring already installed) to CMR at a very good rate. So, it has been decided to set up a separate marketing and sales office in Maidenhead. The office will be staffed by eight people whose main tasks are:

- marketing/public relations
- customer enquiries regarding stock and its availability
- customer order progress.

They will be organised as a separate local network that will have access to local and Slough files from PC terminals. It is also planned that access to services external to CMR will be available via the PTN.

What you have to do

1. Make and state a reasonable set of assumptions as to:

- the nature of the jobs carried out in the new office
- the data that must be made available in the office and at Slough
- data volumes (e.g. orders per day, items per order).

2. Discuss the possible LAN hardware arrangement in the office
3. Make recommendations as to the external services that might be of value in the running of the office

4. Produce a summary report explaining to management, the expected benefits and disadvantages of separating the sales office from the rest of the company.

Assessment

- relevance of assumptions made 20%
- appreciation of systems implications 20%
- usefulness of summary report 20%
- technical comms knowledge 15%
- comms applications knowledge 15%
- presentation/documentation 10%

Workload estimate

- define company data/processing details 4 hours
- specify broad details of new system 4 hours
- define hardware requirements 2 hours
- determine requirements for external services 2 hours
- produce summary report 8 hours

Total 20 hours

Comments

Many students on computer studies and other courses with a heavy systems analysis and design content, will recognise this scenario! The assignment was designed to extend systems analysis work done (see objective 1) and does require some knowledge ofa car spares company that makes use of an in-house computerised system.

The assignment is quite difficult without this knowledge, but keen students can make good use of it if they get some help (or do quite a lot of work) on the first part of the assignment (the assumptions). The remaining parts of the assignment are not difficult once you have sorted the first part.

You may need to think about some the following:

- how will the office be organised
- how will customer order progress be carrried out

- how will the system allow for stock enquiries (price, availability, delivery time etc)
- what data will the office need access to
- how/when will this data need to be updated for them
- what updates will they send back to the main system?
- what computing hardware will be needed.

Assignment 5

Objectives

- to demonstrate an appreciation of the practical problems of PC-to-PC communication
- to demonstrate the ability to design files for a specific application
- to apply OSI layer 2 thinking and specify a sutible protocol.

Scenario

You have been asked to assist in the design of a basic electronic mail system, that will be made available from the company mainframe via a user's PC. The functions to be supported are as follows:

- send a message to Mr. X's terminal
- send a message to everyone's terminals
- ask for a list of messages for you (ie, view your 'in-tray')
- display a particular message
- have hard-copy of a particular message printed and sent to you.

What you have to do

1. State clearly the problems that could arise when each function is requested
2. Produce a recommendation for the file(s) that will be needed at the message centre (the company maniframe) to support the mail functions
3. Produce detailed designs for the user VDU screens associated with the mail system and suggest the data validation that could be carried out by the terminal program to avoid wasteful access to the mainframe

4. Design a set of data frames (from terminal and mainframe) that will be appropriate to the application.

Additional notes

The problem statement does not actually say so, but you are obviously being asked to consider the layer 2 protocol and your submission must make it clear that you know what is involved with starting, maintaining and ending a conversation.

It is assumed that you will not want to write and test a program. If you do, then refer to assignment 3.

Hints:

- restricted access to the system!
- can I get messages from anyone?
- can I send messages to anyone?
- suppose the mainframe is busy?
- maximum number of users?
- maximum number of messages for me?

Assessment

- investigation of application/problem identification 20%
- file design 20%
- usefulness/elegance of dialogue design measures 15%
- completeness of error-handling 20%
- usefulness/elegance of data frames produced 25%

Workload estimate

- problem analysis 2 hours
- file design 3 hours
- dialogue/validation 4 hours
- data frames 4 hours
- documentation/discussion 3 hours

  Total 17 hours

Assignment 6

This scenario has been used several times at Thames Valley College and the specification given relates to our Tapestry network (see chapter 9). It will give much more detail that other assignments, showing how students actually approached the project.

Objectives

- appreciate that an on-line system is still a computerised system
- demonstrate a structured approach to systems investigation and design
- demonstrate an awareness of the problems of inter-networking
- demonstrate an ability to integrate the use of applications and comms software
- appreciate the applications of electronic mail in a typical DP environment
- demonstrate the ability to manage/control the daily operation of a LAN
- demonstrate the ability to work as part of a large team in a complex and integrative project
- demonstrate competence in written communication.

Scenario

A company has a head office and a number of branches each of which has a stores. It sells a fairly simple range of products to a limited range of customers. A branch has several sales clerks, several stores clerks and a manager who is responsible for communications with head office.

Orders are posted by customers and received by sales clerks. They carry out an on-line validation for correct customer and part numbers, invalid orders being passed back to the customer for correction.

After entry and validation, a credit check is carried out on orders and if suspect they are held, pending clearance from head office. Accepted orders are passed to stores who pick goods and arrange for delivery. As goods are picked, stores make a note of items that are getting low and head office will be informed so that it can arrange re-ordering. Once goods have been packed and delivered, orders are sent to head office.

Data is transferred between sales, stores and the manager and as they are all busy people, it will be necessary to 'talk' to each by e-mail when necessary.

The branch manager has the authority to pass suspect orders up to £500, any others must be passed to head office.

A typical branch has about 200 customers and receives about 50 orders per day, with a maximum of four lines per order. On average, about five orders a day need a further credit check by head office.

It has been decided that **all communication between a branch and head office must be carried out through the branch communications manager.**

What you have to do

You are asked to set up appropriate files at head office/branch and simulate the daily operation of one branch using the Tapestry network. You should then execute one overall class project to include:

1. Group presentation to company management
2. Report A - to include *objectives, system design details, test data and actual results*
3. Report B - an appendix to report A called *some problems of internetworking*
4. Progress records (life-history of the project)
5. A clear indication of which students carried out which tasks/activities.

Additional notes

- decide on main report headings and individual responsibilities
- decide on schedule
- decide the logistics of the case study: personnel, locations, responsibilities and privilege
- agree broad DP details and summarise as system flowcharts or logical data flow diagrams
- decide on runs and software to be used
- decide on physical Tapestry configuration
- decide on progress-reporting mechanism

- arrange student training in use of Tapestry and PC-to-mainframe linkage
- produce staff training schedules and manuals
- organise walk-through of proposed work
- set up data on mainframe and Tapestry
- carry out processing
- arrange presentation details
- complete the documentation.

A selection of report sub-headings

- how to configure and set up the system
- (all) the hardware involved
- external communication
- security/privilege
- Tapestry and the user
- the application
- LAN management & control
- internetworking problems.

Assessment

- comprehension and definition of problems arising from the chosen scenario 30%
- completeness of solution 20%
- elegance of solution 10%
- written reports 40% including:

    demonstration of DP knowledge 15%
    demonstration of comms knowledge 20%
    use of diagrams/graphics 5%

Additional notes

- you can ignore the update of files and stock reordering at head office
- this is not a programming project but programs could be written to point out the problems of internetworking.

Tapestry 'sub-networks'

The actual LAN should be configured as three logical networks as follows:

Branch

acts as a gateway, file and printer server, based on XT number 8.

Sales

a supervisor (file and printer server manager) on XT number 1; two clerks (no manager status) based on XTs 3 and 4

Warehouse

a supervisor (file and printer server manager) on XT number 4; two clerks (no manager status) XTs 5 and 6

The network manager (with full manager status) comes from head office, when major configuraton changes are needed at a branch.

User Identification

Staff member	*User number*	*Password*
Head office comms expert	EXPERT	METSYS
Taplow branch manager	BRANCH	WOLPAT
sales office supervisor	SALES	SALESUP
sales clerk 1	SALES	SCL1
sales clerk 2	SALES	SCL2
warehouse supervisor	WHOUSE	WSUP
warehouse clerk 1	WHOUSE	WCL1
warehouse clerk 2	WHOUSE	WCL2

Head office

Harris mainframe, via direct (RS232) link to gateway server
Stand-alone XT (null modem/BASIC link)
Personnel department XT number 8 (null modem/BASIC link)

Suggestions for files

File F1
customer number
customer name
customer address
discount allowed
current balance
credit limit
transaction
details

File F1a
customer number
current balance
credit limit

File F2
item number
description
unit-of-sale
unit price
stock level
re-order level
re-order quantity
sales this month
days since last order

File F2a
item number
description
unit price

File FA
(1 record for each order line)
order number
order date
customer number
item number
price
quantity ordered
flagged indicator (0 = OK, 1 = waiting clearance)

File FL
item number
quantity in stock
unit price

File FS/FS'
order number
customer number
order date
order value
accepted indicator

(In the interests of simplicity, you may choose to abandon many of the fields shown.)

System possible main stages

Head office:

- create customer and stock files in form suitable to pass to branches
- receive e-Mail/FS, check out credit
- return FS' to sales office
- receive re-orders (FL) and pass for manual action
- receive order transactions (FA) and pass for file update.

Sales clerk:

- receive orders
- process credit checking, pass e-mail/FS/FA to manager

Stores clerk:

- receive picking list from sales (via manager after head office check-out)
- pick goods, carry out stock check and delivery set-up
- inform manager of low stock by e-mail/FL

Branch/communications manager:

- receive e-mail/FS from sales
- pass e-mail/FS to head office
- receive FS' from head office and clear flagged FA records
- pass FA to stores (inform with e-mail)
- receive e-mail/FL from stores
- send completed orders e-mail/FA and e-mail/FL to head office
- viewdata access of trade credit list for sales (simulation)
- extract and send sales data to personnel for commissions.

Possible runs

- *run 1* - head office sets up master files customer (F1) and stock (F2)

- *run 2* - daily sub-set (F1a) of sales office's customers (F1) sent to sales office
- *run 3* - daily file F2 sent to stores
- *run 4* - monthly price list (F2a) sent to sales offices
- *run 5* - enter orders at sales office, accepted orders to file FA, suspect orders also on file FA (order flagged): sumary of these held on file FS, details of suspect orders passed (e-mail with file FS attached) to manager
- *run 6* - manager passes FS details to head office for credit control action
- *run 7* - head office checks out file FS and flags as accepted/rejected
- *run 8* - manager receives clearance/refusal on suspect orders FS'. Runs program to set off flags on order records on FA for cleared orders from FS'. Print picking list on relevant stores remote printer (tell them with e-mail)
- *run 9* - stores receive picking list and pick goods. Low stock details passed (via FL and e-mail) to manager
- *run 10* - manager passes FL details to head office for reordering
- *run 11* - manager then transfers FA to head office for update of F1/F2 and invoicing
- *run 12* - manager accesses viewdata source for credit check
- *run 13* - manager sends commission data to Personnel.

Final comments

As you have seen, this is a really enormous assignment, but if you spend some time on it, you should be able to spot quite a number of simple and not-so- simple smaller assignments. Even if you only implement part of a project (eg, by making up fileswith an editor or word processor, rather than writing the create/update programs), you can gain a wealth of systems and comms experience.

To provide an opportunity for one student to write BASIC comms programs, one extension included the need to invent a personnel department.

Every order placed is tagged with the code number of the sales clerk taking the order. The run that updates the branch stock file also collects sales statistics (customer number/order number/date/sales clerk/value) and the file is passed from a Tapestry workstation to another PC linked by null modem. Personnel can then work out sales commissions.

Assignment 7

Objectives

- to provide a vehicle for a range of comms and systems analysis/design assignments
- to provide opportunities for documenting broad system design proposals
- to provide opportunities for document, file and output design
- to assist students in appreciating a range of data transmission services and facilities
- to allow students to demonstrate some knowledge of how these need to be applied to support applications
- to enable students to appreciate the need for and problems associated with distributed systems
- to enable students to appreciate/define the batch-processing back-up needed to support on-line applications
- to enable students to design a DP/e-mail system based on a local area network
- to give students experience in the settting up an running of a LAN-based system.

Scenario

Port and Folio Ltd (PFL) is a company that offers financial and investment advice to pension fund managers, companies and private individuals. It sells information/advice to customers inquiring by phone, letter, fax and e-mail. It has a range of interests such as shipping, insurance, commodities and metals but specialises in advice on the equity market, metals and commodities.

The company operates from one building which holds a computer centre, an administration and sales centre, accounts, an enquiry centre and three service offices.

PFL provides its service in three main areas and intelligence and data processing is carrried out in the service offices, each of which is primarily concerned with its own market area, each office is further divided into 'floors', which deal with particular sections of the market and each floor has a number of 'experts' who carry out the work.

Within a particular floor, any expert can deal with an enquiry although customers may ask for a particular one of a particular enquiry.

Office A deals with *equities (stocks and shares)*, the floors being:

- oils/industrials
- banking/finance
- unclassified.

Office B handles *metals (copper, tin, aluminium etc)* and *commodities (coffee, spices etc)*, the floors being:

- metals
- commodities
- other.

Office C is different in that it deals with intelligence and information on different types of company. The floors are:

- public companies
- private companies
- miscellaneous.

(Note that office A only deals with companies that offer shares. Office C could be asked to look into a partnership, charity or any kind of organisation - even individuals).

All enquiries arrive at the enquiry reception centre which converts it to a standard format and then passes it to the relevant floor/expert. An expert scans his VDU to see the list of queries outstanding and pick one addressed to him or one that he can handle.

The data to support the processing of the query comes from the PFL data base, although each floor and office will have its own sources. Data at head office is updated as often as is necessary from its own sources and external information providers. Its main source of equity and other market data is the *Financial London and Overseas Postings (FLOP)*, a very up-to-date viewdata service with which PFL has a fast, direct link.

The expert handles the query by obtaining any necessary data and making use of a range of software including spreadsheet, statistical packages (for forecasting etc) and will produce a result as text or in some cases graphically (eg, bar-chart, pie-chart) which is passed back to the enquiry centre for invoicing and return to the customer in whatever form was requested.

This data gathering and enquiry processing is very complex and PFL constantly needs to monitor enquiries and how they are processed so that it can keep up a high level of customer service. As results are passed back to the enquiry centre, statistics are gathered on:

- the form in which enquiries arrived (phone, fax etc)
- market area(s) involved
- number of experts involved
- time to process the enquiry
- the form in which returned to customer.

A further feature that adds to the complexity is the operation of office C. When carrying out a complete company investigation, an expert may need advice from other offices eg, about share performance, associated or subsidiary companies. This is carried out by the expert generating an 'internal' enquiry in a very similar form to that received from the enquiry centre.

What you have to do

This is a massive scenario and can provide many assignments, so no particular specification is given. However, a number of recommendations will be made so that you can work out individual or group assignments.

1. Pay attention to the data/information requirements, in particular:-

- what data will be available on a permanent basis
- what can be collected as needed

- what must be held at the enquiry centre
- what can be kept in an office, floor or an expert's terminal
- what floor data might be needed on other floors
- what office data might be needed in other offices.

2. How and in what form do enquiries go:

- from enquiry centre to floor/expert
- from floor to floor, expert to expert and/or office to office
- back to the enquiry office
- back to the customer.

3. What overall processes will be required:

- on-line
- on-line in real-time
- batch (regular)
- batch (as required).

4. What processing does an expert carry out

5. How is data collected, stored, presented and updated

6. What is the scope for:

- external e-mail
- internal e-mail
- computer-integrated telephony
- electronic diary
- external viewdata
- internal viewdata.

7. What DP/comms hardware will be needed to link experts, floors, office and the enquiry centre

8. What comms hardware will be needed for external linkage.

Comments

This scenario hs been used at Thames Valley College using our Tapestry network linked to the mainframe ('enquiry centre'). The LAN was configured as *office A* into three floors, each workstation being an expert.

The share price movement for the last six months on a weekly basis was collected - values are available in the Monday edition of the *Financial Times* and current share information is available in the Tuesday to Saturday editions.

To simplify processing, very elementary statistics and graphical presentation was carried out using Symphony although any integrated package could have been used. (It was felt that the project on this particular occasion, was too complex to allow students to write COBOL or BASIC programs.)

Topics to think about

The following could be considered:

- investigate PFL and define the main functions of a computerised system that might meet their requirements
- produce a system proposal for the processing carried out in the enquiry office
- produce a system proposal for the e-mail transfer of initial, partly-completed and completed enquiries within the building
- produce a detailed design for:
  the expert 'queries outstanding' screen
  a customer invoice
  one of the weekly 'floor processing' summary reports
- suggest designs for replies to typical enquiries, such as:
  which metal has shown the most consistent price over the last four weeks?
  what subsidiaries does XXX Ltd own and how are their shares doing?
  is the ZZZ partnership expanding faster that YYY Ltd?
  give me a weekly summary on the shares of KKK for the last two months
- produce a specification for the batch processes carried out at the computer centre
- use a LAN to simulate the operations of some or all of PFL and produce a report (suggested headings):

objectives of the assignment and the problems of internetworking/operation of a LAN

introduction to PFL and an expansion of the scenario

why the particular LAN was chosen - the actual set-up, processing details, problems of estimating and managing the LAN

notes on software employed

notes on hardware

inputs, files and results

conclusions

notes on standards, protocols, general problems

Finally, note that an equity record could be set up with the following format:

company name
type of business
number of shares issued
current market capitalisation
maximum share price
minimum share price
interim dividend date
final dividend date
interim dividend
final dividend
profit last interim
profit last final
market forecast
earnings per share
gross yield
profit/earnings ratio.

APPENDIX 3: Examination questions/answers and assessment schemes

All the following questions were taken from recent papers set by me for Thames Valley College HND Computer Studies final examinations in *Data Communications* and *On-line and Distributed Systems*.

In all cases, examinations are three hours long and the total mark figure at the end of each question shows the amount of time students are recommended to allocate to their answer.

Try any question that takes your fancy and then refer to the marking scheme to see how you got on.

All questions have a marking scheme and in some cases, brief suggested solutions are given. Not all examiners will use my approach to setting/marking questions, but it is fairly representative.

(The trouble with this appendix is that I will now have to think up a whole new set of questions for my future Data Comms students!!!)

Questions

Question 1

Explain the following terms giving examples of their application where appropriate:

a. synchronous transmission
b. CCITT recommendation V21
c. terminal emulation software
d. forward error checking
e. layered protocol model

f. computer conferencing (6 marks each part)

Total: 36 marks

Question 2

The integrated site for *RCM*, a car spares company, is on the Slough Trading estate. Although this is convenient for the manufacture and storage of spares, it is rather cramped and the 'works' really needs more space than is readily available on the trading estate.

It has been decided to move the marketing and sales activities to a separate office about 800 metres from the main site. The office is to consist of 8 people whose tasks are:

- public relations
- marketing
- customer enquiries regarding stock and its availability
- customer order progress.

They are organised as a separate network connected to the Slough mainframe, so will have access to Slough files from their workstations as well as maintaining local files where needed.

a. make and state reasonable assumptions about timings, data volumes and file sizes (4 marks)
b. give general recommendations for the hardware aspects of a possible local area network for the sales office (8 marks)
c. discuss four alternative methods of providing a link between the two offices and justify their possible use (12 marks)
d. What activities in the office could be supported by computer-aided telephony (2 marks)

Total: 26 marks

Question 3

Discuss the differences between the following pairs of terms:

a. virtual circuit and datagram service
b. WAN and MAN
c. EFT and EDI
d. BSC and HDLC (5 marks each part)

Total: 20 marks

Question 4
Give your views on the following:

a. why do so many different standards apply in data communications? (5 marks)
b. how useful is PC-based BASIC as a language for communications software? (5 marks)

Total: 10 marks

Question 5
Discuss the difference between the following pairs of data communications terms giving examples where possible:

a. data concentration and data compression
b. packet assembler and disassembler packet terminal
c. continuous RQ and idle RQ
d. character-oriented protocol and bit-oriented protocol
e. end-to-end and point-to-point (4 marks each part)

Total: 20 marks

Question 6
A basic electronic message board system is to be implemented for a company.

A central minicomputer will poll a number of authorised, on-line users and collect lines of text to be stored on disk for later reference by authorised users or for forwarding to recipients.

For any 'conversation', there will be three basic data frames, set-up, data and close-down.

a. suggest suitable formats for the sender's data frames once he has responded to the initial poll call (10 marks)
b. from this, develop a set of rules for the 'conversation,' setting out the logic in any convenient form (diagram, pseudocode etc) to represent the steps associated with all aspects of message processing (10 marks)

Total: 20 marks

Question 7

You have been asked to recommend and implement a range of computerised facilities for a car exhaust and tyre company which has three branches and a central warehouse, all within a single town. Branch head office is attached to the warehouse. Branches B and C are both less than 10 miles from Branch A.

The feeling is that a LAN in each building might be the answer with an external link between each.

a. list and discuss **four** of the factors involved in estimating the processing and storage requirements of each LAN (8 marks)
b. describe and give examples of **two** general linkage 'mechanisms' between the buildings (6 marks)
c. suggest and justify a mechanism that might be applied here (2 marks)
d. give two major differences between bus- and ring-stuctured LANs (4 marks each)

Total: 20 marks

Question 8

a. the BASIC statement for setting up a communications port has the following format:

```
OPEN "COMn:speed,parity,data,stop,RS,CS,DS,CD,LF,PE "AS#m(LEN=n)
           |     |      |      | |       |
           A     B      C      D E       F
```

Discuss the sigificance of the six parameters indicated by the letters A to F (3 marks each part)

b. Give three disadvantages of BASIC for communications on a PC (2 marks each)

Total: 24 marks

Question 9

Discuss the following external network facilities and their application to the sales office of *MRC*, a motor car spares company:

a. computer-integrated telephony
b. electronic data interchange
c. viewdata
d. fax (4 marks each part)

Total: 16 marks

Question 10

Explain the following terms and show their application in data communications:

a. ARQ.
b. CSMA
c. digitisation
d. redundancy in data transmission
e. gateway
f. MAN (4 marks each part)

Total: 24 marks

Question 11

On-line systems, by definition, are user-oriented and as you have seen, considerable attention must be paid to the design of suitable dialogue.

With examples taken from videotex and other data communications and on-line applications:

a. explain briefly, **five** hardware facilities available from VDU/keyboard that can assist in general user-friendliness (10 marks)
b. give **five** factors in each of the following three areas showing what might determine the form of dialogue designed:

- the applications supported from the terminal
- the type of user concerned
- the data involved in the application (2 marks each part)

Total: 20 marks

Question 12

You are asked to recommend and implement a number of computerised facilities for *Muffler*, a car exhaust and tyre company which has three branches and a central warehouse, all within a single town. Branch A which is also 'Head Office', is attached to the warehouse. Branches B and C are both about a mile away from Branch A. The feeling is that a LAN in each building might be the answer with an external link between each.

To assist Muffler in making a decision as to the system they will need to implement, produce a preliminary report to the management giving your views and recommendations on the following:

a. estimating processing and storage requirements of each LAN (8 marks)
b. external services that might require 'gatewaying' (6 marks)
c. the range of linkage mechanisms between buildings and the factors affecting a decision as to which might be appropriate (6 marks)

Total: 20 marks

Question 13

Peter Francisco is an off-licence chain with 100 branches (opening hours: 10.30-2.30 and 5.00-8.30). With a view to improving efficiency of operation, a consultant analyst has been asked to give a broad suggestion for a suitable computerised system and he has proposed the following:

- branches are to be equipped with up to two computerised cash registers, with associated VDU and floppy disk drive. Each day, replenishment goods will be delivered to each branch, together with a disk containing for each branch product sold:
    product code/description/price
    VAT code
    start-of-day stock level
- customers will be able to pay by cash, cheque or credit card (an on-line credit check with head office will be required for credit customers)
- as items are checked out through the till, the sales clerk will enter the product code from a label on the item and the number purchased. The information will be expanded and echoed on the VDU (which has a 36-character line and a depth of 16 lines)

- after the purchase is complete, the clerk will check the details and once satisfied, instruct the machine to calculate the total value and print a bill/receipt on an associated 'tally-roll' printer. The clerk will also enter payment details (cash/cheque/credit card)
- the system will record the sale of stock and the payments received on the floppy disk and after closing, this will be collected by a pick-up service which delivers all of the branch floppy disks to head office for overnight processing ofsales/receipts, branch stock replenishments and delivery/pick-up schedules. Management will receive branch sales and overall product analyses.

a. produce a detailed VDU screen design for the existing 'takings analysis' (10 marks)
b. describe and discuss **three** factors you would consider, in particular any additional processing that could be supported, in order to recommend a fully on-line system, (thereby removing the need for the floppy disk delivery / pick-up service) (12 marks)
c. if a full on-line system were implemented, shops would need to be equipped with workstations. Suggest **three** possible 'external services' that might be made available for use by the shops explaining who might provide them and why they might be of use (9 marks)
d. describe **five** components of the hardware that will be needed at the work station to support the intermittnt transmission that will result when the system goes live (5 marks)

Total: 36 marks

Marking schemes

Question 1

a.

Synchronous transmission - the technique showing its advantages over asynchronous transmission, showing the structure of a typical frame and indicating the importance of level 2 synchronous protocols.

Example to show where block transfer is more efficient eg, text or file transfer

4 marks for explanation. 2 marks for example

b.
CCITT recommendation V24
2 marks for appreciation that this is a slow modem specification
4 marks for knowledge of its main details

c.
Terminal emulation
4 marks for appreciation of the need for software to overcome protocol and format differences
2 marks for example such as for PC to DEC VT100 or IRMA for PC to IBM mainframe

d.
Forward error checking
4 marks for noting that the secondary can detect an error and locate and hence correct it as well ie, not just parity checking
2 marks for an example, such as Hamming code

e.
Layered protocol model
4 marks for appreciation of the need to compartmentalise standards in some way because of the complexity of 'conversations' and divergence of standards
2 marks for some explanation of the ISO 7-layer model

f.
Computer conferencing
4 marks for appreciation that is an extension of e-mail and bulletin board.
Users can post questions and examine answers and extensions
2 marks for appreciating problems such as the need for management to avoid abuse and excessive use of facilities

Question 2

a.
Any sensible figures in line with study in other units
4 marks

b.

Students should demonstrate fairly superficial knowledge, but be able to apply general principles to this particular problem. Full marks for a detailed answer that covers the majority of the following, or justified alternatives:

- as most data is held centrally, no workstation has predominance, so a ring structure is reasonable
- intelligent workstation for each staff member eg, IBM AT or Apple Mac (justify hard disk)
- printer service to two draft printers (letters, mailing lists etc) and at least one faster printer
- gateway service to head office and external services, (fax, e-mail to customers, viewdata for technical and trade info)

2 marks for each major point made.

c.

2 marks for each possibility, 1 mark for justification, eg:
Local twisted wire/coax/lazer
PSTN modem dial-up/leased/in-area private line
PDN microwave/Kilostream/Megastream
Justifications based on:
speed, volume, distance, external line costs;
need for intermediate amplifiers, regenerators, balancing etc; security and integrity.

d.

Examples could include:

Order progress - select orders due for delivery today and phone/chase

Sales chase-up - select customers not called for say three months

2 marks each for any reasonable ideas with explanation

Question 3

4 marks each part. Students to show understanding of each term and how they can be confused

a.

Virtual circuit requires a channel to be selected, with associated sender/receiver addressing. When the next block is to be sent, it

is only necessary to specify the channel. The network must guarantee delivery with a very high degree of probability
Datagram contains sender/receiver address and is often used for complete 'messages'. It does not have a specific channel and is delivered 'some how' with as high a degree of probability as is acceptable

b.
A *wide area network* is likely to cover more than a few miles, is probably owned, or partly leased from a PTO and will support multiple gateways
A *metropolitan area network* is limited in geographical area to about one town and will be largely owned by the user although links between different sites may be PTO-supplied (eg, BT Kilostream/Megastream)

c.
Electronic funds transfer involves the transfer of credit from point-of- service terminals (credit-card sales, cash-points).
Electronic data interchange is concerned with the transfer of 'financial' files especially credit transfers, such as bulk salary payments or bulked credit card transactions

d.
Binary synchronous communication is a character-oriented protocol which relies on ASCII frame separator and sub-separator characters. It requires SYN characters at the start of a frame and has limited flow control and ARQ aspects
High-level data link control is a bit-oriented protocol. Frames are headed by a 'frame' byte, are quite complex and can be of various types, allowing primary and secondary to carry out many layer 2 functions. HDLC also has significance at level 3 being fundamental to X25.

Question 4

a.
Students to show that standards originate with manufacturers, user groups, government agencies and international groups, all of whom have different objectives
5 marks for an all-round justification

b.

Students have worked on, or had access to examples of programs during the course and should be able to draw sensible conclusions.

1 mark for each major conclusion

Examples include:

- OPEN statement directly reflects some of V24 in particular timing and primary/secondary not ready or off-line
- a limited number of simple, readable statement-types can be employed for the applications looked at
- half-duplex port usage
- only two ports supported
- only asynchronous transmission possible (PC limitation)
- Difficulty of handling bits unless random files used
- Messy to input/output fields in memory-image format (binary, float....)

Question 5

4 marks each part; 2 marks for explanation, 2 marks for relevant example

a.

Data concentration - bulking of data from slow sources in preparation for transmission at a higher speed eg, collecting till transactions and sending at close of business

Data compression - reducing data to be transmitted so that the number of bits carrying the information is reduced eg, replacing repeated strings by a repeated item and repetition factor

b.

Packet assembler-disassembler - a network protocol conversion unit for use on a public packet network. Conforms to X25 and is responsible for packetising character data from asynchronous terminals, for entry to the network and recovering characters after passage through the network

Packet terminal - terminal that links directly to the packet network; contains the software to form up X25 packets

c.

Continuous RQ - a form of ARQ in which the primary sends frames until the secondary objects and requests either 'go-back-N' or 'selective re-transmission'

Idle RQ or *send-and-wait* - primary sends a frame and waits for a positive acknowledgement of receipt before continuing

d.

Character-oriented protocol - eg, BSC; positive acknowledgement; character- based protocol. Framing and sub-framing is carried out by means of ASCII groupings such as SOH, STX, ETX. Synchronisation by means of SYN bytes

Bit-oriented protocol- eg, HDLC. Much more sophisticated; primary-secondary combined - frame can contain 'send' and 'receive' data and control signals at the same time. Frames synchronised with 'frame' byte.

e.

End-to-end - service or facility between host computers (i.e. user processes) which are transparent to the host or user. Contrast with lower layer services (eg, layer 3 routing or layer 4 internetworking)

Point-to-point - connection between one primary and one secondary, such as PC to PC eg, sharing Symphony files. Contrast with multipoint where for example, one primary could be linked to numerous primaries, such as in a LAN or mainframe to user terminals.

Question 6.

This question is designed to see if students can apply knowledge of OSI level 2 link management and flow control to a particular communication situation. Part of the answer should demonstrate design skills in the structure of the frames sent and the remainder should show that the student can work out what might happen to disturb commmunication.

a.

All frames:

Frame type	Seq. no.	sender ident. / address	receiver ident. / address	---	CRC / BCC

Type 1 initial call in response to poll
Type 2 request to send a message
Type 3 message frame
| Data block | length of data | frame sequence number |
Type 4 request for messages
| Sender identity/address | authority | date/time |
Type 5 close-down, to contain:
count of characters/blocks sent (type 3)
count of characters/blocks received (type 4)
4 marks for a sensible general frame structure
6 marks for understanding/ingenuity/relevance of particular frames

b.

Rules should cover problems such as:

- frame not received
- unrecognised frame type
- frame out of sequence
- frame of wrong type e.g. 3 before 2
- block lost (control failure) on send (type 3)
- block lost (control failure) on receive (type 4).

2 marks for each problem identified

Question 7

a.

Factors such as:

- the effects of the application
- volume/flow/nature of the data
- the users
- file/printing requirements

- software requirements.

1 mark each for identifying
1 mark each for sensible discussion

b.
Students should be able to identify two major classes of link:
Direct - twisted wire, coax, microwave/lazer
Indirect - in-area private line, PSTN, PDN (e.g. Kilostream)
3 marks for each class

c.
Which to choose will depend on: speed of response required; volume of data; external transmission costs; need for intermediate amplifiers, regenerators; security and integrity
2 marks for reasonable selection with justification

d.
Examples include:

- ring with token - deterministic response - can be pre-determined
- broadcast bus is stochastic - probability of response at given level
- bus - all stations can receive message
- ring - only for station addressed
- bus more easy to extend/change since unbounded, while ring is fixed (except for addition of stations).

2 marks for each of 2 suggestions

Question 8

a.
A *speed* - specifies baud rate - usual common rates up to 9600
B *parity* - even/odd/none/0/1, (none for bit data}
C *stop* - number of stop bits to end character frame (1, 1.5 or 2)
D *DSn* - RS232 'data set ready' control. If omitted or n = 0, status not checked. Non-zero, n = milliseconds before timeout
E *CDn* - similar to DS for external (modem) access - checks for carrier present on PSTN link
F *LEN* - maximum number of bytes to/from buffer for GET/PUT: default = 128
3 marks for each sensible explanation

b.

Ideas such as:

- only asynchronous comms supported
- not easy to handle data other than as character strings
- only two comms ports available.

2 marks each for three suggestions

Question 9

a.

Computer-integrated telephony - arranging for a DP application to be integrated with a telephone application eg, selected dialling from a directory - the comms software links with database selection software. A typical example is in telephone sales, where the application software presents background on all customers to be called that day, makes the call when requested and retries on busy

b.

Electronic data interchange - 'paperless' DP, where typical source documents are transferred as transactions between eg, customer host and supplier host. Bulk credit transfer is used for payments - eg, salaries, share dividends. Need for extra data security/secrecy in the protocols

c.

Viewdata - standard format, user-friendly, hierarchical access to data/information. Can be private or via public provider (eg, Prestel). Technical/trade data on cars and components could be accessed by staff

d.

Fax - many suppliers provide fax cards for PCs so that even without a fax machine, it is possible to send documents (such as urgent orders confirmations or delivery schedules) directly from a PC or via a LAN gateway server

For each part:

2 marks for appreciation of what is involved

2 marks for relevance to MRC

Question 10

4 marks each part - 1 mark for each important point made

a.
Automatic repeat request - level 2 acknowledgement scheme for link control. Alternatives - *Idle RQ* - send and wait for reply; continuous RQ retransmit specific block or *go-back-N*

b.
Carrier sense multiple access/Collision detection - broadcast LAN technique for access to facilities - listen for carrier and dont transmit if line busy. If two or more stations try to transmit, system detects 'collision' and takes action eg, back-off algorithm

c.
Digitisation - technique, usually by sampling, where an analogue signal (such as speech, or the input from a point-of-sales terminal) is converted into digital signals. In the modern telephone network, speech is sampled 8,000 times per second and converted to a binary value on a scale from -128 to +127 for later coding and transmission

d.
Redundancy - to enable transmission errors to be detected, several techniques exist which involve operations on bits prior to their being sent which result in further bits being produced. These are then passed along with the data, for checking at the receiver end. The check bits form no actual part of the data itself and from this point of view are said to be redundant. Examples include parity bit/byte, checksum and Hamming code

e.
Gateway - a link between two dissimilar networks. In practice, this is an access path from one network to another, which can cope with the protocol conversion usually necessary. Examples could be a link to telex from e-mail, or PAD access to the packet network from a simple terminal

f.
Metropolitan area network - usually spanning an urban area so too large to be classed as a LAN. The network is usually owned by the user but may rely on PTO-supplied links such as BT's Kilostream or a rented microwave link.

Question 11

a.

1 mark for each item with a brief description of what/why. Examples include:

- window
- pull-down menu
- special function key
- colour
- mouse.

b.

5 marks each part for 3-4 ideas from the list below. Full marks for at least four points demonstrating clear thinking:

- Application

range of facilities available to users
how a choice will be made
how critical is speed of entry
how critical is response time
security/secrecy factors.

- User

the working environment of the user
the user's intelligence level
the keyboard skills acquired
his/her experience of the application area
his/her experience of the application software
how often will the user make use of the facility.

- Data

type of data - text, numeric, graphic, combination
complexity of data eg, complex source documents
volume/frequency of data to be entered
range/scope of output to be expected
the functions that will be initiated by the data entered.

Question 12

a.

Possibilities include:

- the effects of the application

- volume/flow/nature of the data
- the users
- file/printing requirements
- software requirements.

2 marks for identifying and discussing each major point

b.

- telex/electronic mail to suppliers for order chase-up, delivery dates etc
- viewdata for technical information on vehicles, products
- on-line banking/credit transfer - EFT/EDI
- external accounting/stock control software

2 marks for each of three useful examples with justification:

c.
Students should be able to identify two major classes of link:
Direct - Twisted wire, coax, microwave/laser
Indirect - in-area private line, PSTN, PDN
1 mark for identifying each class
Which to choose will depend on:

- speed, volume, distance
- cost
- need for intermediate amplifiers, regenerators etc
- security and integrity.

1 mark for each factor

Question 13

a.
Takings analysis - should make best use of small space available and include shop name, opening and closing cash, takings totals by cash, cheque and credit card, and credits on returns where appropriate.
3 marks for layout/ingenuity
7 marks for usefulness (coverage of above contents)

A typical answer might be:

Date XX/XX/XX TAKINGS ANALYSIS
SHOP xxxxxxxxxxxxxxxxxxxxxxxxxxxx

	Cash at start	£XXXXX.XX	A
Takings:	Cash	£XXXXX.XX	B
	Cheques	£XXXXX.XX	
	P/F cards	£XXXXX.XX	
Credits:	Cash	£XXXXX.XX	C
	Cash at close	£XXXXX.XX	D

PLEASE CHECK THAT -
D + A + B - C

b.
4 marks for each factor selected, such as:

- when - time of day when data needs to be transmitted and cost of data link - possibility of bulking transactions for high-speed transmission at shop
- possibility of intermediate concentrating centre
- volume of data and the amount of on-line processing e.g. possibility of slow link for enquiries etc and fast link for occasional bulk transfer
- adequacy of existing link (already used for credit verification)
- cost of existing delivery service against need for larger stock holding if less deliveries
- extension of DP facilities eg, entry of physical stock-check data, sales commissions.

c. Suggestions such as:

- e-mail between shops for inter-branch transfer of stock/meetings etc

Internal via Company head office or external, e.g. BT Gold, MCL LINK7000

- viewdata for product information to assist in sales promotion: internal, provided by company mainframe; external, via public (such as Prestel) or private (such as Istel)
- credit-verification for credit cards other than PD eg, Access, Barclaycard. External provision by credit-factoring organisation.

2 marks for each service; 1 mark for the provider

d.

1 mark for each suggestion

Suggestions to include the following:

- magnetic card reader for credit cards
- function keys - sale/credit, type of sale, cancel
- small printer (tally roll for receipt and hard copy of VDU)
- autodial modem for card reader and manual terminal
- floppy disk drive.

APPENDIX 4: Answers to typical questions

Answer 1.1

Remote process - in relation to a centralised computer, a remote process is one carried out distant from the main computer, but related to it. For example, a writer at home produces sales and publicity material on his word processor. At the end of the week, his copy is sent to a centralised editing and production facility. To the main production process, all writers are involved with a remote process.

Local process - a local process is not carried out distantly. The production process will involve many local processes such as, taking a security copy of the data sent from writers before it is processed and keeping a record of the amount of data sent in and what correction work needs to be applied to each writer.

Intelligent terminal - a dumb terminal can only be used for remote input and/or output. Intelligence means the ability to process data ie, run programs. A semi-intelligent terminal will be pre-set to run a limited number of programs (usually stored in permanent memory). A fully intelligent terminal is usually a PC in its own right which can run any program written for it (programs usually being loaded from disk).

Point-of-service processing - traditional DP involved collecting data (input or requests for output) and sending it to a computer centre for processing. As remote DP applications have increased, it has become necessary to provide DP at the place and time where the results are wanted, eg, as boxes of goods are checked into a warehouse, they may pass down a chute. If this is fitted with a bar-code reader linked to a microcomputer or transmission line and if the boxes are sutibly labelled, 'head office' can be made immediately aware of deliveries and the increase in stock levels. Similarly when a magnetic credit card is entered into a reader at a supermarket checkout, the customer's account balance is changed immediately and the customer is given an itemised receipt on the spot.

Distributed data base - a data base is an organised collection of all the data that a company needs to support one or more DP applications. If centralised, all the data for all applications is organised in one location. As remote processing becomes important, parts of the data base may be spread around or 'distributed' to the sites that need access to them. This distribution could be on an application, or geographical basis, for example, branch offices will have access to a centralised product data base - they all need description, price, availability etc. But, each branch will only have access to its own customer account details - those for other branches are not of interest to them. Regional offices may have access to the customer details for the branches that make up their areas.

Answer 1.2

Branch terminal

- initial entry of deposits and withdrawals
- initial entry of requests for current balances, statements and chequebooks.

Branch

- bulk transfer of deposits/withdrawals to region
- transfer of current cash, loan and foreign currency balances to region so that they can assess overall positions
- collection of instructions/limits from region so that the branch knows what levels of credit etc it can offer its customers.

Region

- transfer of funds and currency between branches

- issue of instructions/limits to branches
- collection and summarising of branch data.

Head office

- receipt of regional totals, performance figures, projections and balances so that overall bank, region and branch performance can be assessed and plans made
- issue of instructions/limits to regions
- communication of balances and positions to government and central bank so that the national economy can be monitored.

Answer 1.3

We assume that the supermarket has a head office with a number of branches and a factory/warehouse.

Factory/warehouse

- receive requests for supplies from branches
- receive requests for manufacture from head office
- place requests to suppliers for raw materials, packaging kit etc
- receive deliveries from suppliers
- organise delivery of goods to branches.

Branch

- process sales transactions and record stock usage
- inform head office of performance
- inform warehouse of stock usage
- inform head office of sales performance - overall, by product, product group and staff.

Head Office

- receive data relating to performance
- make decisions as to which stock is to be supplied to which branch
- examine performance and make decisions on the running of branches.

Answer 1.4
E-mail - transfer of text material under computer control. Could be used to send expenses claims and weekly progress reports and receive schedules of which customers to call on.

Credit checking - on-line service that enables the creditworthiness of a customer to be looked up from records kept by the credit agency. If the salesman is collecting orders (rather than just chatting up customers), he could do an immediate credit check from his terminal rather than having to refer to 'head office'.

Viewdata - access to a wide range of information, provided in a simple, user-friendly form, either by an external organisation or from the user company. A salsman has access to almost anything he wants, such as:

- weather, traffic and rail conditions - to help in planning journeys
- industry production and sales trends
- marketing information
- product information
- competitor performance.

All of these could assist in deciding on where and how to put in sales effort.

Conferencing - an extension to e-mail, where many people can be involved in an electronic conference - any one can send a question or basic information and receive comments or replies from others such as:

Be careful, product 1234546 seems to be badly packed!
Anyone know the best route to Southampton avoiding the M3?
How do you approach that miserable purchasing clerk at XYZ Ltd?
I broke a customer's phone - I dropped it. How do I enter it on my expenses claim form?

Answer 2.1

Data transfer	*Data transmission*
Usually high-speed (100,000s of chs/sec)	Usually less than 1000s of chs/sec
Usually in parallel	Nearly always serial
Digital	Digital or analogue
Usually involving very high-quality electronics, with low error rates	Could involve low-quality electronics often with quite high error levels
Very short distances (up to 15 metres)	Any distance

Answer 2.2

Private network - a transmission network for voice or data, provided by the company that makes most use of it (as opposed to one supplied by a public network provider). The network could consist of hardware and transmission paths entirely implemented by the owner, but could make additional use of public network facilities to extend it. A private network would normally cover a smaller area than a public one.

PTN - a communications network, available to companies and the general public. Provided mainly for voice calls using analogue transmission and provided currently by five main Network providers. Although primarily intended for analogue transmission, much of the PTN uses the same hardware and transmission paths as the public data network.

Data storage code - computers are digital in nature in particular, handling 0/1 most conveniently, so binary numbers are easy to represent as strings of 0/1s. But it is also necessary to store and handle data in other forms, especially individual characters. Data storage codes such as ASCII, provide a way of doing this, using particular combinations of six, seven or eight bits to represent alphanumeric, special and control characters.

Carrier wave - when data is transmitted, whether broadcast or directed along a cable, rather than send the signals directly in whatever frequency range they were generated, it is often much more convenient to generate a signal of a fixed frequencyand transmit it in such a way that it 'carries' other signals on it (see modulation).

Bandwidth - to enable electrical signals to be transmitted successfully, the medium through which they are sent must allow for a minimum range of frequencies to allow for the electrical components that make up the signal. The difference between the lowest and highest frequencies that the medium can handle is called its bandwidth.

Modulation - for analogue transmission, the carrier signal used is a sine wave of a particular frequency. Both voice and data signals can be carried by this wave. With data (1s/0s), the technique of modulation arranges that individual 1s and 0s change particular aspects of the carrier differently. The receiver can detect these changes (by *demodulation*) and hence determine the values of the original data signals.

In data comms, the two common modulation techniques are *FM*, where 1/0 affects the freqency of the carrier and *DPM* where relative changes of phase in the carrier reflect the value to be transmitted.

Stop bit - when sending data character by character (asynchronous transmission), the bits of each character must be delineated (or framed). The standard is one *start bit* at the beginning of each character and one or more *stop bits* at the end of the character

Synchronous data transmission - with asynchronous transmission, each character is framed with stop/start bits and the receiver has no idea when the next message will arrive. These bits enable the receiver's timer to 'clock in' the bits as they arrive. With synchronous transmission, the data within the message is preceded by signals (particular byte settings) that enable the receiver to set his timer at the start of the message. Whole bytes can then be clocked in until the end of the message.

During transmission of the message, the sender and receiver are in step with each other all the time. With asynchronous transmission, they are in step for each character only - the stop/start bits allow them to resynchronise for each character.

Answer 2.3

a. the same office

- direct null modem link between PCs using proprietary or special-purpose software for the comms and for mail-handling
- the PCs involved being workstations in the same local area network making use of the LAN mail server
- users having dumb terminals linked to a central mainframe or mini to handle mail.

b. *out-of-town*

- using a comms package on a PC to access the friend via a modem through the PTN
- installing a fax card in each PC and communicating by fax via a modem through the PTN
- linking by modem to an external e-mail supplier and making use of its software and storage capacity.

Answer 2.4

a. *Input* - fixed magnetic card reader used for recording employee time when clocking on/off; hand-held bar-code reader for recording stock levels in a warehouse.

b. *Output* - graph plotter displaying a continuous statistical sample analysis from a production line; a remote printer for recording hourly financial results obtained from a private network.

Answer 3.1

a. Most people now accept that a high degree of standardisation in communications is vital. Differing application requirements, different types of computer and other hardware and differing existing standards are applied by manufacturers and network suppliers. Anyone trying to implement a comms network will necessarily have a limited number of options as to **how** the network will operate ie, the internal mechanisms that the network relies on. This means that two organisations might set up networks that offer similar services to their respective users and which perform quite adequately for the owner company, **but** the networks cannot communicate with each other, nor with other public or private networks.

This problem has been recognised as perhaps the biggest of all in the field of communications and anyone with any sense at all bears this in mind when designing a network. The guiding principle is something like this:

- my network is such that it must support communication at various levels - user-to-user, computer-to-computer, modem-to-modem etc
- irrespective of the methods and techniques I employ in the design of my network it needs to be **open**, when communication with the outside is needed
- if the way I do things is not standard, I must provide an interface that converts what I produce to a common form that others recognise.

A simple example of this could be where my computer and internal terminals all make use of the code EBCDIC for representing characters. If messages are to go out of the network, all characters must be converted to ASCII because this is the standard code most systems recognise.

The advantage of an **open system** is that I can be sure it will link in with **any other system** designed with open connectivity in mind.

b. Taking this open system a little further, it makes sense to relate inter-connectivity not just to the network as a whole, but to the various levels at which communication can occur - user-to-user, switching exchange-to-switching exchange, software-to-software etc. Instead of considering the problems of communication and how to design the overall network, it makes life easier to break the problem down and think of the network as operating in a number of simultaneous but independant layers.

For example, user A is sending messages to user B. At the same time, user A's network is talking to user B's network (perhaps via a third network - PTN, PDN etc). User A's modem is talking to user B's and so on.

This kind of thinking means that the problems at one layer can be solved without reference to the problems of other layers - provided they are solved within the standards applying at the particular layer (so that open inter-connectivity is maintained). In this way, improvements and changes at one layer will not affect the design of other layers. The general specification for the layers and how they inter-relate is called a **layered model** of open system inter-connectivity.

c. The term 'peer' implies an equal and is used in the open system sense in the form 'peer-to-peer'. It means two elements of different networks at the same level ie, in the same layer (as above, user-to-user, modem-to-modem and so on).

Answer 3.2

a. In a wide-area, multi-network environment, it is very likely that the different host computers involved support differing kinds of terminal. Similarly, individually-linked user terminals will vary considerably. In practice, one network might support a group of DEC VT200 terminals, another might be handling Sun workstations and individual users might have IBM PC-compatibles. All of these terminals are different, particularly in the control commands (ASCII non-character combinations) needed to make them operate and this would prevent open inter-networking (which here means that users could not communicate at the application level without having to worry about terminal hardware/software).

One possibility would be for each host to convert to/from its terminal type to/from any other type, but a more general approach has been adopted for open systems interconnection. A non-existant, **virtual** terminal has been defined with certain characteristics - any system that wants open communication with any other, must arrange that its terminals appear to act as if they were of the same type as the common, virtual terminal.

b. In this sense, 'messaging' implies a framework for information interchange based on standards for message layout, content and delivery mechanism. In its most basic form, it is concerned with text such as created by word processors and telex machines. The extension, now becoming important is to make provision for users who might have fax machines etc and a true multi-medium messaging service will allow open communication between any kind of text generating device, so that the user can send a communication to another user even if a different device is involved.

The service will need to allow for interconversions, such as different character sets (eg, telex having a smaller range than most ASCII terminals) and representing shapes such as might be part of the material sent from a fax machine or a viewdata terminal.

Answer 3.3

Possible basic definitions might be:

A **standard** is a defined and documented approach to a job, procedure, process or product that can be followed by different people. Reference to and conformity with standards helps to ensure that products, systems etc are more easily developed and maintained

A protocol is a set of rules that allow some aspect(s) of a conversation to proceed.

In the mail system, standards might include the following:

- all terminals must be DEC VT300-compatible
- even parity checking will be applied for all text transmission.
- no user can send more than 20 messages in any one hour
- messages must be created in the same format as the inter-department memo form, with sender, receiver, date and time clearly indicated.

Protocols could include:

- messages will be sent to/from terminals using positive acknowledgement (a particular frame must be acknowledged as received, even if there is something wrong with it)
- if a receiver is not at his terminal, the message must be sent to his supervisor's terminal so that it can be passed on when he gets back
- if the system becomes too busy to handle the message traffic, only users with privilege level '4' or greater will be allowed to send mail: all users will still receive it
- mail delivery takes precedance over mail sending.

Answer 4.1

Note that a good organisation will ensure standards are applied to work procedures, training procedures, documents, manuals and communication and reporting. Reasons for this include:

- standards provide a clear framework for communication - everyone knows where to look for instructions and information and in what form they will be found
- existing staff have a clear idea of procedures, tasks and documents so they can easily explain them to new staff
- if staff are familiar with the existing standards, as new systems and procedures are introduced, they can be taken on-board easily because the framework already exists.

Answer 4.2

Redundancy techniques such as parity checking, checksum and so on, exist to detect errors that arise in received data, but once detected, it is necessary to implement some kind of repeat-request procedure to determine when and how messages in errror can be re-transmitted. This obviously reduces the transmission capacity of the transmission line - a fair part is used up by the receiver sending back repeat requests and the sender re-sending what has been sent before.

As an extended approach, FEC associates more redundancy with data sent so that the receiver can not only **detect** an error but can actually **locate** the error down to the byte/bit concerned. If this can be done, the receiver can then **correct** the error without the need to request a re-transmission. A balance must be struck between the reduction in data that will require re-transmission when FEC is employed and the increase in data transmitted because of the extra redundancy.

Answer 4.3

Some broad guidelines:

- no-one in the office to have LAN manager status (any changes to the network must be requested from the DP department)
- only the supervisor can access the mainframe, either sending or receiving
- 1 person to have access to telex and fax
- 1 person to have control over the printer(s)

- 1 person only for confidential documents with extra password access
- all persons to have password access so that all other staff are blocked out
- all standard forms, letters, paragraphs etc to have 'read' and 'copy' access but not 'write' access.

Answer 5.1

If data communication is to be carried out from a PC, there must be some agreement as to how data and control signals will be exchanged. The RS232 standard allows for this where the 'receiver' is a device such as a printer because it is an output device - it only needs to acknowledge signals received.

When two PCs are linked, they both want to send and receive and the RS232 circuits cannot allow this - they cannot both be 'ready to send' and 'ready to receive' at the same time.

The null modem is one of several re-arrangements of the basic circuits that in effect, fool both PCs into acting as if they were both primaries linked to a modem. In this way, conventional comms software can set up and drive the PC-to-PC link.

Answer 5.2

Two very similar sets of rules, V24 is the CCITT **recommendation** for the signal exchange mechanism between a DTE (e.g. a PC) that wants to connect to an analogue PTN and a DCE (e.g. a modem) that will interface to the network.

RS232 (or more correctly EA-232-C) is the most recent implementation of the USA Electronic Industries Association **standard** for the exchange of signals between a PC and a device (e.g. a printer) and the specification of the connecting medium. V24 suggests what the circuits are to be used for, RS232 additionally specifies how they are used.

Answer 5.3

A mobile terminal links to the PTN via the cellular network, which is a radio broadcasting network. The terminal must link via a special modem which modulates digital data signals, not onto the conventional carrier signal within the 0-4KHz bandwidth of the PTN, but the very much higher frequencies (750-850MHz) employed in transmitting between users and cellular network base stations (receiver/transmitters). The network itself will be responsible for delivering the data to the receiver, either through the PTN, where it will convert signals back to PTN frequency, or to another cellular user, via his nearest base station.

Note that sophisticated error-handling software will be needed because there are many factors external to the hardware involved, that can disturb data transmission.

Applications include any where the user wants to send or receive data at a point where there is no telephone point to connect via a modem - typically, in a vehicle, where connection is via a radio modem. For example, a company sales rep might receive instructions via his terminal as to who to call on. On arrival, he could take his terminal into a customer's office and during the sales pitch, call up specifications, quotations etc for the customer to see (and keep, if the terminal has a printer atached). When the customer places an order, it can be entered directly and costs and delivery dates returned immediately from the terminal.

Answer 5.4

By making use of time-slotting (time-division multiplexing). Each individual terminal will only make use of the transmission capacity of the line for part of the time. The line should be able to handle 80-300 characters/second (depending on the modem), while the terminal, if a keyboard or magnetic card/bar-code reader, will be sending at about 6 characters/second and then only **intermittantly** ie, not continuously.

If all the terminals are connected to a multiplexer, it can collect data, one byte at a time from each terminal in turn and then send them to the modem. It will go round in turn to each terminal and check to see if it is ready to send. If not, it passes to the next. The overall effect is that the line can be thought of as consisting of several channels, each separated in time.

Answer 5.5

Baud rate is a measure of the rate at which the transmission circuity can switch between electrical states and the number of different states will determine the amount of data that can be asociated with each state.

Generally two states (bits) are chosen, representing 0/1; 4 states (di-bits) would enable 00, 01, 10 and 11 and so on. Assuming that there were no problems, 1200 baud would allow 1200 bits per second, 1200 di-bits ps (2400 bps) or 1200 per second of whatever combination was chosen. The limit on the data transmission rate is only determined by the circuit switching capacity.

Unfortunately, errors occur mainly because of outside disturbance and electrical inconsistencies in the transmission circuitry/medium, so not all data sent is received error-free. This means the useful data transfer is reduced because:

- transmissions in error must be repeated when requested
- redundancy must be introduced into the data for error detection (and possible correction).

Answer 5.6

- telephone number and signalling mode (DTMF or pulse-code)
- baud rate (usually between 300 and 2400)
- number of bits in a character (usually 7 or 8 - occasionally 5)
- significance of the parity bit for 7-bit characters (odd, even, ignore, always 1 or always 0)
- number of stop bits after each character (often 2, could be 1 or 1.5).

Answer 6.1

This one is entirely a matter of opinion, but something like this would cover a good part of the rules:

- language used to be English (vocabulary - Webster's English dictionary, 1987 edition)
- disputes over tennis regulations - International Tennis Federation
- no interruption for at least 10 seconds
- no message to last more than 30 seconds

The 'control commands' might include:

- nod head - *I agree*
- shake head - *I disagree*
- raise hand - *I cant understand, please repeat last message*
- wave hand - *going too fast, please slow down*
- shake fist - *I am fed up, goodbye*
- pat head - *I think we have finished*

- pat head - *yes, we have finished*

Answer 6.2

a.

- there was a break in transmission and you did not receive the message
- the message was received but so garbled you did not recognise it as a message
- you were too busy to receive my message
- you received it but there was a break in transmission and I did not get your reply
- your reply was so garbled that I did not recognise it.

b.

- give up
- keep sending the message every 5 seconds until there is a reply, you have sent it 5 times or you have tried for 30 seconds
- send 'can you hear me' 3 times, then give up.

Answer 6.3

Protocols require data to be framed with various control characters such as start frame, start data block etc, all of which are represented by particular ASCII combinations. If the conversation is to consist only of printable (ASCII) characters (such as for data entry, e-mail and so on), there is no problem. However, some data transmission applications could contain other data, for example, when sending word-processed or DTP text, the control characters involved (set margins, turn on italics, skip page) might be the same as those used as control characters in the protocol.

Similarly, when transferring files, it is quite likely that some data fields might be stored in binary or floating point and any particular octet sent could by accident have the same bit pattern as a control character. It would be very unfortunate if we sent a block of data, say a sales transaction, where right in the middle of the 'amount outstanding' field, there was an end-of-block character.

To overcome this problem, some protocols require that all octets are ignored for control purposes, whatever their bit setting, unless they are preceded by the ASCII combination DLE (0010000).

Answer 7.1

- comms software to enable actual connection to the user network
- word-processor or editor to create messages
- mail manager to convert user identifications to actual network addresses. (I send a message to all users in a mailing list by name. The software will need to work out which terminals to send the message to)
- mail service eg, to enable dead messages to be removed from the queue, to handle the sending/receiving of deferred messages (those not to be sent immediately) to enable message receipt confirmation to be implemented and to enable replies to be sent automatically.

Answer 7.2

a. There are many supppliers of terminals (especially VDU/keyboards). These terminals have different characteristics in the way they operate and in the commands that they recognise in order to operate. When a user needs to have his terminal connected to a mainframe or external service which is expecting a different terminal type, software is needed for the user terminal so that it can act like the one expected. A good comms software package will contain options to emulate a wide range of terminals, so the user can connect to a number of different services.

The commonest terminal types in the U.K. are the DEC *VT* range and the IBM *3270* range.

b. The port is 'prepared' for the physical connection and the run-time software is given information to enable it to carry out comms, so that it 'knows':

- the baud rate
- number of data bits and the parity to set/receive
- the serial number to be assigned to a particular file and the size of the buffer to be allocated to the file that is making use of the port
- which of the RS232 lines are to be checked and the timeouts that apply in case of error.

c. Having established a physical connection with the 'outside world' (network, PC, mainframe, external service etc), there may be a number of matters to be covered before the actual service wanted can be provided;

- selection of another network and appropriate user identification - eg, linking into a packet network via the PSTN
- entering user number/password and so on
- selecting the service/application required (perhaps from a menu)
- requesting specific requirements for a particular application.

Much of this information is passed by a simple question-and-answer or menu-selection dialogue, but for a user who makes use of a number of comms services and applications, it is very convenient to have all the data for each individual dialogue stored, so that a log-on can be automated - the comms software can collect all that is needed from a file created as a one-time job by the user.

In a company conferencing application, we might want to indicate:

- replies from within the building/other divisions (ie, external)
- all users/a particular department/a mailing list
- when replies are expected (cut-off date?).

Answer 7.3

Main screen

- Student Union activities - events/activities, bar opening times and so on
- accomodation - what is available, how to book it, where to get advice
- health matters - local doctors/dentists etc, where to get advice.

Sources

If we assume that some software is available for creating screens as well as for displaying carousels, the following are possible:

- hand-collected information entered into the carousel via the software

- external viewdata, collected by logging on to an external information service, capturing relevant screens for storage and later incorporation into a carousel
- downloading data from the college mainframe, formatting it and putting it into the carousel.

One display terminal might be located in the student bar or refectory, while another could be in the main college entrance.

Answer 8.1

a. Mechanisms that select the best route for packets through network switching nodes, to acheive maximum throughput and minimum delay.

b. The specification for the physical interface between a digital network and another digital network (X21) or a PTN (X21bis).

c. A conceptual packet network link that remains available during a conversation. The network may dynamically change the physical link.

d. A means of employing an ISDN connection - 2 data channels (64KB each) and one signalling channel (16KB).

e. A unique, international reference number defining country, network, user organisation identity and individual terminal (if required).

f. A terminal that can generate/receive X25 level 3 packets without linkage via a network protocol converter (e.g. PAD).

Answer 8.2

a. Each switching node must be able to handle varying traffic densities and arrival patterns as there will be slack and high-activity periods. Also, nodes and network links may break down, making other nodes have to work harder in order to handle the level of network traffic. Various routing and back-up policies are possible and all may need to be tried out to see how they affect the overall performance of a node or the whole network.

In addition, network management, control and performance reporting software must be tested. To rely on live data for testing has 3 main disadvantages:

- it may not contain enough errors or problems to enable complete testing
- it is not possible to repeat a batch of live data so that different policies can be tried out and compared
- if inadequate or inefficient mechanisms have been selected, the supplier of the network will lose revenue and users will get a poor service.

If test data generation software is available, system developers can produce a complete set of data to test out whatever is wanted. We can:

- generate it in advance and store it for use
- generate it randomly when needed
- store a copy of a batch of live data and modify it to include the extremes necessary for testing.

b. A matter of opinion, but you might allow for:

- N neighbour nodes, any M of which might be out of service or overloaded - this will enable tests to determine if the node can successfully take on extra work
- a constant, heavy burst of traffic - this will assist in checking whether the node can anticipate overload and communicate with other nodes
- a regular cycle of peak/trough - to test the handling of varying demand.
- a steady burst with occasional large peaks/troughs - can it cope with extreme conditions.

Answer 8.3

JANET is a facility that is mainly designed:

- to enable easy access to academic and technical informtion, facts, figures and software
- to provide a means of communication between educational and research centres

- for a student to be able to obtain on-line information on courses, colleges and universities; books, videos, programmed instruction sets; journals and periodicals; particular subjects
- to obtain lists and specifications for software such as programming languages, statistical packages, word processors and so on
- in many cases, to run such software as an on-line user or down-load it to the terminal and run it off-line
- to provide an e-mail facility to allow messages to be sent so that queries can be answered or discussion groups started
- to allow links to other networks in the UK and abroad so that facilities and services can be obtained or made available world-wide.

Answer 8.4

a. In an analogue network such as the PTN, a conversation usually requires a continuous, point-to-point link between the two parties - the network provides a constant, logical connection (even though it may be a mix of wire, optical fibre, microwave etc).

Digital networks are usually *packet-switched* - messages are chopped up into units (packets) and sent through various network routes from sender to receiver. A digital network could be private or public and could be implemented in many different countries. Hence, one set of standards must be agreed to enable general linkage between national networks and public and private networks.

The nodes that make up a network will operate in a demand-driven manner, which means that they must be sensitive to their environment, so, as well as the messages being transported for the various users of the network, one node needs to pass 'operating' information to another. Standards (such as X25) are needed for this too.

In the same way that standards (eg, V24) are needed for the physical linkage between terminal and analogue network (via the modem), there is a need for standards (X21) to define the linkage between the digital network and the user's digital transmission equipment, similarly between the user's terminal and his transmission equipment.

Not all users of digital networks have digital transmission equipment (even though the device they are using to send/receive is digital), so, although a PC may be the terminal, the link to the outside is modem/PTN.

Different users will be using different data formats (block-sizes, frame types etc) and different transmission profiles (baud rate, stop bits etc). Therefore, another set of standards (X3) is needed to enable the interface (PAD) between PTN and digital network to be able to receive the analogue messages and convert them into packetised digital messages (and the other way round for delivery to an analogue user).

Answer 9.1

a.

- we need to know more about the intelligent terminals. Are they intelligent because they are used for local processing or do they participate in the running of the network? If a user terminal is dumb as far as comms is concerned (but has local intelligence for local DP only), the general network structure is a *star* (even if the smaller building is a 'cluster' off the main processor):

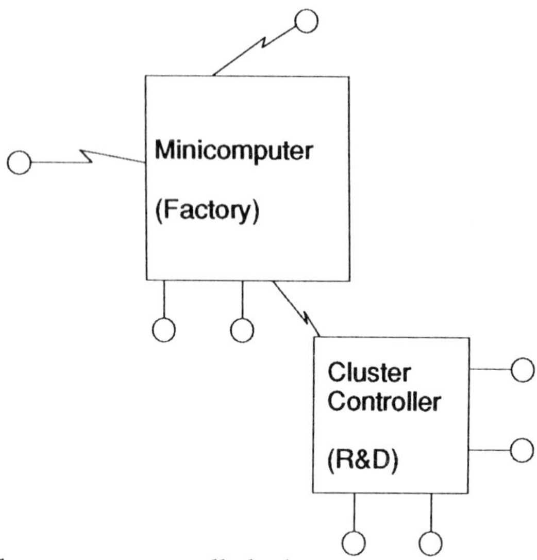

If this is the case, we are really looking at a central computer with lots of satellites

- is the overall area 'local'? The maximum distance between two users is about 200 metres, but if the two sites are not connected over public land, it could be said that the whole network was in a local area (rather than a metropolitan area)

- in view of the distances involved, it is likely that signal regenerators or line drivers would be needed. This is easier to implement with dumb satellites (connected by RS232-like cables) than when trying to extend a bus or ring. Also, ring and tree networks will have limitations on the number of terminals and the total length of transmission medium
- what are the access/contention resolution mechanisms? If the mini is polling each user, we are probably looking at a time-sharing system.

Only by having information on all of these points is it possible to decide on whether we have a LAN.

b. For ease of design and implementation, it might make sense to structure an Ethernet network so that each terminal has an Ethernet card and the whole network is one big tree. It is probably too big for a token-ring particularly because this kind of company has frequent re-organisations of personnel and departments - it is much easier to add users and change the structure of a tree than a ring.

If we look at the general security aspect, both in terms of back-up in the event of failure and the 'need-to-know' nature of some data, it might be more sensible to make the factory the main LAN, with the offices as one subsidiary LAN and R&D/Quality Control as another, both connected by a bridge. Each subsidiary could include local file/mail service and if one of the smaller LANs fails, in an emergency, a user could go to another office and log into the other subsidiary (or the main one).

Without more information about the company's processing requirements, we cannot be more specific.

Answer 9.2

a.

- integrated accounts package to process client fees and expenditure accounts
- database/spreadsheet for personnel and client records
- payroll for staff and temps
- word processing/desk-top publishing for correspondance, contracts, manuals and records

- fax for urgent communications with clients and for publicity fax-mail-shotting (broadcast fax)
- e-mail for general communication with clients and other agencies (possibly staff too if they have a PC at home)
- viewdata for general information - travel news, market information, mailing lists, client credit checking.

b.

- where in the office will users be sited?
- is there any existing cabling/trunking that could be used/modified?
- what level of growth and change can be expected?
- what level of security and back-up is required?
- what user applications will the network support?
- which users for which applications and how many of each?
- What response times will users put up with?
- what restrictions are to be placed on user access to applications?
- what will be the average and peak numbers of users?
- will external access be wanted and by which users?
- how much printing will the users need and what print quality?
- how much file transfer will be involved?
- will LAN management (user, file and printer service) be with one person or spread out?

c. If this company is to rely entirely on the LAN for accounts and administration, it cannot expect to maintain full control by leaving it up to a typist. If the office manager is too busy, the company should consider bringing in someone as the network supervisor. Whoever is in charge must either take full control of the network or have access to an expert who can answer queries and give advice. The network supervisor must have responsibility for:

- adding users and deciding on their network priviledge and authorisation
- ensuring that the right applications software is available with the appropriate level of file security

- monitoring the overall performance of the network including faults and errors and ensuring the users receive the required level of service
- recommending additional or improved hardware and software if necessary.

Answer 10.1

- *postage* - no! not sending documents by post. It may be worth considering the possibility of posting floppy disks. Many people do it and you can buy neat plastic cases with a space for the address and a warning to the Post Office that it contains magnetic material
- *e-mail service* - making use of an electronic mail service. You send a message from your PC to someone's mailbox (a section of disk on the e-mail company computer). The receiver can use his PC to connect up and scan his mailbox to see what is there
- *file-transfer (personal e-mail)* - instead of using an outside service, the two students could buy a comms package (such as Procomm or Kermit or write file-transfer programs. Then, having created messages, perhaps with a word processor or text editor, they could be sent using a simple file-transfer protocol
- *telex* - unlikely, but the big advantage of telex is that acknowledgement and delivery is guaranteed. All other methods of text interchange are only as reliable as the connection network and the error-handling protocols employed. It is just possible that the students might want to exchange something crucial. They would each have to find a telex bureau or a friend in business to handle the transfer - it would not be worth their while to buy telex machines, nor to upgrade their PCs for telex
- *fax* - originally intended for sending photographs, drawings etc as opposed to text that could have be telegrammed or sent by telex. These days, if you expect to send a fair number of documents, you could buy a fax card for your PC and send whole screens directly to the receiver without having to make use of a conventional fax machine. This is OK provided both machines have the same graphics-handling software. It will be difficult to get printout of drawings and photographs, but text should not be a problem.

Answer 10.2

User - he will need to have telephone number, user number, password etc in order to access the service (see 'terminal').

Terminal - this could be a special keypad, such as can be obtained as a 'Prestel Adapter' for receiving viewdata from a TV set. It could also be a PC acting as a dumb terminal. Both will need a modem. Some services such as this require the user to have a magnetic card reader as part of the terminal so that a cheque card can be used for identification purposes (like a high-street cash point).

Connection network - probably a PTN link for dial-up access but increasing use is being made of packet networks. A user could be routed via a gateway (PAD) to such a network without his knowledge, or perhaps be given a packet network identity in order to gain access to the packet network.

Viewdata supplier (VAN supplier) - it is quite possible that the bank may not supply its services directly to customers but rely on another company to provide a 'logical' network from which customers access the bank and other services. This supplier could be a VAN provider or a network supplier such as BT whose logical network here is BTIS (BT Information Service).

The actual link from the customer will initially be via the PTN but gateways are provided to other networks.

Information provider (the bank in this case) - provided the relevant security measures (data encryption, identification etc) are employed, there is no reason why the bank cannot be treated by the VAN supplier just like any other information provider that they service. However, it is more likely that a bank would want a greater level of control over the service being offered to its customers, particularly if it is offering on-line transfer of funds between different accounts. In this case, the bank might bypass the VAN and offer the service directly.

Answer 10.3

All of the following could be considerations:

- all organisations that employ data comms have telephone requirements as well
- when siting terminals and their modems, we need to know about the cabling and junction points of the existing company telephone system.

When planning for the installation of future terminals, it also makes sense to consider the planning of telephones as well

- if terminals are to be installed, we must know something about the capacity of the PABX that handle the company voice system because the same lines will be used by the terminals. Do we need more lines? Can the PABX handle more lines?
- can the system handle *direct dial-out* and *direct dial-in* - it may be convenient to have manual (switchboard operator) control for voice calls, but data terminals need to be able to connect to the network. If the existing system cannot handle this, we may need to set up extra lines. If extra equipment, conditioned lines etc are needed, we will need to liaise with the telephone company.

All of these relate to voice and anyone intending to make decisions on these matters must have a good working knowledge of telephone systems.

A slightly different but very important consideration could be when the DP requirement appears to suggest the use of digital transmission. If the existing telephone system and PABX are analogue, the DP Manager must involve the telecomms people because he will need their voice requirements in order to make a decision as to the cost-effectiveness of the digital linkage.

Answer 10.4

- *E-mail* - constant and regular information needs to be passed between supevisor and programmers and between programmers (teleconferencing of problems etc). Similarly, program specifications, work schedules and progress reports
- *file transfer/download* - as programs are completed, they will have to be passed back to 'head office'. Where a programmer has a program bug he cannot find, he can pass the program and the test output to another programmer to sort out. Similarly, program test data could be passed between programmers
- *diary* - particularly if work schedules are incorporated. Progress meetings could be arranged and booked and since the programmers are nearly always working at home, the diary could be used to schedule test sessions, where programs need to fit together in operation, when a programmer wants to carry out a test and so on. The diary/progress records could indicate to him and other programmers, when test sessions can be arranged

- *viewdata* - programmers spend most of their time at the keyboard and it might be useful to have on-line access to manuals such as for programming standards or programming languages. This kind of text transfer is really the same as the file transfer above, but a viewdata format might be appropriate to the application than straight text
- *on-line programmed instruction* - programmers need to keep up to date and viewdata could be a useful method of presenting the information.

APPENDIX 5: Bibliography

Many of these books and magazines were used for reference in writing this book. Be careful though in their use because some of the US books make little reference to European standards.

I am not prepared to make recommendations as to which books you will find of value, but if you intend to cover the whole subject of comms, you will need to refer to at least four books. I will say however, that items marked * in the list, were found especially useful to me.

Books

Beauchamp, K.G., *Computer Communications*
Van Nostrand Reinhold (UK) 1987

Campbell, Joe, *C Programmers guide to Serial Communications* *
Howard Sams & Co (Indiana USA) 1987

Carter, Roger, *Student's Guide to Information Technology*
Heinemann Newnes 1988

Cole, Robert, *Computer Communications*
Macmillan Education 1986

da Silva, E, *Introduction to Data Communications and LAN Technology*
Collins Professional 1986

Fitzgerald, Jerry, *Business Data Communications - Basic Concepts, Security and Design*
Wiley (USA) 1988

Gandoff, Martin, *Manager's Guide to Telecomms*
Heineman 1987

Halsall, F., *Data Communications, Computer Networks and OSI* *
Addison-Wesley 1986

Held, Gilbert, *Data Communcation Components* *
John Wiley & Sons 1988

Jennings, Fred, *Practical Data Communications - Modems, Networks and Protocols* *
Blackwell Scientific Publications

Marsden, Brian W., *Communication Network Protocols*
Chartwell-Bratt 1988

McConnell, John, *Internetworking Computer Systems*
Prentice-Hall International 1988

Miles, June, *Data Communications Fundamentals* *
CBS College Publishing 1987

Sherman, Kenneth, *Data Communications - a Users Guide*
Reston Publishing Co Inc 1981

Stamper, David A., *Business Data Communications*
Addison-Wesley 1989

Stokes, Adrian, *Concise Encyclopedia of IT*
Gower Publishing 1986

Radio Shack, *Understanding Data Communications* *
Howard W. Sams & Co Publications 1987

Tolhurst, M.R. (Editor), *Open Systems Interconnection*
Macmillan Education 1988

Wheelwright, Geof, *Enhancing your Amstrad PC1512*
Newtech-Heinemann 1987

Willis, Neil, *Computer Architecture and Communications* Paradigm Publishing 1986

Recent purchases

4 books from a large selection offered by NCC Publications, 1989:

Chilton, Paul, *Introducing X.400*

Gandy, Martin, *Choosing a Local Area Network*

Macpherson, Sandra, *What are VADS*

Pye, Colin, *What is OSI*

Useful booklets

British Telecom, *1001 Facts 1988*

British Telecom, *Your Guide to British Telecom*

Case Ltd Rickmansworth. Herts. 09237 76699. *CASE - Pocket book of Computer Communications* *

Philips Business Systems Colchester, Essex. 0206 575115. *Philips - Pocket book of telecomms* *

Telecomms Managers Association November 1988. *Preferred terms for telephone system facilities*

Magazines and journals

Communicate *
Communications
Systems International
Computer Systems
Telecommunications US/International edition

Index